The Blackwell Guide to Literary Theory

BLACKWELL GUIDES TO LITERATURE

Series editor: Jonathan Wordsworth

This new series offers the student thorough and lively introductions to literary periods, movements, and, in some instances, authors and genres, from Anglo-Saxon to the Postmodern. Each volume is written by a leading specialist to be invitingly accessible and informative. Chapters are devoted to the coverage of cultural context, the provision of brief but detailed biographical essays on the authors concerned, critical coverage of key works, and surveys of themes and topics, together with bibliographies of selected further reading. Students new to a period of study or to a period genre (the nineteenth-century novel) will discover all they need to know, to orientate and ground themselves in their studies, in volumes that are as stimulating to read as they are convenient to use.

Published

The English Renaissance	Andrew Hadfield
Renaissance Drama	Peter Womack
The Victorian Novel	Louis James
Twentieth-Century American Poetry	Christopher MacGowan
Children's Literature	Peter Hunt
The Gothic	David Punter and Glennis Byron
Literary Theory	Gregory Castle

The Blackwell Guide to Literary Theory

Gregory Castle

Blackwell
Publishing

BLACKWELL PUBLISHING
350 Main Street, Malden, MA 02148-5020, USA
9600 Garsington Road, Oxford OX4 2DQ, UK
550 Swanston Street, Carlton, Victoria 3053, Australia

First published 2007 by Blackwell Publishing Ltd

1 2007

Library of Congress Cataloging-in-Publication Data

Castle, Gregory.
Literary theory / Gregory Castle.
    p. cm.—(Blackwell guides to literature)
Includes bibliographical references and index.
ISBN-13: 978-0-631-23272-8 (hardback : alk. paper)
ISBN-10: 0-631-23272-9 (hardback : alk. paper)
ISBN-13: 978-0-631-23273-5 (pbk. : alk. paper)
ISBN-10: 0-631-23273-7 (pbk. : alk. paper)   1. Criticism—History—20th
century.   I. Title.   II. Series.

PN94.C38 2006
801′.950904—dc22
2006001706

A catalogue record for this title is available from the British Library.

Set in 11/13.5pt by Dante
by SNP Best-set Typesetter Ltd, Hong Kong
Printed and bound in Singapore
by Markono Print Media Pte Ltd

The publisher's policy is to use permanent paper from mills that operate a sustainable
forestry policy, and which has been manufactured from pulp processed using acid-
free and elementary chlorine-free practices. Furthermore, the publisher ensures that
the text paper and cover board used have met acceptable environmental accreditation
standards.

For further information on
Blackwell Publishing, visit our website:
www.blackwellpublishing.com

To Camille, who taught me the theory of love.

CONTENTS

ACKNOWLEDGMENTS

A book of this sort comes up against two obstacles: the mountain of material on literary theory that must be read and synthesized and another mountain of material, only slightly smaller, that must necessarily be left out. Because *The Blackwell Guide to Literary Theory* is aimed at readers unacquainted with theory – undergraduates especially, but also beginning graduate students, instructors who need a refresher course, and general readers interested in the sometimes forbiddingly arcane world of literary studies – my focus is on fundamental concepts and the most prominent and influential theoretical movements. I have had to be careful at every step to provide clear and concise descriptions and explanations but at the same time to avoid oversimplification. At times, the complexities that are inevitable in theory could not be avoided, but I have tried whenever possible to leaven complexities with definitions of terms and examples drawn from the works of major theoretical writers. It goes without saying that any infelicities are my own and not those of the theorists herein discussed. Indeed, I owe a profound debt to the innumerable fine writers whose work I read in preparing this book. I hope that this *Guide* will inspire students to turn to these writers and see for themselves the richness and diversity of literary theory.

My task in writing this book would have given pause to a hardier soul, but I was helped at every stage of the process by generous professionals and student assistants without whose help I could not have produced this book. To begin with, I want to thank my friend and graduate student William Martin, who was a tireless researcher and provided a sounding board at every step of the way. Among the graduate and undergraduate students at Arizona State University who read portions of the text I want to single out for special thanks Stacey Jackson, Johanna Wagner, and Trevor Helminski. I am also grateful for the support and advice I received from my colleagues on the faculty of the Department of English. I am especially indebted to Neal Lester, Judith Sensibar, Jennifer Parchesky, Claudia Sadowski-Smith, Don Nilsen, Sharon Crowley, Mark Lussier, Joe Lockard, Karen Adams, and Keith Miller. Of course, a project like this entails countless trips to the library, and I am grateful that the Hayden Library at ASU is well stocked. More important, I am grateful for the kindness and expertise of Henry Stevens, Library Supervisor, who came to know nearly as well as I how much research goes into a project of this sort. Finally, I want to thank John Paul Riquelme, whose friendship and encouragement throughout the years have been a boon.

Publishing academic books can be difficult even under the best of circumstances, but I am happy to say that the people at Blackwell have consistently created an environment in which difficulties are minimized and support for authors is readily given. I want to thank Andrew McNeillie, the publisher at Blackwell who gave me the opportunity to write this book. His guidance at an early stage of composition was tremendously important. My highest praise and most sincere gratitude go to my editor, Emma Bennett, whose intelligence, patience, and generosity are exemplary. She worked closely with me at nearly every stage and played an important role in shaping this book. Her sound advice, together with that of the Press's anonymous reviewers, enabled me to avoid many pitfalls. I am grateful also to the wonderful publishing staff at Blackwell, including Karen Wilson, Rosemary Bird, and Leanda Shrimpton, for making the production process go smoothly and painlessly. Authors rarely have the final word: that goes to copy-editors and proofreaders like Sue Leigh and Annette Abel, whose work behind the scenes allows writers like myself to put our best prose forward.

To Radiohead and all the folks at Constellation in Montréal, whose music provided the soundtrack to this project, I am in your debt. And then there's Camille, whose love and support is the air I breathe.

INTRODUCTION

Circumference thou Bride of Awe
Possessing thou shalt be
Possessed by every hallowed Knight
That dares to covet thee.
Emily Dickinson (#1620)

More than eighty years ago, the English literary critic, I. A. Richards, spoke of a "chaos of critical theories," an assessment that would not be wide of the mark in the early years of the twenty-first century. The student of literature today is confronted with an array of theories concentrating on the literary text, TEXTUALITY, language, genre, the reading process, social, historical, and cultural context, sexuality and gender, the psychology of character, and the intentions of the author. In some cases, the specific nature of a given course in literature will make selecting from among these various theoretical approaches easier; in many cases, however, students must choose for themselves which direction their analyses should take. The *Blackwell Guide to Literary Theory* is designed to facilitate this process by offering students and instructors basic information on the major theories, practitioners, and their texts. It also includes a history of literary theory from the late nineteenth century to the dawning of the twenty-first and a series of sample theoretical readings of a variety of literary texts.

The Nature of Literary Theory

Before moving on to describe some of the strategies for using this book, I would like to discuss the nature of theory in general and the problems associated with literary theory in particular. First, I want to make clear that literary theory is distinct from literary criticism, the latter being the practical application of the former. This book is concerned primarily with the theoretical principles and concepts that form the foundation for practical methods and strategies used in literary criticism. Since the 1970s, when literary theory entered a new phase dominated by philosophy, history, politics, and psychoanalysis, a number of introductory texts have emerged that seek to explain the tenets of the main theoretical trends – Marxism, Structuralism, Poststructuralism, Feminism, Cultural Studies, New Historicism, and so on. These many and varied trends have complicated greatly the task of understanding both the nature of theory and of the literary text. Literary theory can be understood, as I have suggested, in terms of principles and concepts, strategies and tactics needed to guide critical practice. But at the same time, many literary theories have as an expressed goal the desire to inspire and guide social and political action. Moreover, students of theory might see a rift in the historical development of the late twentieth century between text-based theories like the New Criticism, Structuralism, and Poststructuralism and historicist theories like Marxism, Feminism, New Historicism, and Postcolonialism. In both of these very broad contexts, theory is understood as fundamentally different: in one, it is restricted to the analysis of language, rhetoric, signs or other systems of signification; in the other, it is directed towards a critique of social, cultural, and historical conditions and the way these conditions are reflected in and altered by cultural forms like literary texts. The differences in method and object of study are often complicated by ideological differences. For example, a New Critical or Deconstructionist approach to literature might strike some readers as conservative or apolitical, while a Marxist or feminist approach might appear radically progressive or even insurrectionary. The methodological and ideological differences multiply once individual theories are examined closely, for each theory has its own complex history of relations with more general theories of society, politics, language, knowledge, history, psychology, and gender.

There is one common element, however; practitioners of all the various theories tend to think in a certain way. Broadly speaking, thinking theoretically might be considered a paradigm for thought itself, at least that form of thought used to understand complexities in the physical and metaphysical worlds. A working definition might run as follows: *theory is the capacity to generalize about phenomena and to develop concepts that form the basis for interpretation and analysis.* The mode of thought suggested by this working definition involves the ability first to think generally about a given set of phenomena (language, social relations, women's experience, the novel as a form); second to develop theoretical concepts (or models) based on assumptions and principles governing the inclusion of elements within the set and the relations between those elements; and, finally, to use these concepts as the starting point from which to interpret and analyze specific instances within a set (the function of metaphor, capitalism, female gender roles, the *Bildungsroman*). A natural scientist will use theory in ways that will yield precise, verifiable, repeatable results; a literary scholar will use it in order to make informed and plausible interpretations that may not be precise, verifiable, or repeatable. To speak of "using" literary theory is to speak of how to recognize and effectively address theoretical problems when they arise in the process of reading. In fact, knowing that one is reading a "literary" text is the first step in this process. The other steps vary, of course, according to which theory is being employed and, indeed, according to how the same theory is applied by different critics.

It would be difficult, in contemporary literary theory, to achieve the kind of stability, uniformity, consistency, and universality that science achieves across social and cultural contexts. Theory inevitably reflects the social world in which theorists operate; but whereas scientists act on the assumption that scientific theory is unaffected by ideology, literary theorists make the point that theory is a product of ideology, that all theorists operate from specific ideological positions. The same can be said for the literary text, which is the product of a particular person or persons in a particular society and culture at a particular time. Literary theory can help us understand both the particular contexts and the ideological points of view that help shape literary texts. We can discern, within practical limits, a good deal about the social and political attitudes of the producers of such texts and the kinds of experiences they make available to the reader. For example, if one is interested in the social or cultural context of a Dickens novel, a Marxist theory would be useful in explaining the author's ideological position and his attitude towards class formations and social problems like poverty; it would also help determine whether the novel in question was read as social criticism or whether it was received primarily as harmless comic realism meant to shore up the social status quo. However, it is important to stress that within a given theory there may be several divergent points of view and methodologies. Thus, one reader of Dickens's *Hard Times* might apply Leninist assumptions and principles and speak mainly of economic disparities and class conflict, while another might draw on **Louis Althusser's** poststructuralist "post"-Marxism in order to discuss the formation of the social SUBJECT under ideological pressures.

Another way in which literary theory differs from theoretical practices in scientific domains is that it is more likely to be bound up in myriad ways with more general (i.e., *non*-literary) theories (of knowledge, of the mind, of interpretation, of desire, of power, and so on). Any attempt to define literary theory that does not explore and describe the relations between general theories and particular (i.e., literary) theories – or between and among particular theories – is bound to be incomplete; the outcome of such an attempt will be a theory cut off from the general PROBLEMATIC in which it has a context and a history. Unlike scientific theories, in which new discoveries tend to displace old ones, literary theories proliferate, with multiple and contesting versions of a given general theory (for example, Marxism or Psychoanalysis) existing simultaneously and with equal claims to validity. This exercise could be repeated with other general theories as well as with the more specialized theories that evolve from them. But, as with the differences between theories, the differences that arise within the conceptual or historical development of a single theory have to do with the construction of new or the modification of existing assumptions and principles. The activities of thinking and working theoretically remain fairly constant. Even theories that attack the very possibility of generalization are grounded on the general principle that generalities are useless.

This leads me to address the problem of style in theory. Many readers are put off by the obscure terms, difficult locutions, allusiveness, self-reflexiveness, and linguistic play that they find in so much theoretical discourse. Deconstruction, Lacanian Psychoanalysis, Marxist theory, Postcolonial theory – all are targets of criticism for stylistic extravagance, logical incoherence, or doctrinal rigidity. To some extent, a specialized vocabulary or a special mode of argumentation or even phrasing is vitally important for theorists addressing new problems which cannot be adequately treated within a discursive framework that is itself, in many cases, the target of critical analysis. I refer here to a framework of Enlightenment thinking, characterized by a universalized subject of knowledge, an empirical orientation to phenomena, and a belief in the universality and instrumentality of reason. In such a critical project, a clear and forthright style could be said to reflect an epistemological self-assurance with respect to the material world that Enlightenment thinkers desired so strongly to master. Contemporary literary theorists for the most part refuse to allow their arguments to fall into this comfortable framework. To be sure, some theorists use obscure terminology or affect a difficult style in order to follow a fashionable trend or mask a trivial or incoherent argument; in such cases, readers are not mistaken in referring to jargon or obscurantism.

Literary interpretation, like any other mode of intellectual inquiry, is subject to the more or less intangible influences of political outlook, gender, social class, race and ethnicity, religious belief, and a host of other social and cultural determinants. Recent developments in the history of science have revealed that even the ostensibly objective methods of science are not immune to such determinations. These developments may result, in time, in substantial modifications to how science is conducted, but for the vast majority of scientists and lay people, scientific method continues to achieve objective results. If literary theory does not seek "objective results," what then does it seek? To answer this question, I want to consider the putative object of literary theory: literature.

What is Literature?

Even if we concede that theory, or theoretical thinking *as such*, operates in similar ways regardless of the specific application of that thinking, the nature of the *object* of theory and the methods for analyzing it remain highly problematic. What, exactly, do we mean when we use terms like "literature" and "literary"? Few theorists agree that literary theory can be adequately defined and even fewer among those who make the attempt can agree on *how* to define it, in large measure because most people founder on the idea of the "literary." It is not possible, in the present context, to pursue this question in any detail. But it might be useful for the student who is new to literary theory to understand that there are numerous ways to describe the nature and function of literature. Though the concept of *literature* is contested today by many theorists, it has had a long history as a term designating an art form devoted to the written word. From Aristotle to Heidegger, philosophers have recognized the value of literary art, and literary theory up until very recently has been strongly influenced by AESTHETIC THEORY. Of special importance is the role that aesthetic theory has played in the development of the New Criticism and the more recent emergence of a Postmodern aesthetics that rejects the Kantian basis of modern aesthetic theory and, as is the case preeminently with **Jean-François Lyotard**, emphasizes the sublime.

Despite the tradition of regarding literature as a fine art and despite the consensus in previous historical eras that literature is *imaginative* writing (a consensus that developed in large measure on the basis of Aristotle's distinction between poetry and history), literary theory has, throughout the twentieth century, called into question the special status of both aesthetics and literature. Anyone who has read a major anthology of literature will discover that a substantial amount of the material in it is not imaginative. One is as likely to find political, historical, or scientific writings as poetry, fiction, and drama. If literature is not simply imaginative, fictional, or poetic discourse, what, then, makes a given written work literary? A common, and commonsensical, response is that literature employs a special form of language, more evocative and "connotative" than that used in other forms of writing; in this sense, literature is "fine" or creative writing, no matter what the content. Thus, we find excerpts from John Stuart Mill, Cotton Mather, Margaret Fuller, and Charles Darwin in literature anthologies. However, one might argue that some of these figures do not produce "fine" writing, and that the criterion itself is hopelessly ambiguous and subjective. The commonsensical response is therefore not sufficient. Nor is it sufficient to appeal to authorial intention – the writer *meant* to write literature – since it suggests the existence of multiple conceptions of literature.

But what definition could ever be sufficient? A brief glance at other possibilities suggests that sufficiency will always elude us. For many readers, literature is that which has stood the test of time. But this criterion is mystifying, for while it suggests an objective temporal process, the "test of time" really amounts to a long historical process of selection and exclusion by cultural elites (publishers, professors, editors, agents) who create CANONS of literature according to criteria that may shift and change rapidly and for no clear or defensible reason. Is literature only that which is readily available to advanced students or is it accessible to general readers as well? Is a forgotten, badly written novel languishing in a library's special collections (or in a secondhand book shop) more or less literary than James Joyce's *Ulysses* or Herman Melville's *Moby Dick*, both of which are regularly written about and assigned in literature courses? Is a forgotten bad novel as literary as a forgotten good one? Who decides whether one is good or bad? And by what criteria: those that existed at the time of publication or those in place at the time of discovery? This raises a question at the heart of Reader-Response theory: Is literariness a quality of the text or of the reading process? Does it have to do with socio-historical context? What about works that were not first read (or written) as literary? One response comes from the tireless and persistent scholar in the special collections archive who has discovered a forgotten text, edits and publishes it, writes about and teaches it: it is literature *now*, despite any doubts in the past.

Inevitably, criteria having to do with a given text being a "classic" or a masterpiece are met with the same objection that arose with "the test of time." Such criteria, the argument goes, have more to do with publishing and marketing, critical opinion, and the vagaries of scholarship and teaching. Few readers, though, will be happy with a definition of literature that is grounded in the marketplace or on the subjective opinions of critics, scholars, and teachers. Therefore, we might consider a definition of literature that emphasizes perennial themes and subject matter. But who is to decide what the important ideas and themes are? This option too appears to be arbitrary and subjective. Would John Milton's *Paradise Lost* be more "literary" than a lyric poem by John Ashbery? Would a Samuel Beckett play about "nothingness" be less "literary" than Tony Kushner's *Angels in America*, which focuses on AIDS and the nature of gay experience in late-twentieth-century US? Indeed, some might regard the latter as indicative of a trend in literature that focuses on social issues to the exclusion of truly literary themes. The question is clear: What is a *truly literary* theme? For many readers, the "truly literary" is that which transcends the social and political spheres. This leads us to still another possible definition: literature is that which is AUTONO-MOUS from these spheres. But how can autonomy be realized or, for that matter, recognized? Books and other works of writing are printed and sold, they are advertised and reviewed, they have demonstrable effects on readers and other writers. Even if we argue that literature is autonomous in the sense that it works according to its own inner laws and principles, we must contend with the objection that authors and readers are inextricably caught up in complex ideological and cultural matrices which, in their turn, have powerful effects on literature's "inner laws." At best, we can speak of what some theorists call AUTONOMIZATION, the attempt to place literature (aesthetic production in general) in a separate sphere or, more accurately, the attempt to create the illusion of such a separation. Even if we were to grant that literature is "relatively" autonomous, what would be the limits of such an autonomy? One logical conclusion is that realistic writing would not qualify, for it relies on a MIMETIC or reflective relation to the social world. Another conclusion would be that writing of a political nature would have to be excluded for the obvious reason that it engages with issues and themes that are clearly part of the social sphere. In the end, the argument that literature is somehow separate from other spheres of society violates good sense as well as logic.

Other possible arguments could be put forward and they could be contested on similar grounds, for most attempts to define literature are based either on inferential reasoning, in which case the definition entails features of an already-existing canon, or on moral or ethical considerations, in which case the definition is based on extra-literary criteria (religious or political ideals are often adduced to limit what is properly literary from what is not). In both cases, new problems arise concerning selection and exclusion. There is clearly no easy way to define *literature* because it is subject to so many determinations, influences, and pressures, any one of which can be arbitrarily elevated to a defining trait. There is no way to determine by formula or by precedent what will become the subject of literary treatment, nor is there any way to determine whether a text written in the past will be reinterpreted as literature at some later date. Today's journalism may be tomorrow's literature, as was the case with Joseph Addison and Richard Steele's essays in the eighteenth-century journal *The Spectator*. Or it may remain, as most journalistic writing remains, ephemeral, useful primarily to historians and students. By the same token, what is considered the highest literary achievement today may become a classic; but it is as likely (if not more than likely) to be forgotten tomorrow. This is a problem of genre as well, for literary history reveals a complex web of influences that reveal the ascendancy now of poetry, now of the novel as the paradigmatic form for "literature" for a given age. The contemporaries of Addison and Steele did not regard their works as literature, nor were their works written in the forms great literature typically took for their age. Saying this is saying nothing about the quality of their work, its popularity, or its influence. That we *do* tend to value their work *now* as literature, however, says a great deal about twenty-first-century reading habits. For in the end, the nature of literature and the literary has to do with how we read, and how we read is fundamentally tied to the social, cultural, and political institutions of a given society at a given time. That some ways of reading have remained constant is less a function of historical continuity than of institutional memory.

The Practice of Theory

The history of literary theory is a history of changing notions of *reading* and *interpretation* and changing notions of what constitutes *literature* and the *literary*. In this book, the term *literary theory* is used to cover an array of principles and assumptions that govern theoretical reflection on the nature and function of literary works. One of my working assumptions, as I have already suggested, is that literary theory often develops out of the application of a more general theory (of art, culture, language and linguistics, aesthetics, politics, history, psychology, economics, gender, and so on) to literary works in the interests of a specific critical aim. Literary theory thus grows out of this experimentation with concepts, terms, and paradigms taken from other spheres of intellectual activity. This emergence and the nature of the relations that are subsequently formed contribute to the *disciplined* nature of most literary theories. In literary studies, this idea of discipline is concerned with (i) the criteria and limits of critical practice, and (ii) the nature and function of the literary object within its historical and social contexts. Literary theory does not possess absolute criteria with regard to the nature, meaning, and significance of literary texts. What it does possess is a set of principles and assumptions that go into *reading* such texts. If there is "truth" to be had from literature, it is very much bound up with the historical experiences that produce the author *and* the reader. Like literature, literary theory is always the product or effect of historical conditions, even when a given theory appears "ahistorical"; chief among these conditions are a context of received ideas, intellectual traditions, academic conventions as well as the complex matrices of social and political relations and forces. The university is where these conditions are most often found together nowadays. The "special" status of the literary text, then, is attributable not to its essential qualities but rather to the reader who reads it according to (more or less) coherent theoretical principles, which are rarely acquired nowadays outside the university. When a new or neglected text comes to light, the scholar's curiosity and skill – sharpened and improved by experience and discipline, by specialized training in strategies of reading and interpretation – are brought to bear in ways unique to the academic reader. An undergraduate English major, a graduate student, a professor of literature all read in similar ways texts that have been created by the specialized reading practices they share. General readers are more or less cognizant of these special ways of reading; conversely, professional readers have become increasingly aware of and sensitive to the ways of reading (no less special, to be sure) to be found among general, non-academic readers. Some academic readers pride themselves on abolishing the distinction between the two kinds of reader; but this perhaps laudable critical gesture flies in the face of evidence everywhere around us, not least in the gulf between seminar reading lists and airport bookshops.

Throughout the latter part of the twentieth century, literary theory found it necessary to develop new approaches to the analysis of traditional literary works as well as social and cultural texts that traditionally had been "claimed" by other disciplines in the humanities and social sciences but which are now being "read" by literary and cultural critics. This trend emphasizes both the profound importance of interpretation and the breakdown of barriers between discrete disciplines, a breakdown that has led to the sharing of theories and interpretive practices and to the formation of new *interdisciplinary* fields of inquiry. Literary theory has long been in the avant-garde of the trend towards interdisciplinarity. Innovative thinkers like **Michel Foucault, Roland Barthes, Julia Kristeva,** and **Pierre Bourdieu** have contributed to the creation of interdisciplinary spaces for the analysis of complex cultural formations of knowledge and power that cannot be adequately described, much less analyzed, from the perspective of a single discipline. Interdisciplinarity entails relations of combination, contiguity, intersection, and imbrication between and among coherent disciplines. But there is also a self-critical element to interdisciplinary approaches, since the possibility that disciplines can be breached easily and productively calls into question the nature and necessity of the boundaries that delimit what counts as a discipline. The implications of interdisciplinary inquiry on the construction of curricula, canons, and professional review processes are at this date still far from clear. The impact on what students and instructors read is easier to discern and is the subject of a good deal of this *Guide*.

Many literary theories can, with surprisingly little modification, be applied to a wide range of cultural forms, events, structures, and spaces. For the *literary* text is not necessarily a work of literature (whatever it is we mean by this term); it can be any "thing" or any signifying practice capable of being subjected to interpretation. The typical student in a modern university today is well aware that films and advertisements, video games and the internet, musical compositions and fashion, historical events and soccer crowds (the possibilities are truly endless) – all can be "read" in much the same "literary" way that one might read a novel by Jane Austen or a play by William Shakespeare. The AMBIVALENCE of the literary text effectively models the critical challenge literary theory offers to disciplinary boundaries. In part, this is the result of Poststructuralism, which made the analytical tools of literary theory available to a wide variety of disciplines. When theorists outside literature departments adapt literary theories to the study of "non-literary" social and cultural texts, they typically modify the methods and strategies of interpretation to fit the signifying systems under analysis. What is uniform is a consciousness of medium (of using language or images or sounds or spaces) and general methods of interpretation and critical understanding. The discipline of Cultural Studies emerged in the 1980s (more or less) in response to this notion that culture and its products can be *read* and *interpreted* in a literary way; and many other theoretical disciplines have been transformed by this idea of the literary. The richness and flexibility of interpretation is one of the principal reasons that literary theory has had such a profound impact on our contemporary ways of perceiving society, cultural production, and human relationships.

The Structure of *The Blackwell Guide to Literary Theory*

The Blackwell Guide to Literary Theory was designed to help students, teachers, and general readers become familiar with literary theory, its history and many manifestations, from a number of different perspectives. Each section offers the student a different kind of research tool. "The Rise of Literary Theory" focuses on the historical development of literary theories into relatively coherent critical trends or schools, each with its own methodology, terminology, and major figures. Of particular importance in this overview are the interrelationships between and among theories and the processes by which general theories (like Marxism or Critical Theory) contribute to the evolution of literary theories. I want to emphasize the diversity of theory and the complexity of theoretical fields and formations as they exist at particular historical moments. The main emphasis is on the twentieth century, especially after the Second World War, when literary theory exploded on college campuses and in scholarly journals and literary quarterlies.

"The Scope of Literary Theory" provides a starting point for those readers who wish to find out more about the main trends and concepts, strategies and practitioners, terms and texts within a given theory. The major theoretical schools and trends are described in entries, alphabetically arranged, each followed by a selected bibliography. "Key Figures in Literary Theory" provides short biographies of some of the most influential theorists of the twentieth century. These short lives are told, for the most part, through bibliography, through institutional affiliations and specific contributions to theory. "Reading with Literary Theory" offers a variety of theoretical readings of literary texts designed to demonstrate techniques of application as well as to suggest how different theories yield different results. They are also meant to show how theories may be used in conjunction with each other.

Throughout the text I have used a system of cross-referencing. SMALL CAPS are used to indicate terms that can be found listed in the Glossary. **Bold face type** is used to indicate that a short biography on a given theorist can be found in "Key Figures in Literary Theory." Generally, I emphasize the first use of the name or term in any given section. Parenthetical cross-references are used to indicate that a given theorist or concept is discussed at length elsewhere in the text. Theories whose names are represented in initial caps (e.g., Postcolonial Studies) are discussed under that name in "The Scope of Literary Theory." A similar system of marking names, theories, terms, and concepts is employed in the glossary and index.

Note on sources. Throughout this book, I have supplied the date of first publication in the original language; for texts not originally written in English, I have supplied the title used for the first English translation. For bibliographic information on theorists mentioned in "The Rise of Literary Theory" and in the biographical sections of "Key Figures in Literary Theory," see the bibliographies in the relevant sections in "The Scope of Literary Theory." Finally, for anthologies and general collections of literary theory, see the "General Resources for Literary Theory" below.

GENERAL RESOURCES FOR LITERARY THEORY

Adams, Hazard, ed. *Critical Theory since Plato.* Rev. ed. Fort Worth: Harcourt Brace Jovanovich College Publishers, 1992.

Eagleton, Terry. *Literary Theory: An Introduction.* 2nd ed. Minneapolis: University of Minnesota Press, 1983, 1996.

Greenblatt, Stephen and Giles Gunn, eds. *Redrawing the Boundaries: The Transformation of English and American Literary Studies.* New York, MLA, 1992.

Groden, Michael and Martin Kreiswirth, eds. *The Johns Hopkins Guide to Literary Theory and Criticism.* Baltimore: Johns Hopkins University Press, 1994.

Leitch, Vincent et al., eds. *The Norton Anthology of Theory and Criticism.* New York: Norton, 2001.

Lentricchia, Frank and Thomas McLaughlin, eds. *Critical Terms for Literary Study.* Chicago: University of Chicago Press, 1995.

Macksey, Richard and Eugenio Donato, eds. *The Structuralist Controversy: The Languages of Criticism and the Sciences of Man.* Baltimore: The Johns Hopkins University Press, 1972.

Murray, Chris, ed. *Encyclopedia of Literary Critics and Criticism*. 2 vols. London: Fitzroy Dearborn Publishers, 1999.

Newton, K. M., ed. *Theory Into Practice: A Reader in Modern Literary Criticism*. Houndmills, Hampshire: Macmillan, 1992.

Richter, David H., ed. *Falling Into Theory: Conflicting Views on Reading Literature*. 1994. 2nd ed. Boston: Bedford/St. Martin's, 2000.

Schreibman, Susan, Raymond George Siemens, and John Unsworth, eds. *A Companion to Digital Humanities*. Malden, MA: Blackwell Publishers, 2004.

THE RISE OF
LITERARY THEORY

Intervene. O descend as a dove or
A furious papa or a mild engineer but descend.
W. H. Auden, "Spain 1937"

The historical life of ideas is typically one of recurrence. Ideas from one era are revived and revised for a new generation of thinkers. It is a variation of the causal variety of history in which we find "one damn thing after another." This could certainly be said about the history of literary theory when looked at in terms of the development of strategies of reading and interpreting literary and cultural texts. As the twentieth century unfolded, literary theory took on a momentum that might be called progressive, each movement or trend building on the blind spots and logical flaws in those that had come before. There was also a good deal of innovation, with literary theories entering the academy and public discourse with all of the excitement and possibility of the genuinely new. As is the case with most historical narratives, the history of literary theory is complicated by the simultaneous development of theoretical movements, schools, trends, and fashions, sometimes interacting with, sometimes contesting each other. There were fruitful collaborations among theorists as well as many HYBRID configurations, some the result of serendipitous synthesis, others the outcome of uneasy truces and strategic coalition-building. This network of creative and conflicting relations gives vivid intellectual life to specific historical epochs: the Modernist era of the 1920s and '30s, the Poststructuralist "turn" in the 1960s and early '70s, the rise of HISTORICISM in the last decades of the century. In such epochs, innovative thinkers and writers redefined decisively the intellectual mission, the academic relevance, and the characteristic methods of literary theory.

This short history of literary theory in the twentieth century will try to do justice both to the general picture of historical development throughout the century as well as to the complexities of specific epochs within it. It will show that there was a marked tendency towards ideological and historicist forms of theory, especially after the Second World War, that appears to coincide, on the one hand, with democratization of universities in Britain and the US and, on the other hand, with the linked processes of globalization and postcolonial emancipation. Along with this dominant historicist orientation, there is another that emphasizes the analysis of formal structures and language. The relation between the two resembles a historical DIALECTIC, a struggle between two incommensurate theoretical perspectives. What the history of literary theory tells us, however, is a much more complicated and pluralistic but in the end no less fruitful story. For literary theory has come to resemble less the dialectical interplay of two formidable orthodoxies than a multitude of alternative methods, coexisting in a vast and growing formation.

As with any historical overview, this one offers a general picture that inevitably gives short shrift to some developments within the history of individual theories. Moreover, such an overview cannot hope to convey adequately the simultaneity of theoretical developments or the convergence and imbrication of theories within a given epoch. For in-depth treatment of the various theories, movements, and trends herein discussed, the reader is advised to consult the texts listed at the end of this section under the heading "Suggestions for Further Reading."

Early Influences on Literary Theory

Literary theory has its roots in classical Greece, in Plato's ideas on mimesis, in Aristotle's *Poetics*, which established classical definitions of tragedy and distinguished poetry from history, and in Longinus (or, as he is now known, Pseudo-Longinus), whose theory of the sublime, in which language is recognized as a powerful means of transporting the mind of the listener, had a profound effect on aesthetic theory well into the nineteenth century. The period from the sixteenth through the eighteenth centuries produced a number of important treatises on literary art. Sir Philip Sidney's *Defence of Poesie* (1595) was instrumental in establishing the importance of the literary artist as an "inventor" or "maker," while John Dryden, in his *Essay on Dramatic Poesy* (1668), followed the lead of Pierre Corneille, whose *Of the Three Unities of Action, Time, and Place* (1660) established the principles of a neoclassical theory of drama. English neoclassicism reached its height in Alexander Pope's *Essay on Criticism* (1711). The emergence of modern AESTHETIC THEORY in the late eighteenth century, in works like Edmund Burke's *A Philosophical Enquiry into the Origin of Our Ideas of the Sublime and Beautiful* (1757), came at the cost of neoclassical didacticism and established the importance of sensation and imagination in artistic judgment. Some years later, Immanuel Kant's *Critique of Judgment* (1790) moved away from the English empirical tradition represented by Burke and established the importance of cognition in aesthetic judgments. For Kant, aesthetic judgments, which are a "freer" form of ordinary cognition, are grounded in an *a priori* principle of taste governed by "common sense." The aesthetic judgment of the beautiful is disinterested, universal, and necessary; such judgments present the beautiful object as possessing "purposiveness without purpose" (that is, they appear to have a purpose, but one that cannot be identified). The aesthetic judgment of the sublime, on the other hand, involves the judgment not of an object but of the relationship between an object's overwhelming size or force and the ability of reason to invoke a concept of "absolute freedom" or "absolute totality" that assimilates the object. From this process a feeling of intense aesthetic pleasure ensues. Friedrich Schiller's consideration of aesthetics, *On the Aesthetic Education of Man* (1795), followed an essentially Kantian line, linking the aesthetic comprehension of the world to the idea of the AUTONOMOUS and harmonious SUBJECT (which the German Enlightenment called *Bildung*).

This Kantian tradition exerted a tremendous influence on English Romanticism, which in its turn inaugurated a tradition of critical reflection on literature and culture that has influenced much of twentieth-century literary theory. One of the chief "conductors" of German aesthetic theory was Samuel Taylor Coleridge, whose *Biographia Literaria* (1817) successfully translated German aesthetics into English terms. The division of imagination into primary and secondary modes and the distinction between imagination and fancy are two of the most famous propositions in that volume, and both are grounded in the aesthetics of Kant, Schiller, and Friedrich Schelling. Coleridge's unique contribution to English literary theory is precisely his role as a cultural translator at a time when England was in danger of losing sight of intellectual developments on the Continent. Frank Lentricchia indicates his continuing relevance when he speaks of the "neo-Coleridgean mainstream of modern theoretical criticism" (215).

William Wordsworth, like many English Romantics, followed Schiller in emphasizing the importance of aesthetic "play" in aesthetic production. He also followed Schiller in distinguishing between naïve and sentimental poetry, the latter characterized by reflection and skeptical self-consciousness, the former by "natural genius" and spontaneous, unselfconsciousness. His preface to *Lyrical Ballads* (co-authored by Wordsworth and Coleridge, 1800) expounds on the nature and function of literary art and the role of the artist in society; it also rejects neoclassical theories of poetic practice and turns to the "natural genius" of the "rustic" man as a model for the poet's aesthetic sensibility. It is a strategy that W. B. Yeats used a century later. A more radical statement of poetic sensitivity at the time was John Keats's "negative capability," a notoriously slippery concept that sought to describe an imaginative absorption in the world outside of oneself, a capacity for surrendering one's personality in the contemplation of an object. It is the opposite of the "egotistical sublime," Keats's term for Wordsworth's poetics. Percy Bysshe Shelley, in *Defense of Poetry* (1821), redefined the egotistical sublime as a form of divine rapture. "Poetry," he writes, "is indeed something divine."

The poet and critic Matthew Arnold was the chief inheritor of the Romantic tradition of literary theory and criticism. The decline in the stabilizing influence of the church and the increasing threat of social and political anarchy led Arnold to argue that literature could provide moral and spiritual guidance for a new secular society. This argument was not new in European intellectual circles. Johann von Goethe, Schiller, and Wilhelm von Humboldt, among many others, had virtually created the modern sense of culture as a harmonious and principled manifold of artistic, social, spiritual, and even political impulses and practices. Arnold's influential *Culture and Anarchy* considers the threat to culture of an increasingly anarchic secular society. His solution was a humanistic education designed specifically to appeal to the burgeoning and restive working classes and a Schillerian vision of criticism that advocated the "disinterested love of a free play of the mind on all subjects, for its own sake" (Arnold 270). He was an important early influence on the efforts of the British government to institute adult education for the working and lower classes and to provide higher educational opportunities for women. However, the redemptive qualities that Arnold discerned in the study of literature tended to lose their importance as English studies came to serve the pragmatic social function of providing a basis of cultural literacy and of forestalling potential social unrest.

The last quarter of the nineteenth century saw a number of alternative voices to Arnold's that emphasized either the social responsibilities of art or, conversely, art's freedom from the social sphere. John Ruskin, from 1869 the Slade Professor of Fine Arts at Oxford, was a central figure in the Pre-Raphaelite Brotherhood of painters and poets and an inspiration to young students who were attracted to his social commitments and fanciful, prophetic style of writing. He was a strong influence on William Morris, the socialist founder of The Firm, an artist and artisan cooperative, and, later, a friend and mentor to both Oscar Wilde and Yeats. Walter Pater, an Oxford professor who made his reputation as an art historian and critic, had a powerful effect on young artists and writers in the late nineteenth and early twentieth centuries. Pater's *Studies in the Renaissance*, especially its brief, stirring conclusion extolling the virtues of AESTHETICISM (with its rallying cry of "art for art's sake"), was part of an avant-garde movement in England that included the Pre-Raphaelites, A. C. Swinburne, and the aesthete dandies clustered around Wilde.

Late-nineteenth-century aestheticism was in part a rejection of Kant's insistence on cognition in aesthetic judgment, but in other ways it clung to Kantian ideas, specifically concerning beauty and the sublime. Friedrich Nietzsche, another important influence on literary artists and, later, literary criticism, had a similarly conflicted relationship with Kant. His vision of the subject who creates new values was clearly a departure from the Kantian subject bound to reason and the "categorical imperative" (moral law as a function of reason). At the same time, the aesthetic and moral dimensions of his GENEALOGICAL method owe a good deal to a critique of Kantian aesthetics, especially the sublime. (On genealogy, see pp. 129–30, 160.) In the end, Nietzsche's affirmation of Life and the "will to power" went beyond Kantian terms to celebrate a new form of the sublime, one no longer answerable to reason, a "Dionysian world of the eternally self-creating, the eternally self-destroying, this mystery world of the twofold voluptuous delight, my 'beyond good and evil,' without goal, unless the joy of the circle is itself a goal" (550).

In one form or another, more or less aggressively, an aesthetics of the sublime dominated the writing of *fin de siècle* aesthetes and continued to dominate throughout the Modernist period, though Structuralism and New Critical formalism introduced new models of aesthetic judgment in literature beginning in the 1920s. New aesthetic models, many indebted to Nietzsche, accompanied the proliferation of literary theories after the 1960s. It is to this long and complex history that I now turn.

Modernist Trends in Literary Theory, 1890 through the 1940s

Modernist literary criticism and theory emerged in distinct phases: an early prewar and wartime phase, 1890–1918; a second inter-war phase, 1919–1939; and, overlapping this second phase, a third phase, 1930s–1940s, which marked the rise, in the US and Britain, of professional academic critics. In the first phase, through the First World War, writers and artists were eager to set themselves apart from their Victorian predecessors and Edwardian contemporaries. Arnold's influence was still strong, especially with regard to the values attached to literary art. His criterion of "high seriousness" and his conception of the literary tradition (with its authoritative "touchstones") can be discerned at the foundation of many neohumanist critics and reviewers at the turn of the century, including such diverse talents as Irving Babbitt, G. K. Chesterton, and Edmund Gosse.

An early and influential alternative to this late-Victorian tradition was provided by the aesthetes gathered around Pater and Wilde in the 1880s and '90s. In a series of lecture tours and critical essays, Wilde challenged the dominant Arnoldean critical tradition. His collected early essays, *Intentions* (1891), redefined the critic as a creative force, whose authority derived not from tradition, as Arnold believed, but from the power and variety of subjective experience. Taking his cue from Pater, Wilde believed that the critic's own impressions were the foundation of criticism. Against Arnold's claim that the critic's responsibility is to see an object as it really is, Wilde counters, in "The Critic as Artist," that the "primary aim of the critic is to see the object as in itself it really is *not*" (144). Whereas Arnold constructed a theory in which criticism served an important, if secondary, role with respect to artistic creation, Wilde insists on the fundamentally *creative* nature of criticism: "[T]he critic reproduces the work that he criticizes in a mode that is never imitative, and part of whose charm may really consist in the rejection of resemblance, and shows us in this way not merely the meaning but also the mystery of Beauty, and, by transforming each art into literature, solves once for all the problem of Art's unity" (149). Wilde's emphasis on beauty and art "for its own sake" and on the creative nature of criticism characterized early Modernist AESTHETICISM.

Modernism was a dynamic international movement, emerging in different forms in the US, Ireland, Britain, and the Continent. Early Modernists were primarily concerned with the "problem" of being human in a world in which the conventions of language, truth, morality, and religion were eroded or eroding, the targets of critical and artistic skepticism. In the run-up to the First World War, the "Men of 1914" – preeminently, T. S. Eliot, Ezra Pound, T. E. Hulme, Wyndham Lewis – announced a decisive break with the aesthetic and literary conventions of their late-Victorian and Edwardian predecessors. Though innovative artists, most of the early Modernists (and many who followed) were cultural conservatives who condemned mass culture and democracy and mourned the passing of integrated, organic societies where fine art and artistic vision had a high social value and authority. Hulme, along with Eliot, called for a new classicism in poetry, while Pound and Lewis promoted the Imagist and Vorticist movements. In the literary and plastic arts, Vorticism used juxtaposition and association to represent the "vortex," a point at which disparate times and places return and intersect with each other in the present. Though these movements did not survive the war, an emphasis on the single sharp image and on a flexible, recursive sense of the past continued to characterize poetry through the 1920s.

The second phase of Modernist criticism coincides with the emergence of the so-called High Modernism, which in one respect designates a certain peak of innovation and experimentation in style, narrative, and language. High Modernist aesthetics privileged SUBJECTIVITY, language, allusion, and allegory over the early Modernist penchant for objectivity, image, impressionism, and symbol; High Modernist texts typically featured non-linear and non-causal forms, stream of consciousness point of view, unreliable narration, and expressive form. The alienation and anomie depicted in Pound's "Hugh Selwyn Mauberley," Eliot's *The Waste Land*, and Woolf's *Mrs. Dalloway* can to some degree be traced to the transformations of social and cultural life that followed the war. To some degree the achievements of High Modernism signaled the dynamism of a movement that was constantly building on previous innovations and seeking ever newer forms of artistic expression. For example, early Modernist fiction had been preoccupied with individual psychology (driven to some extent by greater interest in Psychoanalysis). Joseph Conrad and Henry James wrote prefaces to their work that developed some of the earliest theories of how modern novelistic narrative functions. Conrad's preface to *The Nigger of the "Narcissus"* advocates a form of narrative *impressionism* that relies on temperament and "magic suggestiveness," that assumes as foundational the absolute subjectivity of the artist and the uniqueness of the work of art. James's prefaces explored the theoretical possibilities of point of view, unreliable narration, and the interior monologue style. Their work provided the building blocks for projects as varied as Percy Lubbock's *The Craft of Fiction* (1924) and E. M. Forster's *Aspects of the Novel* (1927). In the inter-war years, the quality of narrative consciousness itself was the chief focus of interest. Novelists sought to go as far beyond realism, even psychological realism, as possible, often experimenting with non-realistic modes of representation. High Modernist prose amplifies and fractures the impressionistic tendencies of early writers like James and Conrad; their psychological realism is radicalized to a stream of consciousness style. From James's unrelenting interiority to Joyce's "odyssey of styles," to William Faulkner's shifting narrative tableaux, experiments in point of view and narrative structure reached further and further into the hidden resources of both human psychology and language.

We see a similar development in the poetry of the inter-war years: the "speaking subjects" we can still discern in early Eliot and Pound, in Yeats's bardic singers, become the august *personae* of such monuments to High Modernist poetry as *The Waste Land* and Pound's *Cantos*. The associational or "pastiche" style of High Modernism (with its mixing of rhetorical and generic idioms) not only suppressed the personality of the creator, it fractured personality at the level of "speaker" as well. There is no singular personality generating the content of *The Waste Land* or

Cantos; it is an arrangement of utterances, perhaps "ventriloquized" by a single voice, but arranged quite deliberately to create new lyrical and narrative effects. The High Modernist poem (and, in some cases, novel) used style in deliberate and deliberately innovative ways; it was often the most significant variable in the text's meaning. As Gwendolyn says, in Wilde's *The Importance of Being Earnest*: "In matters of grave importance, style, not sincerity is the vital thing." Neither Gwendolyn nor Wilde is joking. For Modernists generally, artistic style was not an affectation; it was the responsibility, not lightly taken on, of the individual who maintained a living connection with an artistic tradition.

A good deal of High Modernist criticism appeared in the "little magazines," the most prominent of which were *The Criterion, The Dial, The Little Review, The English Review, The Freewoman/Egoist, Poetry, The Masses,* and *transition*. These magazines were published in London, New York, Chicago, and Paris. In Ireland, Yeats, under the auspices of the Abbey Theatre, edited *Beltaine* and *Samhain*, journals dedicated to issues concerning theater in Ireland at the turn of the century. Eliot's journal, *Criterion* (which began publication in 1922), was long running and influential. Pound's early essays and reviews, especially early writings on Vorticism, were widely published in the "little magazines" and had a significant impact on other writers, especially Yeats and Eliot, in the 1910s and '20s. Eliot's critical essays, beginning just after the war, became a standard, not only because of their insights and judgments but also because of their style. His "Tradition and Individual Talent," which has since been widely anthologized, stands as an emblematic critical work of High Modernism. Eliot saw the literary tradition as an evolving and transforming CANON. He believed that the past, in the form of a literary tradition, informed and enlivened the present and that individual writers of talent became a part of and transformed that tradition if they could create "the new (the really new) work of art" (5).

In many of his critical essays, Eliot hinted at an alternative view of tradition, one that was not supported by a Hegelian or progressivist theory of history. For many early Modernists, history was neither TELEO-LOGICAL (as Hegel believed) nor always tending towards the betterment of human life (as the progressivists believed) but cyclical. They wrote as if past times could revisit the present and create a "vortex" of pliable, recursive, simultaneous moments. This new perspective on time and history attempted to make a virtue of the "dissociated sensibility" that

Eliot believed had "set in" in the seventeenth century. The classical rigors of Imagism and Vorticism provided a hedge against dissociation, which makes it impossible to "devour any kind of experience" (247).

Another important source of Modernist innovation, in both creative and critical writing, was the Bloomsbury group. Loosely centered around Virginia Woolf, Lytton Strachey, and E. M. Forster, the group adopted the ethical philosophy of G. E. Moore, which placed a high value on personal friendships and conversation and fostered a critical sensibility characterized by refined taste, nuanced judgments, and an openness to experimentation and innovation. Woolf's reviews and critical essays were influential throughout the 1920s and '30s. Her widely-read "Modern Fiction" made the distinction between "materialist" writers (e.g., Arnold Bennett, John Galsworthy, and H. G. Wells) and "spiritual" writers (e.g., Joyce and, presumably, Woolf herself). Woolf clearly preferred the latter style of writing, which for her was dedicated to representing life "as it really is" – not "a series of gig-lamps symmetrically arranged" but "a luminous halo, a semi-transparent envelope surrounding us from beginning of consciousness to the end" (Woolf 160). Woolf was one of many women writers in the Modernist period who gained strength and inspiration from the suffragette movement. To this extent, Modernist literary criticism contributed to the first phase of modern feminist criticism.

The Modernist era of literary criticism also saw the emergence of Formalism, which followed on the pioneering work of the Swiss linguist, Ferdinand de Saussure. Saussure created a framework of structural linguistics that was later adapted to the uses of a wide range of disciplines, from anthropology and folklore studies, to sociology and textual studies. His *Course in General Linguistics* (1916) taught that language was grounded in the structural differences of phonemes, very basic sound units, rather than in the mimetic relation of the sign to an external referent. Unlike the nineteenth-century philologists, who were interested in the history of languages, Saussure was concerned with the way that language functioned as a system. He posited a distinction between the systematic nature of language (*langue*) and the specific instances of usage within the system (*parole*). A structuralist understanding of language, according to which universal forms were found to govern the seemingly endless variety and mutability of languages, dialects, argots, and jargons, thus depended on the interrelation of specific instances within a given system rather than on a referential relation to the external world. In the decades following the publication of Saussure's *Course*, a number of leading European theorists expanded the potentialities of a structuralist approach to language. (On Saussure, see 181–4.) The most prominent early figures were Vladimir Propp, Roman Jakobson, and Viktor Shklovsky. Jakobson was associated with the Moscow Linguistic Circle and the Prague Linguistic Circle from 1915 to the 1930s. His theories of language, especially of the metaphoric and metonymic poles of literary discourse, were to have a profound impact on other formalists and structuralists as well as on the poststructuralist movement of the 1960s and '70s. Propp used formalist methods to analyze folktales and derive a typology of narrative structures that was to prove instrumental in establishing a structuralist theory of narrative. His work was also important for the structuralist semiotician A. J. Greimas and the structuralist anthropologist Claude Lévi-Strauss. Viktor Shklovsky, like Jakobson associated with the Moscow Circle, produced a quite different theory of narrative in his *Theory of Prose* (1925). Of particular note is the concept of *estrangement* or *defamiliarization*, a technique whereby naturalized or clichéd language usages and literary conventions are "laid bare." Estrangement permits a reevaluation of literary language and the world it purports to represent. Like so many other formalists, Shklovsky conducted his intellectual life on the periphery of the Communist Party. He was an exile in Berlin for a while after the First World War (at one time in hiding at Jakobson's house), one of many Social Revolutionaries to evade arrest by the Bolsheviks in the early 1920s. His resistance to the Party line on matters of aesthetics led to intense criticism from Marxist literary critics, but he eventually capitulated to Marxism, signaled by the publication of *A Monument to Scientific Error* in 1930.

The third phase of Modernist literary criticism coincided with the rise of Formalism. The dominant mode of formalist criticism in the US and Britain in the 1920s and '30s was the New Criticism. But whereas Formalism grew out of the science of linguistics and provided a theoretical basis for innovation in a wide variety of other disciplines, the New Criticism emerged out of poetry and poetics as a set of interpretive strategies that did not have a wide impact outside literary studies. There was always something patrician, even elitist, about the New Criticism, the legacy of the great Modernist poet-critics, whose highly refined, mandarin sensibilities were behind much artistic and critical innovation in the inter-war years. By the 1930s, Modernist literature and criticism were staples in mainstream journals, including Eliot's *Criterion*, the *Nation and Athenaeum* (two early journals consolidated in 1931), *Vanity Fair*, the *Times Literary Supplement* and, beginning in 1932, *Scrutiny*. F. R. Leavis and his wife, Q. D. Leavis, were the intellectual center of *Scrutiny*, which emphasized the moral and ethical dimensions of literature. Another critical voice was that of Edmund Wilson, whose *Axel's Castle* (1931) and *The Wound and the Bow* (1941) treated the innovative texts of the High Modernist era with a seriousness and professional attentiveness that was often lacking in the mainstream literary establishment. His work was widely read and provided an alternative to the New Critics who were to dominate criticism and theory for the next thirty years.

The rise of English departments in the opening decades of the twentieth century, especially in the US, helped to create the social conditions that enabled the rise of the professionally-trained academic critic. The New Criticism, which privileged the kind of esoteric and erudite poetry that invited close reading and that was eminently suited both to the teacher in the classroom and to the professional critic, was crucial to this development. It encompassed a variety of interpretative methods that shared certain key elements, the most important of which was the notion of the literary work as AUTONOMOUS and self-contained – a "verbal icon," as W. K. Wimsatt and Monroe C. Beardsley famously put it. I. A. Richards' *Principles of Literary Criticism* (1924), one of the first works to employ the New Critical method, explored the psychology of reading and the relationship between emotional responses to literature and the values that literature articulates. Literature records experiences, and it is the critic's job to be able to evaluate those experiences as they are expressed in literary form. Richard's comment in the Preface – "A book is a machine to think with" (1) – neatly sums up both the autonomous self-sufficiency of the literary text and the mechanistic nature of the reading process. An appendix on T. S. Eliot's poetry added to the second edition (1926) testifies to the prestige that the poet enjoyed as a motive force in the New Criticism. Richards speaks of the difficulty of Eliot's poetry and asserts that the various elements of his work "are united by the accord, contrast, and interaction of their emotional effects": "The value lies in the unified response which this interaction creates in the right reader" (290). The ideal of unity and the assumption that a "right" kind of reader of such poetry actually exists reflects the abiding values of the New Criticism.

Richards' second book, *Practical Criticism* (1929), continued this program of criticism, with an emphasis on controlled studies of reading and evaluation and an empirical form of literary scholarship better suited (or so Richards thought) to the modern research university.

Academic critics in the US propelled New Critical techniques of close reading to the forefront of pedagogy and scholarship. Cleanth Brooks, William Empson, and Wimsatt and Beardsley developed methods of close reading that sought to describe the internal dynamics and the range of signification in literary (typically poetic) works that stressed irony, PARADOX, ambiguity, and other rhetorical features. A literary text was more or less "well-wrought," autonomous, and self-regulating. New Critical formalism extended to the study of the novel as well. Leavis, in *The Great Tradition* (1948), found that such Modernist writers as Joyce lacked the kind of formal integrity and unity that he found in the realist tradition of George Eliot, Henry James, Joseph Conrad and, somewhat grudgingly, Charles Dickens and D. H. Lawrence. Alternatives to this view of the novel form – for example, Edmund Wilson's more sympathetic judgments of Joyce's *Ulysses* and other Modernist experiments in symbolic narrative – sought to enlarge the focus of New Criticism beyond issues of form and tradition. But Leavis's influence defined powerful limits within which thinking about the novel remained stalled, until Ian Watt's still-influential *The Rise of the Novel* (1957) inaugurated a historicist theory of the novel.

Another aspect of the New Criticism, one that underscores the pedagogical importance of the new modes of interpretation, was the creation of college textbooks focusing on poetry and fiction. Brooks and Robert Penn Warren edited a number of popular textbooks – including *Understanding Poetry: An Anthology for College Students* (1938) and *Understanding Fiction* (1959) – in which the new modes of interpretation were made available as practical tools for the classroom. It is hard to underestimate both the CANON-forming impetus behind the New Criticism and the extent to which it transformed the nature of scholarship and teaching. And while the importance of close reading in the New Critical style in scholarly writing begin to wane in the 1960s, with the advent of Structuralism and Poststructuralism, it remained dominant in the classroom for much longer – indeed, many instructors in the twenty-first century, especially in undergraduate classrooms, continue to rely on New Critical methodologies.

Social and Political Theory from the 1930s to the 1960s

The same professionalization, the same drive for methodological rigor and argumentative nuance, that characterizes New Criticism and Formalism can also be seen in the development of social theory. One of the most significant early figures was the Hungarian Marxist Georg Lukács who was a vocal critic of the Modernist novel and a champion of "critical realism." In 1920, after the failure of the Hungarian Soviet Republic and in exile, Lukács published *Theory of the Novel*, a study strongly influenced by Hegel's dialectical method and Marx's sociology. He regards the novel as a "problematic" genre: "The novel is the epic of an age in which the extensive totality of life is no longer directly given, in which the immanence of meaning in life has become a problem, yet which still thinks in terms of totality" (56). TOTALITY, as Lukács uses it here, refers to idealist conceptions of perfect unity and fullness.

The same problems that preoccupied Lukács also determined the nature and direction of the new social theory that emerged in the 1920s and '30s from the Frankfurt Institute of Social Research, founded by Felix Weil and incorporated into Frankfurt University in 1923 under the directorship of Carl Grünsberg, who made Marxism its theoretical basis. Max Horkheimer became director in 1930 and continued the emphasis on Marxist studies of society and culture. The rise of Hitler and Nazism in Germany forced a relocation of the Institute, many of whose members where Jewish, first to Geneva in 1933 and then to California in 1935. These geopolitical developments were largely responsible for the shift, in the late 1930s and '40s, from an interest in economics and the modes of production to an interest in the SUPERSTRUCTURAL side of social development, with a strong emphasis on ideology critique. This shift was discernible as well in the work of the Italian Marxist Antonio Gramsci, who was active in the Italian Communist Party throughout the 1920s, until he was arrested in 1926 by Mussolini's fascist government under the "Exceptional Laws." He remained in prison, working on his *Prison Notebooks* until his death in 1937. From his prison vantage point, without reference books and under censorship, Gramsci meditated on the structure of complex capitalist societies and concluded that dominant social classes exercise power primarily through HEGEMONY, through modes of indirect and "spontaneous" consensus; DOMINATION was the power in reserve, authorized by the State, for those "moments of crisis of command and direction when spontaneous consent has failed" (12). (On Gramsci, see 110–11.)

Gramsci's theory of the superstructure as a domain divided between "civil society" and "political society" – between "private" realms of hegemonic connection and a State that uses domination to crush resistance – was similar to theories put forward by Horkheimer, **Theodor Adorno**, **Walter Benjamin**, and Herbert Marcuse. Horkheimer was interested in a Marxist analysis of culture that stressed sociological methods, while Adorno and Benjamin were more interested in the analysis of philosophy, literature, film, music, and other cultural productions. Marcuse, like Horkheimer, was involved in sociological studies, but his work on Freudian psychoanalysis underscored the importance of psychology in the study of social formations and institutions. Their common theoretical project was the systematic investigation of MODERNITY, mass and commodity culture, authoritarianism, anti-Semitism, and capitalist ideology. Horkheimer's and Adorno's collaboration on *Dialectic of Enlightenment* (1944) is one of the signal achievements of the Frankfurt school. This text is a wide-ranging analysis of the "culture industry" – Adorno's term for the concentrated efforts of media corporations to convert cultural productions into COMMODITIES – and other features of modern society (including anti-Semitism). Adorno wrote extensively on philosophy, aesthetics, music, and literature, as did Benjamin, whose friendship with Adorno constituted an informal collaboration. Benjamin was not an official member of the Institute and did not embrace conventional Marxism and social science methodologies, though he was in agreement with the Institute's general aim of analyzing culture. He produced thoughtful and provocative materialist analyses of literature, philosophy, film, and social phenomena like the Parisian arcades. He was far more willing to see the potential for positive social transformation in the technologies of culture that for Adorno were the engines of an increasingly demoralizing and dehumanizing State. In the early years of the Second World War, Benjamin tried to escape from Europe, only to find himself held up at the Spanish frontier. Certain that Hitler's Gestapo was on his trail, he committed suicide on September 26, 1940. This event underscores the utter alienation of the intellectual in totalitarian regimes, where the options were absolute conformity, exile, or death.

The Frankfurt Institute was able to relocate in Frankfurt in 1953 and Adorno and Horkheimer became co-directors in 1955. With Adorno's death in 1969 and Horkheimer's in 1973, the first generation of critical theorists came to an end, though Marcuse would remain influential throughout the 1960s and early '70s as an intellectual mentor of anti-war activists in Europe and the US. Beginning in the 1960s, Jürgen Habermas emerged as the leading figure of a new generation of critical theorists. He was far more critical of Marxist theory than the earlier generation, and consequently his work on the public sphere concentrates not on the struggle between social classes or on the inevitability of a proletarian revolution but on the authority behind political and cultural discourses and institutions and how they achieve and maintain legitimacy. For Habermas, the crucial issue was the legitimation crisis of late modernity. New forms of legitimacy had to be found that would account for both the AUTONOMY of social groups and their interconnectedness within a larger social framework. Habermas and his student, Seyla Benhabib, were the key figures in the Frankfurt school tradition from the 1980s. They advocated forms of social TOTALITY and consensus, which Habermas termed "communicative action," that would, theoretically at least, resolve legitimation crises. In an important early essay, he invoked Max Weber's analysis of modernity and emphasized the developments that led to the creation of autonomous social spheres for science, morality, and aesthetics. He decried the "negation of culture" that some social theorists had promoted as a way to resolve contradictions in the social sphere as a whole. But locating the problems of the social totality in the sphere of aesthetics detracts attention from problems in the other spheres and from problems that arise when the spheres function as a single, social totality. This project of cultural renewal would bring the sphere of aesthetics back into contact with those of morality and science, thus achieving a condition of totality in which modern culture could connect to everyday life. As Habermas put it, in a rejoinder to Postmodernists, the "project of modernity has not yet been fulfilled" (12). (On this debate, see pp. 38–9, 69–70.)

There are some points of overlap between Critical Theory and Post-colonial theory, which began to attain its disciplinary shape in the 1950s, drawing on the same works of Hegel and Marx that served as the foundation for mainstream European social theory. Early theorists committed to nationalism and anti-colonial resistance drew for ideological sustenance on a Marxian critique of IMPERIALISM. The key figures in this early phase were Albert Memmi and **Frantz Fanon**, men who occupied complex positions in colonial societies that inspired literary and theoretical works now widely regarded as the foundations of Postcolonial theory. Albert Memmi, a Tunisian Jew, was a novelist and social theorist; his major theoretical work, *The Colonizer and the Colonized*, was published in 1957 in the midst of the anti-colonial struggles in Tunisia and Algeria. One of the chief virtues of this book is its dialectical analysis of the relationship between the colonizer and the colonized. Fanon, born in Martinique, was trained as a psychiatrist and spent considerable time examining combatants in Algeria during the nationalist insurgency against France in the 1950s. Before he was assigned to the Psychiatry Department at the Blida-Joinville Hospital in Algeria, he published one of his most important works, *Black Skin, White Masks*, which dealt with the problems of a black man living in a "whitened" world. In *The Wretched of the Earth* (1961), he argued that the task of anti-colonial struggle was to "reintroduce mankind into the world, the whole of mankind" (106). No longer would the colonized have to suffer the indignity of being "submen," an indignity that arose from the central contradiction of colonialism: "Laying claim to and denying the human condition at the same time" (20). It is significant that *The Wretched of the Earth*, like Memmi's *The Colonizer and the Colonized*, was introduced to European intellectual communities by Jean-Paul Sartre, who wrote prefaces for both. In part because of this association with European radical politics, *The Wretched of the Earth* had a wide-ranging impact, influencing not only anti-colonial resistance but also the Black Power movements in the US in the 1960s.

The other major theoretical trend to take root in this post-war period was Cultural Studies. In the early years, Richard Hoggart and **Raymond Williams** brought materialist and sociological methods of analysis to bear on the study of culture. Williams, who focused on links between literature and culture as well as on the new modes of mass communication that were transforming the very nature of culture, best represents the Marxian influence in Cultural Studies. His *Culture and Society: 1780–1950* (1958) inaugurated a tradition of British cultural Marxism informed by sociology and anthropology, while his *Communications* (1962) was instrumental in defining new the disciplines of communications and media studies. (On Williams, see pp. 72–4.) The foundation, in 1964, of the Centre for Contemporary Cultural Studies at the University of Birmingham was pivotal in establishing the field initially in Britain. In this first phase of Cultural Studies (a second phase in the US would begin to emerge in the 1980s), theorists were primarily interested in literary and cultural traditions, new technologies, and marginal social groups. Hoggart's work on literacy and Stuart Hall's on politics and the police exemplify the sociological tenor of early work in British Cultural Studies. Some theorists, notably Williams, were strongly influenced by CULTURAL MATERIALISM, which emphasizes the influence of economic conditions on social and cultural works and practices.

The Poststructuralist Turn, 1966 through the 1980s

Poststructuralism grew out of developments in Structuralism, which had reached a culmination in 1958 with Lévi-Strauss's *Structural Anthropology* (1958). Lévi-Strauss's anthropology, which brought together cultural observation and structuralist analysis, was a clear divergence from the theories of functionalism and cultural diffusion that had dominated the field since the turn of the century. The idea that myth and kinship patterns could be studied as coherent and stable signifying systems and that these systems operated in a similar fashion in diverse societies had a galvanizing effect on **Roland Barthes**, whose early work, from *Mythologies* (1957) to "Introduction to the Structural Analysis of Narrative" (1966), was indebted to Lévi-Strauss. Barthes' work is significant not only for what it accomplished within the Structuralist movement but also for how quickly and decisively it turned away from Structuralist conventions. By 1970, *S/Z*, a study of a short story by Balzac, marked Barthes' transition to a poststructuralist understanding of how narrative works and indicated the productive potential of the contradictions, gaps, and APORIAS found in texts from a wide variety of fields.

Another remarkable indication of this turn from structuralist to poststructuralist thought was a symposium, "The Languages of Criticism and the Sciences of Man," held under the auspices of the Johns Hopkins University Humanities Center in October, 1966 (the proceedings were published in 1970 as *The Structuralist Controversy*). Among those participating were René Girard, Georges Poulet, Tzvetan Todorov, Jean

Hyppolite, Barthes, **Jacques Lacan**, and **Jacques Derrida**. Among the papers was Derrida's "Structure, Sign, and Play in the Discourse of the Human Sciences," which was to have a transformative effect on literary criticism and theory in the US. The essay was a tour de force critique of the "concept of centered structure" ("Structure" 279) and an analysis of the concept of PLAY, Derrida's term for the decentering capabilities of language and texts. (On Derrida, see pp. 79–82, 154–5.) The participants in the symposium, especially Barthes, Lacan, and Derrida, staked out new domains of theoretical inquiry grounded in a critique of Saussurean Structuralism. This poststructuralist "turn" changed utterly the way literary theory constituted itself and its objects of analysis.

All of this took place at a time, the late 1960s and early '70s, when many theoretical schools and trends were coming to the realization that the cherished assumptions of Western culture were neither natural nor universally valid. In many ways, Poststructuralism coincides with Postmodernism, though the two terms are not synonymous. While Postmodernism is concerned primarily with a critique of MODERNITY and a repudiation of aesthetic Modernism, Poststructuralism is committed to the ongoing critique of Structuralism and the development of new theories of language, TEXTUALITY, and SUBJECTIVITY. Like Postmodernism and Postcolonialism, Poststructuralism does have a historical valence – it emerges in the 1960s during the peak period of Structuralism and effectively supplanted it – but the main point of Poststructuralism is not that it comes *after* Structuralism but that it puts Structuralism to the test.

The Saussurean idea that language is formed not in the relation of word to thing but in the relation between words led to provocative new ways of looking at literary texts. For poststructuralists, meaning lies precisely in the slippage between SIGNIFIER and SIGNIFIED, in the gap or space or DIFFERENCE between them. Deconstruction, the name given to the analytical method Derrida favored, focuses on how difference renders texts internally unstable and self-contradictory. Derrida used deconstructionist methods to examine a wide variety of social and cultural texts. Though it has acquired the reputation for being ahistorical and uninterested in social and political questions, poststructuralist strategies have proven quite useful in the analysis of race, gender, ideology, and history. Derrida, for example, used Deconstruction to critique the system of apartheid in South Africa, while **Homi Bhabha** and **Gayatri Chakravorty Spivak** used Poststructuralist methods to interrogate colonial discourses. Finally, Foucault's work on the nature of social institutions (the clinic, the madhouse, and the prison) had a tremendous impact on the politicization of theory. Indeed, after 1968, his political commitments became a model for the "engaged" theorist, both in Europe and the US. His many interviews on politics and social power have provided the inspiration for many intellectuals who wished to combine Poststructuralist theory with radical politics.

As I have suggested, these theoretical trends were not restricted to France. The Johns Hopkins symposium in 1966 was a historical watershed, for it marked the point at which "French theory" became accessible to US audiences. By the mid-1970s, with the publication of the English translation of Derrida's *Of Grammatology* (1976), Poststructuralism had become the dominant theoretical trend in US universities. The leading edge of this theoretical avant-garde was a group of US theorists in French and comparative literature departments who developed distinctive varieties of deconstructionist critique, in some cases derived from the work of Derrida. This group, the so-called Yale Deconstructionists, consisted of **J. Hillis Miller**, **Paul de Man**, Geoffrey Hartman, Barbara Johnson, and Harold Bloom. Beginning in the early 1970s, with de Man's *Blindness and Insight* (1971), US deconstruction focused new attention on interpretation and stressed the value of philosophy (especially Nietzsche's) in the formation of literary theory. Miller's essays at this time emphasized the labyrinthine qualities of textuality and reading. He concentrated on the canonical figures of English and American literature, with a strong emphasis on nineteenth-century English novelists. Miller's work amounted to the most significant reconsideration of the English novel tradition since Leavis's *Great Tradition* in 1948. Hartman and Bloom were involved in a similar project of rehabilitating Romantic poets, particularly Wordsworth and Shelley. (Though often included as part of the Yale group, Bloom's work was idiosyncratic, lacking that common background in European phenomenology and linguistics that the major Deconstructionists shared.) Barbara Johnson's work pioneered the application of Derridean theory to problems in Feminism and African American literature and points up the crucial role played by Feminist theory in the poststructuralist era.

Poststructuralism and Deconstruction had an obvious appeal to Feminism. Beginning with Simone de Beauvoir's *The Second Sex* (1949), Feminism was dedicated to the critique of gender and sexual difference. De

Beauvoir articulated in philosophical terms some of the same issues raised by Virginia Woolf and other early feminists, and she was to enjoy tremendous influence in the 1960s and '70s, at a time when US and French feminists took this groundbreaking work as the starting point for their own critiques of masculinist, LOGOCENTRIC discourses. De Beauvoir's work inaugurated a second wave of Feminism concerned with civil rights, social equality, and the critique of patriarchy. The first crest of that wave occurred in the US, where three major works appeared within seven years – Betty Friedan's *The Feminine Mystique* (1963), Kate Millet's *Sexual Politics* (1970), and Germaine Greer's *The Female Eunuch* (1970) – and they set the stage for the feminist revolution that, for many US observers, was inseparable from the sexual revolution. The chief concerns of these feminists – equal rights in the workplace, representation in literature and politics, sexual freedom – index the social and political climate of the times. By the end of the 1970s, Feminism had become a powerful force in US universities and intellectual circles. **Elaine Showalter**, **Sandra Gilbert**, and **Susan Gubar** wrote pioneering works in feminist literary history and created models of feminist literary theory and criticism that were widely adapted and productively modified.

In contrast to US feminism, French feminism was at this time oriented towards philosophy, linguistics, psychoanalysis, and politics. Developments in psychoanalysis were fundamental for poststructuralists generally and for feminists in particular. French Feminism, which included preeminently **Luce Irigaray**, **Hélène Cixous**, and **Julia Kristeva**, was aptly described by Toril Moi as the "child of the student revolt of May 1968" (93), when anti-war and anti-government protests nearly shut down Paris. Cixous' "The Laugh of the Medusa" (1975) and Irigaray's *Speculum of the Other Woman* (1974) were critical challenges to patriarchal and masculinist discourse, particularly Psychoanalysis and philosophy. This new French feminism was strongly connected to the main lines of development in poststructuralist thought, although dissent from some of the key elements of that thought was characteristic of the field. Kristeva's work blended the methodologies of linguistics, SEMIOTICS, Lacanian Psychoanalysis, and Bakhtinian Formalism to create what she called "semanalysis." Kristeva, along with Cixous, pioneered a style of ÉCRITURE FEMININE (women's writing, writing the body). For the most part, Cixous conformed closely to the assumptions and methodologies of Derridean Deconstruction and Lacanian psychoanalysis, as did Irigaray, though both were critical of Freud's and Lacan's writings on femininity. Irigaray's *Speculum*, which includes a lucid and incisive critique of Freud's discourse on female sexuality, led to her dismissal from Lacan's *École freudienne de Paris*. Lacan's action was emblematic not only of the embattled state of French psychoanalysis in the mid-1970s but also of the increasing independence of Feminism from a masculinist, patriarchal intellectual culture. This independence was reinforced when Cixous established, in 1974, the Centre d'Etudes Féminines at the University of Paris VIII. (On French Feminism, see pp. 97–9, 156–9.)

The 1960s and '70s also saw the expansion of narrative theory, beginning with a formalist phase that was to have a long-lasting influence. As noted above, Barthes published his landmark essay, "Introduction to the Structural Analysis of Narrative," in 1966. In the same year, Gérard Genette began publishing *Figures* (1966–72), portions of which were published in the US as *Narrative Discourse* (1980). Mieke Bal and Tzvetan Todorov developed their own theories of narrative structure, much influenced by A. J. Greimas's semiotics and the theories of DIALOGISM and HETEROGLOSSIA put forward by **M. M. Bakhtin**. The US theorist Seymour Chapman, borrowing terms from Russian Formalism and building on the work of Christian Metz in France, developed a theory of narrative that he applied to both fiction and film. New work was also going forward on the theory of the novel, building on the foundation laid by James and Conrad. Wayne Booth's *Rhetoric of Fiction*, for example, offered a rhetorical typology of the novel, some aspects of which – the reliable narrator and the implied narrator – are still in wide use today. By the late 1970s a substantial new trend emerged that concentrated on contemporary or Postmodern fiction. Robert Scholes and **Linda Hutcheon** developed theories of FABULATION and METAFICTION, respectively, and argued that Postmodern fiction tended to comment on and thematize its own linguistic and narrative practices. The impulse towards more open-ended theories of novelistic narrative – a reaction, more or less directly, to Booth's rhetorical theory – was quickened by the publication of Bakhtin's *Dialogic Imagination*, which introduced a new element of political critique to the study of the novel, one later pursued by critics like D. H. Miller and R. Brandon Kershner.

The new interest in interpretation at this time was in part linked to developments in hermeneutics, especially innovations regarding the reader and the reading process. The hermeneutical tradition of the nineteenth century, associated with Friedrich Schleiermacher and Wilhelm Dilthey, was dedicated to understanding the state of mind of a consciousness distant in time or space. Though hermeneutics of this sort was often associated with sacred texts, by the late nineteenth century its importance for secular literature was becoming increasingly apparent. The conceptual leap involved in fathoming another's consciousness is a nearly mystical experience between the self and the alien OTHER, an experience that unifies subject and object in a single conscious intention. Early in the century, with the work of Edmund Husserl and Martin Heidegger, a phenomenological hermeneutics emerged that shifted attention away from an alien consciousness inscribed in a text to a pure realm of being in which the text could be understood as a present experience. Hans Georg Gadamer, a student of Heidegger's writing at mid-century, was the leading theorist of this new hermeneutical tradition. For Gadamer, the text was not something that lay on the far side of a temporal gap but rather something that could be understood within the "horizon" of the present moment, a moment in which interpretation is grounded not in the historical difference of texts but in the "historicality" of the interpreter.

Reader-Response theory brought some of the theoretical rigor of hermeneutics to bear on the pragmatics of reading. Some of the earliest work in this field was done in the 1930s by the phenomenologist Roman Ingarden, and it was this work that later inspired Umberto Eco and **Wolfgang Iser**. Iser's *The Act of Reading: A Theory of Aesthetic Response* (1978) created the foundation for a theory of reading that explained how texts are constructed or completed by the active response of the reader to the challenges issued by them. In the US, **Stanley Fish** introduced the concept of "affective stylistics," which was grounded in the reader's response to and construction of the literary text. His most popular and influential work, *Is There a Text in This Class?* (1980), combined the aesthetic dimension of Hans Robert Jauss's reception theory with an interest in the way that academic and other social institutions created "interpretive communities" that could account both for shared reading experiences among diverse individuals and for divergent interpretations of the same text.

While new theories began to emerge in the 1970s, more traditional theoretical approaches to literature enjoyed a resurgence of interest. One of the most important of these revitalized theories was Marxism, especially as it was reinterpreted by **Fredric Jameson** and **Louis Althusser**.

These theorists had clearly learned much from Gramsci, who was less interested in the economistic analysis of the modes of production than in IDEOLOGY critique. The new emphasis on politics and culture and their role in the formation and maintenance of what Althusser calls "ideological state apparatuses" led to a theoretical discourse that was both politically relevant and sharply attuned to the complexities of social life in POSTMODERNITY. However, as Graeme Turner has noted, the so-called "Gramscian turn" towards the study of ideology and HEGEMONY limited the capacity "to theorize the forms of political conflict and relations specific to the functioning of particular cultural technologies." The "cultural technologies" of the late twentieth century required analytical models not constrained by Marxist materialism, even Gramsci's and Althusser's nuanced versions of it. These models often relied on Foucault's work on power in order to expand the critical potential of Marxist critique so that theorists might "work with" ideology rather than "write it off" as a producer of false consciousness (Turner 31).

Jameson's own work ranged from the DIALECTICAL MATERIALISM of the early works through *Political Unconscious* (1981) to the critique of Postmodernism in the 1980s and '90s. His career has shown how a Marxist theorist could adapt to changing theoretical environments and become one of the leading theorists of Postmodernism. Like Louis Althusser's poststructuralist Marxism, which paved the way for a new generation of "post-Marxist" theorists, Jameson's writings on postmodernity retained a strong commitment to Marxism at the same time that they acknowledged fundamental changes in both society and social critique. By emphasizing ideology, determination, and hegemony, post-Marxists were better able to analyze the complex relations of power at the superstructural (broadly, cultural) level where dominant ideologies achieve hegemony and where radical politics take a stance of resistance. His work continued throughout the 1990s to explore the potential of post-Marxist social and cultural analysis. If the volume of essays edited by R. L. Rutsky and Bradley J. Macdonald, *Strategies for Theory: From Marx to Madonna* (2003), is any indication, the future direction of post-Marxist theory is both continuous with its nineteenth-century origins and divergent from them in its attention to the most evanescent of superstructural phenomena.

In the late 1970s and early '80s, a debate took place in the pages of scholarly journals between Critical Theorists and Marxists who were committed to the idea of theoretical and social TOTALITIES and Postmodernists who rejected models of totality for theories of dispersion, simulation, incommensurability, and chaos. Postmodernists were generally united in their stand against MASTER NARRATIVES that sought to explain, legitimize, and perpetuate universal truth, historical destiny, Providence, evolution, and a host of other ideals. Lyotard's *Postmodern Condition* (1979) is a powerful critique of such narratives and their legitimation of knowledge. It argues that the grand narratives of the Enlightenment had become delegitimated and replaced by language games and a "pragmatics of knowledge" (61). Jameson, in his foreword to *The Postmodern Condition*, finds this view problematic because it leaves no productive role for the kind of historicist critique crucial to Marxist theory. He suggests that master narratives were driven underground, so to speak, and formed part of a "political unconscious" that could be detected in the close analysis of literary and social texts. Jürgen Habermas more forcefully countered Lyotard's critique with his advocacy of a form of "communicative action" that kept theory engaged with historical conditions and political action and that offered at the same time a reasonable hope for social unity. In opposing the perceived anti-historical tendencies of Postmodernism, Habermas and Jameson were instrumental in creating the intellectual conditions for the dominance of historicist theories in the 1980s. (On the Lyotard–Habermas debate, see pp. 69–70.) The work of Steve Connor, especially *Postmodernist Culture* (1989), John McGowan, and Steven Best challenged those critics of Postmodernism who saw it as unhistorical and nihilistic or who believed that it lacked the potential for progressive social critique. They also extended the warrant of Postmodernism, which, by the early 1990s, could boast of being, as Connor put it, a general "theory of the contemporary."

"Always Historicize!": Historicism and Cultural Critique from the 1980s

The growth of theory since the 1970s has created a mind-boggling variety of approaches to social and cultural texts, and this variety itself presents a problem to many students and teachers who want to achieve a greater awareness of the theoretical nature of their intellectual labors. Equally troubling are the conceptual difficulties that theory present. Perceived as unduly erudite, arcane, obscure, and jargon-ridden, theory is regarded by many readers as far removed from the realities of both the university and society at large. In his essay "Traveling Theory," **Edward Said** raises some important questions about the proliferation of theory and its critical and social relevance:

> What happens to [theory] when, in different circumstances and for new reasons, it is used again and, in still more different circumstances, again? What can this tell us about theory itself – its limits, its possibilities, its inherent problems – and what can it suggest to us about the relationship between theory and criticism, on the one hand, and society and culture on the other? The pertinence of these questions will be apparent at a time when theoretical activity seems both intense and eclectic, when the relationship between social reality and a dominant yet hermetic critical discourse seems hard to determine, and when, for all of these reasons . . . it is futile to prescribe theoretical programs for contemporary criticism. (230)

One response to this crisis was the rise of historicist discourses, including a resurgent CULTURAL MATERIALISM, that rejected the often abstruse methods and nomenclature of Poststructuralism, especially Deconstruction, which relied on complex concepts and strategies drawn from philosophy and linguistics. Literary and cultural analysis from a materialist standpoint presupposes that the SUBJECT is neither stable nor AUTONOMOUS, but the *subject of* social, cultural, and historical forces. Negotiating among these forces, consciously performing the various functions of the subject (and subjectivity), constitutes what for many is the *Postmodern* subject.

In 1981, Fredric Jameson, one of the most influential Marxist critics in the US, declared, "Always historicize!" For Jameson, this meant that the critic of culture must examine the material, social, and political DETERMINATIONS that constitute every historical moment. He was recommending that readers and critics practice what Marxist theorists had been doing all along. As I have already indicated, the 1970s saw the rise of Gramscian and Althusserian modes of historical analysis that had redefined the way that Marxists, as well as a host of other historicist critics, looked at society and culture. Jameson's exhortation was another moment of redefinition. Amid Postmodernist attacks on history, he was exhorting us to think of history all the time. The New Historicism, which started to emerge at this time, made similar exhortations. **Stephen Greenblatt**, who was influenced by Marxism and Poststructuralist theories of TEXTUALITY, developed a popular New Historicist mode of analysis that has had a strong presence in literary studies, but especially in Renaissance studies, where Greenblatt's own work is situated. The mainspring of New Historicist thought in the 1980s was the journal *Representations*, co-edited by Greenblatt. Greenblatt's most important early work, *Renaissance Self-Fashioning* (1980), developed a mode of reading literary texts that relied on contextualizing them within a context (or "archive") of other (typically "non-literary") texts. This "thick" historical description of the discourse environment in which the literary text in question is produced and first consumed constitutes a CULTURAL POETICS, one that owes a great deal to the TEXTUALIST anthropology of Clifford Geertz. (On Greenblatt, see pp. 130–1.) The other major theorists in the early years were Catherine Gallagher, whose interests included feminism and American left-wing radicalism, Louis Montrose, whose essays throughout the 1980s insisted on the dialectical interplay between textual formalism and historical context, and Jonathan Goldberg, whose work focused on the importance of sexual identities, especially queer identities, and opened up a whole new terrain for Renaissance scholars. The New Historicism was not solely concerned with Renaissance literature, however. Early on, we find important works in US literature and culture. For example, Walter Benn Michaels, in *The Gold Standard and the Logic of Naturalism* (1987), employed new historicist methodologies to examine the intersection of economics and literary representation.

Many Marxist critics reject New Historicism and its textualist strategies of interpretation and take a CULTURAL MATERIALIST position less interested in the textual quality of history than in the impact of material social forces on people and institutions. Cultural materialism offers a dialectical critique of the relationship between social and economic forces and cultural production. Important figures in the British tradition include Jonathan Dollimore and Alan Sinfield, whose work carries on a tradition of materialist analysis that goes back at least to the cultural histories of **Raymond Williams** and E. P. Thompson. In the US, the materialist analyses by Elizabeth Fox-Genovese and Eugene D. Genovese drew the attention of literary scholars to new historical evidence concerning slavery and other social problems in the US. Their *Fruits of Merchant Capital: Slavery and Bourgeois Property in the Rise and Expansion of Capitalism* (1983) was a landmark work that considered hitherto marginalized and excluded subjects and social groups as meaningful historical agents. By the 1990s, Jameson's "Always historicize!" had ceased to be a radical call to arms and had become instead a theoretical ORTHODOXY.

The historicist orientation in literary studies was accompanied by an expansion of its geographical ambit. Nowhere is this more apparent than in the new field of Postcolonial Studies – though "new" is not quite accurate, since theoretical work on the phenomenon of postcolonialism had been going on since at least the 1950s. What renovated the field was **Said**'s *Orientalism* (1978). Drawing on **Foucault**'s theories of DISCOURSE and POWER and Nietzsche's theories of critical history and genealogy, Said analyzed a vast structure of knowledge and mythology emanating from the West (or Occident) that had, for at least two hundred years, determined how the West conceived of the East (or Orient). The "cultural strength" of the West led to an assumption "that the Orient and everything in it was, if not patently inferior to, then in need of corrective study by the West" (41). Some theorists have criticized Said for not representing the reverse process – representations of the West produced by colonial and postcolonial intellectuals and artists – but just this kind of work had been produced by the theorists of the 1950s, as well as by others in the 1960s and '70s, including Aimé Césaire and C. L. R. James writing in the Caribbean and Wole Soyinka and Chinua Achebe writing in Nigeria. In part as a reaction to Said's work, a number of important new figures began to emerge, and in them we can discern a coherent field of study taking shape. South Asian theorists took the lead in the early 1980s. Ashis Nandy's *The Intimate Enemy* (1983) and the early work of the Subaltern Studies Group, especially that of Ranajit Guha, revealed both the nature of the effects of colonialism in India and the outlines of a nativist and revisionist historical discourse that could serve as an alternative to colonialist and nationalist MASTER NARRATIVES. Influential essays by Partha Chatterjee, **Gayatri Chakravorty Spivak**, and **Homi Bhabha** appeared in the mid-1980s. These theorists brought to Postcolonial Studies the insights of Feminism, Deconstruction, and Psychoanalysis, and showed how such theories could be used for progressive political ends. The postcolonial critique of Western Feminism that we see in the work of Spivak, Chandra Talpade Mohanty, and Sara Suleri was instrumental in making Feminism more responsive to the problems of non-Western women.

Although South Asian theorists in some ways dominated the field, especially in the US and England, there was significant work going on all over the world. From the mid-1980s, important work appeared by Peter Hulme and Antonio Benitez-Rojo on the encounters between European explorers and indigenous peoples in the Caribbean. Achebe's and Soyinka's work was followed by a new generation of African philosophers and theorists, including preeminently Kwame Anthony Appiah and V. Y. Mudimbe. Former and current British Commonwealth countries – especially Australia, whose colonial development was complicated by the penal colonies established in the eighteenth century – have their own peculiar postcolonial conditions. Work by Helen Tiffin, Bob Hodge, and Vijay Mishra has been especially important since 1990 for drawing our attention to the problems faced by Aboriginal peoples and to the impact of large-scale immigration and SETTLER COLONIZATION. In a similar manner, Irish studies has forged its own brand of postcolonial inquiry which emphasizes Ireland's character as a METROCOLONY and its long history of intimate mismanagement by the British Parliament and the Anglo-Irish ruling class. Because of its close proximity to the center of Empire, Ireland experienced colonialism in a unique fashion. In this regard, it resembled India, where the English language and English political and cultural traditions had become entrenched after centuries of colonial administration. As Luke Gibbons, Declan Kiberd, and other theorists have pointed out, Ireland's metrocolonial status did not immunize it against the problems faced by other colonial and postcolonial territories.

All of the above-mentioned theorists were attempting, in an era dominated by theory rooted in European and US intellectual traditions, to promulgate alternatives that could respond to the special situations that had arisen in the former colonies and that also could contribute to a greater understanding of the role postcolonial nations played within an increasingly globalized political framework. We might regard this as the legacy of Fanon, who argued that "National consciousness, which is not nationalism, is the only thing that will give us an international dimension" (247). Taken together, the work in the 1980s and '90s reflects the special problems faced by postcolonial nations as they overcame the difficulties of DECOLONIZATION (which for many of these nations began in the 1950s and '60s) and confronted the pressing difficulties of establishing new national traditions and international relations. One of the possibly unintended consequences of these developments is that many postcolonial theorists now have positions at prestigious US and European universities, where they have become valuable members of a new global intelligentsia.

Some of the same developments that we see in Postcolonial Studies – especially the new emphasis on non-Western and non-traditional social groups – were occurring in other fields as well, notably in British Cultural Studies, which in the 1980s began to look more closely at the complex interrelations between postcolonial and METROPOLITAN cultures. The mainstream tradition of British Cultural Studies at this time – represented in the influential reader, *Culture, Ideology and Social Process* (1981), edited by Tony Bennett and others – was primarily concerned with a critique of IDEOLOGICAL HEGEMONY, which took the form of a critique of cultural representations, and with the analysis of counter-hegemonic alternatives proffered by immigrant groups, popular media, and subcultures. Dick Hebdige's *Subculture: The Meaning of Style* (1979), for example, concentrates on the fracturing of social groups into increasingly smaller subgroups. Hebdige looked closely at the social and cultural significance of popular media and challenged traditional hierarchies of high and low culture in the arts. But this was not an insular British affair, for Hebdige's work with subcultures, and the way that social status is negotiated within them, bears a disciplinary kinship to that of **Pierre Bourdieu**. The latter's *Distinction: A Social Critique of the Judgment of Taste* (1979) argued that the determining power in the SOCIAL FIELD is HABITUS, the "socialized subjectivity" of an active agent in the world whose *dispositions* (skills and competences acquired in a given social field) are the mark of social status and *distinction*. The limits and rules that structure the social field, in which the social agent achieves distinction, are neither arbitrary nor external but are constituted by the aggregate of successful social experiences (or "moves") that constitute the field. The limits of the *habitus* and the social field are not unlike Foucault's "historical *a priori*," the governing limits of a DISCURSIVE FORMATION, which Foucault links to the "archive," a "general system of the formation and transformation of statements" as well as the "law of what can be said, the system that governs the appearance of statements as unique events" (127, 129). (On historical *a prioris*, see 159.) Like Clifford Geertz, whose *Interpretation of Cultures* (1973) pioneered textualist ethnography, Bourdieu was interested in how cultures represent themselves, how they use dance, ritual, and other practices to establish and communicate hierarchies of status and ranks of distinction.

From the 1950s, US Cultural Studies was mainly concerned with historical and political analysis, though Geertz's work in the 1970s adumbrated one form Cultural Studies would take in the 1980s, when textualist anthropology would produce its first set text, *Writing Culture: The Poetics and Politics of Ethnography* (1986), edited by James Clifford and George E. Marcus. In other respects, US Cultural Studies began to resemble its British counterpart. The study of so-called popular or mass cultural formations and artifacts in both the US and Britain became widespread from the 1980s, leading to serious academic projects focusing on rock and roll, fashion, genre fiction, and subcultures. Many of these new Cultural Studies theorists, in the US and Britain, were interested in problems of Gender and Sexuality. Angela McRobbie and Janice Radway, for example, combined textualism and Feminism in nuanced readings of popular music and literature, youth culture, and middle-class literary tastes. Work on film theory by **Teresa de Lauretis** and Laura Mulvey revealed the gendered dynamics of representation, particularly the *gaze* that is doubly represented in film, once by the film maker whose gaze constructs or composes human actors as objects in a visual medium and again by the audience member whose own gaze reduplicates the film maker's but can also criticize it, especially if the audience member is a woman reflecting on the gaze required of her by a male film maker. **Donna Haraway** sought the same gendered dynamics in nature and made some controversial claims in *Simians, Cyborgs, and Women* (1991), a book that sought at bottom to redefine the relationship between culture and nature. In the late 1990s, the study of "material culture" – especially the areas of consumer product design and collecting – stressed the fundamental importance of consumerism and thereby expanded the theoretical warrant of Cultural Studies. One of the latest and most innovative trends in Cultural Studies is the project of digital humanities, which entails the use of computer technologies in the study of a broad array of disciplines. Applications in literary studies include stylistic and linguistic analysis, electronic editing, thematic research, cognitive stylistics, speculative computing, and "robotic poetics."

The new emphasis on culture and history in the 1980s and '90s was accompanied by a concern with the SUBJECT and SUBJECTIVITY. These concepts were addressed from a number of perspectives. Historicist and cultural theorists tended to emphasize context and situation, framing social and historical problems in terms of subjects hitherto ignored: slaves, ethnic and religious minorities, workers, women, children, prisoners, the disabled, and so on. The critique of the subject took on a new complexion with the resurgence of Psychoanalysis in the 1980s, following upon the English translation of **Jacques Lacan's** *Écrits* (1977). Lacan claimed to be promoting a "return to Freud," who had been all but eclipsed in the academy by feminist critique and other models of psychotherapy. As it turned out, returning to Freud meant unveiling whole new vistas that Freud had glimpsed but lacked the theoretical tools to explain. The most important insight Lacan derived from his return was that the unconscious was structured like a language; Freud himself had suggested as much in *The Interpretation of Dreams*, when he argued that dreams function by condensing and displacing images. Lacan, drawing on Saussure's work, went further and declared that the unconscious, in dreams for example, operates through the play of signifiers, much as language does. The most important implication of this insight was that unconscious operations were fundamentally *linguistic* and that language could be said to penetrate to the very basis of human existence. He also posited orders of human experience, which he described as the Symbolic (law and language), the Imaginary (fantasy), and the Real (unmediated material existence). Lacanian psychoanalysis provides a means to chart the formation of subjectivity in its traversal of these orders. (On Lacan, see pp. 158–9, 168–71.)

It is difficult to overestimate the extent of Lacan's influence at this time. His ideas can be found in French and US Feminism, in theories of Gender and Sexuality, in the Critical Theory of **Slavoj Žižek** and Ernesto Laclau, and in the study of literature and culture, from Homer to Hitchcock. **Homi Bhabha** drew on Lacan's work in order to describe the peculiar nature of the postcolonial subject, while **de Lauretis** and Mulvey stressed Lacan's notion of the gaze in order to develop a Feminist theory of film and visual culture. **Gilles Deleuze** and **Félix Guattari's** *Anti-Oedipus* (1977), which emerged in part as a critique of Lacan's seminars, challenged the dominant themes of Psychoanalysis – especially the Oedipus complex – and replaced the Freudian concept of desire as lack with a new conception of desiring machines that produce intensities and flows of libido that course through systems ("bodies without organs") creating effects no longer grounded in the repressive logic of Oedipus (or, for that matter, Lacan's Symbolic order).

Questions of the subject and subjectivity became central to French Feminism in the 1980s, though as Toril Moi points out in her widely-read *Sexual/Textual Politics* (1985), US feminists were slow in following suit. It did not take long for US feminists like Jane Flax, Jane Gallop, Alice Jardine, and Barbara Johnson to develop sophisticated new theories informed by Lacanian psychoanalysis and Deconstruction. Of crucial importance was the consideration of the SUBJECT in terms of SOCIAL CONSTRUCTIONISM, according to which gender and sexuality are regarded not as essential aspects of individual identity but rather as constructions of social and cultural power. Foucault's theories of discourse and power and **Judith Butler's** work on PERFORMATIVITY have been especially influential in developing constructionist theories of identity that seek to avoid the ESSENTIALISM of traditional sexual and gender roles. Performative strategies grew out of a desire to move beyond the essentialist notions of the subject that, to varying degrees, still dominated much theoretical discourse. In part a result of poststructuralist critiques of the subject, performativity grounds gender and sexual identity in the personal choices made by men and women in concrete social situations. Butler's *Gender Trouble* (1990) followed de Beauvoir's *The Second Sex* in proffering a constructionist thesis of female identity. In addition to questioning the essentialist notion that a single "common identity" can apply to all women, she also argued that there is no common oppressor, no "universal or hegemonic structure of patriarchy or masculine domination" (3). Her chief concerns were to challenge the fixity and masculine character of the social and legal subject and to expose the compulsory nature of social regulations that determine gender identity.

Butler's *Gender Trouble* was followed in 1993 by *Bodies that Matter: On the Discursive Limits of "Sex,"* which continued her critique of gender, with an emphasis on the material body. This development was not new for Feminism. As I have indicated already, it was an abiding concern for Irigaray, Cixous, and other French feminists who were often accused of essentialism, of claiming that a woman's body was the indivisible and irrefutable core of female identity and self-expression. In Butler's work, and that of Susan Bordo and Elizabeth Grosz, the body was recognized as the site of complex social, cultural, and political inscriptions. This turn towards the politicized and inscribed body in Feminism also had some precedent in the work of African American Feminism. Prominent in this regard was Barbara Smith, who published, in 1977, what was arguably the first important work on black Feminism, *Toward a Black Feminist Criticism*, and **bell hooks**, whose work from the mid-1980s was at the forefront of a third wave of Feminism that emphasized the experiences of women of color, both in the West and in a variety of postcolonial locations. Just as Moi's *Sexual/Textual Politics* criticized US feminists for their lack of class analysis and their philosophical naïveté, hooks' *Feminist Theory: From Margin to Center* (1984) called on Feminism to broaden its horizons and consider the circumstances of women of color and the role of race in the PROBLEMATICS of identity, gender, and sexual violence. By the turn of the twenty-first century, Feminism had become a global discourse, one that had overcome many of its own limitations by becoming more open to the myriad experiences of women from all walks of life.

As Feminism gained prominence in the 1980s, questions of Gender and Sexuality were posed in ways that were often provocative but always innovative and refreshing. The new interest in gender and sexual identities was propelled by Butler's theories of performance and performativity. From the mid-1970s, with Monique Wittig's *The Lesbian Body* (1975) and the essays and poetry of Adrienne Rich, greater attention was being paid to lesbian sexuality, a trend that accelerated in the mid-1990s with work by de Lauretis, Judith Roof, Laura Doan, and Lynda Hart. Indeed, it is possible to argue that the feminist critique of gender and sexuality made possible the explosive interest in male homoeroticism and homosexuality inaugurated by **Eve Kosofsky Sedgwick's** pioneering study, *Between Men: English Literature and Male Homosocial Desire* (1985). This volume drew on theories of "triangular desire" put forward by René Girard and Gayle Rubin, in which women mediate the desire of men. In the literary contexts explored by Sedgwick, HOMOSOCIAL DESIRE is a form of displacement. Desire between men, which could threaten to become eroticized, even genitalized (that is, result in sexual activity), was thus displaced onto a relationship in which a woman serves as the common object of desire. (On homosocial desire, see 105–6.) Sedgwick's second book, *Epistemology of the Closet* (1990), and Jonathan Dollimore's

Sexual Dissidence (1991) explored further the problems of male homosexuality and helped to establish the foundations of queer theory.

The new ideas concerning language, the subject, and the social construction of identity – ideas that transformed so much literary and
cultural theory in the 1980s and '90s – were instrumental in transforming Ethnic Studies. One of the most significant works in African
American studies at this time, **Henry Louis Gates's** *The Signifying
Monkey: A Theory of Afro-American Literary Criticism* (1988), explores the
complex and dialectical interplay of native traditions, like the "signifying
monkey" motif found in African and early slave literatures, and how
native traditions intersect with poststructuralist theories of language
and signification. To some extent Gates's work, and that of his mentor,
Houston Baker, is indebted to the pioneering work of W. E. B. Du Bois
who, in 1903, put forward the idea of "double consciousness. This was
a provocative idea, one that emphasized not only a consciousness of
racial DIFFERENCE but also a sense of radical internal division, a sense of
"two-ness" that Du Bois understood in terms of a doubling of the soul,
of the struggle to be human in America. If Gates offered a way to
syncretize Western and African approaches to literary theory, the
Afrocentrism of Martin Bernal and Molefi K. Asante advocated the rein-
statement of Africa and African culture at the center of Western cultural
and intellectual history. Bernal's *Black Athena: The Afroasiatic Roots of
Classical Civilization* (1987) and Asante's *The Afrocentric Idea* (1987) were
radical and controversial revisions of history that had a profound
impact on the constitution of African American programs in the US.
Cornel West, one of the leading advocates of multiculturalism, though
more moderate in his approach than Asante, was perhaps more effective
in his appeal to a nonacademic audience. In 1992, Gates and Kwame
Anthony Appiah released *Encarta Africana* (first published 1998). Published by Microsoft, this electronic resource, the first of its kind on such
a large scale, not only marked a pivotal moment in scholarly publishing
but also announced, in no uncertain terms, that the African American
experience would not be marginalized by its own radical discourse.
Rather than advocate a separatist or multiculturalist agenda, Gates and
Appiah situated African American theory and criticism within the
broader context of Western discourse. In a sense, they found a middle
ground between the Afrocentrism of Asante and the multiculturalism
of West.

In a parallel development to the rise of African American studies, Chicano/a studies emerged in the late 1960s as part of a movement, initially centered in California and Texas, that included strikes and boycotts initiated by Cesar Chavez's United Farm Workers. In the wake of this political activism came a vibrant theoretical and critical movement. Gloria Anzaldúa's foundational *Borderlands/La Frontera: The New Mestiza* (1987) introduced students and scholars to a new perspective on the Feminism of women of color and was one of the first works to focus on the impact of borders on the formation of ethnic identities. Ramón Saldívar's *Chicano Narrative* (1990) focused on Chicano experience in the US Southwest as it is explored dialectically in narrative fictions. As with other movements concerned to reveal the social and political foundations of literary productions, Chicano literature explores the links between politics and art. "Especially with the beginning of Chicano social activism in the 1960s," Saldívar writes, "narrative could root itself in the concrete social interests of historical and contemporary events" (24). Though in some important ways connected to the Anglo-American societies against which they struggled, Chicano writers remained profoundly connected to their "other" homeland. Like African American studies, Chicano/a studies was in the avant-garde when it came to theorizing race, ethnicity, and cultural difference. Cherríe Moraga, Sonia Saldívar-Hull, and others have diversified the theoretical base of Chicano/a studies with work on the legal system, Feminism, bicultural experience, and the status of race in the twenty-first century. This ongoing project suggests the complexity of problems still facing US theorists of race and ethnic identity in the context of POSTMODERNITY.

Like Chicano/a studies, Native American studies has had a long history of resistance to the social and cultural institutions responsible for the decimation and displacement of native peoples. For example, Vine Deloria, in *Custer Died for Your Sins* (1969), critiqued the anthropological representation and social repression of native peoples. The next year, Dee Brown's *Bury My Heart at Wounded Knee* offered a revisionist history of Native Americans. Subsequent work, mostly in the late 1980s and 1990s, contextualized Native American experience within the broader framework of cultural diversity in the US and created greater awareness of native intellectual thought. Of special importance from the 1980s was the work of Gerald Vizenor who combined a deep knowledge of native literatures with an interest in Western theoretical discourse, including the concerns of Poststructuralism and Postmodernism. Native American studies, like Chicano/a studies, had become, by the 1990s, deeply invested Cultural Studies and Postcolonial theory, which could be used to explore the form and social function of native literatures. Vizenor was involved in this endeavor, as was Arnold Krupat, whose *Ethnocriticism* (1991) was part of the "writing cultures" movement associated with James Clifford and George Marcus. This movement, which stressed the problems of Western anthropology and the potential of indigenous alternatives, had a vital impact on studies of US ethnic literatures and cultures. Krupat's *Red Matters: Native American Studies* (2002) and Elvira Pulitano's *Toward a Native American Critical Theory* (2003) consolidated the gains made in the 1990s and indicate the direction of Native American studies in the twenty-first century.

The movements I have been discussing are characterized by a strong HISTORICIST orientation, but there is another significant element that links them together: theorizing DIFFERENCE. Of course the desire to theorize difference – including cultural, ethnic, sexual, gender, and other forms of difference – has its roots in the general concept of linguistic difference that emerged in the work of poststructuralist theorists beginning in the 1960s. But it is plain that for these new theorists, difference is a function of specific social, cultural, and historical contexts. It is important to emphasize that the historicization of difference does not constitute a departure from or break with Poststructuralism; on the contrary, it testifies to the continued relevance of poststructuralist innovations. It also gives further evidence of the tendency towards HYBRIDIZATION at all levels of theoretical discourse.

Theory at the *Fin de Siècle*

In the last decade of the twentieth century, the general trend towards HISTORICISM continued, with new developments in Postmodern theory, Feminism, and Critical Theory. Chief among these developments was the critical rehabilitation of certain categories – specifically the SUBJECT and UNIVERSALITY – that could be deployed in the service of social and cultural transformation. Feminism at the *fin de siècle* played a leading role in forming a critical theory of Postmodernism. From the early

1990s, Butler, Seyla Benhabib, and Drucilla Cornell began to use Critical Theory in conjunction with Feminist critique to address social and political issues concerning women. Postcolonial Feminism, especially in the work of Spivak and Mohanty, continued at this time to call into question the politics of postcolonial nations in which women continue to suffer under patriarchal rule. Vital to the feminist critique of POSTMODERNITY was Mary Joe Frug's *Postmodern Legal Feminism* (1992), which challenged masculinist assumptions underwriting the subject of legal discourse. Her groundbreaking work was developed by Jennifer Wicke and Barbara Johnson who addressed problems of gender, identity, and social justice. According to Wicke, Feminism needed "to catch up to a reality we barely have a name for, the Postmodern situation of a theory of identity that seeks to overcome the limitations of fixed, immutable, and hierarchical identities, with a feminism still involved in a straightforward identity politics" (33). The critical questioning of fundamental aspects of social life – the legal status of women, the ethics of reproduction, intellectual and aesthetic life, class and racial identity – continue to be the focus of a Postmodern Feminist theory that does not lose track of the subject of identity politics.

Questions about the possibility of social activism and identity politics became increasingly important in a post-Cold War era in which **Lyotard**'s "Postmodern condition" had leapt from the domain of esoteric science and technology to the mainstream of social life. The 1990s saw a number of theorists working across theoretical disciplines in an attempt to understand complex new developments, including the paradoxical coexistence of globalization and the resurgence of nationalism and the equally paradoxical desire to approach these new social and political realities with recourse to theoretical concepts and strategies belonging to another, simpler era. This trend is evident in the increased interest in the Enlightenment and MODERNITY. Adorno and Habermas had long held conflicting views about the Enlightenment and its effects on late modernity – Adorno was highly skeptical of the benign force of reason, while Habermas held that reason was crucial for gaining social consensus – and saw their work as part of a larger critique of the Enlightenment. By the last decade of the century, modernity and the Enlightenment were once again subjects of critical conflict and debate. A variety of theorists, including Perry Anderson, Charles Taylor, Anthony J. Cascardi, and Anthony Giddens, weighed in on the character and consequences of modernity. A strong consensus has emerged, among many theorists, that Enlightenment philosophers (especially Kant and Hegel) still exert a considerable influence on Postmodernist thinking. **Fredric Jameson**, in *A Singular Modernity* (2002), alludes to the paradox of this situation when he argues that the contemporary (so-called *Postmodern*) world is a fundamentally *modern* one.

The impulse to revise received notions of MODERNITY and to call into question the fundamental difference between it and POSTMODERNITY is seconded by a renascent Critical Theory, strongly influenced by Feminist Theory and by Althusserian and Gramscian reconsiderations of Marx. Of particular note was the renewed focus on Kant and Hegel, whose conceptions of universality and TOTALITY were submitted to an essentially Postmodernist critique; one of the results of this critical operation was that these concepts were made available in new ways for the analysis of gender, sexuality, the subject, the State, and political action. Butler, along with **Slavoj Žižek** and Ernesto Laclau, exemplified this trend, often called "postfoundationalism," in an important volume of essays, *Contingency, Hegemony, Universality: Contemporary Dialogues on the Left* (2000), which draws on post-Marxism, Feminism, and Lacanian psychoanalysis to argue for forms of "provisional totality" and "contingent universality" that could ground collective political action. What is truly striking is the willingness on the part of these theorists to rethink Kantian and Hegelian concepts as provisional and performative within a specific framework of social critique. Thus, Žižek can claim that "Kantian formalism and radical historicism are not really opposites, but two sides of the same coin" (Butler et al. 111). This willingness to see continuities across the historical field – continuities that hitherto had seemed impossible – characterizes a theoretical perspective at once unrelentingly critical and persuasively constructive.

Conclusion

No history of literary theory can hope to give a full account of the rich and varied developments that in this section have been sketched in only the broadest strokes. What is inevitably left out is a sense of the complexity of individual theories and the relationships between and among them that have produced innumerable hybrid configurations. The remaining sections of this *Guide* offer the reader some sense of these complexities.

One of the arguments made throughout this section is that literary theory in the twentieth century developed along two main pathways: one that emphasized language, linguistic difference, and formalism and another that emphasized historicism, ideology, and the determining influence of social and cultural forces. From one perspective it appears that one pathway or another has dominated the course of theory in any given epoch; however, from another perspective, both pathways appear interdependent. This is nowhere more evident than in the account of theory in the last quarter of the twentieth century, an epoch during which formalism and historicism interacted and imbricated with one another, producing exciting new combinations and raising new and controversial questions about the subject, language, identity, textuality, race, gender, and a host of other topics. If anything remains constant in this variegated history, it is the impulse to understand how literary and cultural texts create meaning and how we, as readers, can understand the value and variety of being human.

WORKS CITED

Arnold, Matthew. "The Function of Criticism at the Present Time." In *Lectures and Essays in Criticism*. Vol. 3 of *Complete Prose Works*. Ed. R. H. Super. 11 vols. Ann Arbor: University of Michigan Press, 1960–77. 258–85.

Butler, Judith. *Gender Trouble: Feminism and the Subversion of Identity*. New York: Routledge, 1990.

———, Ernesto Laclau, and Slavoj Žižek. *Contingency, Hegemony, Universality: Contemporary Dialogues on the Left*. London and New York: Verso, 2000.

Du Bois, W. E. B. *The Souls of Black Folk*. New York: Vintage Books/Library of America, 1990.

Derrida, Jacques. "Structure, Sign and Play in the Discourse of the Humanities." In *Writing and Difference*. Trans. Alan Bass. Chicago: University of Chicago Press, 1978. 278–93.

Eliot, T. S. *Selected Essays, 1917–1932*. New York: Harcourt, Brace, 1932.

Fanon, Frantz. *The Wretched of the Earth*. Trans. Constance Farrington. New York: Grove Weidenfeld, 1963.

Foucault, Michel. *The Archaeology of Knowledge and the Discourse on Language*. 1969, 1971. Trans. A. M. Sheridan Smith. New York: Pantheon, 1972.

Gramsci, Antonio. *Selections from the Prison Notebooks of Antonio Gramsci.* Ed. and Trans. Quintin Hoare and Geoffrey Nowell Smith. New York: International Publishers, 1971.

Habermas, Jürgen. "Modernity versus Postmodernity." *New German Critique* 22 (Spring 1981): 15–18.

Lentricchia, Frank. *After the New Criticism.* Chicago: University of Chicago Press, 1980.

Lukács, Georg. *The Theory of the Novel.* 1920. Trans. Anna Bostock. Cambridge, MA: M.I.T. Press, 1971.

Lyotard, Jean-François. *The Post-Modern Condition: A Report on Knowledge.* Trans. Geoff Bennington and Brian Massumi. Minneapolis: University of Minnesota Press, 1984.

Moi, Toril. *Sexual/Textual Politics: Feminist Literary Theory.* 2nd ed. London and New York: Routledge, 1985, 2002.

Nietzsche, Friedrich. *The Will to Power.* Ed. Walter Kaufmann. Trans. Walter Kaufmann and R. J. Hollingdale. New York: Vintage, 1968.

Richards, I. A. *Principles of Literary Criticism.* New York: Harcourt, Brace; London: K. Paul Trench, Trubner, 1924, 1926.

Said, Edward. *Orientalism.* 1979. London: Penguin, 1985.

———. "Traveling Theory." In *The World, the Text and the Critic.* Cambridge, MA: Harvard University Press, 1983. 226–47.

Saldívar, Ramón. *Chicano Narrative: The Dialectics of Difference.* Madison: University of Wisconsin Press, 1990.

Turner, Graeme. *British Cultural Studies.* London; New York: Routledge, 1996.

Wicke, Jennifer. "Postmodern Identities and the Politics of the (Legal) Subject." In *Feminism and Postmodernism.* Eds. Margaret Ferguson and Jennifer Wicke. Durham: Duke University Press, 1994. 10–33.

Wilde, Oscar. *Intentions: The Decay of Lying, Pen, Pencil and Poison, The Critic as Artist, The Truth of Masks.* New York: Brentano's, 1905.

Woolf, Virginia. "Modern Fiction." In *The Essays of Virginia Woolf. Vol. VI 1925–28.* Ed. Andrew McNeillie. London: Hogarth Press, 1986. 157–65.

RECOMMENDATIONS FOR FURTHER STUDY

The following texts are concerned primarily with the history of literary theory. Readers interested in general studies of theory should consult the short list at the end of "The Rise of Literary Theory" and the individual sections of "The Scope of Literary Theory."

Baldic, Chris. *Criticism and Literary Theory 1890 to the Present*. London and New York: Longman, 1996.

The Cambridge History of Literary Criticism. 9 vols. Cambridge, UK and New York: Cambridge University Press, 1989–2001.

Cassedy, Steven. *Flight from Eden: The Origins of Modern Literary Criticism and Theory*. Berkeley: University of California Press, 1990.

Dosse, François. *History of Structuralism*. 2 vols. Trans. Deborah Glassman. Minneapolis: University of Minnesota Press, 1997.

Lentricchia, Frank. *After the New Criticism*. Chicago: University of Chicago Press, 1980.

Graff, Gerald. *Professing Literature: An Institutional History*. Chicago: University of Chicago Press, 1987.

Wellek, René. *A History of Modern Criticism*. 8 vols. New Haven: Yale University Press, 1955–92.

Wimsatt, William K., and Cleanth Brooks. *Literary Criticism: A Short History*. 2 vols. Chicago: University of Chicago Press, 1957, 1978.

Timeline

1951	Theodor Adorno, *Minima Moralia: Reflections from Damaged Life*
1953	Roland Barthes, *Writing Degree Zero*
1954	W. K. Wimsatt and Monroe C. Beardsley, *The Verbal Icon: Studies in the Meaning of Poetry*
1955	Theodor Adorno and Max Horkheimer, co-directors of the Institute of Social Research
	Herbert Marcuse, *Eros and Civilization*
1956	Roman Jakobson and Morris Halle, *Fundamentals of Language*
1957	Ian Watt, *The Rise of the Novel*
	Albert Memmi, *The Colonizer and the Colonized*
	Roland Barthes, *Mythologies*
1958	Raymond Williams, *Culture and Society: 1780–1950*
	Claude Lévi-Strauss, *Structural Anthropology*
1961	Frantz Fanon, *The Wretched of the Earth*
1963	Betty Friedan, *The Feminine Mystique*
1964	Founding of the Centre for Contemporary Cultural Studies at the University of Birmingham
1966	Roland Barthes, "Introduction to the Structural Analysis of Narrative"
	Symposium, "The Languages of Criticism and the Sciences of Man," Johns Hopkins University Humanities Center
	Wayne Booth, *Rhetoric of Fiction*
	Jacques Lacan, *Écrits*
	Kenneth Burke, *Language as Symbolic Action: Essays on Life, Literature and Method*
1966–72	Gérard Genette, *Figures*
1967	Jacques Derrida, *Writing and Difference, Of Grammatology*
1968	Walter Benjamin, *Illuminations*
1969	Michel Foucault, *The Archaeology of Knowledge and the Discourse on Language*
	Vine Deloria, *Custer Died for Your Sins*
1970	Kate Millet, *Sexual Politics*
	Germaine Greer, *The Female Eunuch*
1971	Paul de Man, *Blindness and Insight*
	Louis Althusser, *Lenin and Philosophy, and Other Essays*
	Michel Foucault, *The Order of Things: An Archaeology of the Human Sciences*

Ihab Hassan, *The Dismemberment of Orpheus: Toward a Postmodern Literature*

1974   Luce Irigaray, *Speculum of the Other Woman*

1975   Hélène Cixous, "The Laugh of the Medusa"

Jürgen Habermas, *Legitimation Crisis*

Michel Foucault, *Discipline and Punish: The Birth of the Prison*

Monique Wittig, *The Lesbian Body*

1976   J. Hillis Miller, "Ariadne's Thread: Repetition and the Narrative Line"

Elaine Showalter, *A Literature of Their Own: British Women Novelists from Brontë to Lessing*

Terry Eagleton, *Criticism and Ideology: A Study in Marxist Literary Theory*

1976–84   Michel Foucault, *The History of Sexuality*

1977   Roland Barthes, *Image-Music-Text*

Gilles Deleuze and Félix Guattari, *Anti-Oedipus: Capitalism and Schizophrenia*

Tzvetan Todorov, *The Poetics of Prose*

1978   Wolfgang Iser, *The Act of Reading: A Theory of Aesthetic Response*

Edward Said, *Orientalism*

1979   Robert Scholes, *Fabulation and Metafiction*

Jean-François Lyotard, *The Postmodern Condition*

Pierre Bourdieu, *Distinction: A Social Critique of the Judgment of Taste*

Sandra Gilbert and Susan Gubar, *The Madwoman in the Attic: The Woman Writer and the Nineteenth-Century Literary Imagination*

1980   Linda Hutcheon, *Narcissistic Narrative: The Metafictional Paradox*

Stanley Fish, *Is There a Text in This Class?*

Stephen Greenblatt, *Renaissance Self-Fashioning*

Pierre Bourdieu, *The Logic of Practice*

Gilles Deleuze and Félix Guattari, *Thousand Plateaus: Capitalism and Schizophrenia*

Frank Lentricchia, *After the New Criticism*

Julia Kristeva, *Desire in Language: A Semiotic Approach to Literature and Art*

Jane Tompkins, *Reader-Response Criticism: From Formalism to Post-Structuralism*

1981   M. M. Bakhtin, *The Dialogic Imagination* (composed 1930s and '40s)

Barbara Johnson, *The Critical Difference: Essays on the Contemporary Rhetoric of Reading*

Jürgen Habermas, "Modernity versus Postmodernity"

Fredric Jameson, *The Political Unconscious: Narrative as a Socially Symbolic Act*

1982   J. Hillis Miller, *Fiction and Repetition*

Shoshana Felman, *Literature and Psychoanalysis*

Jacques Lacan, *Feminine Sexuality: Jacques Lacan and the École Freudienne*

Gerald Prince, *Narratology: The Form and Functioning of Narrative*

Jane Gallop, *Feminism and Psychoanalysis: The Daughter's Seduction*

1983   Jean Baudrillard, *Simulations*

Terry Eagleton, *Literary Theory: An Introduction*

Louis Montrose, "Of Gentlemen and Shepherds: The Politics of Elizabethan Pastoral Form"

1984   bell hooks, *Feminist Theory: From Margin to Center*

1985   Eve Kosofsky Sedgwick, *Between Men: English Literature and Male Homosocial Desire*

Ernesto Laclau, and Chantal Mouffe, *Hegemony and Socialist Strategy: Towards a Radical Democratic Politics*

Toril Moi, *Sexual/Textual Politics: Feminist Literary Theory*

1986   Peter Hulme, *Colonial Encounters: Europe and the Native Caribbean, 1492–1797*

1987   Teresa de Lauretis, *Technologies of Gender: Essays on Theory, Film, and Fiction*

Martin Bernal, *Black Athena: The Afroasiatic Roots of Classical Civilization*

Molefi K. Asante, *The Afrocentric Idea*

Gloria Anzaldúa, *Borderlands/La Frontera: The New Mestiza*

1988   Gayatri Chakravorty Spivak, "Can the Subaltern Speak?"

Henry Louis Gates, *The Signifying Monkey: A Theory of Afro-American Literary Criticism*

1989   Laura Mulvey, *Visual and Other Pleasures*

Slavoj Žižek, *The Sublime Object of Ideology*

1990   Judith Butler, *Gender Trouble*

Eve Kosofsky Sedgwick, *Epistemology of the Closet*

Ramón Saldívar, *Chicano Narrative: The Dialectics of Difference*

1991   Donna Haraway, *Simians, Cyborgs, and Women*

Jonathan Dollimore, *Sexual Dissidence*

Fredric Jameson, *Postmodernism, or, The Cultural Logic of Late Capitalism*

1992   Judith Butler and Joan W. Scott, *Feminists Theorize the Political*

Mary Joe Frug, *Postmodern Legal Feminism*

Slavoj Žižek, *Looking Awry: An Introduction to Jacques Lacan through Popular Culture*

1993   Judith Butler, *Bodies that Matter: On the Discursive Limits of "Sex"*

1994   Homi Bhabha, *The Location of Culture*

1995   Ann McClintock, *Imperial Leather: Race, Gender, and Sexuality in the Colonial Conquest*

Robert Young, *Colonial Desire: Hybridity in Theory, Culture and Race*

1996   Declan Kiberd, *Inventing Ireland*

Stuart Hall, *Critical Dialogues in Cultural Studies*

1999   Henry Louis Gates and Kwame Anthony Appiah, *Africana: The Encyclopedia of the African American Experience*

2000   Sonia Saldívar-Hull, *Feminism on the Border: Chicana Gender Politics and Literature*

2000   Judith Butler, Slavoj Žižek and Ernesto Laclau, *Contingency, Hegemony, Universality: Contemporary Dialogues on the Left*

Terry Eagleton, *The Idea of Culture*

2002   Arnold Krupat, *Red Matters: Native American Studies*

Fredric Jameson, *A Singular Modernity*

THE SCOPE OF
LITERARY THEORY

To die for one's theological opinions
is the worst use a man can make of his life;
but to die for a literary theory!
It seemed impossible.
Oscar Wilde, *Intentions*

Each entry in this section is a general introduction to a theoretical field. Key ideas, themes, issues, concepts, and arguments are surveyed, with illustrative quotations from major works. **Bold-face** type throughout is an indication that a relevant biography exists in "Key Figures in Literary Theory." Parenthetical notes are used to alert the reader to relevant discussions elsewhere in the *Guide*. At the end of each entry, readers will find a short note directing them to another part of this section for further study. For additional titles, see "Recommendations for Further Reading."

Pursuing these cross-references will provide a better sense of the variety and complexity of individual theories as well as the potentiality for combining them. While this section is organized according to discrete theories, theoretical practice is often characterized by hybrid approaches that combine one or more of these theories. Whenever possible, I will note the kinds of hybrid formations that are commonly found. See "The Rise of Literary Theory" for additional discussions of these formations.

Critical Theory

Critical Theory is, by and large, concerned with the critique of MODERNITY, MODERNIZATION, and the modern state. The first generation of critical theorists – Max Horkheimer, **Theodor Adorno**, Herbert Marcuse, **Walter Benjamin**, Erich Fromm – came together in the early 1930s from different disciplines within the humanities and social sciences in order to analyze and critique ideologies, institutions, discourses, and media as well as to research the social psychology of disturbing new trends like fascism and the "administered society." All of these figures, except Benjamin, were officially connected with the Institute for Social Research which was founded by Felix Weil in the years following the First World War and became part of Frankfurt University in 1923. They were dedicated to studying society from a Marxian perspective, but diverged from classical Marxism in their emphasis on "superstructural phenomena" (e.g., problems of culture, class formation, and ideological hegemony) as opposed to the modes of production and economic forces that for classical Marxism determine such phenomena more or less mechanistically. Though rooted in Hegelian or Kantian traditions, Frankfurt school theorists were critical of the visions of TOTALITY (social, political, historical, and aesthetic) associated with these two philosophers.

The aim of the Institute in its early years (1930–64) was to develop a comprehensive social theory that would both describe relations of power and domination *and* facilitate and encourage radical social transformations. Adorno's main concerns, like Horkheimer's, were for the quality and value of human life, for the preservation of happiness, leisure, and aesthetic experience. The most important work of this period was their *Dialectic of Enlightenment* (1944), a critique of modernity in the form of "philosophical fragments," critical analyses of Enlightenment thinking, anti-Semitism, the "culture industry," and the administered society. The Enlightenment is here regarded as incorporating within its dialectical trajectory the very thing it seeks to overcome: mythology. "Mythology itself sets off the unending process of enlightenment," and "[j]ust as the myths already realize enlightenment, so enlightenment with every step becomes more deeply engulfed in mythology" (11–12). This dialectical interaction is already at work in Homer, whose epic organization is at variance with mythic reality: "The venerable cosmos of the meaningful

Homeric world is shown to be the achievement of regulative reason, which destroys myth by virtue of the same rational order in which it reflects it" (44). The disenchantment of the mythic unity of nature ultimately led to the alienated SUBJECTIVITY of modernity and the rationalization and COMMODIFICATION of culture. It also created the conditions in which anti-Semitism and the "final solution" could flourish amid all of the advances of human science, philosophy, and art.

The cultural industry is Adorno's phrase for the commodification of cultural production. He believed that the cultural productions of capitalist societies, especially those dominated by high quality media technologies, were a debasement of human potentiality, little more than instruments in the general pacification of the masses. His analysis of the culture industry reveals that in the modern era, social life is rationalized and "administered" by highly sophisticated media technologies and entertainment industries. The idea of the administered society, like Herbert Marcuse's of the "one-dimensional man" typical of such a society, was profoundly important for the Institute theorists and chimed with work being done by sociologists like Thorstein Veblen on the leisure class and C. Wright Mills on new class formations and power elites in US society. Marcuse argued that advanced industrial societies were characterized by a form of "one-dimensional thought" that reduced all human potential and transcendence to the limited domain of capitalist material production. Adorno's analysis of these same societies is characterized by an unstinting attack on the debasement of culture under capitalism. He argues that the technologies of popular culture (radio, television, films, advertising, the music and book industries) serve a subtle form of social control that relies less on persuasion (overt and subliminal) than on creating contexts, moods, attitudes, and "lifestyles" in order to transform the living individual who experiences the world into a consumer of commodities. The individual comes to have only an abstract and alienated relation to the material world of authentic experience.

In this environment, consumers of culture become the primary producers, but they are limited to the reproduction of existing social conditions. Thus, " 'consumer culture' can boast of being not a luxury but rather the simple extension of production" (*Prisms* 26). The culture industry thus produces popular forms of entertainment in order to lull individuals into conformity with dominant ways of thinking and consuming. Adorno's later critique of jazz, which he rejected as commercialized and debased, indicates the extent to which even marginal cultural forms reproduce dominant values and tastes. For Horkheimer and Adorno, people in administered societies no longer have aesthetic experiences; there is only the spectacle of consumption itself, the never-ending round of entertainments that never satisfy and also never fail to manufacture the desire for more. To feel these desires is to conform to the consumerism that has transformed the way political and economic interests determine increasingly complex, technological societies. In a consumerist society, competition and the logic of the marketplace infiltrate all levels of social, cultural, and political practice.

Adorno's work underscores the new emphasis in Marxist theory on art, aesthetics, and the artist's commitment to social change. The Holocaust underscored the limits both of culture and of critique: "The critique of culture is confronted with the last stage in the dialectic of culture and barbarism. To write poetry after Auschwitz is barbaric. And this corrodes even the knowledge of why it has become impossible to write poetry today" (*Prisms* 34). In other words, it is difficult to reflect on the impossibility of art, because even that critical reflection is tainted by the barbarism latent in Enlightenment visions of progress. The rationalization of culture makes it difficult for Adorno to see any emancipatory potential in humanism, which means that he must turn to the radical innovations of anti-humanist, avant-garde artists like Arnold Schoenberg, Samuel Beckett, and Franz Kafka. For Adorno, the negative aesthetics exemplified in their work proffers the only authentic alternative to the administered culture of advanced capitalism. Adorno's theory of NEGATIVE DIALECTICS is one of the most important tools for analyzing social and cultural problems without becoming entrapped in traditional concepts of SUBJECTIVITY and IDENTITY. Negative dialectics preserves the "negativity" of the NEGATIVE, which resists being appropriated by the positive term of DIALECTICAL processes. It is not a reversal of standard dialectical operations. As Adorno warns, "a purely formal reversal" of the formula "identity in nonidentity" merely reinscribes conventional dialectical relations (154). Negative dialectics avoids such a reversal by rescuing NONIDENTITY from a dialectical process that would subsume it in the production of identity. Nevertheless, the process of rescue remains tied "to the supreme categories of identitarian philosophy as its point of departure" (147).

Adorno's friend and colleague, Walter Benjamin, was less committed to dialectical method. He is best known for his work on the Parisian arcades and the *flâneur*, the quintessential figure of modernity, adrift in the city, in thrall to a constant barrage of people, objects, and commodities. He combined the sociological and philosophical rigor of the Institute with a messianic point of view best illustrated by his "Theses on the Philosophy of History." For Benjamin, HISTORICAL DETERMINISM is not a dialectical process but rather a form of mystical simultaneity in which the "angel of history" faces the past, which is piled like wreckage at its feet, its back to the future towards which it is irresistibly propelled.

Benjamin was, as Hannah Arendt puts it, "the most peculiar Marxist ever produced" by the Frankfurt school (qtd. in Benjamin 10). In line with other Critical Theorists, Benjamin regarded the vast array of cultural productions – popular music and films, literature, fashion, consumer products – in terms of how they reproduced the logic of capitalism. But unlike them, he attempted to identify what had been gained in the process of COMMODIFICATION. In "The Work of Art in the Age of Mechanical Reproduction," Benjamin argues that traditional works of art were "one of a kind," that they possessed an "aura" of authenticity inseparable from a ritual function. However, there is at least partial compensation for the loss of aura that occurred once works of art were mass produced. Film and other new art forms could now create an emancipatory popular culture in which the once-sacred artwork would be "de-sacralized" and "de-aestheticized," its infinite reproducibility making it both more democratic and less tied up with mystifying ritual: "for the first time in world history, mechanical reproduction emancipates the work of art from its parasitical dependence on ritual" (224). The loss of aura signals an AMBIVALENCE at the heart of modern culture, for the very means by which traditional culture is robbed of its authenticity are the means by which art becomes available to the masses. With the loss of aura came the loss of the idea that the work of art is a timeless, unified structure. For this reason Benjamin explored new avenues for expressing his views about literature and culture. Because he was drawn to the materiality of things, to the telling detail, he became adept at the use of quotation. "In this," according to Arendt, "he became a master when he discovered that the transmissibility of the past had been replaced by its citability and that in place of its authority there had arisen a strange power to settle down, piecemeal, in the present and to deprive it of 'peace of mind,' the mindless peace of complacency. 'Quotations in my works are like robbers by the roadside who make an armed attack and relieve an idler of his convictions'" (qtd. in Benjamin 38). Benjamin developed a model for critical understanding based not on a conception of organic or synthetic unity, but on a CONSTELLATION of texts, concepts, and ideas that constitutes a provisional and effective TOTALITY as well as a mode of social practice.

Jürgen Habermas's emergence in 1964 as the chair in philosophy and sociology at the Institute marked a second phase of Critical Theory. He and his followers, especially Seyla Benhabib, carried on a tradition of social theory associated with the Frankfurt school. At this time, we see a shift away from a critique of modernity as the dead-end of capitalism to a critique in which the emancipatory potential of the "unfulfilled" project of modernity could be realized in new strategies for social transformation. Something of Benjamin's hope for new cultural technologies is evident in Habermas's belief that new forms of "communicative action" could provide a means of achieving social and political consensus. These were noncoercive, rational forms of consensual action based on a principle of mutual criticism and a shared acceptance of the values and risks entailed in rational consensus. By 1975, with the publication of *Legitimation Crisis*, Habermas was able to offer a systemic alternative to Adorno's view of society. Along with Hans Blumenberg, Claus Offe, and Ernest Mandel, Habermas argued that crises in advanced, "technocratic" capitalist societies provided critical opportunities for social change. In this context, the welfare state theorized by Offe is a symptom of a capitalist system that is far from exhausted, that is simply taking risks in producing social programs that contribute to a *de-commodification* process in which, contrary to the logic of commodity production and consumerism, the State gives away resources without a commensurate enrichment in the form of capital or other commodities.

In the late 1970s, Habermas entered into a debate with **Jean-François Lyotard**, who argued, in *The Postmodern Condition* (1979), that the project of modernity was indeed finished and a new one had already begun. Habermas's claim to the contrary, in his oft-cited 1979 essay, "Modernity versus Postmodernity" – that the "project of modernity has not yet been fulfilled" (12) – can be regarded as an expression of Critical Theory's optimism with respect to modernity. His *Lectures on the Discourse of Modernity* (1987) reinstates modernity as the "positive" force, the philosophical ground and material condition for Critical Theory and social practice. Many other theorists at this time were writing on MODERNITY, though not from a Frankfurt school perspective. Anthony Giddens, for example, in *The Consequences of Modernity* (1990) and *Modernity and Self-Identity* (1991), put forward a social theory grounded in the idea of reflexivity, a social process in which IDENTITY is conceived as a dynamic process involving the individual's access to and management of information. While Postmodernists concentrated on the nature and effect of language games and media simulations, Giddens focused on the way individuals acquired competence within information environments. He distinguished between the *self* (a "generic phenomenon") and SELF-IDENTITY, which "is not something that is just given, as a result of the continuities of the individual's action-system, but something that has to be routinely created and sustained in the reflexive activities of the individual" (*Modernity and Self-Identity*, 52).

The renewed interest in modernity marks a third phase of Critical Theory, one very much influenced by the revisionist Marxism of **Antonio Gramsci** and **Louis Althusser**. In some respects, this phase responds to the very problems that the study of modernity made evident. What is to be done, asks Wendy Brown, when the "constitutive narratives of modernity" are "tattered," when challenges to such concepts as "progress, right, sovereignty, free will, moral truth, reason" have not yielded any alternatives? (3–4). One response to this question was a greater openness to Postmodern and poststructuralist theories and to ideas coming from Feminism, Lacanian psychoanalysis, Deconstruction, Postcolonial Studies, and Cultural Studies. Critical Theory at this time sought to redefine social TOTALITY as "the totality of conditions under with social individuals produced and reproduced their existence" (Benhabib 2). For Ernesto Laclau and Chantal Mouffe, the hegemony of dominant classes in capitalist societies is grounded on inauthentic totalities – that is to say, the particular and limited interests of a dominant group are represented as the universal foundation for justice, morality, and politics. They advocate the production of a *counter*-hegemony in the form of strategic coalitions of political groups mobilized to exploit weaknesses, contradictions, crises, and other gaps in the hegemony of advanced capitalism. Laclau has advocated the use of "quasi-transcendentals," which can serve as the starting point for cultural and political discourses that seek consensus across broad audiences or constituencies, and **Judith Butler**, in her analysis of feminist politics, calls for "contingent foundations" to allow for coalition building and political activity. In 2000, Laclau and Butler joined **Slavoj Žižek** in publishing a volume of polemical essays – *Contingency, Hegemony, Universality: Contemporary Dialogues on the Left* – whose general warrant was to explore the possibility for social theory of contingent or provisional totalities and to "account for the enigmatic emergence of the space of UNIVERSALITY itself" (Butler et al. 104).

Note. For more on Adorno, Gramsci, Althusser, and others, see Marxist Theory; on Butler, Laclau, and Žižek, see Postmodernism and Psychoanalysis.

WORKS CITED

Adorno, Theodor. *Negative Dialectics.* Trans. E. B. Ashton. New York: Seabury Press, 1973.

——. *Prisms.* Trans. Samuel and Shierry Weber. Cambridge, MA: MIT Press, 1981.

Benhabib, Seyla. *Critique, Norm, and Utopia: A Study of the Foundations of Critical Theory.* New York: Columbia University Press, 1986.

Benjamin, Walter. *Illuminations.* Ed. Hannah Arendt. Trans. Harry Zohn. New York: Harcourt, Brace & World, 1968.

Brown, Wendy. *Politics Out of History.* Princeton, NJ and Oxford: Princeton University Press, 2001.

Butler, Judith, Ernesto Laclau and Slavoj Žižek. *Contingency, Hegemony, Universality: Contemporary Dialogues on the Left.* London and New York: Verso, 2000.

Giddens, Anthony. *Modernity and Self-Identity: Self and Society in the Late Modern Age.* Stanford: Stanford University Press, 1991.

Habermas, Jürgen. "Modernity versus Postmodernity." *New German Critique* 17 (Spring 1979): 3–22.

Horkheimer, Max and Theodor Adorno. *Dialectic of Enlightenment: Philosophical Fragments.* Ed. Gunzelin Schmid Noerr. Trans. Edmund Jephcott. Stanford: Stanford University Press, 2002.

Cultural Studies

Cultural Studies first emerged as part of a tradition of British cultural analysis best exemplified by the work of **Raymond Williams**, whose *Culture and Society: 1780–1950* (1958) and *The Long Revolution* (1961) mark the decisive point at which an Arnoldian idea of culture as a coherent and self-regulating tradition of serious artistic achievement cut off from historical conditions undergoes a radical transformation. These works were revolutionary in that they sought to analyze culture by way of a concept of TOTALITY that had been refined by new ways of conceiving the relationship between (to use Marxian terms) BASE and SUPERSTRUCTURE. Following Antonio Gramsci, Williams addressed the unique forms of cultural and ideological HEGEMONY that characterize advanced capitalist societies; he also pioneered the analysis of "structures of feeling" that create and sustain complex organic communities. Williams delineates "three general categories" in the definition of culture: 1) the "ideal, in which culture is a state or process of human perfection, in terms of certain absolute or universal values"; 2) "the 'documentary,' in which culture is the body of intellectual and imaginative work, in which, in a detailed way, human thought and experience are variously recorded"; and 3) "the 'social' definition of culture, in which culture is a description of a particular way of life, which expresses certain meanings and values not only in art and learning but also in institutions and ordinary behaviour" (*Long Revolution* 41). Each of these categories offers something of value to the critic, but none of them alone is sufficient. A theory of culture must take into account elements from each and respond to the complexity and significance of specific cultural organizations. Williams thus defines the theory of culture "as the study of relationships between elements in a whole way of life. The analysis of culture is the attempt to discover the nature of the organization which is the complex of these relationships" (*Long Revolution* 46).

With Williams, and British Cultural Studies generally, we see a movement away from an elitist and idealist vision of culture (of the sort found in Matthew Arnold and his successors), towards an alternative vision that recognizes the dynamism and complexity of late-capitalist society, the web-like connections that link subcultures and the various class formations within overlapping regional and national frameworks. Williams used the phrase "structure of feeling" to describe the experience of living within these frameworks. A structure of feeling constitutes "the culture of a period . . . the particular living result of all the elements in the general organization." It often "corresponds to the dominant social character" (*Long Revolution* 48, 63). In some ways, Williams anticipates **Michel Foucault** and **Pierre Bourdieu** in his conception of culture as a dynamic network of relations and links, but in other ways he is limited by his organic conception of culture as a *whole*, as a living totality of elements. However, his consciousness of social DETERMINATION as a complex function of IDEOLOGY (rather than economics) meant that he, like Gramsci, would not make the mistake of those Marxists who saw a simple and mechanical relation between the productive base of society and superstructural phenomena. He was able, according to Stuart Hall, to counter "vulgar materialism and an economic determinism," with "a radical interactionism: in effect, the interaction of all practices in and with one another, skirting the problem of determinacy" (23). In this, Culture Studies shared many concerns with the Critical Theory of the Frankfurt school. (On ideology, see pp. 110–13.)

Richard Hoggart, a contemporary of Williams and, like him, a teacher of adult education, embarked on a similar project of revisionary cultural analysis in *The Uses of Literacy: Changing Patterns in English Mass Culture* (1957). For the early British theorists, the emphasis on mass culture entailed the analysis of new modes of cultural production, especially the popular media (newspapers, magazines, television, film), as well as patterns of cultural consumption, including individual behaviors as well as the audiences of new mass events and entertainments. The study of high-tech media societies using traditional methods of empirical sociology achieved disciplinary legitimation in 1964 with the foundation of the Centre for Contemporary Cultural Studies at the University of Birmingham, which was pivotal in establishing the field initially in Britain (Turner 71–72). Hoggart became the first director of the Centre, and his emphasis on sociology and empirical research methods was designed to facilitate a rigorous, empirical study of cultural trends, practices, and institutions. By the late 1960s, it was clear that new media technologies would not only change the meaning and significance of culture; they would also change the function and value of cultural analysis. A transformed idea of culture required a transformed project of Cultural Studies, and Williams was not slow to see the significance of this general social transformation. His *Communications* (1967) reflects his recognition of the importance of new media technologies as well as his dissatisfaction with the concept of "mass culture," which for him relied on an outmoded difference between high and low cultural productions.

Stuart Hall, who took over as director of the Centre in 1968, sought to legitimize not only new methods for defining and studying culture but also whole new domains of cultural production. Especially influential was Hall's work on Critical Race Theory, ethnicity, immigration, and "diasporic identities," which signaled a new direction in British Cultural Studies that intersected with the emerging discourses of Postcolonial Studies. Of special note is *Policing the Crisis: Mugging, the State and Law and Order* (1978), by Hall and his colleagues at the Centre, which focuses on the way the British media linked crime to race. Dick Hebdige approached the study of culture from another perspective in *Subculture: The Meaning of Style* (1979), a study of ethnic and musical subcultures (Rastafarians, "hipsters, beats and teddy boys," glam and glitter rockers, and so on) and the function of *style* as a signifying practice. These works analyze cultural formations on their own terms, something which Hoggart, working within an older, humanistic, top-down model of culture, had failed to do (Turner 68). Iain Chambers' *Migrancy, Culture, Identity* (1994) pursued a similar critical goal. Hebdige and Chambers were able to expand on Williams's interest in marginalized social groups by rethinking the idea of marginalization: a subculture is not an excluded or ignored class with a distinct identity and sense of solidarity; it is a contingent, often nebulous formation, characterized by a specialized *activity*, such as playing darts, nightclubbing, or reading fashion magazines, rather than by class consciousness. The emphasis on subcultures also highlights the fact that culture is not a homogenous and evenly distributed matrix of forces and relations. With these developments, the *idea* of culture became the *problem* of culture.

By 1980, when Hall published "Cultural Studies: Two Paradigms," Cultural Studies was faced with a dilemma: Should it embrace Claude Lévi-Strauss's structuralist anthropology and analyze cultures as coherent, predictable structures? Or should it adopt the "culturalist" approach associated with Williams, an approach that stresses the dynamic quality of cultural formations? Early British cultural theorists were generally hostile to Structuralism largely because it ignored the social and cultural determinations that shaped institutions, beliefs, and social practices. For this reason, the culturalist trend was more popular, especially after the "Gramscian turn" to the study of HEGEMONY, which was highly effective in shifting the emphasis in Cultural Studies towards "the PROBLEMATIC of relative autonomy and 'over-determination,' and the study of *articulation*" (Hall 32). Though British Cultural Studies tended to avoid Structuralist approaches, some theorists found the innovations of French Poststructuralism to be useful in critiquing received ideas about culture, language, and representation. On the whole, however, poststructuralist developments were not generally favored, in part because of Poststructuralism's AMBIVALENT relation to the absolute. As Hall notes: "Foucault and other post-Althusserians have taken [a] devious path into the absolute, not the relative autonomy of practices, via their necessary heterogeneity and 'necessary non-correspondence'" (Hall 32).

But it is just this "devious path" that Catherine Belsey has attempted to demystify. Belsey was one of the first British cultural theorists to consider seriously the critical potential of Poststructuralism. Her controversial volume, *Critical Practice* (1980), takes to task the concept of common sense, "the collective and timeless wisdom whose unquestioned presence seems to be the source of everything we take for granted" (*Critical Practice* 3). Common sense, which forms the basis of what she calls "expressive realism," presupposes an "empiricist-idealist interpretation of the world," a form of humanism that constitutes the basis of traditional conceptions of culture (*Critical Practice* 6). "To challenge common sense is to challenge the inscription of common sense in language" (*Critical Practice* 43). Her study of the major poststructuralists helped to clarify their arguments and also to introduce into British academic discourse a practical tool for the analysis of texts and modes of reading. Her more recent work continues this project, but it also acknowledges an important trend in Cultural Studies. If "culture subsists as the meanings in circulation at a specific moment, the relations between separate genres or cultural forms might be as illuminating as the distinctions between them. . . . English is spilling over into the terrain of cultural studies, cultural history into the history of art and architecture" (*Culture and the Real* xiii). Belsey's analysis not only acknowledges this trend but submits it to a critique that serves as a reminder that culture is not as easily "materialized," through language and discourse, as some theorists (e.g., **Judith Butler**) believe.

As Graeme Turner and Patrick Brantlinger have demonstrated, there are significant differences between British and US Cultural Studies. The British form emerged out of the sociological and materialist studies of people like Williams and Hoggart, who were associated with the Birmingham Centre. By the early 1980s, with Hall at the head of the Centre, new emphases on multiculturalism and the problems of immigration, exile, and diaspora brought Cultural Studies into the postcolonial orbit. US Culture Studies from the 1950s to the '80s was primarily concerned with the historical analysis of national characteristics (major political figures and parties, economics). By the mid-1980s, new forms of cultural critique were beginning to gain ground. One of the most important of these was the "writing cultures" movement in anthropology, which advocated a TEXTUALIST approach to the representation of culture. The influential collection of essays edited by James Clifford and George E. Marcus, *Writing Culture: The Poetics and Politics of Ethnography* (1986), built on the seminal work of Clifford Geertz in the 1970s. Geertz had argued that certain aspects of Balinese culture (e.g., the cock-fight) could be read and interpreted like a text. The contributors to *Writing Cultures* elaborated on this new mode of cultural analysis and turned as well to an investigation of the problem of ethnography itself, particularly its claims to scientific objectivity. A form of "cultural science" (as Turner puts it), textualist ethnography was primarily interested in the problems of translating and representing so-called primitive cultures, but it would ultimately have an impact on the analysis of Western cultures as well.

By the end of the 1980s, British and US Cultural Studies had converged on many theoretical and thematic points. Iain Chambers and Angela McRobbie in Britain and Janice Radway in the US were focusing increasingly on popular culture (especially film), with a strong emphasis on the analysis of gender and sexual identity. McRobbie's *Feminism and Youth Culture: From "Jackie" to "Just Seventeen"* (1991), for example, explored subcultures from a feminist perspective, focusing on the unique experiences of young women, while Radway's *Reading the Romance* (1984) considered the importance of genre fiction in a critique of patriarchal culture. The intense interest in popular culture, especially alternative textual forms that involved individuals in sustained "fantasy" environments (e.g., film, rock and roll, the internet, video games), was part of a more general critique of cultural CANONS in literature, art, music, and elsewhere. Throughout the 1990s, as "discourse" became increasingly prominent in the analysis of cultural "formations," **Michel Foucault** and **Pierre Bourdieu** offered to Cultural Studies important new paradigms for DISCOURSE ANALYSIS. In some cases, the category of culture is itself challenged, in part by challenging traditional notions of the "natural." **Donna Haraway**'s *Simians, Cyborgs, and Women: The Reinvention of Nature* (1991) is a controversial instance of this radical revision of the culture concept. The importance of nature as a category that imbricates with and defines culture continues to define the limits of Cultural Studies, as is evidenced in Beth Fowkes Tobin's *Colonizing Nature* (2005), which examines the flora and fauna of tropical outposts of empire and how they contribute to our understanding of British culture in the eighteenth and nineteenth centuries.

    Teresa de Lauretis and Laura Mulvey, influenced by poststructuralist theories of language and Lacanian Psychoanalysis, have made inroads into popular culture by focusing on the power of the male gaze in film and its role in defining culture as a space in which women are constructed as objects of desire and instruments in the fashioning of masculinist social institutions. (On Lacan, see pp. 158–9, 168–71.) Perhaps the most celebrated practitioner of Lacanian Cultural Studies is **Slavoj Žižek**, whose *Looking Awry: An Introduction to Jacques Lacan through Popular Culture* (1992) considers a wide variety of subjects, including detective fiction, the films of Alfred Hitchcock, pornography, politics, and Postmodernism. More recent developments, especially the study of material culture, have focused on cultural objects and their production, consumption, collection, and preservation.

    A common criticism of Cultural Studies is that it regards literary and cultural texts as pretexts for the study of culture as such. The text is therefore, as Richard Johnson argues, "only a *means* in cultural study." It is "no longer studied for its own sake . . . but rather for the subjective or cultural forms which it realises and makes available" (qtd. in Turner 22). But trends in the US and elsewhere belie this claim, for in many analyses of popular culture there is an almost obsessive attention paid precisely to literary and cultural texts, including clothing, sporting events, jazz and popular music, film and video, advertisements, and "collectibles" of every description. Indeed, in the analysis of *material culture* it is precisely artifacts that count. Susan Pearce, who has studied museums and the theory and practice of cultural preservation, argues that the analysis of the way individuals collect objects has much to say about how material culture impacts broader issues such as gender and class. Yet the very inclusiveness that has opened up the idea of culture to "elements in a whole way of life" (as Williams put it) not traditionally regarded as cultural has led some people, in and out of the academy, to condemn Cultural Studies for overvaluing the ephemeral and insignificant. This condemnation, however, betrays a serious confusion about the social and analytical value of objects and the function and goals of Cultural Studies. The charge of insignificance rests on the assumption that objects in the cultural field are *not* (or should not be) of equal value. If *any* object is open to critique on the same terms, then *all* objects are of equal value – which is to say, they have no real value at all. However, the work of Cultural Studies theorists in the twenty-first century suggests that the issue is less one of regarding all cultural phenomena as equally valuable but rather of developing new modes of analysis suited to specific cultural practices and products. Innovations of this sort have made Cultural Studies both popular and controversial and have significantly altered the study of literature.

WORKS CITED

Belsey, Catherine. *Critical Practice*. 2nd ed. London: Routledge, 1980, 2002.
——. *Culture and the Real: Theorizing Cultural Criticism*. London: Routledge, 2005.
Hall, Stuart. "Cultural Studies: Two Paradigms." In *Culture, Ideology and Social Process: A Reader*. Eds. Tony Bennett, Graham Martin, Colin Mercer, and Janet Woollacott. London: Batsford Academic and Educational, Ltd., 1981. 19–37.
Turner, Graeme. *British Cultural Studies*. London; New York: Routledge, 1996.
Williams, Raymond. *The Long Revolution*. New York: Columbia University Press; London: Chatto & Windus, 1961.

Deconstruction

Deconstruction emerged out of a tradition of French philosophical thought strongly influenced by the phenomenological projects of Edmund Husserl and Martin Heidegger. The main concern of phenomenology is consciousness and essence. For Husserl, consciousness entailed an intention towards the essence of an object, whether it be material or imaginary. As Robert Holub puts it, "Consciousness is always consciousness *of* something; it has a direction towards or a goal in the object" (291). Heidegger's critique of Husserl led him to shift the emphasis from an epistemological phenomenology (knowledge or consciousness *of* the world) to an ONTOLOGICAL phenomenology (knowledge *of* Being, which precedes and conditions consciousness of the world). This general context of Heideggerian critique, together with the new existentialist phenomenology of Jean-Paul Sartre, was the environment in which **Jacques Derrida** developed his deconstructionist method. Of special interest to him was Heidegger's critique of the "transcendental temporality of consciousness," which revealed the latent idealism of Husserl's phenomenology and shifted attention to the essence of Being, which is always understood as "worldly," as Being-in-the-world or human-*being* (*Dasein*). Derrida was quick to expose in his turn the (ma)lingering influence of a metaphysical tradition discernible in the privilege Heidegger accorded Being, a presence that "dwells" in the world, a transcendental foundation for philosophy, an indivisible point of origin and departure. "The privilege granted to consciousness signifies the privilege granted to the present; and even if one describes the transcendental temporality of consciousness, and at the depth at which Husserl does so, one grants to the 'living present' the power of synthesizing traces, and of incessantly reassembling them. This privilege is the ether of metaphysics, the element of our thought that is caught in the language of metaphysics" (*Margins* 16). Derrida identifies here the chief object of philosophical analysis: the metaphysics of PRESENCE. Out of his critique of this philosophical tradition came the revolutionary idea that language does not refer in some stable and predictable way to the world outside of it but rather designates its own relationships of internal DIFFERENCE.

Like other thinkers in the late 1950s and early '60s, Derrida was drawn to the emerging discipline of Structuralism, especially the structural linguistics of Ferdinand de Saussure. Saussure's lectures in the first decade of the twentieth century provided the foundation for many post-structuralist thinkers. Saussurean linguistics refutes the "Adamic" theory of language, which holds that there is an essential link between words and the things they signify, and argues instead that phonemic difference (*bat* v. *cat*), which parallels but is not reducible to conceptual difference, is the primary operative feature of language. The SIGN, according to Saussure, consists of a SIGNIFIER (word or sound pattern) and a SIGNIFIED (concept). Its importance lies not in designating an aspect of the material world but rather in functioning as part of a system. The significance of the sign is thus entirely arbitrary. (On Saussure, see pp. 181–4.) One of the important implications of Deconstruction is that the signifier is just as important as the signified, that the word is just as important as the world it purports to designate. Deconstruction, as a form of analysis, calls our attention to the failure of philosophy to achieve or describe PRESENCE (the SELF-IDENTITY of the signified, the "transcendental signi-fied"). Deconstruction distrusts the valorization of presence as the more authentic register of discourse (i.e., "speech" is more authentic and present than "writing"). Instead, it focuses on the way in which language constitutes meaning through a play of differences, the slippage or "spacing" of the signifier. In his seminal essay, "Structure, Sign and Play in the Discourse of the Human Sciences," Derrida argues for a theory of PLAY that calls into question the "structuration of structure," the tran-scendental signified that stands behind and authorizes the very possibil-ity of stable and centered structures. The play of difference within language is "permitted by the lack or absence of a center or origin" – it is "the movement of *supplementarity*" (*Writing* 289). For Derrida, SUPPLE-MENTATION means more than simply adding something, "a plenitude enriching another plenitude, the *fullest measure* of presence." It means also, and perhaps primarily, a substitution, something that "insinuates itself *in-the-place-of.* . . . If it represents and makes an image, it is by the anterior default of a presence" (*Of Grammatology* 167, 144–45). The sup-plemental difference within language oscillates between nostalgia for lost unities and a joyful embrace of their loss.

In *Of Grammatology* (1967), Derrida argues that the priority of speech over writing generally assumed by theorists of language and human development has obscured the problem of language and its relation to presence. On this view, Deconstruction emerged as both a critique of "phonocentrism" and an elaboration of a "general science of writing" (27). Writing, in this special sense, refers to the play of differences within language or, to use Derrida's neologism, DIFFÉRANCE (the French term combines two meanings, "differing" and "deferring"), which marks the arbitrary condition of language in which signifiers endlessly refer to each other, in a process that Umberto Eco calls "infinite semiosis." However, while the free play of signification nullifies the possibility of presence or a transcendental signified, it does not sanction subjectivist claims that only language exists or that the material world is a conjuring trick, an illusion of words. Derrida's famous remark, *"il n'y a pas de hors-texte,"* there is nothing outside of the text (*Of Grammatology* 158), is not a repudiation of the material world. It is rather a testament to the text's radical ONTOLOGY, its otherness, its "being-as-text," its freedom from a merely mimetic mode of reference. Deconstruction takes place within the horizon of the text, at the moments of rupture, in those APORIAS in which the text throws itself into doubt. These moments of instability provide the starting point for a critique of the philosophical, scientific, moral, ethical, or critical assumptions underlying a given text. The presumption of an adequate language – one that could faithfully represent the true being of things in the world – is precisely what Deconstruction seeks to criticize. All purportedly singular and unified texts can be shown to be internally inconsistent and this inconsistency, or aporia, is constitutive of those very texts. Deconstruction demonstrates that Western thought has *always already* been defined by inconsistency, PARADOX, contradiction, incommensurability. Deconstruction is not nihilistic, however. To *de*-construct is not to destroy; it is rather to unveil the seemingly hidden workings of language that constitute the very basis of linguistic and textual meaning. In the "Plato's Pharmacy" section of Derrida's *Disseminations*, for example, we learn that the term *pharmakon* means both remedy and poison. Other examples of this paradoxical concept in Derrida's work include *hymen*, which can signify both a barrier (between men and women) and a fusion (marriage), and the *gift*, which signifies a relation to the presence of the OTHER that grounds all philosophy but also all deconstructionist critiques of philosophy.

In the later part of his career, Derrida explored the ethical implications of the *gift* as it has been represented since Abraham offered up Isaac to God. Derrida's "ethics of the possible" (to use Richard Kearney's phrase) offered a compelling alternative to nihilistic relativism and an

amoral Postmodernism. The *gift* also provided a focal point for meditations on history, epistemology, biography, and autobiography. Derrida's
powerful last works deal precisely with the reality of, even the desire
for, presence. Indeed, presence haunts the later works in the form of the
specter, the uncanny presence of what can never be present but manages
to survive as the trace of pure presence that neither Deconstruction nor
philosophy can achieve.

Though Deconstruction began as a critique of phenomenology, it
very soon became a valuable critical tool in the analysis of literature,
film, and other cultural phenomena. Derrida wrote several important
works on literature (particularly on the work of Jean-Jacques Rousseau
and James Joyce), but it was the work of the US theorists **Paul de Man**
and **J. Hillis Miller** that made Deconstruction a popular tool for the
analysis of literature (especially in US universities). De Man and Miller
were, like Derrida, influenced by phenomenology, but they arrived at
their deconstructionist methodologies through their own understanding
of the implications of difference and contradiction within literary texts.
Miller's early work on Dickens and other Victorian novelists, strongly
influenced by the phenomenology of Georges Poulet, advanced new
ideas about the structure and significance of narrative and linguistic
consciousness. For Miller, language created the world of the text, a point
of view that undermines the naïve sense, to some degree a product of
phenomenology itself, that language can capture the immediacy of one's
experience of the world. By the late 1970s, Miller had become the leading
advocate of Deconstruction. In a brilliant and influential response to M.
H. Abram's accusation that deconstructionist criticism was parasitical on
definitive or univocal readings of literary texts, Miller deconstructed the
opposition host/parasite, demonstrating through detailed etymological
analysis that the word "parasite" can be traced back to the same roots as
the word "host." "On the one hand, the 'obvious or univocal reading'
always contains the 'deconstructive reading' as a parasite encrypted
within itself, as part of itself, and, on the other hand, the 'deconstructive'
reading can by no means free itself from the metaphysical, logocentric
reading which it means to contest" ("Critic" 444–45). Miller draws from
Friedrich Nietzsche and Gilles Deleuze to put forward a theory of "differential repetition" that attempts to account for the way that literary
narratives work. Differential repetition lacks a ground or fixed origin
against which to compare succeeding copies. Rather than produce copies,

which is what we find in conventional, MIMETIC, or "unifying" repetition, differential repetition produces SIMULACRA: "ungrounded doublings which arise from differential interrelations among elements which are all on the same plane. This lack of ground in some paradigm or archetype means that there is something ghostly about the effects of this . . . kind of repetition" (*Fiction and Repetition* 6). Reading, on this view, is not a matter of tracing language to its referents outside the text (either in the author's consciousness or in the external world) but of following the labyrinthine trajectory of language as it produces significations in a theoretically endless process of repetition. Instead of the exact repetition of a signifier in harmony with its signified, we find the "infinite semiosis" of signifiers linked in chains of signification.

One of the most important influences on Miller was the work of de Man, his colleague at Yale. De Man's *Blindness and Insight* is perhaps the best known text of American deconstructionist criticism. De Man argues that becoming aware of the "complexities of reading" is the necessary first step towards "theorizing about literary language" (viii). These complexities are the function of the critic's "blindness" with respect to a gap between practice and the theoretical precepts guiding it. Literary critics are thus "curiously doomed to say something quite different from what they meant to say" (105–106). And while critics may remain unaware of the discrepancy that informs their work, "they seem to thrive on it and owe their best insights to the assumptions these insights disprove" (ix). De Man illustrates his thesis in a detailed analysis of Derrida's reading of Rousseau, arguing that it is actually a *mis*reading. Derrida believes that Rousseau's theory of language is a reflection of his desire to link language to the world of objects in a direct and unmediated fashion – a reflection, in short, of his desire for presence. De Man, however, argues that Rousseau is always aware of the fundamentally *rhetorical* nature of language, that he in fact uses language not to make mimetic statements about the world but rather to make rhetorical statements that refer only to themselves, to their own figural nature. By working in this rhetorical mode, Rousseau's text "prefigures its own misunderstanding as the correlative of its rhetorical nature" (136). When Derrida deconstructs Rousseau, claiming that his theory of language and representation is committed to the "metaphysics of presence," he misses the point. For de Man, Rousseau "said what he meant to say" (*Blindness* 135). Part of the problem is that Derrida refuses to read Rousseau as literature and thus fails to see the figural or rhetorical nature of Rousseau's language. His reading of a "pseudo-Rousseau" is nevertheless instructive, for he seems to be aware of his own *mis*reading, which is "too interesting not to be deliberate" (*Blindness* 140).

According to de Man, Rousseau, like all literary authors, is well aware of the figural nature of his discourse; in fact, he occupies the privileged position of *not* being blinded by his own practice. The importance of the rhetorical dimensions of language is explored in de Man's most famous essay, "The Rhetoric of Temporality," which focuses on two of the most common rhetorical tropes, symbol and allegory. De Man is chiefly concerned with the privilege historically granted to the symbol. The Romantic notion that the symbol exists in a kind of synthesis or union with what it designates is called into question, as is the denigration of allegory as a disjunctive figure, lacking any intimate association with what it signifies. De Man argues that the disjunctive quality of allegory is owing to its *temporal* nature: "in the world of allegory, time is the originary constitutive category" (*Blindness* 207). Allegory, like irony, always points to another sign that precedes it; it is always an instance of differential repetition in which the sign can never coincide, as the symbol is purported to do, completely and without remainder, with its object. It is, in a word, a *narrative* form of signification. This narrative temporality is precisely the *différance* that Derrida believes to be the function language: deferral, spacing, the trace, play, specter, survival – all of these terms indicate the temporality of rhetorical figures that refer not to the world of objects but to the world of signs and traces, a mode of reference that is interminable and vertiginous, leading the reader not to some definite referent or origin beyond language but to the very heart of language itself: its engagement with time along an endless series of significations. For de Man, it is rarely possible to decide, when reading a literary text, whether we are reading, or should be reading, in a rhetorical or literal fashion. This critical "undecidability" is a property of both literary and critical language.

Though Deconstruction is primarily understood as a theory of TEX-TUALITY and as a method for reading texts, it constitutes for many a radically new way of seeing and knowing the world. Barbara Johnson and **Gayatri Chakravorty Spivak**, for example, both translators of Derrida's work, were instrumental in bringing Deconstruction into Feminism, Psychoanalysis, and the critique of gender and racial difference.

Derrida, de Man, and other deconstructionists may no longer stand in the limelight of literary theory, but their ideas are part of the foundation of contemporary theories of sexuality, gender, race, history, and culture.

Note. For more on Derrida, see Poststructuralism.

WORKS CITED

Derrida, Jacques. *Margins of Philosophy.* Trans. Alan Bass. Chicago: University of Chicago Press, 1982.

———. *Of Grammatology.* Trans. Gayatri Chakravorty Spivak. Baltimore: Johns Hopkins University Press, 1976.

———. *Writing and Difference.* Trans. Alan Bass. Chicago: University of Chicago Press, 1978.

Holub, Robert. "Phenomenology." In *The Cambridge History of Literary Criticism.* Vol. 8: *From Formalism to Poststructuralism.* Ed. Raman Selden. Cambridge, UK and New York: Cambridge University Press, 1995. 289–318.

Miller, J. Hillis. "The Critic as Host." *Critical Inquiry* (Spring 1977) 3.3: 439–47.

———. *Fiction and Repetition: Seven English Novels.* Cambridge: Harvard University Press, 1982.

De Man, Paul. *Blindness and Insight: Essays in the Rhetoric of Contemporary Criticism.* New York: Oxford University Press, 1971.

Ethnic Studies

Ethnic Studies, the theoretical study of race and cultural pluralism, began in the US with the work of African American writers in the late nineteenth and early twentieth centuries. African American studies has revealed the theoretical richness of African American literature and philosophy and shown how contemporary European theories of language, TEXTUALITY, gender, and SUBJECTIVITY can be used to critique discourses of race and racial difference. African American studies is by no means alone in furthering these aims. Chicano/a studies has, at least since the 1960s, been building an impressive canon of theoretical works, and Native American studies has more recently started to explore the links between native literary and cultural practices and mainstream Anglo-European theory. In Britain, some of these same developments can be discerned, especially from the 1970s, in part as a response to the presence in the UK of formerly colonized peoples.

Speaking from an African American perspective, W. E. B. Du Bois in 1903 articulated succinctly the central issue: "The problem of the twentieth century is the problem of the color-line" (16). For Du Bois, race and the difference that it marks have a profound effect on the social development of individuals. For if race is a problem, so too is the individual whose race differs from that of the dominant group. "It is a peculiar sensation," Du Bois writes in *The Souls of Black Folk*, "this double-consciousness, this sense of always looking at one's self through the eyes of others, of measuring one's soul by the tape of a world that looks on in amused contempt and pity. One ever feels his two-ness, – an American, a Negro; two souls, two thoughts, two unreconciled strivings; two warring ideals in one dark body, whose dogged strength alone keeps it from being torn asunder" (8–9). Quintessential expressions of this syndrome in literature are Richard Wright's *Native Son* and Ralph Ellison's *The Invisible Man*, novels that depict the alienating and destructive effects of double consciousness on young men growing up black in the US. The problem of double consciousness, however, was not a simple MANICHAEAN one in which an authentic African American experience is opposed to an inauthentic and oppressive Anglo-American norm. For example, in the phenomenon of "passing" the same double consciousness that pits African Americans against the dominant culture is itself doubled within African American communities, where light-skinned individuals often find themselves in the position of having to choose between a "native" black culture and a "foreign" white one. As novelists and critics alike have shown, both choices create a burden of inauthenticity. The Harlem Renaissance, which flourished in the 1920s and '30s, articulated the specific personal, social, and cultural manifestations of double consciousness in the urban contexts not addressed by Du Bois. As **Hazel Carby** has shown, the "Talented Tenth" of Northern intellectuals tended to propagate the view of an IDEALIZED rural "black folk." As a result, there emerged a conflict between middle-class intellectuals, often accused of imitating white middle-class culture, and an emergent radical working class. Especially problematic was the representation of black women, in literature and other social discourses, as the responsibility of professional black men who were obligated to protect them from both dominant culture and their own sexuality. Novelists like Nella Larsen and Zora Neale Hurston defied the stereotypes of black women at the same time that they questioned the responsibility to "uplift" the race.

Du Bois was tremendously influential in defining the terms of debate in contemporary discourse on race in African American studies. However, as Kwame Anthony Appiah has shown, Du Bois confused biological and socio-historical conceptions of race: "what Du Bois attempts, despite his own claims to the contrary, is not the transcendence of the nineteenth-century scientific conception of race – as we shall see, he relies on it – but rather, as the dialectic requires, a revaluation of the Negro race in the face of the sciences of racial inferiority" (25). Contemporary African American studies by and large regards race as a function of ideology, a construction deployed by political and nationalist groups that have inevitably "engendered the seeds of essentialism": "if 'race' is real, it is so only because it has been rendered meaningful by the actions and beliefs of the powerful, who retain the myth in order to protect their own political-economic interests" (Darder and Torres 5, 12). Critical Race Theory, which developed out of African American studies (particularly the work of Du Bois), similarly approached race as an ideological construct and investigated the ways in which race had become a factor in civil rights legislation and in the legal system. Derrick Bell and Alan Freeman, both legal scholars influenced by the Critical Legal Studies movement, provided initial impetus to the movement in the

1970s, though it soon expanded beyond legal issues to embrace education, public policy, and economics.

The issue of race lay at the heart of a number of projects seeking to "de-essentialize" discourses of ethnicity. One of the most influential of these projects was Martin Bernal's *Black Athena*, a work that demonstrates the extent to which race is an effect of specific historical conditions. Bernal posits that Africa (specifically Egypt) lies at the center of Western civilization, rather than on its periphery. On this view, racial difference is the result of the "fabrication" of ancient Greek culture. Extensive geological, archaeological, and linguistic analysis led Bernal to argue that the origin of Greece lies in "Egyptian and Semitic cultural areas" and that "there seems to have been more or less continuous Near Eastern influence on the Aegean" in the period during which Greek culture emerged (2100–1100 BCE) (1, 18). His assertion that we must rethink "the fundamental bases of 'Western Civilization'" and "recognize the penetration of racism and 'continental chauvinism' into all our historiography" (1–2) has been hotly contested by classicists, archaeologists, historians, and other scholars. To some degree, *Black Athena* is part of a larger "Afrocentric" project associated with the work of Molefi K. Asante. For Asante, Afrocentricity is a general challenge to "established hierarchies" (14); it takes difference as the mark of African identity and consciousness, the mark of a "recentering" of Africa in response to its "peripheralization" by Western cultures. Afrocentricity is not a separatist discourse; it does not argue for the exclusion of other traditions of thought, nor does it designate practices of cultural revival. It is a way of thinking about Africa as central to the development of civilizations and of Africans as important contributors to African *and* Western culture. "Afrocentricity liberates the African by establishing agency as the key concept for freedom" and "provides the shuttle between the intransigence of white privilege and the demands of African equality" (21, 41). Though it is dedicated to African agency, Afrocentricity seeks to join with other theoretical enterprises that value human freedom.

Chief among these other enterprises were those that sought either to reject or to appropriate and refashion the Euro-American theoretical tradition as the first stage of developing a black literary theory. Of particular importance in this context is **Henry Louis Gates's** theory of African and African American literature. Gates builds on Houston Baker's early work, which argues that "Black America" possessed its "own standards of moral and aesthetic achievement" and distinguished itself from white America by virtue of its commitment to an oral tradition and a collectivist ethos. Additionally, "black American culture is partially differentiated from white American culture because one of its most salient characteristics is an index of repudiation," especially of Western cultural theory (6, 16). Like Baker, Gates develops a theory of African American literature based on a black vernacular tradition. In *The Signifying Monkey* (1988), he analyzes various trickster figures found in the literature of Africa (especially of Yoruba cultures) and in the black vernacular of African American slave cultures. He singles out Esu-Elegbara and the "signifying monkey," which can be found in Africa, the Americas, and the Caribbean. These figures are bound up with the idea of Signification or Signifyin(g) (capital *S*), which differs from the poststructuralist conception of signification (lower-case *s*); in Signifyin(g) the signifier itself becomes the signified in a self-consciously rhetorical performance of language. (On the function of the SIGN, see pp. 181–3.) Black vernacular performances like "the dozens," which Gates traces to sources in Africa, exemplify this Signifyin(g) practice. As he demonstrates in his analysis of Esu-Elegbara and signifying monkey stories, the PROBLEMATIC of language and of representation is itself the centerpiece and subject of the stories. "Esu is our metaphor for the uncertainties of explication, for the open-endedness of every literary text. . . . Esu is discourse upon a text; it is the process of interpretation that he rules." The related trope of the signifying monkey is "the great trope of Afro-American discourse, and the trope of tropes, his language of Signifyin(g), is his verbal sign in the Afro-American tradition" (21). Signifyin(g) is about naming and revising discourse, a process of revision and repetition that works within a black vernacular tradition but also within (and against) a dominant Euro-American one. It is a form of "double voiced" utterance (an idea Gates borrows from **M. M. Bakhtin**), a "speakerly" text in which parody, pastiche, and a general facility with language permits a negotiation between two discourse communities as well as the creation of a new oppositional discourse. (On Bakhtin, see pp. 115, 157, 184–6.)

Gates's influence has been powerful, and one result has been to urge African American studies to continue to question the theoretical models it employs. African American Feminism has been especially productive in this regard. Barbara Smith's *Toward a Black Feminist Criticism* (1977) anticipated Baker's call for a black literary theory and drew much-needed attention to writing by African American women. Her groundbreaking work was followed by that of **bell hooks**, who called white Western feminists to task for failing to address the fundamental problems of race and racism: "Although ethnocentric white values have led feminist theorists to argue the priority of sexism over racism, they do so in the context of attempting to create an evolutionary notion of culture, which in no way corresponds to our lived experience." In fact, argues hooks, racism is the very means by which white women "construct feminist theory and praxis in such a way that it is far removed from anything resembling radical struggle" (53–54). For Smith and hooks, race is the category that orients thinking about women's experience because it is the "color-line" that dominates individual experience and collective political action. Recent work in African American studies has maintained the focus on race but has developed new methodologies from Cultural Studies, Psychoanalysis, and Postcolonial Studies. Of particular note are Toni Morrison's work on "constructing social reality" and Hortense Spiller's on race and gender.

The focus on race, ideology, and Cultural Studies defines much of the work going on in Chicano/a studies and Native American studies, particularly in the 1990s, when both fields began to develop strong institutional presences. Unlike African American studies, however, slavery was not part of this focus. Instead, theorists turned to the special problems of foreign conquest and the question of native identity and native rights. As Ramón Saldívar puts it, Native Americans and Mexican Americans "became ethnic minorit[ies] through the direct conquest of their homelands" (13). However, though this important condition differentiates the experiences of these groups from African Americans, whose minority status is the result of slavery and its aftermath, all of them are committed to the same theoretical category, DIFFERENCE. Saldívar agrees with Gates that the Mexican American experience, like the African American, is defined by the interrelationship of two cultures, a "minority" and a "dominant." His analysis departs from Gates's primarily in its insistence on a form of dialectical materialism. For Saldívar, Chicano narrative "has provided a mediated truth about a culturally determinate people in a historically determinate context." The function of these narratives differs "from what readers normally expect from literary texts. Not content with mirroring a problematic real world of social hardship and economic deprivation, Chicano narratives seek systematically to uncover the

underlying structures by which real men and women may either perpetuate or reformulate that reality" (5–6). These structures often entail
a struggle between the dominant culture and "the opposing group's
traditional culture," a struggle that has come to characterize the "stance
of resistance that Mexican American culture develops and its dialectical
relationship to both of its original contexts" (17).

Many Chicana feminists also question the dominance of Euro-American theory and its tendency to ignore the role of race and racism in the
constitution of gender and sexual identity. For Gloria Anzuldúa, racial
difference must intersect with gender and sexual difference. Moreover,
in the analysis of gender and sexuality in Chicano/a contexts, difference
is never simply binary, for identity, female and male, is determined by
multiple contacts and intersections. To be sure, this is a concern for
African American intellectuals, as Du Bois pointed out in his discussion
of "the phenomena of race-contact" (120). What differs is the Chicano/a
experience of geographical borderlands, spaces of difference that complicate binary structures of knowledge. Contemporary Chicano/a studies
regards borderlands as both a concrete sociohistorical context of social
action and cultural production *and* a state of mind characterized by
ethnic, linguistic, and sexual HYBRIDITY. "Positioned between cultures,
living on borderlines," writes Saldívar, "Chicanos and their narratives
have assumed a unique borderland quality, reflecting in no uncertain
terms the forms and styles of their folk-based origins" (24–25). The
border is a space of pain and merger, of struggle and communication.
"The US-Mexican border *es una herida abierta* where the Third World
grates against the first and bleeds. And before a scab forms it hemor-
rhages again, the lifeblood of two worlds merging to form a third country
– a border culture" (Anzuldúa 3). Anzuldúa, like so many other Chicano/
a writers, opposes a MANICHAEAN "counterstance" that "locks one into
a duel of oppressor and oppressed." It is not enough, she writes, "to stand
on the opposite river bank, shouting questions, challenging patriarchal,
white conventions" (78). Anzuldúa and Sonia Saldívar-Hull focus on the
conflicts between and within dominant, immigrant, and *mestizo* cultures. "Life as feminists on the border," writes Saldívar-Hull, "means
recognizing the urgency of dealing with the sexism and homophobia
within our culture; our political reality demands that we confront institutionalized racism while we simultaneously struggle against economic
exploitation" (34). The PROBLEMATIC of race within this context of

cultural pluralism and cultural critique intensifies as each new wave of immigration, as each new *mestizo* formation brings new voices into the dialogue. Indeed, in the twenty-first century, it is difficult to speak of white Anglo-Americans as a majority population (though it is quite easy to speak of them as forming a dominant group).

Many of these same issues can be found in the emergent theoretical discourse in Native American studies. For example, Arnold Krupat's theory of "cosmopolitan comparativism," which is committed to a form of "cross-cultural translation" (ix–x), in a similar way argues for greater understanding of racial and cultural "contact points." Building on the work of Gerald Vizenor, Vine Deloria, Jr., and others, Krupat outlines a Native American literary theory that acknowledges multiple perspectives. Krupat isolates three of these. The nationalist perspective frames the struggle for sovereignty within a context of "anticolonial nationalism." For the indigenous critic, "the source of the values on which a critical perspective must be based" is not the "world of nations and nationalisms" but "the animate and sentient earth" (11). The cosmopolitan perspective is linked to Appiah's notion of "cosmopolitan patriotism," a sense of transportable rootedness. Krupat elaborates on this notion in his development of cosmopolitan comparativism, which situates Native American literatures "in relation to other minority or subaltern literatures elsewhere in the late-colonial or postcolonial world" (19). Like **Gayatri Spivak**'s "transnational cultural studies," Krupat's Native American literary theory seeks to transcend the necessarily narrow limits of national and indigenous literatures in order to find a space for the consideration of such literatures in contact with other literatures elsewhere in the world. Its engagement with Western forms of theoretical reflection has been criticized by Elvira Pulitano, whose quarrel with Krupat appears less a matter of the measure of his commitments to the West than one of how he positions himself with respect to those commitments.

Note. On Native American studies and Postcolonial theory, see p. 141.

WORKS CITED

Anzuldúa, Gloria. *Borderlands/La Frontera: The New Mestiza.* 1987. 2nd ed. San Francisco: Aunt Lute Books, 1999.

Appiah, Kwame Anthony. "The Uncompleted Argument: Du Bois and the Illusion of Race." In *"Race," Writing, and Difference.* Ed. Henry Louis Gates. Chicago: University of Chicago Press, 1986. 21–37.

Asante, Molefi K. *The Afrocentric Idea.* 1987. Rev. ed. Philadelphia: Temple University Press, 1998.

Bernal, Martin. *Black Athena: The Afroasiatic Roots of Classical Civilization.* Vol. 1. London: Free Association Books, 1987.

Darder, Antonia and Rodolfo D. Torres. *After Race: Racism after Multiculturalism.* New York: New York University Press, 2004.

Du Bois, W. E. B. *The Souls of Black Folk.* New York: Vintage Books/Library of America, 1990.

Gates, Henry Louis. *The Signifying Monkey: A Theory of Afro-American Literary Criticism.* New York: Oxford University Press, 1988.

hooks, bell. *Feminist Theory: From Margin to Center.* 1984. Cambridge, MA: South End Press, 2002.

Krupat, Arnold. *Red Matters: Native American Studies.* Philadelphia: University of Pennsylvania Press, 2002.

Saldívar-Hull, Sonia. *Feminism on the Border: Chicana Gender Politics and Literature.* Berkeley: University of California Press, 2000.

Saldívar, Ramón. *Chicano Narrative: The Dialectics of Difference.* Madison: University of Wisconsin Press, 1990.

Feminist Theory

Modern Feminism began with Mary Wollstonecraft's *Vindication of the Rights of Women* (1792), a work that criticizes stereotypes of women as emotional and instinctive and argues that women should aspire to the same rationality prized by men. A product of the Enlightenment, Wollstonecraft believed that women should enjoy social, legal, and intellectual equality with men and drew for support from the work of progressive social philosophers. Liberal intellectuals like John Stuart Mill and his wife, Harriet Taylor, developed this argument, infusing it with the principles of individualism that Mill had developed out of the utilitarian philosophy of Jeremy Bentham. In 1866, Mill introduced a bill in parliament that called for an extension of the franchise to women and, in 1869, published *The Subjection of Women* (1869). In that essay he argued that women ought to enjoy equality in the social sphere, especially in marriage, and condemned "forced repression" and "unnatural stimulation" (276): "All women are brought up from the very earliest years in the belief that their ideal of character is the very opposite to that of men; not self-will, and government by self-control, but submission, and yielding to the control of others" (271). Mill's views, influenced strongly by Taylor, marked a significant advance for women and provided the inspiration for the New Woman movement at the end of the nineteenth- and the early-twentieth-century suffragette movements committed to social equality and individual freedom.

The first phase or "wave" of modern Feminism, then, was concerned primarily with the issue of suffrage (the right to vote). The dominant figures at mid-nineteenth century in the US were Elizabeth Cady Stanton and Susan B. Anthony, whose political roots were in anti-slavery activism and, to a lesser degree, temperance movements. Stanton composed the "Declaration of Sentiments" for the Seneca Falls women's rights convention in 1848, a watershed moment in US Feminism. Modeled on the US Constitution, the Declaration asserts "that all men and women are created equal," and indicts a patriarchal culture for repressing the rights of women: "The history of mankind is a history of repeated injuries and usurpations on the part of man toward woman, having in direct object the establishment of an absolute tyranny over her" (*Sourcebook*). Together with Matilda Joslyn Gage, Stanton wrote the "Declaration of

Rights of the Women of the United States" for the Centennial celebration in Washington in 1876. Though not officially invited, Anthony read the address. Anthony and Stanton later founded the National Woman Suffrage Association, which in 1890 merged with the more conservative American Woman Suffrage Association. These organizations were instrumental in securing suffrage for women – in 1920, with the Susan B. Anthony Amendment – and served as the foundation for modern Feminism.

Not all feminist movements involved political activism in this early period. Literary Modernism produced foundational feminist writers, including preeminently Virginia Woolf, H.D. (Hilda Doolittle), and Djuna Barnes. Their work dramatized the potentially damaging effects of the rationalism that Wollstonecraft and Mill proffered as the birthright of women and the social entitlement called for by the New Woman movement, which emerged in the late nineteenth century. Woolf's *Room of One's Own* (1929) was a landmark work in which representations of women by male authors are roundly criticized and a new model for female IDENTITY and AGENCY is proffered. Woolf also insisted that women be allowed the economic and social freedom to follow their aspirations and to forego the traditional role of serving as an enlarging mirror for male identity. "How is he to go on giving judgement, civilising natives, making laws, writing books, dressing up and speechifying at banquets, unless he can see himself at breakfast and at dinner at least twice the size he really is?" (60).

A second wave of Feminism, cresting in the 1960s, focused attention on civil rights, specifically social and economic equality. Simone de Beauvoir's *The Second Sex* (1949) was a foundational text. Claiming that "one is not born, one becomes a woman," de Beauvoir challenged the idea that a woman's essence was distinct from a man's, that she was born with certain inherent potentialities and qualities that defined her personal, social, and legal existence. This insight, and the SOCIAL CONSTRUCTIONIST thesis it entails, was further developed by US feminists in the 1960s. In *The Female Eunuch*, Germaine Greer, like de Beauvoir, argues that there is no "natural" distinction between the sexes. She is critical of Freud's influence on American culture and rejects his ideas about femininity as largely irrelevant to understanding modern women. Her book begins with a number of quotations from middle-class, suburban housewives she had interviewed, and the picture she paints is of a pervasive sense of dissatisfaction: "I have heard so many women try to deny this dissatisfied voice within themselves because it does not fit the pretty picture of femininity the experts have given them. I think, in fact, that this is the first clue to the mystery; the problem cannot be understood in the generally accepted terms by which scientists have studied women, doctors have treated them, counselors have advised them, and writers have written about them" (27). For Kate Millet, the problem was fundamentally political. Also like de Beauvoir, she argued against the concept of "biologism," the idea that gender difference is "natural." But unlike others in the 1960s, Millet took aim at the "power-structured relationships" of domination (23) characteristic of PATRIARCHY, relationships that condition gender and cause the oppression of women. She dismissed the arguments of contemporary science, religion, philosophy, and law that insisted upon patriarchy as the original and therefore most natural form of social organization, calling them the "evanescent delights afforded by the game of origins" (28). Anticipating the work of radical feminists of the 1980s and 1990s, Millet criticized "cultural programming," especially the infantilization of women perpetuated by social surveillance and the violence directed against them, a "patriarchal force" that is "particularly sexual in character and realised most completely in the act of rape" (42–44).

What all of these women have in common is an interest in exposing patriarchal forms of power as the cause of the unequal and subordinate status of women in Western societies. However, these early feminist theorists speak from the standpoint of white, middle-class privilege – even as they criticize that very privilege in the form of suburban complacency. And while these early critiques are aimed at the patriarchal authority of Enlightenment politics and science, they nevertheless retain something of that Enlightenment heritage, particularly the tendency to think in terms of UNIVERSALS, to presuppose a generalized, abstract idea of "woman." **Elaine Showalter**, **Sandra Gilbert**, and **Susan Gubar** were instrumental in developing revisionist literary histories of women's writing, though they concentrated largely on white women writers in the nineteenth century. Showalter's A Literature of Their Own examines innovative work by the Brontë sisters, George Eliot, and writers in the suffragette movement and compares it to the sensationalist "feminine novel" of the day that did little to combat sexist stereotypes. Gilbert and Gubar, too, fought against the tendencies of conventional fiction and the patriarchal culture that nurtured it. Their landmark work, *Madwoman in the Attic*, draws on phenomenology and Harold Bloom's theories of influence to describe new relationships between women writers and their audiences and between these writers and their male predecessors. In part by deconstructing or re-visioning male discourses and images of women, in part by exploring the unexplored terrain that sustained women's writing, Gilbert and Gubar examine "the crucial ways in which women's art has been radically qualified by their femaleness" (82).

For some critics, Showalter, Gilbert, and Gubar had not gone far enough. Toril Moi, for example, in her widely-read *Sexual/Textual Politics* (2002), takes "humanist feminism" to task for its rejection of theory and its adoption of New Critical aesthetics. "What 'knowledge,'" Moi asks, "is ever uninformed by theoretical assumptions?" (76). For Moi, an alternative can be found in the work of **Luce Irigaray**, **Hélène Cixous**, and **Julia Kristeva**, French feminists whose critique of PATRIARCHY and the gendered SUBJECT extends the concerns of second-wave Feminism into the realms of philosophy, Psychoanalysis, linguistics, SEMIOTICS, and radical politics. French feminists critiqued the foundational principles of a patriarchal culture that developed the concept of "rights" as part of a stable, AUTONOMOUS subjectivity. The Centre d'Etudes Féminines at the University of Paris VIII (Vincennes), founded by Cixous in 1974, provided an institutional structure for the ongoing critique of patriarchal culture, a critique that was to a significant degree fashioned by borrowing concepts and methodologies from poststructuralist discourse written by men. Irigaray's critique of Freud exemplifies this approach. Borrowing from Derridean Deconstruction and Lacanian psychoanalysis, Irigaray calls into question the Freudian discourse on femininity, particularly the role played by the Oedipus and castration complexes and their total lack of relevance for little girls. Her chief point is that women are trapped in a masculine world of representation, forced to be the reproductive medium or essence in which men find their ESSENTIAL being, but are themselves debarred from actually possessing essence. "The girl," she writes, "has no right to play in any manner whatever with any representation of her beginning, no specific mimicry of origin is available to her: she must inscribe herself in the masculine, phallic way of relating to origin, that involves repetition, representation, reproduction. And this is meant to be 'the most powerful feminine wish'" (78). Cixous and Catherine

Clément, in *Newly Born Woman* (1975), critique the Freudian seduction scene, in which the daughter seduces the father, the "pivotal" point at which the Symbolic order enters into the young girl's life. However, the daughter, though pivotal, is relegated to the margins, sexually and socially, and takes the blame for "fantasiz[ing] a reality that, it seems, is to remain undecipherable" (47). She is thus an unreadable, non-essential ground for masculine sexual identity. As such, the woman's body becomes available for the type of symbolic exchange between men that Gayle Rubin analyzes in "The Traffic in Women" (1975).

Alternatives to PHALLOCENTRIC discourse are offered by Irigaray and a number of other French feminists. Collectively these practices are known as ÉCRITURE FEMININE (variously translated as "feminine writing" and "writing the body"). This view of Feminism, which Diana Fuss and others have described as a form of strategic essentialism, holds that a woman's body determines not only her identity but also a mode of writing and thinking fundamentally different from and in revolt against masculine modes. Irigaray called it "hysteria scenario, that privileged dramatization of feminine sexuality" (60). This practice is strongly associated with Cixous' literary and theoretical work, especially her influential essay "The Laugh of the Medusa." "It is impossible to define a female practice of writing," Cixous claims, but she goes on to insist that such a practice "will always surpass the discourse that regulates the phallocentric system" in part because it lies outside the arena of "philosophico-theoretical domination" (46). The space marked out by this new practice is a woman's body, where her own desires, banned from patriarchal discourse, can find expression. It is also a space defined by the blanks and gaps in that discourse where a woman's voice can find its "silent plasticity" (142). The Lacanian concept of JOUISSANCE is often used to define this inexplicable site of "female writing," where women's experience can be freed from the unforgiving dialectic of Oedipus and the HEGEMONY of the Symbolic in order to embrace the Imaginary realm of mystical and pre-Oedipal experiences, the "oceanic" unity with the body of the mother. (On Lacan, see pp. 158–9, 168–71.) These experiences are linked, in Kristeva's "semanalysis," to the "semiotic *chora*," the pre-Oedipal dissolution of boundaries. Thus the maternal body becomes the foundation for both a resistance to patriarchal discourse and for a feminist ethical practice ("herethics") that does not derive from it. Like other French feminists of her generation, Kristeva struggled to lift prohibitions on the maternal body imposed by the Oedipal and castration complexes. In the Preface to *Desire in Language* (1980), she confesses that "[i]t was perhaps also necessary to be a *woman* to attempt to take up that exorbitant wager of carrying the rational project to the outer borders of the signifying venture of men" (x). (On Kristeva, see pp. 156–9.)

However, the concerns of many feminists, particularly of lesbians and women of color, were remote from those of straight, white, middle-class intellectuals working in Western universities. These feminists, who began to emerge in the late 1970s, gaining momentum in the 1980s, constituted a third wave of feminist critique that took issue with abstract, UNIVERSALIST notions of the idea of woman that either ignored women of color or relegated them to the status of "third world woman," yet another form of abstraction. Adrienne Rich has famously critiqued the "compulsory heterosexuality" at the heart of patriarchal cultures and advocated new forms of community based on lesbian desire, which she believed was an unacknowledged and powerful force for social change. In a similar way, Monique Wittig emphasizes the "lesbian body" and lesbian consciousness as a precondition for a more inclusive and politically effective Feminism. Just as Rich and Wittig emphasize sexuality as the key to Feminism, so **bell hooks** and other women of color insist that the fight against racism is the fundamental conflict, the one that all feminists must fight who desire an end to sexism. hooks, in her landmark work, *Feminist Theory: From Margin to Center* (1984), articulated the principal problems with Western Feminism. She took issue, as did Gayatri Spivak and other postcolonial feminists, with the notion that race and class can be ignored or downplayed in the formulation of a feminist politics. "Racism is fundamentally a feminist issue," hooks argues, "because it is so interconnected with sexist oppression" (53–54). According to hooks, sexist oppression is the foundation of patriarchal culture and should be the chief concern of a progressive Feminism. Violence against women, whether in the form of domestic abuse or ritualized social practices like *sati* and genital mutilation, is the physical manifestation of this oppression on women's bodies. Responding to what she sees as a dominant trend in US Feminism towards seeking "social equality with men" (19), hooks advocates a more general critique of male domination and a transformation of social relationships, especially marriage and child rearing. Gloria Anzaldúa and Cherríe Moraga were involved in similar projects at this time, with an emphasis on the way that borders, both geographical and psychological, determine gender and sexual identity. What all of these women have in common is a desire to overcome a two-fold domination, for they are oppressed not only because of their gender but also because of their race.

Most of the trends I have discussed above continued into the 1990s and beyond. Postmodern Feminism, particularly the work of **Judith Butler** and Nancy Fraser, continue to explore some of the issues that interested the early French feminists and tackle with new theoretical vigor the problem of the gendered SUBJECT. Of critical importance for the study of Gender and Sexuality is Butler's work on PERFORMANCE and PERFORMATIVITY (see pp. 104–5). The future of Feminism, and its principal intellectual value, lies in its continued ability to critique its own assumptions and, by doing so, to open up the discourse to the new problems created by the globalization of economies, cultures, and discourse.

Note. For more on Feminism, see entries on Ethnic Studies, Gender and Sexuality, Postcolonial Studies, Postmodernism, and Psychoanalysis.

WORKS CITED

Cixous, Hélène. "The Laugh of the Medusa." *Signs* 1.4 (Summer 1976): 875–93. Rpt. of "Le Rire de la Méduse." *L'Arc* 61 (1975): 39–54.

—— and Catherine Clément. *The Newly Born Woman.* 1975. Trans. Betsy Wing. Minneapolis: University of Minnesota Press, 1986.

Gilbert, Sandra and Susan Gubar. *Madwoman in the Attic: The Woman Writer and the Nineteenth-Century Literary Imagination.* 1979. 2nd ed. New Haven and London: Yale University Press, 2000.

Greer, Germaine. *The Female Eunuch.* London: MacGibbon & Kee, 1970.

hooks, bell. *Feminist Theory: From Margin to Center.* 1984. Cambridge, MA: South End Press, 2002.

Internet Modern History Sourcebook. "The Declaration of Sentiments, Seneca Falls Conference, 1848." http://www.fordham.edu/HALLSAL/MOD/Senecafalls.html.

Irigaray, Luce. *Speculum of the Other Woman.* 1974. Trans. Gilliam C. Gill. Ithaca: Cornell University Press, 1985.

Kristeva, Julia. *Desire in Language: A Semiotic Approach to Literature and Art.* Ed. Leon S. Roudiez. Trans. Thomas Gora, Alice Jardine, and Leon S. Roudiez. New York: Columbia University Press, 1980.

Mill, John Stuart. "The Subjection of Women." 1869. In *Essays on Equality, Law, and Education*. Vol. XXI of *The Collected Works of John Stuart Mill*. Ed. John M. Robson. Toronto: Toronto University Press, 1984. 259–340.

Millett, Kate. *Sexual Politics*. Garden City, NY: Doubleday, 1970.

Moi, Toril. *Sexual/Textual Politics: Feminist Literary Theory*. 2nd ed. London and New York: Routledge, 1985, 2002.

Woolf, Virginia. *A Room of One's Own*. London: Hogarth Press, 1929.

Gender and Sexuality

Since the late 1980s, theories of Gender and Sexuality have redefined how we think about culture and society. They have raised new questions about the construction of the gendered and sexualized subject and put forward radical new ideas about PERFORMANCE and PERFORMATIVITY as the means by which the body becomes a SIGNIFYING SYSTEM within SOCIAL FORMATIONS. At the foundation of most theories of Gender and Sexuality is a thoroughgoing critique of the SUBJECT and SUBJECTIVITY. As a social and political category, the subject cuts across all disciplinary and theoretical boundaries. Being a subject can mean many things – a citizen of a particular community, an AUTONOMOUS being in possession of a sense of personal wholeness and unity, the subject of an oppressive ruler or of a discourse. Being a subject and possessing subjectivity are not the birthrights of all human beings, however; they are specialized attributes, more or less unique to Western or Westernized cultures. This notion of the modern subject begins in the Enlightenment, with the reflections of John Locke, who regarded personal identity as unique, sovereign, and autonomous. Subjectivity, the consciousness of one's historical and social agency, was the prerogative of the Western individual who defined himself in opposition to the OTHER, to that which was not a subject and did not possess subjectivity. The classic philosophical expression of this relationship of the subject to what is not the subject is Hegel's dialectic of the master and slave. As is so often the case in Enlightenment thought, the potential for subversion and AMBIVALENCE is contained in what appears to be a universal concept. For Hegel's dialectic also suggests the possibility of the disenfranchised slave or non-subject acquiring subjectivity by overpowering the master. By the end of the nineteenth century, Friedrich Nietzsche could speak of the "subject as multiplicity," and by the 1920s, Freud would call into question most of our preconceived notions about of selfhood and sexual identity.

Closely linked to the concept of the subject is the concept of IDENTITY, which is typically used to cover the process by which a subject becomes a particular *kind* of subject. Rather than a fixed quality or ESSENCE, identity is understood by theorists of Gender and Sexuality as an ongoing process of construction, performance, appropriation, or mimicry. This perspective, strongly influenced by **Michel Foucault**'s theories of sexuality, came be known as SOCIAL CONSTRUCTIONISM, the idea that subjectivity and identity are not natural categories or essential features of human existence, unique and indivisible aspects of one's being; they are rather the material effects of the discourses and images that surround us. The crucial questions raised by theories of Gender and Sexuality have to do with agency and determination: Who or what determines the construction of gender and sexuality? How is social AGENCY acquired and maintained by these constructions? Is one constructed solely by social ideologies and institutions? Or do individuals have the freedom to act reflexively, to engage in what Anthony Giddens calls "projects of the self"? For Foucault, sexuality has played a fundamental role in developing modern modes of social organization and regulation. In his landmark study, *History of Sexuality* (1976), Foucault argues that sexuality, far from being proscribed or repressed in the nineteenth century, became part of a discourse that sought to identify and regulate all forms of sexual behavior. "Instead of a massive censorship," he claimed, "what was involved was a regulated and polymorphous incitement to discourse" (34). Religious confession, Psychoanalysis, sexology, literature – all were instrumental in this incitement, which simultaneously made sexuality a public matter and a target of social administration. "Under the authority of a language that had been carefully expurgated so that it was no longer directly named, sex was taken charge of, tracked down as it were, by a discourse that aimed to allow it no obscurity, no respite" (20).

Foucault's critique of sexuality brilliantly exposed the ideological mechanisms by which sexual identities are maintained and regulated by institutional authorities. In this regard, his work paralleled that of **Louis Althusser** whose theory of IDEOLOGY held that the subject is always already "interpellated," coercively recruited by ideological apparatuses of the State. (On Althusser, see pp. 112–13.) Subjectivity, selfhood, and citizenship are the products of socialization; agency, that quantum of will that enables the subject to move within social spheres, is a product of those very spheres. In another direction, Giddens argues that the individual has many significant opportunities to intervene in the ideological construction of subjectivity; she is able to choose from an array of available discursive strategies and write the narrative of herself. These techniques of self-development guarantee freedom even in contexts of overwhelming social power. In his later work, Foucault recognized that the individual possessed a necessary freedom from POWER, which is "exercised only over free subjects . . . and only insofar as they are free. By this we mean individual or collective subjects who are faced with a field of possibilities in which several ways of behaving, several reactions and diverse comportments may be realized" ("Subject" 221).

Judith Butler is perhaps the most influential theorist to explore the idea of sexual and gender identity as a social PERFORMANCE, a site of power and discourse. "To what extent," she asks, "do *regulatory practices* of gender formation and division constitute identity, the internal coherence of the subject, indeed, the self-identical status of the person?" (*Gender Trouble* 16). As an alternative to such naturalized regulatory practices, she developed a model of PERFORMATIVITY, which she distinguished from a normative model of PERFORMANCE:

> [performance] presumes a subject, but [performativity] contests the very notion of the subject. . . . What I'm trying to do is think about performativity as *that aspect of discourse that has the capacity to produce what it names.* Then I take a further step, through the Derridean rewriting of [J. L.] Austin, and suggest that this production actually always happens through a certain kind of repetition and recitation. So if you want the ontology of this, I guess performativity is the vehicle through which ontological effects are established. Performativity is the discursive mode by which ontological effects are installed. ("Gender" 111–12)

According to Butler, gender and sexual identity (self-consciousness about the ontology or "being" of the self) has always been a matter of performance, acquiescence to social norms and to mystifications about sexuality and gender derived from philosophy, religion, psychology, medicine, and popular culture. Performativity upsets these norms, sometimes appropriating them in a transformed fashion, at other times parodying or miming them in a way that draws out their salient elements for criticism. The "ontological effects" to which Butler refers are all that we can see or know of "true" gender or sexual identity, a situation dramatized most clearly in drag and other forms of transvestism. For while the drag queen prides himself on getting every detail right and being true to a particular vision of femininity, his performance is in the end a critique of the very category of woman he strives to imitate faithfully. These reflections on the ontology of sexual identity have led Butler and others to argue that the so-called biological notion of "sex" may itself not be free from a performative dimension. Performativity, as a mode of subject- and identity-formation, is clearly indebted to poststructuralist notions of language and TEXTUALITY premised on the idea of the subject *as the subject of a discourse*. It is the quintessential expression of personal agency in a context of late MODERNITY, a context in which naturalistic, biological, or ESSENTIALIST conceptions of the subject and of gender and sexual identity are no longer operative. Performativity is, paradoxically, the provisional result of a process of construction *and* the material sign of an authentic self. Butler's later work, especially *Excitable Speech: A Politics of the Performative* (1997), indicates the decisive role that public language – her chief example is "hate speech" – plays in constituting the performative element of social life.

Innovations in queer theory have made it evident that performativity is a function of the choices that gay and lesbian individuals make every day and in all walks of life. To a certain extent, such individuals have always known that the performative is the real. This is why, as Alan Sinfield argues in *The Wilde Century* (1994), Oscar Wilde's life experience is as valuable for queer theory as his literary works, for it posits performativity at the foundation of queer identity.

Queer theory seeks, among other things, to describe or map out the ways homosexual or homoerotic desire manifests itself in literary and cultural texts. It is strongly reliant on psychoanalytic categories and concepts, but seeks to overcome the heterosexual limits of psychoanalytic theory. **Teresa de Lauretis**, who was one of the first to use the term queer theory, has since rejected it because of its appropriation by mainstream media. Certainly popular television shows like *Queer Eye for the Straight Guy* have made the word "queer," which had been appropriated by the gay and lesbian movement as a symbol of political empowerment, into a sanitized label for homosexuals with no political agenda. Others feel that queer theory privileges gay male experience at the expense of lesbian and bisexual experience. To some degree, the male bias is due to the strong influence of gay male theorists. It is also due to the enormous influence of **Eve Kosofsky Sedgwick's** *Between Men* (1985), which, along with Foucault's *History of Sexuality*, provided the theoretical scaffolding for academic queer theory. One of her most powerful formulations, the concept of *homosociality*, has come to enjoy rather widespread use across academic disciplines. HOMOSOCIAL DESIRE is grounded in René Girard's theory of "triangular desire" and in Gayle Rubin's theory of the "sex/gender system," specifically her critique of Lévi-Strauss's analysis of kinship systems in which women function as gifts in economic exchanges between men. According to Sedgwick, homosocial desire between men is expressed in a triangular structure with a woman (or a "discourse" of "woman") standing as a putative object of at least one of them: "the ultimate function of women is to be conduits of homosocial desire" (99). These relationships need not be sexual; in fact they are far more potent whenever the sexual element is sublimated in the MIMICRY of a heterosexual identity that effectively disguises homosexual "deviancy." Homosocial structures frequently elicit homophobia as an institutionalized check on repressed homosexual desire, but they more often lead to "changes in men's experience of living within the shifting terms of compulsory heterosexuality" (134). Her chapter on Henry James in her *Epistemology of the Closet* (1990) illustrates the divide between homosocial networking, which confirms the heterosexual status quo, and "homosexual panic," which reacts violently against any manifestation of eroticism or "genitalized" behavior that might emerge out of such networks.

Queer theory has come to encompass a substantial body of work in lesbian studies. Monique Wittig's *Lesbian Body* attacks the tradition of anatomy based on the orderly and ordered male body and offers instead the lesbian body as a model of the desiring subject. Like other feminists who challenge the authority of PATRIARCHAL discourse, Wittig openly confronts the problem of the SUBJECT POSITION she occupies as a theorist and writer; she disrupts the texture of her writing and thus repeats at the level of her discourse the disorderly nature of the lesbian body itself. Adrienne Rich, in her much-anthologized essay, "Compulsory Heterosexuality and the Lesbian Existence," attacks "heterocentricity" as a covert mode of socialization that seeks willfully to repress the "enormous potential counterforce" (39) of lesbian experience. Because heterosexuality is the compulsory cultural norm, the oppression of women – their sexual slavery – is more difficult to name. Rich revalues the so-called perversity of lesbian desire, more frightening even than male homosexuality, and posits a "lesbian continuum" free of invidious binary sexual typologies. Lesbian Feminism is not concerned with hating men but rather with celebrating the life choices of women who love women. It is not that heterosexuality is in and of itself oppressive, it is that "the absence of choice remains the great unacknowledged reality" (67).

Acknowledging this reality and creating and preserving choice is what motivates the successors of Rich and Wittig. Thus Theresa de Lauretis, in *The Practice of Love: Lesbian Sexuality and Perverse Desire* (1994), challenges psychoanalytical theories of normative sexuality that would limit such choices, and Lynda Hart, *Fatal Women: Lesbian Sexuality and the Mark of Aggression* (1994), attacks the pathologization and appropriation of lesbian sexuality by the "male Imaginary" and defends women who respond criminally to men who attempt to foreclose lesbian desire. In both cases free choice is celebrated, for without it there can be no chance for free subjects to combat the fortified positions of social and cultural power.

Note. For more on issues related to gender and sexuality, see Feminism, Ethnic Studies, and Postcolonial Studies.

WORKS CITED

Butler, Judith. "Gender as Performance." Interview. In *A Critical Sense: Interviews with Intellectuals.* Ed. Peter Osborne. London: Routledge, 1996. 108–25.

——. *Gender Trouble: Feminism and the Subversion of Identity.* New York: Routledge, 1990.

Foucault, Michel. *The History of Sexuality.* 1976. Vol. 1. Trans. Robert Hurley. New York: Pantheon Books, 1978.

——. "The Subject and Power." In *Michel Foucault: Beyond Structuralism and Hermeneutics.* Eds. Herbert L. Dreyfus and Paul Rabinow. Chicago: University of Chicago Press, 1984. 208–26.

Sedgwick, Eve Kosofsky. *Between Men: English Literature and Male Homosocial Desire.* New York: Columbia University Press, 1985.

Rich, Adrienne. "Compulsory Heterosexuality and the Lesbian Existence." In *Blood, Bread and Poetry: Selected Prose 1979–1985.* New York: Norton, 1986. 23–75.

Marxist Theory

Marxist literary theory is predicated on the idea that literature is a product of social forces and ideology. However, **Terry Eagleton** insists that "The literary text is not the 'expression' of ideology, nor is ideology the 'expression' of social class. The text, rather, is a certain *production* of ideology, for which the analogy of a dramatic production is in some ways appropriate. . . . The relation between text and production is a relation of *labour*" (64–65). Marxism is a form of DIALECTICAL MATERIALISM; it holds that all social realities are fundamentally material, that they have their origin and being in specific forms of labor and production, and that the history of society is the history of dialectical transformations in the relationship between labor and production. For Marx, there were two social classes, the capitalist and the proletariat. The antagonism he discerned between these classes was part of a long history of social development. Western civilization began with agrarian societies structured along tribal lines, which ultimately evolved into the feudal organizations of medieval Europe. Slowly, as indentured serfs secured their freedom from feudal lords, they established themselves as artisans and craftsmen in towns. Guilds and other professional organizations, along with the apprentice system, followed and, by the eighteenth century, the rudiments of an industrialized society and capitalist economy. "With the advent of manufacture the relationship between worker and employer changed. In the guilds the patriarchal relationship between journeyman and master continued to exist; in manufacture its place was taken by the monetary relation between worker and capitalist – a relationship which in the countryside and in small towns retained a patriarchal tinge, but in the larger, the real manufacturing towns, quite early lost almost all patriarchal complexion" (*German Ideology* 74). The division of labor in capitalist societies led to the creation of private property and the contradictions that arise because of its uneven distribution. The class struggle at the heart of capitalist society is the logical outcome of a historical process, which would come to its conclusion after the working classes seized the modes of production and created the "dictatorship of the proletariat," a classless, communist society. Classical Marxism was thus a form of HISTORICAL DETERMINISM, which means that the analysis of history could conceivably proceed along scientific lines. In fact, **Louis**

Althusser called Marxism "a *new* science: the science of history" (19). While contemporary Marxists still regard these materialist and deterministic theses to be important for social and cultural analysis, they have devised complex theories of DETERMINATION that rely less on the mechanistic aspect of the modes of production than on superstructural phenomena.

A chief concern of classical "economistic" Marxism is the concept of the COMMODITY (that which is produced out of the materials of nature) and the values that are given to that commodity. "A commodity is . . . a mysterious thing," Marx muses in *Capital*, "simply because in it the social character of men's labour appears to them as an objective character stamped upon the product of that labour; because the relation of the producers to the sum total of their own labour is presented to them as a social relation, existing not between themselves, but between the products of their labour" (*Marx–Engels* 320). The process Marx describes here is also known as REIFICATION. At issue here is a distinction between form and content. The form of the commodity corresponds with its *exchange value* while the content corresponds with its *use value*. Exchange values have to do with specific systems of economic exchange in which a commodity's value may rise or fall depending on its desirability. Use values, which are derived from the labor expended in creating the commodity, are constant and may bear no logical or intrinsic relation to the exchange value. *Surplus value* is what accrues to the capitalist who owns the modes of production; it is the difference between wages paid and the actual work done by workers. In a capitalist society, workers are, in principle, underpaid; the value of labor expended in a day's work exceeds the wages paid for that work. *Money* functions in this system of values as another form of value, one that is determined within the economic system in which it is used as an equivalent value for a specific commodity. The excess in value between the cost of producing a commodity and the price paid for it constitutes *capital*. Money in the form of capital is always subject to fluctuations of the market, boom periods and crises which cause the value of money to rise or fall depending on whether or not capital is in high demand. The commodity form is essential to understanding Marx's vision of the social TOTALITY.

Marxist social theory begins with a base/superstructure paradigm. The BASE (or infrastructure) refers to the modes of production as well as to the class formations and class relationships generated by them; the

SUPERSTRUCTURE refers to the social and cultural institutions and traditions that promulgate and sustain the specific ideologies of the ruling class. The term IDEOLOGY refers to ideas and beliefs that guide and organize the social and cultural elements of the superstructure. Ideology is typically associated with the ideas and beliefs of the ruling class, which controls the means of production; this is the sense in which Marx himself used the term. Since Marx, the term has undergone a number of refinements and complications, with the relationship between ideology and the modes of production receiving special attention. For example, Georg Lukács argues, in *History of Class Consciousness* (1923), that materialist analysis must concern itself with "the relation to society *as a whole*," by which he meant "*society as a concrete totality*, the system of production at a given point in history and the resulting division of society into classes." Only when this relation to a social totality is established "does the consciousness of their existence that men have at any given time emerge in all its essential characteristics" (50). Ideology, for Lukács, is a form of *false consciousness* that arises whenever the subjective consciousness of a specific class (typically, the ruling class) is taken to be the objective consciousness of society at large. It is not merely a question of good or bad judgment, but rather of ignoring the fundamentally dialectical process of historical development. The Italian Marxist Antonio Gramsci refined Lukács view of ideology and argued for a two-tier model of the superstructure: "civil society" ("private") would correspond to "the function of HEGEMONY which the dominant group exercises throughout society," while "political society" (the State) would correspond to "'direct' DOMINATION or command exercised through the State and 'juridical' government. The functions in question are precisely organisational and connective" (*Selections* 12). Hegemony works through institutional modes of consensus and consent (e.g., universities, political parties, state bureaucracies, corporations). The goal for the dominant social group is to achieve hegemony by extending its ideology – its values, beliefs, and ideals – to every level of society. Gramsci and his successors put forward the idea of *articulation* to describe the myriad links between social institutions and individuals, points of ideological consensus and consent that create a tightly woven social and cultural fabric.

Like Fanon after him, Gramsci was interested in the role of the intellectual, especially those who are engaged, passively or actively, in supporting the dominant class and its ideology. "The intellectuals are the dominant group's 'deputies' exercising the subaltern functions of social hegemony and political government" (*Selections* 12). Gramsci describes two distinct groups: *traditional* intellectuals (the clergy, professors, writers, artists, and others), who enjoy relative AUTONOMY, and *organic* intellectuals, the "specialists" that "every new class creates alongside itself" (*Selections* 6). Both work within and sustain existing social conditions. Organic intellectuals in capitalist societies are mostly ineffective and "standardized," willing promoters of the dominant ideology. Traditional intellectuals belong to professions and guilds, they are "ecclesiasts" or "medical men" and "put themselves forward as autonomous and independent of the dominant social group" (*Selections* 7). Gramsci suggests that the only alternative to this all-pervasive social net is to create forms of COUNTER-HEGEMONY especially among working-class activists and intellectuals. The need for the development of an organic intellectual tradition in the working classes led Gramsci to a radical reconception of "intellectual activity": "Each man, finally, outside his professional activity, carries on some form of intellectual activity, that is, he is a 'philosopher', an artist, a man of taste, he participates in a particular conception of the world, has a conscious line of moral conduct, and therefore contributes to sustain a conception of the world or to modify it, that is, to bring into being new modes of thought" (*Selections* 9).

Raymond Williams understood early on the significance of Gramsci's rethinking of ideology. For him, ideology is a complex and multivalent phenomenon. He notes that ideology can refer not only to "a system of beliefs characteristic of a particular class or group" but also to "a system of illusory beliefs" (Lukács called this "false consciousness") in contrast with "true or scientific reality," the discovery of which is the function of MATERIALIST criticism. The second definition can be combined with the first if one holds, as some Marxists do, that all class-based beliefs are at some level illusory. To further complicate matters, Williams adds a third possibility: ideology is "the general process of the production of meanings and ideas" (55). Williams concludes that despite the difficulties in forming a singular definition, it is necessary to arrive at a general term "to describe not only the products but the processes of signification, including the signification of values." Following V. N. Volosinov, he advocates using the terms "ideological" and "ideology" to refer to the production of signs and "the dimension of social experience in which meanings and values are produced" (70). Theoretical speculation on the concept of ideology, especially after the Second World War, is a good indicator of the tremendous importance that has been attached to the superstructural aspects of society. (On Williams, see also pp. 72–4.)

Williams also drew on Gramsci in his discussion of overlapping epochs of social and cultural formations, in which different functions of ideology operate simultaneously. At any given historical moment, one can locate not only a *dominant* ideology but also *residual* and *emergent* ideologies that represent, respectively, the cultural formations of an earlier time and those of new social groups on the margins of the dominant group. This model not only accounts for the complexities and contradictions of late capitalism, it also acknowledges the presence of counter-hegemonic potentialities within the social totality. This "Gramscian turn" in Williams's work is evident in many Marxist thinkers of the 1970s. Of special note is **Louis Althusser**, who drew on Poststructuralism, linguistics, and psychoanalysis in his highly influential rereading of Marx. Althusser is most famous for his elaborations on Gramsci's theory of ideology and the specific mechanisms of ideological hegemony that create the social subject. Following **Jacques Lacan**, he argues that false consciousness is an IMAGINARY construction: "Ideology represents the imaginary relationship of individuals to their real conditions of existence" (109). Althusser here refers to the Lacanian Imaginary, which corresponds to the pre-Oedipal phase of development when the individual has not yet experienced differentiation from the mother, a space of fantasy formations, of resistance to mimesis, reason, rationality, the entire order of the SYMBOLIC. According to Althusser, the "ideological formations that govern paternity, maternity, conjugality and childhood" (211) produce a double distortion of reality: they substitute for the REAL we cannot know and they disguise the real nature of social relations (i.e., the Symbolic order). The Real also represents a *potential* for critique of and intervention into the Symbolic order of ideology. As Ernesto Laclau puts it, "the Real becomes a name for the very failure of the Symbolic in achieving its own fullness. The Real would be, in that sense, a retroactive effect of the failure of the Symbolic" (Butler et al. 68). In the fantasia of ideology, JOUISSANCE is put to work sustaining what Althusser calls "ideological state apparatuses," into which "individuals are always-already interpellated by ideology as subjects." Ideology " 'recruits' subjects among the individuals (it recruits them all), or 'transforms' the individuals into subjects (it transforms them all) by that very precise operation which I have called *interpellation* or hailing and which can be imagined along the lines of the most commonplace everyday police (or other) hailing: 'Hey, you there!'" (174). This "imaginary mis-recognition of the 'ego'" (219) is the first and foremost ideological function of the capitalist state. (On Lacan, see pp. 158–9, 168–71).

By the mid-1980s, Ernesto Laclau and Chantal Mouffe could "state quite plainly that we are now situated in a post-Marxist terrain" (4). For **Fredric Jameson**, as for other post-Marxists, the analysis of class struggle and the problems of commodity production, which was well suited to the era of industry capitalism and the initial formation of modern classes, did not adequately account for the way that ideology was increasingly being used to organize classes and social relations. Jameson, one of the first major Marxist critics in the US, employs another important Althus-serian concept, "structural causality," which helps account for a non-mechanistic mode of historical determination. What matters is not a direct economic or material relation between modes of production and the social and political spheres but rather the structure of relations between these modes and spheres *and* across the spectrum of social and cultural institutions. In many cases, this structure of relations is not easily perceivable. For Jameson, as for other post-Marxists, HISTORICAL DETERMINISM remains a vital concept, though it is no longer regarded in mechanistic terms. History is driven by necessity, but it is not the iron necessity of classical Marxism. It is instead the necessity of structure, of structural relations and of the subject's own saturation by these rela-tions. The turn to ideology and hegemony reflects the importance of relations of social power at the level of the superstructure; it has captured totally new social formations and relations of power, totally new forms of ideological hegemony and social totality. At the turn of the twenty-first century, one could discern a turn to postfoundationalism, which seeks to reinstate the idea of UNIVERSALITY on a provisional or contin-gent basis in order to provide theory with the grounds for making state-ments about new political needs and new social relations. In part, this is a response to the politics of Postmodernism, in which difference, PER-FORMATIVITY, pragmatics, game theory, and SIMULATION deconstruct any demonstrable and material social totality about which one can theo-rize. But it is also a response to the reality of a globalized, universalized marketplace and the dizzying pace of technological transformation. It is on this shifting, globalized field that contemporary post-Marxism crafts new strategies for combating ideological hegemony.

Note. For more on ideology and related concepts, see Critical Theory.

WORKS CITED

Althusser, Louis. *Lenin and Philosophy, and Other Essays.* 1971. Trans. Ben Brewster. New York: Monthly Review Press, 2001.

Butler, Judith, Ernesto Laclau and Slavoj Žižek. *Contingency, Hegemony, Universality: Contemporary Dialogues on the Left.* London and New York: Verso, 2000.

Eagleton, Terry. *Criticism and Ideology: A Study in Marxist Literary Theory.* London: NLB; Atlantic Highlands: Humanities Press, 1976.

Laclau, Ernesto and Chantal Mouffe. *Hegemony and Socialist Strategy: Towards a Radical Democratic Politics.* London and New York: Verso, 1985, 2001.

Lukács, Georg. *History and Class Consciousness: Studies in Marxist Dialectics.* 1923. Trans. Rodney Livingstone. Cambridge, MA: MIT Press, 1983.

Marx, Karl and Fredrick Engels. *The German Ideology.* Ed. C. J. Arthur. New York, International, 1972.

——. *The Marx–Engels Reader.* Ed. Robert C. Tucker. 2nd ed. New York: Norton, 1978.

Selections from the Prison Notebooks of Antonio Gramsci. Ed. and Trans. Quintin Hoare and Geoffrey Nowell Smith. New York: International Publishers, 1971.

Williams, Raymond. *Marxism and Literature.* Oxford: Oxford University Press, 1977.

Narrative Theory

Modern Narrative Theory begins with Russian Formalism in the 1920s, specifically with the work of Roman Jakobson, Yuri Tynyanov, and Viktor Shklovsky. Tynyanov combined his skills as a historical novelist with Formalism to produce, with Jakobson, *Theses on Language* (1928), a treatise on literary structure. Like Shklovsky and other formalists at this time, Tynyanov and Jakobson employed a systematic and holistic theory of language, drawing on Saussure and the idea of language as a binary structural system. Shklovsky was interested in what distinguished the language of prose fiction from "ordinary" language and sought to demonstrate the AUTONOMY of prose on the same lines that Jakobson established the autonomy of poetry. His earliest work, his essay "Art as Technique" (1917), introduced the concept of *ostranenie* ("making strange") or *defamiliarization*, one of the "devices" that constitutes the work of art, and challenged novelistic realism by drawing the reader's attention to the strangeness of what is most familiar and thus calling into question the referential function of language. (On Shklovsky, see pp. 183–4.) A few years later, in *Problems of Dostoevsky's Poetics* (1929), **M. M. Bakhtin** proffered a similar theory of novelistic form based on what Caryl Emerson calls "aesthetic distance": "the observing self must be distanced from what it perceives if art is to happen" (640). While for Shklovsky, distance is a function of the reader's "estrangement" from a *thing*, for Bakhtin it is largely a function of a relationship "between one person and another person, between two distinct living centers of consciousness" (656), a relationship that he describes in terms of DIALOGISM. Bakhtin argues that novelistic narrative is multi-voiced or polyphonic; it is characterized by a condition of HETEROGLOSSIA, Bakhtin's term for the stratification of discourses in novelist narrative – from the monologic "voice" that we associate with traditional omniscient narrators, to the interpolated dialogue of characters, to the various ideolects and jargons available to those characters. His notion of the "carnivalesque," a mode of discourse or ritual in which traditional hierarchies are turned upside down, suggests that the destabilization of social and discursive stratifications can liberate both author and reader from the restrictions of social and literary orthodoxies. (On Bakhtin, see pp. 115, 157, 184–6.)

The other major figure of the 1920s was Vladimir Propp, whose *Morphology of the Folktale* (1928) influenced in its turn French Structuralists. According to Propp, folktales are made up of specific narrative functions (leaving home, confronting danger at the hands of a villain, the realization of a lack, combat between hero and villain, marriage of the hero, and so on). "Function is understood as an act of a character," writes Propp, "defined from the point of view of its significance for the course of the action" (21). There are thirty-one possible functions, all or some of which may appear in a given tale, but in any case, they invariably appear in the same order. These functions are stable and independent of the particular character who fulfills them. The "dramatis personae" of the folktale consists of seven different character types: villain, donor (provider), helper, princess ("a sought-for person"), dispatcher, hero, false hero (Propp 79–80). This limited number of characters and narrative situations nevertheless permits an almost infinite number of story possibilities. In the 1960s, A. J. Greimas modified Propp's structuralist model, refining the typology of functions, which he called *actants*, and the articulation of *actors* (Propp's "characters"). "The result is that if the actors can be established within a tale-occurrence, the actants, which are classifications of actors, can be established only from the corpus of all the tales: an articulation of actors constitutes a particular *tale*; an articulation of actants constitutes a *genre*" (200). In his restructuring of Propp, Greimas employed the science of *semantics* (concerned with the meaning of signs) to posit a structure of actantial relations that stresses binary pairs: subject v. object, sender v. receiver, and helper v. opponent. Each of these pairs makes a number of "thematic investments." Greimas's *structural semantics* is driven by desire. Actantial relationships do not operate on the primary level of action ("to be able to do," "to do") but rather express a "specialized relationship of 'desire' . . . which transforms itself at the level of the manifested functions into 'quest'" (207). Greimas gives the example, greatly simplified, of a "learned philosopher of the classical age" who desires knowledge; his story would be a "drama of knowledge" in which the subject is "philosopher" and the object "world"; the sender "God" and the receiver "mankind"; the opponent "matter" and the helper "mind" (209–10). Any number of actors might be employed, depending on the genre, to fulfill these actantial functions.

Greimas's modifications of Propp's Formalism coincide with the rise of Structuralism in anthropology and literary studies. As the early Structuralists demonstrated, the form of a given narrative does not necessarily follow the sequence of events that constitute the story it tells. In fact, literature and film often depend on the tensions created between the expected temporal ordering of the story and the actual structure of narrative. These different levels of narration have been theorized in a number of different ways – as story/discourse, *histoire/récit, fabula/sjuzet* – but in each case, the same fundamental distinction is maintained. Propp and Greimas, with their emphasis on the meaning of functions and character, are both interested in what is narrated, the level of story. In the work of Tzvetan Todorov, Meike Bal, Gérard Genette, and **Roland Barthes**, the level of narrative discourse is preeminent, with the result that character and event are subordinated to processes and problems of narration.

In his "Introduction to the Structural Analysis of Narrative" (1966), Barthes takes linguistics as the starting point for a structuralist theory of narrative as a *functional syntax*. Narratives function like sentences, but they operate on different levels of description. There are two primary relations: "distributional (if the relations are situated on the same level) and integrational (if they are grasped from one level to the next)" (86). Narrative elements can be arranged in a variety of predictable and stable ways within the acceptable limits of a narrative syntax or grammar. The arrangement of elements operates according to a "hierarchy of instances": units, action, narration. At the "atomic" level, *units* perform distributional functions, ordering elements around "hinge-points" of the narrative while at the integrational level they connect and order the levels of character and narration. These units are often fairly minor elements of the story (Barthes's offers the example of a cigarette lighter in a James Bond film); however, they can serve important functions by linking or "distributing" narrative elements in a causal chain or by integrating different aspects of the narrative across temporal and spatial contexts. The level of *action* is dominated by character, which is not a "being" in the psychological sense, but a "participant" enacting a function within a specific sequence: "every character (even secondary) is the hero of his own sequence" (106). Finally, the level of *narration* (often called "point of view") concerns the specific structure of linguistic presentation and the site of reading. At this level, we see a shift from the story being told to the structure of narrative itself. The mechanisms of conventional realism – a straightforward and transparent means of referring to the external world – do not apply at this level: "The function of narrative is not to 'represent'; it is to constitute a spectacle still very enigmatic for us but in any case not of a MIMETIC order" (124).

Throughout the 1970s and '80s, Genette and Bal further extended the possibilities of narrative by devising tripartite models of narrative structure. In Bal's arrangement, *narrative text* denotes the level of narration and the narrator, *story* denotes the sequencing of events, and *fabula* denotes "a series of logically and chronologically related events that are caused or experienced by actors" (5). The central problem is the relationship between *story* and *fabula*, between "the sequence of events and *the way in which* these events are presented" (6). *Fabula* refers both to the signifying level of narrative and the deep structure of the narrative text, that which "causes the narrative to be recognizable as narrative" (175). Bal follows Barthes and other structuralist narratologists in arguing for a deep structural aspect of narrative, though she recognizes the problematic nature of such structures. In a similar manner, Genette's tripartite theory of narrative distinguishes between *story* (the level of the signified or narrative content, which he also called diegesis), *narrative* (the level of the signifier, discourse or narrative text), and *narrating* (the level of the "narrative situation or its instance" [31], including narration and narrators). Genette stresses the temporality of narrating: "it is almost impossible for me not to locate the story in time with respect to my narrating act, since I must necessarily tell the story in a present, past, or future tense" (215). Another important category is *point of view* (or *mood*), especially the concept of *focalization*. Genette is especially forceful in drawing the distinction between *mood*, which refers to "the character whose point of view orients the narrative perspective," and *voice*, which refers to the question, "who is the narrator?" (Genette 186). Finally, he posits three narratorial functions: *narrative function* (where the emphasis is on telling a story); *directing function* (where the emphasis is on the narrative text; a metanarrative function); and *function of communication* (where the emphasis is on the relation between narrator and reader). The third function underscores the differences between a fictive *narratee* within the text and the reader or implied reader outside of it. Tzvetan Todorov offers another way of explaining how the structural analysis of narrative emphasizes the structure of a discourse. Thus, the object of structural analysis "is the literary discourse rather than works of literature, literature that is virtual rather than real." It is not to offer a paraphrase or "a rational résumé of the concrete work," but "to present a spectrum of literary possibilities, in such a manner that the existing works of literature appear as particular instances that have been realized" (436–37).

Structuralist narrative, or narratology, remains a vital field of scholarly research and advanced teaching, with Gerald Prince dominating the field in the US, but it has been eclipsed by theories of the novel. Modern novel theory begins with Georg Lukács, who argued, in his seminal *Theory of the Novel* (1920), that the novel is "the epic of a world that has been abandoned by God," a world "in which the extensive totality of life is no longer directly given, in which the immanence of meaning in life has become a problem, yet which still thinks in terms of totality" (88, 56). The problem of the novel was the problem of a world in which the old notions of religious and social totality no longer provided solace. The representation of social totalities was best achieved, Lukács believed, not in the experimental Modernist novel, which tended to emphasize fragmentation and alienation, but in the realist novel, which had the potential of capturing the complexity of class relations and class consciousness. Early theorists in the Anglo-American tradition, like Percy Lubbuck and F. R. Leavis, also favored the realist novel, but for very different reasons. For them, novelistic realism was the most effective way to explore human consciousness and the motivations that led to moral action. By the 1960s, Wayne Booth's rhetorical approach had successfully displaced these earlier models. Like Genette, Booth focused on problems of point of view, mood, and narrative voice, but he was less interested in the structure of narrative than in the rhetorical function of narration. Booth and his followers (especially James Phelan) were the successors of a theoretical tradition that originated with Henry James and Joseph Conrad. Of special importance for Booth were narrative irony and narrative distance, devices which represented the gap between the narrator and the narrated and between author and narrator. Dorrit Cohn in a similar fashion posited a theory of *free indirect discourse*, a mode of third-person narration in which speech and thought are represented in terms very close to a character's own syntactical and idiomatic usages.

Since the 1980s, the theory of the novel has been concerned primarily with historicist and materialist approaches. One of the most influential studies was **Fredric Jameson's** *The Political Unconscious* (1981), which argues that the Modernist novel harbors a deeply sublimated narrative structure shaped by ideological forces. Jameson is indebted not only to

Freud and Lacan, but to Althusser as well who provided a "post-Marxist" theory of IDEOLOGY. A related development can be discerned in Post-modern theory. Fundamental in this context is **Jean-François Lyotard's** *Postmodern Condition* (1979), which is interested in how MASTER NARRA-TIVES reproduce and legitimize dominant ideologies and social and cultural institutions, norms, and values. Lyotard analyzes the status of master narratives and speculates on the viability of alternative models of narrative based on "paralogy," a mode of narrative legitimation that is not concerned with promulgating "law as a norm," but rather with making moves within a "pragmatics of knowledge" (8, 60–61). Lyotard's Postmodernist perspective, like that of **Linda Hutcheon**, Robert Scholes, and other theorists of METAFICTION and FABULATION, is a response to a crisis in narrative representation and narrative legitimation. (See also pp. 149, 285–6.) The translation of Bakhtin's work in the early 1980s led to the proliferation of new modes of interpreting the novel that focused on the DIALOGIC structure of narrative and the ideological investments that dialogism both makes possible and lays bare. A promising new direction for Narrative Theory combines the insights of Reader-Response theory with Bakhtinian DIALOGISM and is best described as an *ethics of narrative*, which is concerned primarily to find out why and to what ends and under whose auspices we read. Inspired by the work of ethical philoso-phers, especially Emmanuel Lévinas, Booth and **J. Hillis Miller** have emerged as early and influential contributors to this new ethical theory of the novel.

Note: For more information on the reader, see Reader-Response Theories.

WORKS CITED

Bal, Mieke. *Narratology: Introduction to the Theory of Narrative.* Toronto and Buffalo: University of Toronto Press, 1985.

Barthes, Roland. "Introduction to the Structural Analysis of Narrative." 1966. *Image-Music-Text.* Trans. Stephen Heath. New York: Hill and Wang, 1977. 79–124.

Emerson, Caryl. "Shklovsky's *ostranenie*, Bakhtin's *vnenakhodimost*" (How Dis-tance Serves an Aesthetics of Arousal Differently from an Aesthetics Based on Pain). *Poetics Today* 26.4 (Winter 2005): 637–64.

Genette, Gérard. *Narrative Discourse*. 1972. Trans. Jane E. Lewin. Ithaca: Cornell University Press, 1980.

Greimas, A. J. *Structural Semantics: An Attempt at a Method*. 1966. Trans. Daniele McDowell, Ronald Schleifer, and Alan Velie. Lincoln: University of Nebraska Press, 1983.

Lukács, Georg. *The Theory of the Novel*. 1920. Trans. Anna Bostock Cambridge, MA: M.I.T. Press, 1971.

Lyotard, Jean-François. *The Postmodern Condition: A Report on Knowledge*. Trans. Geoff Bennington and Brian Massumi. Minneapolis: University of Minnesota Press, 1984.

Propp, Vladimir. *Morphology of the Fairy Tale*. 1928. Trans. Laurence Scott. 2nd rev. ed. Austin: University of Texas Press, 1968.

Todorov, Tzvetan. "Structural Analysis in Narrative." In *Modern Literary Criticism, 1900–1970*. Eds. Lawrence I. Lipking and A. Walton Litz. New York: Atheneum, 1972. 436–41.

New Criticism

The New Criticism is an Anglo-American variety of Formalism that emerged in the early decades of the twentieth century and dominated teaching and scholarship until the early 1960s. It is less a coherent literary theory than a congeries of critical and theoretical approaches all of which agree that the literary work is AUTONOMOUS, that its unity and meaning are constituted primarily by formal and rhetorical features, and that it is free from any burden of reflection on the social world in which it is produced or from any connection to the author who produces it. New Critical practice strongly favors poetic texts, in large part because they exemplify to a greater degree the ambiguity, irony, and PARADOX considered by New Critics to be crucial elements of poetic form. As T. S. Eliot, the poet and critic who had a significant effect on the New Critics, wrote, "poets in our civilization, as it exists at present, must be *difficult*" (248). It was this difficulty that New Criticism privileged through the development of strategies of explication that remain relevant, not only in the classroom, where they have an undeniable pedagogical value, but also in critical practice, where they are often informed by social and cultural contexts that had, for the New Critics themselves, been bracketed off as extraneous to the meaning of the literary text.

Decades of biographical and *belle lettristic* criticism, which focused on the author's intentions or on aesthetics in the most general sense, had reduced the study of poetry to what Eliot called "opinion or fancy" unconnected to technical and rhetorical accomplishments. In part, this was the legacy of Matthew Arnold's criticism, which emphasized tradition and high seriousness and tended to treat literature as a means for conveying normative moral and ethical ideals. By the end of the First World War, a new generation of poets were experimenting with form and language, and their work could no longer be judged according to the biographical and aesthetic criteria used by traditional critics. Moreover, these poets were publishing their own criticism, and it was this work, especially Eliot's, that created a theoretical foundation for the New Criticism. According to Eliot, the critic's task was to understand and explain the "new combinations" of feeling that poetry was capable of expressing. The only legitimate context in which to judge a literary work was the tradition in which it emerged, the "organic wholes" of literature itself, "systems in relation to which, and only in relation to which, individual works of literary art, and the works of individual artists, have their significance." This does not mean that literature cannot serve ends outside of itself, only that "art is not required to be aware of these ends, and indeed performs its function, whatever that may be, according to various theories of value, much better by indifference to them" (12–13). Though art is best understood as existing autonomously (or, to use Eliot's word, "autotelically"), criticism must rely on shared principles. Eliot decries the state of criticism in the early 1920s, which consisted "in reconciling, in hushing up, in patting down, in squeezing in, in glozing over, in concocting pleasant sedatives" (14) – in doing everything but agreeing on the aim of criticism. Instead of "narcotic fancies" and "nebulous" appreciation, Eliot advocated a form of practical criticism that could transform the apparently nebulous into "something precise, tractable, under control." The practical critic "is dealing with facts, and he can help us do the same" (20).

The first generation of New Critics set about forming the "various theories of value" according to which literature best performed its functions. In *Principles of Literary Criticism* (1924), the English critic I. A. Richards put forward a psychological theory of practical criticism that emphasized an essentially phenomenological approach that valued above all the "capacity for satisfying feeling and desire in various ways" (47). He does not have in mind the vague sort of sentiments that earlier critics substituted for analysis, but a scientific approach to the "mental events" that governed the act of reading a literary work. He is most interested in the attitudes that emotional responses signal, the "imaginal and incipient activities or tendencies to action" that come into play whenever one is aroused by a work of art (112). The value of criticism, therefore, lies in the "total mental effect" produced by the relations of elements within the work of art (174). For Richards, the "standard experience" against which a poem is judged is that of the poet "when contemplating the completed composition," and the most effective critics are those "whose experience approximates in this degree to the standard experience" (226–27). Like Eliot's depersonalized poet, Richards' ideal reader must be disinterested and detached, open to many "channels of interest," a standpoint that paradoxically increases the reader's involvement in the text, for "to say that we are *impersonal* is merely a curious way of saying that our personality is more *completely* involved" (251–52).

In Richards' view the formal unity of a literary text is a function of the subjectivity of the critic, who must not ascribe "peculiar, unique and mystic virtues to forms in themselves," since the effects of form are bound up with the mental effects that literary works excite (173). Subsequent theorists, especially in the US, downplayed the psychological dimension of the reader and stressed the verbal and rhetorical dimensions of the literary work. The Agrarian-Fugitive movement, centered at Vanderbilt University, was dominated by Cleanth Brooks and poet-critics like John Crowe Ransom, Allen Tate, and Robert Penn Warren. Brooks's studies of English and US poetry set the tone for a new kind of Formalist criticism that emphasized PARADOX as a constitutive feature of poetic language. Paradoxes are not "some sort of frill or trimming" external to the work; they "spring from the very nature of the poet's language: it is a language in which the connotations play as great a part as the denotations" (8). Our greatest poems are "built around paradoxes" (194). Where previous critics might have detected only "mere decoration" or "sensuous pictures," the New Critic finds "meaningful symbolism," purposeful ironies and ambiguities (142). Though Brooks agrees with Richards that the poem is an "organic thing," he does not believe that poetry serves primarily to communicate an emotional experience. "The poem, if it be a true poem is a simulacrum of reality – in this sense, at least, it is an 'imitation' – by *being* an experience rather than any mere statement about experience or any mere abstraction from experience" (194). Poems are created objects that contain within themselves a unity of rhetorical effects, quite different from the unity of responses that Richards describes. Like the "well-wrought urn" in John Keats's "Ode on a Grecian Urn," the poem is entirely self-contained and irreducible to any meaning not located in the poem's structure. The "principle of unity" that informs poetry "seems to be one of balancing and harmonizing connotations, attitudes and meanings" which are all "subordinated to a total and governing attitude" (178, 189). Any attempt to capture this attitude by means of a summary interpretation constitutes what Brooks calls the "heresy of paraphrase."

Irony, ambiguity, and paradox are also the predominant elements in the English critic William Empson's *Seven Types of Ambiguity*. Empson echoes Brooks in his insistence that ambiguity is a constitutive feature of the work and also a significant element of the work's unity. *Ambiguity* is itself an ambiguous term, one that can lead the critic in a number of directions: it "can mean an indecision as to what you mean, an intention to mean several things, a probability that one or other or both of two things has been meant, and the fact that a statement has several meanings" (5–6). Ambiguity constitutes the literary work as a situational unity or TOTALITY. Though the "forces" that hold such a unity together may originate "in the poet's mind," they can be discerned only in the context of specific rhetorical contradictions and tensions. "An ambiguity, then, is not satisfying in itself, nor is it, considered as a device on its own, a thing to be attempted; it must in each case arise from, and be justified by, the peculiar requirements of the situation" (235). The only way for a writer to impress upon the reader a conception of unity is to present a "total meaning" in the form of a "compound," "to arrange that [the reader] can only feel satisfied if he is bearing all the elements in mind at the movement of conviction" (238–39). The influence of Richards' practical criticism is apparent in Empson's emphasis on the reader's role in constructing meaning and in his willingness to attribute ambiguity to the author's intentions, as opposed to the inevitable effects of literary language.

The Chicago school critics, particularly R. S. Crane, were less interested in celebrating ambiguity and paradox than in creating the rhetorical tools necessary for a rigorous formalist critical method. In this sense, Chicago school Aristotelianism offered an alternative to the New Critics, though there were some salient similarities between the two movements. Crane envisioned "a general critique of literary criticism" that would "yield objective criteria for interpreting the diversities and oppositions among critics and for judging the comparative merits of rival critical schools." For Crane, as for the Chicago school at large, pluralism is a reassertion of the Aristotelian notion that "poetry exhibits a multiplicity of structures not capable of reduction to any single type" (*Critics* 5). His own theory of "practical criticism" – "a pluralistic view of critical languages" (*Languages* 27) – is echoed in a somewhat idiosyncratic fashion in the work of Kenneth Burke, whose approach to literature borrows insights from anthropology, sociology, semantics, and other areas of study. According to Burke, poetic meanings "cannot be disposed of on the true-or-false basis," which is the case with what he calls "semantic meanings." "Rather, they are related to one another like a set of concentric circles, of wider and wider scope. Those of wider diameter do not categorically eliminate those of narrower diameter. There is, rather, a progressive *encompassment*" (144). Where Burke departs from the New Criticism is in his insistence that literature is an expression of human motives and desire, a form of "symbolic action" that extends beyond the confines of the literary work's formal structure to touch upon the experiences of writing and reading. In his theory of "dramatism," he elaborates on this essentially rhetorical idea by defining the five levels of meaning production in literary works: act, agent, scene, agency, and purpose. Though Burke's emphasis on rhetoric and the special role of poetic language situates him within a tradition of Structuralism and Formalism, his interest in human behavior and motivation and his desire to see human actions as essentially symbolic are rooted in sociology and psychology.

All of the theories discussed above share some common assumptions, chiefly the importance of form and the AUTONOMY of the literary work. With the exception of Burke, they also share a common reluctance to admit moral or ethical considerations into their interpretative methodologies. This is not the case with F. R. Leavis, a literary and cultural critic and editor of the journal *Scrutiny* (1932–53), who combined New Critical Formalism with the Arnoldian belief that literature concerns itself with moral and ethical ideas. Unlike Richards, Brooks, and others who wrote extensively about Modernist poetry, Leavis focused on the novel, specifically a closed system of CANONICAL "great" works in the nineteenth and early twentieth centuries. In *The Great Tradition* he notes that the "great novelists" are "very much concerned with 'form'; they are all very original technically, having turned their genius to the working out of their own appropriate methods and procedures" (7). While Gustave Flaubert and the aesthetic writers of the late nineteenth century who sought to emulate him elevated formalism above all else, English writers were concerned with a "formal perfection" that did not come at the expense of "the moral preoccupations that characterize the novelist's peculiar interest in life" (8). James Joyce does not qualify as "great" in part because his work possesses "no organic principle determining, informing, and controlling into a vital whole . . . the extraordinary variety of technical devices"; it is rather a "pointer to disintegration" (25–26).

The different and often conflicting strands of the New Criticism are considered in Wimsatt and Beardsley's *The Verbal Icon* (1954). The authors are critical of romantic idealism and the sort of "practical affective rhetoric" found in Richards and some of the Chicago school critics (201–202). They expose two fundamental errors in contemporary theory: the *intentional fallacy* and the *affective fallacy*. The intentional fallacy, a form of the genetic fallacy found in philosophy, refers to the common assumption that the meaning of a work corresponds with the author's intentions. "The design or intention of the author is neither available or desirable as a standard for judging the success of a work of literary art" (3). Only objective criticism can arrive at a sense of a work's value, "which enables us to distinguish between a skillful murder and a skillful poem" (6). And even if we could gain access to the author's intentions, through archival sources or personal communication, the results would be of no use for criticism, for "[c]ritical inquiries are not settled by consulting the oracle" (18). The affective fallacy refers to a category mistake, "a confusion between the poem and its results" (21). Poetry does not acquire its meaning by producing a particular kind of result in the reader, but rather by simply existing as a verbal object: "A poem should not mean but be" (81). For Wimsatt and Beardsley, a poem exists by virtue of its linguistic and rhetorical materiality; it is a *thing*, and it is this physical character that is the sole object of criticism. The only value the critic need uphold is the autonomy of a dynamic and self-regulating "verbal icon," a "positive and structural complexity, the varied fabric of organic unity" (269). If poetry is also "a fusion of ideas with material" (115), it is not because it is somehow less than verbal, nor because it bears an intimate relation to its referents in the external world, but because of its very "hyperverbal" "counter-logical" nature. The New Critic, who must always be aware of "the ambiguous or polysemous nature of verbal discourse" (268) ironically anticipates the poststructuralist, whose vision of language and literature is often regarded as the antithesis of New Critical Formalism.

WORKS CITED

Brooks, Cleanth. *The Well-Wrought Urn*. New York: Harcourt, Brace & World, 1947.

Burke, Kenneth. *The Philosophy of Literary Form: Studies in Symbolic Action*. 1941. 2nd ed. Baton Rouge: Louisiana State University Press, 1967.

Crane, R. S. *The Language of Criticism and the Structure of Poetry*. Toronto: University of Toronto Press, 1953.

——, ed. *Critics and Criticism: Ancient and Modern.* Chicago: University of Chicago Press, 1952.

Eliot, T. S. *Selected Essays 1917–1932.* New York and London: Harcourt Brace Jovanovich, 1932.

Empson, William. *Seven Types of Ambiguity.* London: Chatto and Windus, 1947.

Leavis, F. R. *The Great Tradition: George Eliot, Henry James, Joseph Conrad.* 1948. London: Chatto and Windus, 1950.

Richards, I. A. *Principles of Literary Criticism.* New York: Harcourt, Brace; London: K. Paul Trench, Trubner, 1924.

Wimsatt, W. K. and Monroe C. Beardsley. *The Verbal Icon: Studies in the Meaning of Poetry.* Louisville: University of Kentucky Press, 1954.

New Historicism

New Historicism is the general term given to a wide variety of theories and methodologies that are HISTORICIST in orientation. Unlike prior forms of historicism, the New Historicism is strongly influenced by poststructuralist theories of language and TEXTUALITY and is indebted to Friedrich Nietzsche, whose "On the Uses and Disadvantages of History for Life" set out the terms for a historicism that calls its own assumptions into question and that rejects the dominant modes of historiography (i.e., antiquarian and monumental). Nietzsche recommends *critical history* as the form that could best combat the oppression of a "present need" ("Uses" 72). "If he is to live, man must possess and from time to time employ the strength to break up and dissolve a part of the past: he does this by bringing it before the tribunal, scrupulously examining it and finally condemning it; every past, however, is worthy to be condemned" ("Uses" 75–76). There are two alternatives to history "proper," the *unhistorical*, which is "the art and power of *forgetting* and of enclosing oneself within a bounded horizon," and the *supra-historical*, which "lead[s] the eye away from becoming towards that which bestows upon existence the character of the eternal and stable, towards *art* and *religion*." The unhistorical and the supra-historical are "the natural antidotes to the stifling of life by the historical, by the malady of history" ("Uses" 120–21). In his later work, Nietzsche developed a theory of GENEALOGY that traces the progress of human values as they are (re)interpreted in different contexts, for different aims: "the whole history of a thing, an organ, a custom, becomes a continuous *chain* of reinterpretations and rearrangements, which need not be causally connected among themselves, which may simply follow one another" (*Genealogy* 210). Nietzsche's critique of morality in *Genealogy of Morals* brilliantly shows how moral values emerge and remerge along multiple and often scattered points in time and place. The genealogical challenge to conventional ways of thinking about the past created the conditions for a "transvaluation of all values." It is also the theoretical foundation for **Michel Foucault**'s ARCHAEOLOGICAL method, another "anti-historical" approach to history.

Foucault argues that genealogy is a fundamentally interpretative attitude towards the past. "Genealogy does not pretend to go back in time to restore an unbroken continuity that operates beyond the dispersal of forgotten things. . . . Genealogy does not resemble the evolution of a species and does not map the destiny of a people" ("Nietzsche" 146). For Foucault, a historical "event" is not a stable phenomenon that can be captured by documentary evidence; nor is it the result of purposeful human action. It is instead a sign of domination, of the shifting of power relations. It is "the reversal of a relationship of forces, the usurpation of power, the appropriation of a vocabulary turned against those who had once used it, a feeble domination that poisons itself as it grows lax, the entry of a masked 'other'" ("Nietzsche" 154). A good example of Foucault's method is his *History of Sexuality*, which looks at how social and cultural power created the modern notion of sexuality: "The history of sexuality . . . must be written from the viewpoint of a history of discourses" (*Sexuality* 69). The discourse on sex is the articulation of POWER, "a rule of law" (*Sexuality* 83). Foucault's method here, and in his other genealogical works, abandons conventional ideas about historical events, diachronic sequence, causality, and origin. Following Nietzsche, he focuses instead on interpretations of the relations of power and how they shape human experience through the agency of discourse.

The emphasis on interpretation and power, in both Nietzsche and Foucault, is found in much New Historicist writing, especially that which takes a TEXTUALIST approach to history. This tendency towards textualism provoked **Fredric Jameson** to describe New Historicism as a form of nominalism (a belief that ideas represented in language have no basis in reality). Catherine Gallagher resolves the dilemma by constructing a hybrid methodology that accommodates both Foucauldian and Marxian theories in a critical discourse suited to a localized and highly mobile "micro-politics of daily life" (Gallagher 43). **Stephen Greenblatt** offers a similar resolution. His vision of CULTURAL POETICS draws from both materialist and textualist traditions and entails a flexible and self-critical framework for historical criticism and a commitment to a rigorous methodology. Though Greenblatt privileges literary texts, at times ascribing to them "relative" AUTONOMY from social conditions, he maintains that such texts are embedded in specific relations of power and "systems of public signification" (Greenblatt 5), even though they may at times elude these relations and systems. When reading "powerful" texts, "we feel at once pulled out of our own world and plunged back with redoubled force into it" (Gallagher and Greenblatt 17).

In *Renaissance Self-Fashioning* (1980), Greenblatt draws on a Foucauldian notion of POWER to fashion a POETICS OF CULTURE capable of reading the complex web-like disposition of languages, literatures, and other sign systems that he finds in Renaissance literature. He reads Shakespeare's *Othello* as "the supreme expression of the cultural mode" of improvisation (232), a mode of self-fashioning that entails the displacement and absorption of symbolic structures found in the culture at large and that is made possible by "the subversive perception of another's truth as ideological construct" (228). Identity in the Renaissance, according to Greenblatt, is not a matter of achieving or sustaining autonomy but of negotiating among social and cultural discourses whose DETERMINATIONS impose constraints on self-fashioning. Shakespeare's play exists within a socio-historical matrix in which such discourses, emanating from institutions (for example, the Church and the State), help to determine its meaning. The same is true of the work of Christopher Marlowe, whose achievement can best be understood by looking not "at the playwright's literary sources, not even at the relentless power-hunger of Tudor absolutism, but at the acquisitive energies of English merchants, entrepreneurs, and adventurers, promoters, alike of trading companies and theatrical companies" (194). It is the task of the New Historicist to "map" the various connections and relations between literary texts and the social and cultural contexts. The result of these discursive negotiations and exchanges is the construction of what Tony Bennett calls a *reading formation*, a set of determinations that "mediate the relations between text and context" (qtd. in Montrose 398). In a reading formation, context does not lie outside of discourses but is established by them and their interrelations. This textualist approach to historical context and TEXTUALITY is characterized, as Louis Montrose puts it, by "a reciprocal concern with the historicity of texts and the textuality of histories." All texts and all modes of reading must be understood as historically embedded; but at the same time, "we can have no access to a full and authentic past, to a material existence that is unmediated by the textual traces of the society in question" (Montrose 410).

As a form of cultural poetics, New Historicism assumes that historical phenomena can be read like a text. H. Aram Veeser has isolated five key assumptions: 1) "every expressive act is embedded in a network of material practices"; 2) every critique inevitably "uses the tools it condemns and risks falling prey to the practice it exposes"; 3) literary and non-literary texts "circulate inseparably"; 4) no discourse "gives access to unchanging truths" nor "expresses inalterable human nature"; and 5) critical methods under capitalism "participate in the economy they describe" (xi). While these assumptions can be traced to poststructuralist and cultural materialist discourses, New Historicism owes much to the textualist anthropology of Clifford Geertz, for whom "local knowledge" is not an impersonal function or structure but rather a "readable" cultural practice, as in the famous Balinese cock-fight: "a story [the people] tell themselves about themselves" (448). Hayden White and other theorists of history refute the charge that textualism itself is ahistorical and argue that at some level all history is textual. The critical issue is whether or not one can get beyond the textual level of analysis (of primary documents and historical accounts) to say something meaningful about the concrete social world. If the past can be known only through the negotiation of competing interpretations of the archival evidence and through the critical awareness of the historian's own role in the selection and representation of it, then an exploration of the archive is a prerequisite to understanding fully the relations of power in any given epoch and to subverting prevailing historical explanations.

All of this has led some critics to claim that if history is only a text or, more broadly, an archive, there can be no historical "truth." Yet New Historicism has emerged in part out of a desire to say something "true" about the past. It is caught up in the dilemma that **Stanley Fish** describes: "the problem of reconciling the assertion of 'wall to wall' textuality – the denial that the writing of history could find its foundation in a substratum of unmediated fact – with the desire to say something specific and normative" ("Commentary" 303). The possibility of "saying something specific and normative" is especially relevant to CULTURAL MATERIALISM, according to which ideas, beliefs, and IDEOLOGIES are formed by material conditions, by constraints imposed by social, cultural, and political policies and forces. The British tradition of cultural materialism, from Christopher Caudwell and Raymond Williams to E. P. Thompson and Eric Hobsbawm, has focused attention on the specific relationships between material and cultural production. Literature and the arts, though at times granted autonomous status, are no exception. Indeed, aesthetic forms are highly sensitive sites of social, political, even economic conflict; as such, they can reveal contradictions in social conditions and foster a standpoint for a

materialist critique of them. For **Raymond Williams**, cultural materialism was bound up with the representation of "structures of feeling," the
"distilled residue" of a particular community's cultural organization
independent of its ideological determinations. In recent years, materialist
theorists like Jameson and Jonathan Dollimore have adopted poststructuralist theories of the text. It is important to emphasize, however, that
while such theorists may draw on the work of Foucault, **Louis Althusser**,
and **Jacques Lacan**, they do not subscribe to a radical form of textualism.
Indeed, Jameson has pointed out "that history is not a text, not a narrative,
master or otherwise, but that, as an absent cause, it is inaccessible to us
except in textual form, and that our approach to it . . . necessarily passes
through its prior textualization, its narrativization in the political unconscious" (35). For the cultural materialist, the text is always an opening to
the material conditions that may not be otherwise available to us.

WORKS CITED

Fish, Stanley. "Commentary: The Young and the Restless." In *The New Historicism*. Ed. Veeser. 303–16.

Foucault, Michel. *The History of Sexuality*. 1976. Vol. 1. Trans. Robert Hurley.
New York: Pantheon Books, 1978.

——. "Nietzsche, Genealogy, History," In *Language, Counter-Memory, Practice:
Selected Essays and Interviews*. Ed. Donald F. Bouchard. Trans. Donald F.
Bouchard and Sherry Simon. Ithaca: Cornell University Press, 1977.
139–64.

Gallagher, Catherine. "Marxism and New Historicism." In *The New Historicism*.
Ed. Aram H. Veeser. 37–48.

—— and Stephen Greenblatt. *Practicing New Historicism*. Chicago: University
of Chicago Press, 2000.

Geertz, Clifford. *The Interpretation of Cultures*. New York: Basic Books, 1973.

Greenblatt, Stephen. *Renaissance Self-Fashioning: From More to Shakespeare*.
Chicago: University of Chicago Press, 1980.

Jameson, Fredric. *The Political Unconscious: Narrative as a Socially Symbolic Act*.
Ithaca: Cornell University Press, 1981.

Montrose, Louis. "New Historicism." In *Redrawing the Boundaries: The Transformation of English and American Literary Studies*. Eds. Stephen Greenblatt and
Giles Gunn. New York, MLA, 1992. 392–418.

Nietzsche, Friedrich. "On the Uses and Disadvantages of History for Life." In *Untimely Meditations*. Ed. Daniel Breazeale. Trans. R. J. Hollingdale. Cambridge and New York: Cambridge University Press, 1997. 57–123.

——. *On the Genealogy of Morals*. Ed. Keith Ansell-Pearson. Trans. Carol Diethe. Cambridge, UK and New York: Cambridge University Press, 1994.

Veeser, H. Aram, ed. *The New Historicism*. New York: Routledge, 1989.

Postcolonial Studies

The emergence of Postcolonial Studies is tied to a number of factors, the most important of which is the relation of postcolonial nations to colonialism and the colonial era. Hence the prefix *"post-"* refers to a historical relation, to a period after colonialism. Strictly speaking, the postcolonial era begins with the American revolution in the late eighteenth century and the Haitian revolution of the early nineteenth century. However, the emergence of America as a leading industrial nation and colonizing power in the later nineteenth century and Haiti's neocolonial situation extending well into the twentieth century render them somewhat exceptional with respect to the current usage of the term *postcolonial*. As many theorists have noted, the historical relation alone is insufficient to describe the meaning of this *"post-."* The title of Kwame Anthony Appiah's influential essay – "Is the Post- in Postmodernism the Post- in Postcolonial?" (1991) – implies that the significance of the term *postcolonial* extends beyond the historical relation of colonialism to include other times, themes, and discourses. Adapting **Jean-François Lyotard**'s description of the Postmodern as that which cannot be *"presented"* in the modern, we might say that the postcolonial refers to the unpresentable in the colonial: racial difference, legal inequality, subalternity, all of the submerged or suppressed contradictions within the colonial social order itself. In this sense, the *postcolonial* presents itself in the colonial epoch, especially during periods of DECOLONIZATION, when social contradictions are expressed in intensified nationalist organization and anti-colonial struggle. The processes of decolonization often continue well past the official establishment of a postcolonial state in the form of NEO-COLONIAL (or neo-imperialist) relations of economic and political dependence on the former colonizer. Entities such as the World Bank and the International Monetary Fund often play a part in neocolonial relations, while the United Kingdom retains something of its old colonial structure in the Commonwealth of Nations, which consists mostly of former British colonies.

Frantz Fanon and Albert Memmi, the leading figures of the first generation of Postcolonial theorists, wrote their most important works in the 1950s and early '60s and were strongly influenced by the dialectical and materialist traditions of Hegel and Marx. Both were interested in understanding the psychology of colonialism, specifically of the absolute sense of difference that characterized colonial relations. Fanon began his short career with *Black Skin, White Masks*, a study of racial difference in colonial and postcolonial societies. Fanon's ideas about the nation, nationalism, and national consciousness have been especially influential. He rejected the Western conception of the nation as a "universal standpoint" that subsumes all particulars (i.e., individual human lives) in the fulfillment of its own abstract freedom. Universality instead belongs to the people who comprehend themselves as a nation. The people's struggle is largely the struggle "to make the totality of the nation a reality to each citizen" (Fanon 200). It inevitably entails the spontaneous violence of the masses, for only through violence can the native become human and enter into history as something other than a mere slave. Violence and the "permanent dream to become the persecutor" (Fanon 52–53) constitute the tools of the anti-colonial revolutionary.

However, Fanon noted a deep chasm between the people in the countryside and the national bourgeoisie in the urban areas whose members fill the former colonial bureaucracies and enjoy the fruits of Western-style corruption. Little by little, accommodations are made with former colonial rulers in order to sustain the privileges of power. This stage of decolonization, when nationalist groups consciously and unconsciously mimic the political formations of the IMPERIAL state, inevitably reveals the complicity that tempts even the most progressive anti-colonial groups to build political parties and unions on METROPOLITAN models. Some theorists, in response to Fanon, have embraced the idea of "emancipatory complicity," the idea that nationalist or postcolonial critique can sustain itself within a social and political environment shot through with neocolonial relationships and lingering colonialist habits, historical DETERMINATIONS that can, if not overcome, work against the creative, forward-looking power of postcolonial nationhood. As Fanon points out, nationalism is concerned not with inheriting power but with "the living expression of the nation" which "is the moving consciousness of the whole of the people; it is the coherent, enlightened action of men and women" (204). Only this form of national consciousness will enable solidarity movements with other emergent postcolonial nations. "National consciousness, which is not nationalism, is the only thing that will give us an international dimension" (247).

Fanon's investments in Western philosophy and social theory, particularly Marxist thought, make for a very AMBIVALENT relationship with colonialism. The very nature of the relationship – the unequal binary struggle of master and slave, dramatized famously by Hegel as a parable of self-consciousness – appears to the colonized as predetermined and merciless. It is a classic example of MANICHAEANISM in a modern social context: the civilized West ("good") conquers, tames, and civilizes the barbarous East ("evil"). Fanon was, like Memmi, limited by the Marxian or at least Hegelian terms of his intellectual response to the Algerian struggle. The second wave of Postcolonial Studies had to surmount the intellectual legacy of the Marxian anti-colonial struggles of the 1950s and '60s, shed the habit of dialectical, "us and them" thinking. **Edward Said** threw down the gauntlet in 1978 with *Orientalism*, a foundational work that has exerted extraordinary influence. Drawing on Michel Foucault's theories of DISCURSIVE FORMATIONS and Althusser's idea of the PROBLEMATIC (a system of problems and questions that constitute the "unconscious" of a text), Said studied the discursive relationship between the West (the Occident) and the East (the Orient) and pioneered a form of colonial DISCOURSE ANALYSIS. He maps the complex relations of power in a long tradition of philological and scholarly writing about the East in an attempt to "unlearn" "the inherent dominative mode" (28) of imperialism. Orientalism is a form of "executive" knowledge that can be used to gain information on native peoples in order better to control them. It is also archival in nature, for its ambitions are to gain total knowledge about these peoples and their cultures. These ambitions have their roots partly in a long tradition of anthropological intervention in colonial territories that contributed not only to authoritative academic discourses on PRIMITIVISM but also to official colonial actions to pacify or eradicate those cultures. Finally, it is a form of knowledge that circumscribes and delimits, constructing the East as an OTHER in relation to the West. Orientalism is thus a form of *Manichaeanism*, which posits an absolute difference "between the familiar (Europe, the West, 'us') and the strange (the Orient, the East, 'them')" (43). Discourses about the East, like the massive Napoleonic *Description de l'Égypte*, bear no "natural" or MIMETIC relation to the geographical and social realities of eastern nations. Said notes a distinction between *latent* Orientalism, what a traveler or a native might experience in a specific geographical space, and *manifest* Orientalism, the discourses produced by Western intellectuals. New knowledge gained by direct experience at the latent level (e.g., E. M. Forster traveling in India) flows into the manifest level in the form of a novel representing India, *Passage to India*. The parallel with Freudian dream-work suggests that Orientalist discourse represses a good deal more than it represents.

Though widely read and well received, Said's *Orientalism* attracted criticism. Aijaz Ahmad, for example, took Said to task for his Nietzschean and Foucauldian anti-humanism, his unwillingness to critique the idea of "third world" authenticity, and his reluctance to include COUNTER-HEGEMONIC alternatives. Said addresses many of these criticisms in later work, though the issues at hand are addressed more forcefully by a new generation of theorists that emerged in the 1980s, including **Homi Bhabha** and **Gayatri Chakravorty Spivak**. For these theorists, the main issues are the SUBJECT and SUBJECTIVITY, nationalism, and COLONIAL DISCOURSE. In "Can the Subaltern Speak?," for example, Spivak uncovers the dynamics of a SUBALTERN subjectivity silenced by Western theory which, despite its "radical" stance, remains committed to an Enlightenment vision of a universal and sovereign subject. She addresses the possibility of the subaltern finding a voice "inside *and* outside the circuit of the epistemic violence of imperialist law and education" ("Subaltern" 283). Spivak's analysis of power relations in colonial and postcolonial India reveals dramatic and persistent gender inequalities. "Both as object of colonialist historiography and as subject of insurgency, the ideological construction of gender keeps the male dominant. If, in the context of colonial production, the subaltern has no history and cannot speak, the subaltern as female is even more deeply in shadow" ("Subaltern" 287). Her example of *sati* (widow sacrifice) illustrates the ways that imperialism codified and redefined a native practice as a crime, transforming a realm of free choice and power into one of juridical repression. Because the female subaltern disappears into a violent shuttling between tradition and modernization, she cannot speak.

As Fanon points out, one of the most pressing problems facing postcolonial states after independence is the continuance of the struggle in the form of a resistance to NEOCOLONIAL relations that keep new states economically and politically (in some cases, culturally) dependent on former colonial powers. The commitment to continue the struggle against neocolonialism has led Said to develop a conception of secular criticism that would offer a "contrapuntal" perspective on a divisive and polarized terrain. **Bhabha**'s work is similarly committed to what he calls "vernacular cosmopolitanism," a sense of what Said calls worldliness that is grounded in local knowledge of local needs. These modes of engagement take place within a "temporality of continuance," a local historical process with international implications. However, as recent history has shown, anti-colonial resistance succeeded in ousting colonial governors and establishing native states, but the international dimension of the struggle was set aside because of the pressing needs of nation-building. Of special interest in this context is the prominence of nationalism and national identity in the work of theorists in Ireland, South Asia, and the Caribbean. Myriad possibilities for HYBRID IDENTITY formation spring from the very ethnic, racial, and religious differences that delimit and destabilize colony and postcolony alike. Bhabha's highly influential *Location of Culture* defined COLONIAL MIMICRY as "the sign of a double articulation; a complex strategy of reform, regulation and discipline, which 'appropriates' the Other as it visualizes power. Mimicry is also the sign of the inappropriate, however, a difference or recalcitrance which coheres the dominant strategic function of colonial power, intensifies surveillance, and poses an immanent threat to both 'normalized' knowledges and disciplinary powers" (86). Mimicry is double-edged; it is the sign of a colonial discourse that desires a "reformed, recognizable Other" but it is also the means by which the colonized subject challenges that discourse. In the latter sense, mimicry reverses the process of disavowal inherent in "colonial representation and individuation" and permits "'denied' knowledges" the opportunity to "enter upon the dominant discourse and estrange the basis of its authority – its rules of recognition" (114, 120). The HYBRID subject is the subject of a discourse of mimicry, forced to speak from multiple, typically antagonistic locations.

Linked to this concept of hybridity is **Stuart Hall**'s theory of DIASPORIC IDENTITIES. Hall claims that Caribbean peoples experience cultural identity "as an enigma, as a problem, as an open question" (286):

> everybody [in the Caribbean] comes from somewhere else. . . . That is to say, their true cultures, the places they really come from, the traditions that really formed them, are somewhere else. The Caribbean is the first, the original and the purest diaspora. . . . [I]n the histories of the migration, forced or free, of peoples who now compose the populations of these

societies, whose cultural traces are everywhere intermingled with one another, there is always the stamp of historical violence and rupture. (283–84)

African, European, Indian, Chinese, and indigenous peoples have been dispersed throughout a system of islands bound together, in the modern era at least, primarily by colonial commerce, which had its roots in the slave trade. Aimé Césaire, a poet and dramatist from Martinique, used Shakespeare's *The Tempest* as a point of departure for a critique of Western IMPERIALISM and its notions of racial difference. His *Une Tempête* (1969) tells Caliban's story from the native's point of view. Peter Hulme's *Colonial Encounters: Europe and the Native Caribbean, 1492–1797* (1986) was one of the first major studies to analyze the phenomenon of cultural contact from a postcolonial perspective. In order to recover the full discursive context of the "discovery" of America, Hulme explores the DISCURSIVE FORMATION constituted by the letters, journals, ship log entries, and other documents associated with the voyages of Columbus, but he also includes the discourse of the Carib people, a discourse that was frequently misunderstood and, for that very reason, had a profound impact on colonial discourse about "primitive" peoples.

Despite general agreement concerning the objects of postcolonial critique – colonial discourse and IDEOLOGY, nationalism, gender relations, religious sectarianism – divergences can be found whenever we look closely at specific colonial and postcolonial contexts. The most important distinction within COLONIALISM is between *settler* and *administrative* colonies. Administrative colonies are those which supervise exports (rubber, ivory, spices and, until the early nineteenth century, slaves), participate in world markets, guarantee freedom of movement for religious missions and for sociological and anthropological inquiry. Settler colonies were developed by the colonial powers to absorb populations from the home country. In some cases, as in Rhodesia and French Algeria, these new populations were working- and middle-class settlers seeking land and a fresh start; many in the middle classes regarded the colonies as a way to find advancement that would otherwise be out of their reach. In Australia and New Zealand, through the nineteenth century, the new populations were primarily impoverished Irish, Scottish, and English families and transported convicts. In Ireland, the Anglo-Irish had a long history of occupation and many considered themselves culturally Irish. Northern Ireland has emerged as an extremely complicated special case in that it no longer fulfills the requirements of a settler or an administrative colony; England's rule in the region is largely a police action, designed to maintain order and, until recently, to shore up Protestant "home rule." Since the peace talks of the late 1990s, however, England's role has been ambiguous, for it continues to maintain its role as a police force but is also joined with the Republic of Ireland in ongoing efforts to transfer power to a joint Catholic–Protestant administration in Northern Ireland. As with the situation in the Palestinian Occupied Territories, the Northern Irish problem points up the difficulties of negotiating settlements without due attention to the question "who has the right to settle where?"

This is, of course, the underlying question in so many postcolonial discourses. Indeed, it is the same question that Native Americans have been asking since at least the middle of the nineteenth century. The situation in the US has been particularly intriguing because of the long history of oppression endured by native peoples and enslaved Africans. Such instances of domination and oppression redefine the very concept of colonialism. The segregation and resettlement of Native American Indian tribes on reservations is the most compelling example of "domestic colonization," far-flung colonial practices brought to the imperial backyard. The work of Arnold Krupat and Gerald Vizenor has contributed much to expand the warrant of Postcolonial theory to include those social and cultural situations in which DOMINATION takes on specific characteristics of widespread lack of social services, chronic unemployment, relocation of populations, and suppression of native traditions, languages, and cultural practices.

Postcolonial Studies is profoundly involved in a project of *historical revisionism* that makes possible the representation of historical subjects and conditions of existence that had been ignored or suppressed by European historians. The Irish postcolonial experience, for example, has yielded a long tradition of revisionist historiography, beginning at the time of the Literary Revival in the 1890s and accelerating after the formation of the Irish Free State in 1922. The Subaltern Studies Group, a South Asian collective, similarly combats the representations of India and the Indian peoples generated by Orientalist and colonialist discourses. One result of this revisionist impulse is the displacement of the *postcolonial* as the primary category of theoretical reflection. For example,

Spivak has recently advocated the development of a "transnational cultural studies" that would supplant traditional modes of comparative study and encourage greater sensitivity to native languages and cultures. As for the term *postcolonial*, she argues that its original use was to designate "the inauguration of neo-colonialism in state contexts. Now it just means behaving as if colonialism didn't exist." Moreover, the emphasis in Postcolonial Studies on the nation-state is no longer timely: "we can't think of post-coloniality in terms only of nation-state colonialism. We have to think of it in different ways. Otherwise, it becomes more and more a study of colonial discourse, of then rather than now. You can no longer whinge on about imperialism. We're looking at the failure of decolonization" ("Setting" 168).

It may be that Fanon's dialectical fusion of "national consciousness" and "an international dimension" is no longer possible. There appears to be little common ground between well-developed postcolonial states (e.g., Ireland, India, Egypt) and the new transient internationalism of migrants, refugees, exiles, émigrés, and stateless peoples like the Kurds. This problem of transience illustrates from another perspective Bhabha's "temporality of continuance," for it is the failure of nationalism and the triumph of neocolonial exploitation that have remained constant in the second half of the twentieth century. This is especially true of the Arab lands, which were carved up by the colonial powers and redistributed without regard for tribal, ethnic, and religious boundaries. This remapping of territories created and continues to create innumerable problems for national governments that are virtually powerless to remedy the lingering effects of colonial domination. Another factor in the ongoing development of postcolonial states is the neo-imperial project of GLOBALIZATION that links developed nations to the burgeoning labor forces and consumer markets in developing and undeveloped regions around the world. As a result, the postcolonial nation, often modeled on the nineteenth-century European nation-state, is left out of the "international dimension" because it has failed to develop sufficiently. The nullifying, destabilizing effects of theological and ideological absolutism so evident in the formerly colonized regions of the world may be the result of incomplete nation-building and thus of incomplete nationalism. Fanon charted an itinerary from subjugation to revolution, and along that itinerary was the difficult process of building a nation that represented the spirit of the people. In many cases, the nation-building process got stalled in the early years of independence, and the national consciousness, or *Bildung*, that Fanon foresaw seems to have been arrested as well. As for the "international dimension," it no longer seems possible to forge socialist alliances along traditional European lines. In the opening decade of the twenty-first century, we tend to regard the international dimension in different terms. We tend now to think of terrorism, of free-floating, stateless collectivities and networks of "sleeper cells" whose members are often marginalized or excluded by the nationalism of their home countries. Once international socialism fell with the Berlin wall, the Islamic world alone maintained any interest in a vision of an international community bound by religious and historical ties. In this new context, the question of neocolonialism continues to be urgent.

WORKS CITED

Bhabha, Homi. *The Location of Culture*. London and New York: Routledge, 1994.

Fanon, Frantz. *The Wretched of the Earth*. Trans. Constance Farrington. New York: Grove Weidenfeld, 1963.

Hall, Stuart. "Negotiating Caribbean Identities." In *Postcolonial Discourses: An Anthology*. Ed. Gregory Castle. Oxford: Blackwell, 2000. 280–92.

Said, Edward W. *Orientalism*. 1978. London: Penguin, 1985.

Spivak, Gayatri Chakravorty. "Can the Subaltern Speak?" *Marxism and the Interpretation of Culture*. Ed. Cary Nelson and Lawrence Grossberg. Urbana: University of Illinois Press, 1988. 271–313.

——. "Setting to Work (Transnational Cultural Studies)." In *A Critical Sense: Interviews with Intellectuals*. Ed. Peter Osborne. London: Routledge, 1996. 163–77.

Postmodernism

The term *Postmodernism* designates a number of theories dealing with a broad array of themes across disciplinary and theoretical lines. In architecture, where the Postmodern movement is prominent, the term refers to a critique of the dominant Modernist trend of Le Corbusier and Ludwig Meis van der Rohe as well as to a playful, pastiche style. To some degree, art and art history use Postmodernism in a similarly dual fashion. In history, philosophy, and political science, Postmodernism is regarded, when it is given credence at all, as a new epoch or episteme in which knowledge, language, and texts function in new and highly diversified ways. In literary and cultural studies, many of these ideas would find a firm following among scholars interested in the challenge that modernity poses to art and aesthetics in the late twentieth century.

As with Postcolonialism and Poststructuralism, the *"post-"* in Postmodernism is problematic. Postmodernism, from one perspective, is a critical reaction to the Enlightenment project of MODERNITY and the Modernist movements in art and literature. In this sense, the prefix *"post-"* signifies an *epistemological shift* in how we see and know the world. It implies the end of modernity and the beginning of something new. This historical conception suggests that the Postmodern comes *after* the modern, and to a certain extent this is the case. But, as with other usages, the *"post-"* in Postmodernism denotes something other than historical sequence; it denotes a general condition of innovation in technologies, especially the technologies of art and writing, and a general transformation (in some cases, Nietzschean *transvaluation*) of social, cultural, and aesthetic values. There is still another sense in which the *"post-"* signals a counter-movement within the modern itself. This is the view of **Jean-François Lyotard**, one of the leading proponents of Postmodernism: "The postmodern world would be that which, in the modern, puts forward the unpresentable in presentation itself, that which denies itself the solace of good forms" (*Postmodern Condition* 81). Though some early theorists, preeminently Ihab Hassan, attempted to identify positive characteristics of Postmodernism, the tendency in many theorists is to define by NEGATION, to make statements about what Postmodernism is *not* or to describe the Postmodern as lack, negativity, and the *un*presentable.

In literary theory, Postmodernism typically embraces a set of practices, strategies, and techniques that either repudiate Modernist tendencies (i.e., expressive form, mythic structures, stream of consciousness)
or develop those tendencies in extreme forms. Postmodernist thought is
characterized by a principled skepticism about language, truth, causality,
history, and SUBJECTIVITY. This skepticism extends to method as well,
which means that Postmodernism rejects the kind of methodological
coherence that we find in the New Criticism, Deconstruction, Critical
Theory, and Psychoanalysis – fields in which a common terminology
and shared strategies of analysis and interpretation link otherwise disparate critical practices. In some ways, Postmodernism resembles Cultural Studies in the sense that it lacks disciplinary and methodological
coherence, yet has acquired a distinct profile within the broader context
of literary and cultural theory. In some form or another, the major Postmodernists maintain a stance of incredulity with respect to MASTER
NARRATIVES, the unifying and TOTALIZING discourses (narratives of
liberty and knowledge, Hegelian and Marxian TELEOLOGICAL narratives,
Christian Providence, and so on) that organize knowledge (into systems,
laws, beliefs, institutions) and account for all aspects of human experience. Postmodernism rejects the notions of authenticity and origin,
regarding them as little more than romanticized myths that disguise
interminable conditions of repetition, deferral, and self-reference. The
Postmodern world is indeterminate and contingent; there can be no
stable foundations for truth, law, ethics, language, consciousness, even
perception. Postmodernism rejects UNIVERSALS and embraces the unpredictable and ever-changing reality of particulars. Pragmatics and what
Lyotard calls "paralogy" triumph over idealism and TOTALIZATION.
Binary functions, which lie at the heart of Structuralism and are the
starting point of so many poststructuralist critiques, have little or no
relevance for Postmodernism. Though many Postmodernists are in
agreement with poststructuralist theories of language and sign systems,
they tend to bypass the solutions of linguistics, semiotics, and discourse
analysis in favor of language games, chaos theory, and information
theory. That is to say, Postmodernism seeks to discover entirely new
ways of thinking about communication and expression, in many cases
drawing on the resources of the internet and other electronic media.

With respect to literary texts, Postmodernism shares with Poststructuralism a strong aversion to traditional notions of authors, texts, and

canons and an equally strong attraction to INTERTEXTUALITY and PLAY. In some respects, Postmodernism appears to depart significantly from what **Fredric Jameson** calls "aesthetic Modernism." Hassan, in *Dismemberment of Orpheus* (1971), defined Postmodernism as a rejection of the commitment to realism behind Modernist experimentation in favor of a literature of ludic self-reference, a METADISCOURSE that eschews old-fashioned plot lines and character development in favor of what **Hutcheon** calls "narcissistic narrative" and Robert Scholes FABULATION. Both concepts refer to a self-conscious attitude towards literary structure and writing that often serves as the central theme of the work itself. This is in part an effect of the rejection of realistic or MIMETIC representation, for if there is no intrinsic relation between language and the "real" world, then language becomes the only thing that literary works can effectively "re-present." But this tells only part of the story, for, as Lyotard suggests, the Postmodern movement is caught up in the presentation of the *un*presentable, that which has been ignored, occluded, or repressed. METAFICTIONAL strategies, therefore, are more than simply narcissistic, or at least they should be, for presenting the *un*presentable is an act of liberation. For Hutcheon, metafiction aims to revolutionize literature as well as the society that produces it by forcing readers to look at language and texts in new ways: "the narcissistic novel as incitement to revolutionary activity would be the ultimate defence of self-conscious fiction against claims of self-preening introversion" (155). However, from the materialist perspective of someone like Jameson, the self-referentiality and lack of affect that characterizes the "narcissistic novel" would appear far from revolutionary.

Many of the characteristic features of Postmodernism suggest a retreat from material social existence. The pervasive use of irony, parody, and other modes of *citation* announce Postmodernism's radical skepticism with respect to mimetic representation and reference. Citation conventionally signifies a relation of authority within a discourse, one in which certain statements serve a regulatory or evidentiary function: one *cites an authority* in order to advance an argument. Postmodern citation is a strategy of repetition and appropriation; texts cite each other not with the intent of invoking an authority or showing indebtedness but with the desire to create new expressive connections, new opportunities for enunciation and articulation, new models of cultural production and social action. Jameson describes a related practice, *pastiche*:

Pastiche is, like parody, the imitation of a peculiar or unique, idiosyncratic style, the wearing of a linguistic mask, speech in a dead language. But it is a neutral practice of such mimicry, without any of parody's ulterior motives, amputated of the satiric impulse, devoid of laughter and of any conviction that alongside the abnormal tongue you have momentarily borrowed, some healthy linguistic normality still exists. Pastiche is thus blank parody, a statue with blind eyeballs. (17)

Pastiche, like other forms of INTERTEXTUALITY, sustains a linguistic universe in which reference to the external world is neither necessary nor desirable. Disenchanted with material existence, living in a world of simulated reality, the Postmodern subject experiences a "waning of affect," in which psychological and cultural depth is replaced by SIMULACRA. Cultural products still produce "feelings" (which **Gilles Deleuze** and **Félix Guattari** call "intensities") but they are "free-floating and impersonal," no longer anchored to a stable, AUTONOMOUS subjectivity (Jameson 15–16).

The anti-foundationalism of Postmodernism, its aversion to absolutes, universals, and general truths is rooted in Nietzsche's critique of idealist metaphysics and Christian morality. Nietzsche's importance in this regard is easy to underestimate without a fairly extensive knowledge of his work, in which an aphoristic style, a gift for translating ideas into literary figures and episodes, and a background in philology combined to produce a searching critique of the ontology of concepts and ideas. Nietzsche pioneered new ways of knowing such things as the past, moral and ethical systems, languages and what they actually do, our belief in God and our propensity to go on believing even after we have, so it would seem, killed Him. In one of his earliest essays, Nietzsche celebrates the artist's "good deception," which is the use of metaphors to "smash" existing frameworks or throw them into confusion. It is only when we have forgotten that we are *artistically creating subjects*," when we begin to believe that Truth can be uncontaminated by any trace of human construction, that we fall into error ("Truth and Lies" 90, 86). In *The Genealogy of Morals* and *Beyond Good and Evil*, Nietzsche challenged the transcendent origin and unchanging nature (the "truth value") of moral concepts and beliefs. Opposed to the Truth, located in the depths or in the core of things, is an "Olympus of appearance":

> Oh, those Greeks! They knew how to *live*. What is required for that is to
> stop courageously at the surface, the fold, the skin, to adore appearance,
> to believe in forms, tones, words, in the whole Olympus of appearance!
> Those Greeks were superficial – *out of profundity!* . . . Are we not, pre-
> cisely in this respect, Greeks? Adorers of forms, of tones, of words? And
> therefore – *artists?* (*Gay Science* 38)

Many Postmodernist theorists take this aspect of Neitzsche's work,
together with poststructuralist theories of language (themselves often
indebted to Nietzsche), as the starting point for an interrogation of Modernism and modernity. **Lyotard** is one of the more important of these
figures. Drawing on Edmund Burke and Kant, he developed a conception of the *Postmodern sublime* that designates an excess (or NEGATION) of
representation in the form of a gap between reality and its presentation,
between "presentation" and the "unpresentable." In part, Lyotard is combining two paradoxical elements of Nietzsche's thought (and of Postmodernist thought as well): the attention to linguistic and artistic surfaces
and the capacity to plunge to great and even terrible depths. Nietzsche's
work on language and philosophy points to a firm belief in the infinite
depth of surfaces; the interminable and vertiginous qualities of language
and TEXTUALITY, the sheer existence of what Lyotard calls "heterogeneous genres of discourse," open the surface of discourse to the sublime.
In *The Differend*, he writes that "the despair of never being able to present
something within reality on the scale of the Idea [. . .] overrides the joy
of being nonetheless called upon to do so. We are more depressed by the
abyss that separates heterogeneous genres of discourse than excited by
the indication of a possible passage from one to the other" (179). Unlike
the Romantic sublime, which was typically located in nature, the Postmodern sublime has no object, there is no reference point in nature that
can trigger a sublime reaction. It is a function of language and discourse,
specifically of the despair of ever finding language or a genre adequate
to experience. The Postmodern sublime is caught up in the currents of
nostalgia for something that can never be re-possessed or re-presented;
indeed, it underscores the fact that this "something" has never been possessed or presented, has always been a matter of deferral and displacement. "A sorrow felt before the inconsistency of every object, [the
sublime] is also the exultation of thought passing beyond the bounds of

what may be presented. The 'presence' of the absolute is the utter contrary of presentation" (*Postmodern Fables* 29).

In *The Postmodern Condition* (1979), his most famous work, Lyotard critiques the problem of *delegitimation* and "the contemporary decline of narratives of legitimation," traditional or modern. This process "is tied to the abandonment of the belief" that science or anything else can provide "metaprescriptions" to unify all language games (*Postmodern Condition* 64, 66). Over against the MASTER NARRATIVES of emancipation and speculation that had, in modernity, served as the "quintessential form of customary knowledge," Lyotard proffers the concept of *paralogy*, a language game "played in the pragmatics of knowledge" (*Postmodern Condition* 60–61). Joining Lyotard in his critique of knowledge and representation was **Jean Baudrillard**, whose theory of SIMULATION suggests that the Postmodern world is one in which the real has been replaced by simulations of reality. "It is no longer a question of imitation, nor of reduplication, nor even of parody. It is rather a question of substituting signs of the real for the real itself, that is, an operational double, a metastable, programmatic, perfect descriptive machine which provides all the signs of the real and short-circuits all its vicissitudes." Whereas dissimulation involves "feign[ing] not to have what one has," simulation involves "feign[ing] to have what one hasn't" (4–5). In the "hyperreal" space of simulation, there is no truth, causality, temporality, law – even nature and the human body are irrelevant in a world in which "signs of the real" replace the real and "God, Man, Progress, and History itself die to profit the code" (111).

Lyotard's Postmodern vision provoked a debate with Jürgen Habermas, who wrote in response that the "project of modernity has not yet been fulfilled" (12). He was committed to a reintegration of social spheres based on "communicative action" and consensus, on the essentially humanist notion of an organic and meaningful social TOTALITY. Though Habermas's humanist political project did not require a "correspondence" model of truth, it did presuppose, as part of a meaningful social totality, the possibility of social and political consensus. Like **Michel Foucault, Jacques Derrida, Roland Barthes**, and other poststructuralists, Lyotard and Baudrillard critique the ESSENTIALIST foundations of humanism and offer new paradigms for understanding the nature of SUBJECTIVITY and the relations between subjects in social formations.

Also like them, they reject the idea of the unified SUBJECT with its indivisible and essential core of being.

Perhaps the most devastating Postmodern critique of humanism comes from **Gilles Deleuze** and **Félix Guattari**, whose *Anti-Oedipus* and *Thousand Plateaus* challenge the main achievements of the Enlightenment: capitalism, philosophy, Psychoanalysis (Freudian and Lacanian), medical science, even physics. Deleuze and Guattari believe that desire does not function according Freud's Oedipal theory, in which desire for the mother inaugurates the Oedipus complex and the mechanisms of repression; nor do they agree with Lacan's emphasis on lack as the primary motivation of desire. Against the dyadic or binary structure of Freudian and Lacanian subjectivity, Deleuze and Guattari advance the notion of *schizophrenia*, which more aptly describes the heterogeneous and discontinuous experience of postmodernity. Their model of *schizoanalysis* replaces Psychoanalysis and counters the Oedipal scene of repressed desire and lack with the flows of *desiring machines* – individuals, collectivities, social institutions – that are capable of creating new forms of solidarity as well as new forms of social control. No longer a singular and unified producer of desire – a *subject* – the human being and body become "machinic." The "major enemy" of Deleuze and Guattari's experiment in Psychoanalysis and Marxism is fascism. As Foucault puts it in his preface to *Anti-Oedipus*, "the strategic adversary is fascism. . . . And not only historical fascism, the fascism of Hitler and Mussolini – which was able to mobilize and use the desire of the masses so effectively – but also the fascism in us all, in our heads and in our everyday behavior" (xiii).

This fight against fascism is waged by "desiring machines" that generate and direct the flows and intensities of a "libidinal economy" throughout the entire social structure. The specific structure of this economy is determined by processes of DETERRITORIALIZATION and RETERRITORIALIZATION that traverse the social body, inscribing and reinscribing psychological, geographical, political, or social boundaries. TERRITORIALIZED space is not governed by a "schizo" logic but rather by the logic of the Law, the Lacanian Symbolic. Deterritorialization refers to the process of breaking down these boundaries and mapping "demographic flows" of intensities that emanate from different points of the social matrix. Reterritorialization occurs once new boundaries are inscribed on this matrix-in-process. All of this plays out on a social landscape that resembles a "rhizome," which Deleuze and Guattari describe as "a subterranean stem" that is "absolutely different from roots and radicles. Bulbs and tubers are rhizomes. Plants with roots or radicles may be rhizomorphic in other respects altogether. . . . Burrows are too, in all their functions of shelter, supply, movement, evasion, and breakout" (*Thousand Plateaus* 6–7). Following Antonin Artaud and Spinoza, Deleuze and Guattari develop a theory of social space as a "body without organs," the "full egg" prior to the organization of the organs. A body without organs designates a node through which intensities or flows of forces pass and create interconnections, openings, passages, assemblages: "the BwO [body without organs] is not a scene, a place, or even a support upon which something comes to pass. It has nothing to do with phantasy, there is nothing to interpret" (*Thousand Plateaus* 153). Desire is the operation of the body without organs. Even when that body is threatened with annihilation, "it is still desire. Desire stretches that far: desiring one's own annihilation, or desiring the power to annihilate. Money, army, police, and State desire, fascist desire, even fascism is desire. There is desire whenever there is the constitution of a BwO under one relation or another" (*Thousand Plateaus* 165).

Postmodernism does not reject the political sphere or political action. Deleuze and Guattari are committed to revolutionary social change and their work has been extremely useful to those who reflect on radical new forms of social organization and political activism. The same can be said of other Postmodernists, especially those who turn their attention to legal and ethical matters. In *Contingency, Hegemony, Universality* (2000), **Judith Butler, Slavoj Žižek**, and Ernesto Laclau revisit Kant and Hegel in order to fashion new theoretical foundations, no matter how contingent, while Lyotard's late work is dedicated to analyzing and reflecting on the problem of ethics in a Postmodern frame of reference. Lyotard's *The Differend* is a good example of Postmodern ethical reflection. The term *différend* refers to an aporia or contradiction that occurs when the parties in a legal dispute occupy incommensurate positions; they are unable to "phrase" their case because there is no common language or universal ground on which to base an appeal. The alternative to this impasse is to arrive at a "practice of justice that is not linked to that of consensus" (*Postmodern* 66).

Feminism has developed its own critique of the legal and ethical implications of postmodernity. **Judith Butler**, Jennifer Wicke, and Mary

Joe Frug have used Postmodernist theory in a feminist critique of the legal conception of the SUBJECT. Lyotard and Baudrillard, who celebrate "the liberating potential of local, interlocking language games, which replace the overall structures," leave little room for reflection on "collective identities" and the "historical terrain of struggle" (Wicke 17–18). Greater awareness is needed of the distinction between *identity politics*, which is tethered to traditional notions of the AUTONOMOUS, legal subject, and *relational politics*, which denotes "a multiple political dynamic that can see itself at work in the world in the back and forth of actual political engagement" (Wicke 33). **Donna Haraway** takes the critique of the gendered subject beyond ethics and law and challenges the foundations of science and the limits of nature. Her aim, in *Simians, Cyborgs, and Women* (1991), is to deconstruct binomial models of human experience – mind/body, subject/object, nature/artifice, art/science, body/machine – and to posit an alternative model, the cyborg, which links biological nature structurally to the "interface" opportunities made possible by computer generated and mediated environments. Especially for women, the cyborg model is better adapted to a relational politics and can help bridge the gap between Postmodernism and a Feminist theory that still presupposes, for political purposes, the existence and necessity of an autonomous subject. (On Butler, see pp. 104–5.)

As Lyotard has famously argued, Postmodernism is a *condition*. The precise nature of that condition has been the object of much debate. Lyotard's own position – Postmodernism entails lost faith and skepticism, an attitude of incredulity towards traditional modes of legitimation – has been quite influential. By envisioning a world that can no longer be comprehended by dialectics and totalities, unities and "nations," subjects and laws, Deleuze and Guattari, like many Postmodern feminists, offer a vision of the Postmodern that avoids the Kantian and Hegelian concepts that lie at the foundation of Lyotard's view. Others, like Laclau and Žižek, see social and political implications in textualist theories that seem to foreground language and representation at the expense of social action. To some degree the quarrel is over the political function of representation, but a more fundamental issue is at stake: the status of representation in a world that exists *only* as representation. The desire for stable categories of social subjectivity is in part a recognition that there is more than representation at stake, but it is also a sign that the *subject* – along with the nation, history, the text, the author, and even time and space themselves – is a thing of the past.

WORKS CITED

Baudrillard, Jean. *Simulations*. Trans. Paul Foss, Paul Patton and Philip Beitchman. New York: Semiotext(e), 1983.

Deleuze, Gilles and Félix Guattari. *Anti-Oedipus: Capitalism and Schizophrenia*. 1977. Trans. Robert Hurley, Mark Seem and Helen R. Lane. Minneapolis: University of Minnesota Press, 1983.

——. *A Thousand Plateaus: Capitalism and Schizophrenia*. Trans. Brian Massumi. London: Athlone, 1988.

Hutcheon, Linda. *Narcissistic Narrative: The Metafictional Paradox*. Waterloo, Ont.: Wilfred Laurier University Press, 1980.

Jameson, Fredric. *Postmodernism, or, The Cultural Logic of Late Capitalism*. Durham: Duke University Press, 1991.

Lyotard, Jean-François. *The Differend: Phrases in Dispute*. 1983. Trans. Georges Van Den Abbeele. Minneapolis: University of Minnesota Press, 1988.

——. *The Postmodern Condition: A Report on Knowledge*. Trans. Geoff Bennington and Brian Massumi. Minneapolis: University of Minnesota Press, 1984.

——. *Postmodern Fables*. Trans. Georges Van Den Abbeele. Minneapolis: University of Minnesota Press, 1997.

Nietzsche, Friedrich. *The Gay Science*. Trans. Walter Kaufmann. New York: Vintage-Random, 1974.

——. "On Truth and Lies in a Nonmoral Sense." In *Philosophy and Truth: Selections from Nietzsche's Notebooks of the Early 1870s*. Ed. and trans. Daniel Breazeale. Atlantic Highlands, NJ: Humanities Press, 1979. 79–97.

Wicke, Jennifer. "Postmodern Identities and the Politics of the (Legal) Subject." In *Feminism and Postmodernism*. Eds. Margaret Ferguson and Jennifer Wicke. Durham: Duke University Press, 1994. 10–33.

Poststructuralism

Poststructuralism designates a number of distinct theoretical principles and practices with a common aim: a critique of Structuralism, the idea that human societies and their traditions can be understood according to universal and unchanging structures that are replicated in texts, artworks, rituals, and other modes of expression. Of special importance in the development of Poststructuralism were Ferdinand de Saussure's linguistics and Claude Lévi-Strauss's structural anthropology. (See below, "Structuralism" pp. 181–90.) The "structurality of structure," according to **Jacques Derrida**, in his groundbreaking essay "Structure, Sign and Play in the Discourse of the Human Sciences" (1966), is the concept of the *center*: "The function of this center was not only to orient, balance, and organize the structure – one cannot in fact conceive of an unorganized structure – but above all to make sure that the organizing principle of the structure [i.e., *structuration*] would limit what we might call the *play* of the structure. By orienting and organizing the coherence of the system, the center of a structure permits the play of its elements inside the total form." It is play "based on a fundamental ground" that is itself beyond play (*Writing* 278–79). In the poststructuralist critique of structure, the center is deconstructed, exposed as contradictory, incoherent, a "mythology of presence." "The center is at the center of totality," Derrida claims, "and yet, since the center does not belong to the totality (is not part of the totality), the totality *has its center elsewhere*. The center is not the center. The concept of centered structure – although it represents coherence itself, the condition of the *episteme* as philosophy or science – is contradictorily coherent" (*Writing* 280). Poststructuralists question the ability of language to designate the center, to remain structured around a center, if there is *no* center, if there is only irresolvable contradiction. If there is no guarantee of stable and stabilizing authority, no absolute criterion for assessing the truth, then disciplines grounded in structuralist paradigms of truth, especially scientific truth, are deprived of their legitimacy.

Poststructuralism rejects what Derrida calls "onto-theology," a world view in which meaning and value are invested in the transcendent ESSENCE (*onto*, being) of an unchanging principle or divinity (*theo*, God). Nor does it accept PHALLOGOCENTRISM, a world view in which social and cultural power are invested in a symbol of pure abstract presence (*phallus*) and articulated in the unchanging concepts of reason (*logos*). Poststructuralism, in its principal modes – Deconstruction, SEMIOTICS, and DISCOURSE ANALYSIS – precisely by focusing its critical energies upon structured systems, especially binary systems, commits itself to discovering alternatives precisely *through* the critical project itself. Derrida invites us "to seek new concepts and new models, an *economy* escaping this system of metaphysical oppositions. This economy would not be an energetics of pure, shapeless force. . . . If we appear to oppose one series to the other, it is because from within the classical system we wish to make apparent the noncritical privilege naively granted to the other series by a certain structuralism. Our discourse irreducibly belongs to the system of metaphysical oppositions" (*Writing* 20). Derrida famously warned that we cannot step outside of the metaphysical tradition of philosophy and humanism in order to critique it, that critique must be conducted immanently. There is no possibility of stepping outside the (con)text: *il n'y a pas de hors-texte*, there is nothing outside of the text. If this vision of the world resembles Postmodernism, it is because some of the same deconstructionist strategies are employed in both fields; the key difference lies in Poststructuralism's requirement of structure, not only as an object of critique but as a means of measuring alternatives. The chief concepts of Poststructuralism – DIFFERENCE, openness to the OTHER, resistance to dialectical and binary operations – derive their power precisely from the NEGATIVE or deconstructionist critique that alone creates a space for the production of new theoretical values and techniques *within* structured systems.

One of the most innovative poststructuralists, **Roland Barthes**, began his career in SEMIOTICS and structural narratology. His early work drew on Saussure's semiology and Lévi-Strauss's structuralist analysis of mythology; by the late 1960s, he had taken structuralist analysis to a certain limit, discovering in literary and cultural texts a plurality of possible interpretations and a dizzying kind of bliss in the contemplation of them. Though his "Introduction to the Structural Analysis of Narrative" (1966) is, in many ways, an exemplary structuralist analysis, it also stands at a transition point in Barthes career, a point at which the idea of a regulated and centered structure is transformed into the idea of an unregulated, decentered *process of reading*. Like Foucault, he rejected the conventional figure of the author who *originates* the work. In "The Death of the Author" (1968), Barthes argued that authorship is a linguistic function, "never more than the instance writing, just as *I* is never more than the instance saying *I*" (*Image* 145). The Author is a subject position in a text or discourse, not a psychological being, locus and origin of aesthetic and ethical values. In place of the "author," Barthes produces the "modern scriptor," a force "in no way equipped with a being preceding or exceeding the writing"; nor is this scriptor a "subject with the book as predicate." It is "born simultaneously with the text" (*Image* 145). So too is the reader, but "at the cost of the death of the Author" (*Image* 148). It is a decisive moment in Barthes's development, and a critical turn from structuralist orthodoxies, to link the reader and the work joined in "a single signifying practice" (*Image* 162).

Barthes follows Derrida in recognizing that language is fundamentally "dilatory," a play of differences, deferrals, and displacements of meaning within semiotic and linguistic systems. Unlike the AUTONOMOUS "work," which fixes signification and reference, the "text" takes its shape and meaning from a fluid and multifarious network of signs. The distinction between "work" and "text" is coupled to a distinction between *writerly* and *readerly* texts. The writerly text is a text of bliss, "pleasure without separation" (*Image* 164); it induces JOUISSANCE and leaves the contented reader behind: it is "the text that imposes a state of loss, the text that discomforts (perhaps to the point of a certain boredom), unsettles the reader's historical, cultural, psychological assumptions, the consistency of his tastes, values, memories, brings to a crisis his relation with language" (*Pleasure* 14). Over against this notion of the writerly text is "what can be read, but not written: the readerly. We call any readerly text a classic text" (*S/Z* 4). It is a text of pleasure, "a *comfortable* practice of reading" (*Pleasure* 14).

Barthes' poststructuralist semiology has much in common with the work of **Julia Kristeva**. Both theorists proceeded from similar foundations in semiotics and structuralist linguistics and both found much of value in Psychoanalysis. Perhaps because she was a practicing analyst herself, Kristeva was more inclined to "graft" psychoanalytic theory onto semiology. Her practice of "semanalysis" is an "*analytical discourse on signifying systems*" (*Desire* 125). Kristeva's early poststructuralist semiology is driven by a *desire for language*. Like many French Feminists, Kristeva focuses attention on the body and the ways in which ideology penetrates and inhabits the body, sometimes leaving signs and significations on the flesh (as in tattoos and scars). She also looks at how *libido* – Freud's word for sexual energy as it is expressed in psychological and physiological systems – interlocks with language and discourse to form a *libidinal economy*. The structure, trajectory, and outcome of libidinal drives become the model for new forms of SEMIOTIC activity. Kristeva treats language, especially literary language, as an exemplary conduit for libidinal energies that inevitably flow between readers and texts. She developed a theory of INTERTEXTUALITY to explain the way that language, especially non-representational language, maps "historical and social coordinates" at "different structural levels of each text" (or "semiotic practice") (*Desire* 36). Drawing on **M. M. Bakhtin's** theory of DIALOGISM and the CARNIVALESQUE in Rabelais and Dostoyevski, Kristeva emphasized the polyphonic nature of the novel and its constitutive AMBIVALENCE, its oscillation between monological and dialogical narrative structures. "Bakhtinian dialogism identifies writing as both subjectivity and communication, or better, as intertextuality" (*Desire* 68). For Bakhtin, literary texts were dialogized and stratified by a variety of languages and idioms. His essays of the 1930s and '40s, which were later republished in *The Dialogic Imagination* (1981), challenged the limits of Formalism and raised the kinds of questions that poststructuralists would ask in the 1960s and '70s. Intertextuality integrates and translates discourses within interlocking and interdependent sign systems; it is a fundamentally rhetorical and semiological concept, that "situates philosophical problems *within* language; more precisely, within language as a correlation of texts, as a reading-writing that falls in with non-Aristotelian syntagmatic, correlational, 'carnivalesque' logic" (*Desire* 88–89). (On Bakhtin, see pp. 115, 157, 184–6.)

Early critics of Poststructuralism point out that Kristeva's "semanalysis" lacks a concrete ground and therefore lacks an effective defense against arbitrary practice. "The problem for *any* intertextual reading," writes Toril Moi, "is to counter the charge of arbitrariness. Paradoxically, it is precisely because there is, in principle, no limit to the number of possible intertexts to any given text, that it becomes necessary explicitly to justify one's choice of any *particular* intertext" (Moi 1043). Kristeva is less interested in a *"particular* intertext" than in understanding the operations of the "speaking subject" of language and TEXTUALITY, which is not to be confused with the autonomous bourgeois SUBJECT. Structural linguistics falls short, she argues, by refusing to recognize the speaking subject of discourse: "[I]n order to move from sign to sentence the place of the subject had to be acknowledged and no longer kept vacant" (*Desire* 127–28). On this point, Kristeva follows Lacan's groundbreaking critique of SUBJECTIVITY founded on the primacy of the ego. **Lacan**, like other poststructuralists, rejected the "unity of the subject" (*Écrit* 281), positing instead a subject who accepts "the signifier as the determinant of the signified," "through an enunciation that makes a human being tremble due to the vacillation that comes back to him from his own statement" (288–9). This trembling marks "the moment of a fading or eclipse of the subject – which is closely tied to the *Spaltung* or splitting he undergoes due to his subordination to the signifier – to the condition of an object" (301).

Lacan follows Freud in grounding his theory of the subject in neurosis, specifically in the structure of the symptom. The symptom "speaks in the Other, I say, designating by 'Other' the very locus evoked by recourse to speech in any relation in which such recourse plays a part. If it speaks in the Other, whether or not the subject hears it with his ear, it is because it is there that the subject finds his signifying place in a way that is logically prior to any awakening of the signified" (275). But whereas Lacan remains committed to the Oedipal paradigm and the castration complex as fundamental to the construction of speaking subjects, Kristeva concentrates on the pre-Oedipal, pre-symbolic possibilities of poetic language. These possibilities signal "a *heterogeneousness* to meaning and signification" that "operates through, despite, and in excess of [meaning] and produces in poetic language 'musical' but also nonsense effects that destroy not only accepted beliefs and signification, but, in radical experiments, syntax itself" (133). In a manner similar to Lacan's *jouissance*, which is caused by proximity to unconscious processes, Kristeva's *chora* designates an ecstatic experience of the IMAGINARY grounded on the "oceanic" bond of mother and child. In both cases, a structured system (the ego, language) is disrupted by an excess of signs, a boundless, oceanic state, a "semiotic disposition" rooted in the maternal body. For poststructuralist feminists, the body is the ultimate structure: systematized at multiple levels, intricately cross-referenced, coded but capable of a wide range of random de- and recodings, fluid but contained. The structuralist conception of the relationship between *énoncé* (utterance) and *énonciation* (the act of uttering in a specific material and social context) tended to privilege the *énoncé*, the utterance or text that embodied linguistic (or semiotic) information. This privilege is challenged in Kristeva's semiotics, which focuses on *énonciation*, on context and place, on the site of discourse. Understood in this radical sense, the body itself is simultaneously *énoncé* and *énonciation*, message and site of inscription. (On Lacan's terms, see pp. 112, 168–9.)

Foucault's theories of GENEALOGY and ARCHAEOLOGY offer innovative ways to map the complex networks of language and text, discontinuous and decentered, with which poststructuralists grappled. They are both anti-historicist modes of DISCOURSE ANALYSIS, interested not in chronology, causality, precedent and continuity but rather in POWER and its emergence and the discontinuities and ruptures it occasions in DISCURSIVE FORMATIONS. In *The Archaeology of Knowledge*, Foucault offered a detailed account of the archaeological method and the principles governing discursive formations. A discursive formation is a *"system of dispersion,"* a series of statements (e.g., on medicine or madness), "an order in their successive appearance, correlations in their simultaneity, assignable positions in common space, a reciprocal functioning, linked and hierarchized transformations" (*Archaeology* 37). Archaeological analysis, which is concerned primarily with synchronic relations, infers and describes the patterns of emergence, dispersion, and disposition of statements and events within a formation. The historicity of formations is purely discursive or textual; it is an "enunciative past," an "acquired truth," a form of *recurrence* that is not a return, but rather a refiguring, modification, and accumulation of discursive material. What we often think of as a "unity through time" is really the effect of a "temporality of accumulation," which Foucault calls *historical a prioris*. This term designates not historically constituted conditions for judgment but rather the concrete, material aspect of discursive statements, the "condition of reality for statements" as well as "the group of rules that characterize a discursive practice" (*Archaeology* 127). The "rules of enunciation" for each formation determine what constitutes a "legitimate" statement; they determine the horizon of what is sayable, the limit of a particular discursive formation beyond which enunciations simply cannot be heard. The practice of archaeology produces a "series full of gaps, intertwined with one another, interplays of differences, distances, substitutions, transformations" (*Archaeology* 37). By mapping conceptual and methodological similarities, continuities, connections, and imbrications, the archaeologist can see patterns in the production and consumption of discourse and, inferring from these patterns, can derive the rules of enunciation of a given formation.

A related conception, *genealogy*, is less interested in language and the function of statements in discursive formations than in the emergence of concepts and forms of knowledge through the specific practices of social and cultural institutions. In *Discipline and Punish*, for example, Foucault built on Nietzsche's theory of genealogy, which does not seek to find the origin of ideas and values, but rather to establish their *emergence* as functions of institutional POWER (or "power/knowledge") in its various forms. Genealogy is not interested in TELEOLOGICAL theories of history, for it does not give credence to historical origins and ideals. Instead, it looks for the "the hazardous play of dominations," "the emergence of different interpretations" (*Language* 148, 152); it identifies the ruptures in the flow of events, "the accidents, the minute deviations – or conversely, the complete reversals – the errors and the false appraisals, and the faulty calculations that gave birth to those things that continue to exist and have value for us" (*Language* 146). In his late essays, Foucault elaborated on the way that power effects the constitution of social subjects. Perhaps his most influential genealogical work was *The History of Sexuality*, in which he considered the emergence of a discourse of sexuality, which he called a "slow surfacing of confidential statements" (*History of Sexuality* 61, 63) produced and regulated by particular matrices of power.

Foucault (and his predecessor, Nietzsche) is often criticized for being abstract and reductive, for substituting one idealist and ahistorical value for another, DIFFERENCE (or signification or discourse) for transcendence (or being, presence, consciousness), power for Truth. At a more pragmatic level, Foucault is criticized for not asking more penetrating questions: for example, who "composes" the rules of enunciation within a given discursive formation? What are the options for concrete political action within them? **Pierre Bourdieu's** theory of SOCIAL FIELDS is one attempt to theorize the relationship between DISCURSIVE FORMATIONS and concrete fields of social action. Bourdieu regards the social field as a sphere of social action, a site of power games between individuals and social institutions. "Social fields," Bourdieu notes, "are the products of a long, slow process of AUTONOMIZATION, and are therefore, so to speak, games 'in themselves' and not 'for themselves'" (*Logic of Practice* 67). They exist on two levels: the level of material production and the level of symbolic production. The ability to manipulate the HABITUS formed within a given social field is the measure both of "cultural capital" and of social distinction. The term HABITUS refers to the half-conscious, unspoken (because always already consented to) limits of a given field, the "acquired, socially constituted dispositions" formed by experience with the rules of a particular social practice. It is a "'creative,' active, inventive capacity" of an "active agent," not "a transcendental subject in the idealist tradition" (In Other Words 12–13). Like discursive formations, social fields perform a mediating function, allowing the critic or historian to formulate provisional TOTALITIES that are not completely arbitrary, that are fashioned out of perceived systematic relations (of dispersion and contiguity), even though these relations are often antagonistic, contradictory or coercive, in which case they can be regarded as a form of "symbolic violence."

Foucault's final works on the "care of the self" and the rise to prominence of feminist theories of the body and subjectivity reflect general developments in literary and cultural theory grounded in the poststructuralist critique of the ESSENTIAL or UNIVERSAL SUBJECT. Foucault's late interviews and essays on the relationship between individuals and social power recognize the subject's freedom to negotiate among structures and discourses of power. "At the very heart of the power relationship," Foucault claims, "and constantly provoking it, are the recalcitrance of the will and the intransigence of freedom. Rather than speaking of an essential freedom, it would be better to speak of an 'agonism' – of a relationship which is at the same time reciprocal incitation and struggle; less of a face-to-face confrontation which paralyzes both sides than a permanent provocation" ("Subject" 221–22). However, **Slavoj Žižek** criticizes Foucauldian theories of identity for failing to offer a decisive critique of existing social conditions: "The predominant form of ideology today is precisely that of multiple identities, non-identity and cynical distance. This includes even sexual identities. . . . these Foucauldian practices of inventing new strategies, new identities, are ways of playing the late capitalist game of subjectivity" (40). This is perhaps an unsurprising outcome of a theoretical formation rooted in philosophical modernity.

Note. For more on Derrida, see Deconstruction; on Foucault and Nietzsche, see New Historicism; on Barthes, see Structuralism; on Kristeva, see Feminism; on Lacan, Deleuze and Guattari, see Psychoanalysis; on Saussure, see Structuralism.

WORKS CITED

Barthes, Roland. *Image-Music-Text*. Trans. Stephen Heath. 1977. New York: Hill and Wang, 1977.

——. *The Pleasure of the Text*. Trans. Richard Miller. New York: Hill and Wang, 1975.

——. *S/Z*. Trans. Richard Miller. New York: Hill and Wang, 1974.

Bourdieu, Pierre. *In Other Words: Essays Towards a Reflexive Sociology*. Trans. Matthew Adamson. Stanford: Stanford University Press, 1990.

——. *The Logic of Practice*. Trans. Richard Nice. 1980. Stanford: Stanford University Press, 1990.

Derrida, Jacques. *Writing and Difference*. Trans. Alan Bass. Chicago: University of Chicago Press, 1978.

Foucault, Michel. *The Archaeology of Knowledge and the Discourse on Language*. 1969, 1971. Trans. A. M. Sheridan Smith. New York: Pantheon, 1972.

——. *The History of Sexuality*. 1976. Vol. 1. Trans. Robert Hurley. New York: Pantheon Books, 1978.

——. *Language, Counter-Memory, Practice: Selected Essays and Interviews*. 1962–72. Ed. Donald F. Bouchard. Trans. Donald F. Bouchard and Sherry Simon. Ithaca: Cornell University Press, 1977.

——. "The Subject and Power." In *Michel Foucault: Beyond Structuralism and Hermeneutics*. Eds. Herbert L. Dreyfus and Paul Rabinow. Chicago: University of Chicago Press, 1984. 208–26.

Kristeva, Julia. *Desire in Language: A Semiotic Approach to Literature and Art*. Ed. Leon S. Roudiez. Trans. Thomas Gora, Alice Jardine, and Leon S. Roudiez. New York: Columbia University Press, 1980.

Moi, Toril. "Appropriating Bourdieu: Feminist Theory and Pierre Bourdieu's Sociology of Culture." *New Literary History* 22.4 (Autumn 1991): 1017–1049.

Lacan, Jacques. *Écrits: A Selection*. Trans. Bruce Fink. New York: Norton, 2002.

Žižek, Slavoj. "Postscript." Interview. In *A Critical Sense: Interviews with Intellectuals*. Ed. Peter Osborne. London: Routledge, 1996. 36–44.

Psychoanalysis

Psychoanalysis offers a systematic accounting of the psychic apparatus (especially the unconscious) and a theory of the mind and human psychic development. Sigmund Freud initially theorized a "topographical" relation between the *ego* and the *unconscious*; the former encompassed consciousness and the individual's contact with the external world, while the latter was a quite different space of instinctual drives and repressive mechanisms. In the topographical model, the ego and the unconscious occupied different areas and the problem was to understand how libidinal energy moved back and forth between the two. Much of Freud's early work centered around the analysis of *neurotic symptoms* (particularly *hysteria*) which he believed were derivatives of memories that had been repressed and existed only in the unconscious. (*Neuroses* are psychological disorders with no organic basis and include hysteria, obsessive and compulsive disorders, depression, phobias, and so on; they are the focus of psychoanalysis and can be treated. *Psychoses* are more serious disorders, often with an organic basis, that are typically not treatable by psychoanalysis. The most common psychoses are schizophrenia and manic depression.) The early case histories – for example, "Dora: A Case of Hysteria" and "History of an Infantile Neurosis (Wolf Man)" – show the development of Freud's thinking about unconscious processes and the way in which dreams provide insight into the etiology, or cause, of neurotic symptoms. Like the symptom, the dream is an indirect or coded message, the interpretation of which holds the key to resolving the original traumatic memory. Dream interpretation is a complex process involving considerable skill on the part of the analyst; but Freud was confident that proper training would ensure reliable, *scientific* results.

Freud argues that dreams have two kinds of content, the *manifest* and the *latent*. The manifest level is the dream itself, the object of interpretation; the latent level is the actual thought that cannot be known or expressed consciously because it has been repressed or "censored." "[A] dream is not an intention represented as having been carried out, but a wish represented as having been fulfilled" (*SE* 7: 85). The distortions that convert wishes into often bizarre and obscure dreams Freud called the *dream-work*, a process in which unconscious material is allowed a disguised or coded expression during sleep, when the dream-censor relaxes its vigilance. This dream-work entails the primary mechanisms of *displacement* and *condensation* by which unconscious material is formed into the manifest content of the dream. In other words, the dream-work performs what many (including Freud) recognize as a literary activity in which metaphor, metonymy, and other figures represent in a disguised form the secret wish that lies hidden in the unconscious. In order to comprehend the manifest content of the dream, the analyst must lead the analysand to the latent level of unconscious, repressed meaning. It is a difficult and time-consuming process, and the analysand very often will resist the analyst's interpretations. The analyst must be a skilled interpreter, able to work back from the dream to the underlying wish. "The dream's interpretation had to disregard everything that served to represent the wishfulfilment and to re-establish distressing latent dream-thoughts from these obscure remaining hints" (*SE* 15: 225).

Dreams are important because they hold the key to neurotic symptoms that usually originate in an individual's earliest experiences of instinctual satisfaction and repression. For this reason, childhood sexual experiences are fundamentally important. Freud's *Three Essays on Sexuality* argues that these experiences are structured diphasically, which means that sexual development is interrupted by a latency period that effectively separates it into two distinct phases, pre-genital (oral and anal states) and genital, each incorporating multiple stages and, quite often, regressions to prior stages. Children are *polymorphously perverse* and can therefore respond along a number of erotic pathways (or "sexual aims") to a number of "sexual objects" (including the child herself). For Freud, "normal" development entailed the integration of the component "perversions" (scopophilia and exhibitionism, auto-eroticism, sadism and masochism) into a healthy, heterosexual instinct. He was also well aware that normal sexuality and sexual identity were not often achieved, that an individual could fixate at one or another of the early stages; but he strongly believed that this norm was best suited to fulfill the destiny of the human species, to fend off death and produce more life. The *pleasure principle*, which is the pure and unfettered energy of the sexual instinct, motivates childhood polymorphous perversity. In normal sexual development, particularly during the genital phase and the "dissolution" of the Oedipus complex, the narcissistic pursuit of pleasure associated with early sexual development "comes under the sway of the reproductive function" and the instincts are "organized" more firmly "towards a sexual aim attached to some extraneous sexual object" (*SE* 7: 197). This form of *primary narcissism*, which refers to the auto-erotic tendencies of infants, is to be distinguished from *secondary narcissism*, the unhealthy fixation of the ego on itself at later stages of sexual development. The *reality principle* keeps individuals from succumbing to the whim of their sexual instincts and forces them either to sublimate some of their libido in non-sexual or non-violent activities (art, religion, philosophy) or to repress the desire for such activities through *reaction-formation*, the mental forces that come into play to oppose or block perverse impulses (moral reactions like disgust and shame). Under the influence of the reality principle, the child learns to direct sexual libido away from the ego (in order to avoid the danger of secondary narcissism) and onto a suitable sexual object.

Freud's understanding of object choice dynamics led to the central event in psychoanalysis: the working out of the *Oedipus complex*, which allows the individual to overcome "incestuous phantasies" and permits "one of the most painful, psychical achievements of the pubertal period . . . detachment from parental authority" (*SE* 7: 227). The young boy must not desire his mother, but this prohibition throws up defenses against the father, who is perceived as a threat to the boy's bond with his mother. Freud believed that a point is reached when the mother or a caregiver, less often the father, notices the child's curiosity about his own genitals and issues a warning that his penis will be cut off if he does not leave it alone. This threat of castration is made all the more real when the young boy happens to see a young girl undressing or his own mother in bed with his father and realizes that women have already suffered castration. A "normal" dissolution of the Oedipus complex would involve the child repudiating his mother, with whom he was closely identified and to whom he was most attracted, and identifying with his father. His desire must now find another object. For young girls, this process is slightly different. First, the threat of castration is a past event, her own body is evidence of its terrible effects; second, while the boy is free to find a female substitute for his mother, the girl is absolutely prohibited from finding another female object of desire and is also separated from the very person with whom she would "normally" attach herself. These events lead little girls to experience a loss or lack which they attempt to alleviate by having a baby, a phallic gift from the father. The Oedipal process for girls (sometimes called the *Electra complex*) thus begins with a double imperative:

preserve life through heterosexual object choices and repudiate the most natural bond of attachment (the mother), which would entail an identification with the father. For boys and girls, the Oedipus complex installs repression as a means by which to manage prohibited desires; it involves "the transformation into affects, and especially into anxiety, of the mental energy belonging to the instincts" (*SE* 14: 153). The onset of repression is simultaneously the destruction of the Oedipus complex. Subsequent repressions are made under the aegis of the super-ego that emerges as a result of a successful Oedipal experience. The super-ego is thus "the heir of the Oedipus complex" (*SE* 19: 36).

The importance of the Oedipus complex in psychoanalysis is hard to underestimate. It is the basis of the "family romances" in which "the young phantasy-builder" (*SE* 9: 240) replaces his family with one of a higher rank or rescues his mother from an abusive father. It guarantees the structural integrity of the nuclear family and, in a broader cultural context, could be regarded as the foundation of civilization. In *Totem and Taboo*, Freud suggests that "[t]he beginnings of religion, morals, society and art converge in the Oedipus complex" (*SE* 13: 156). He speculates that there existed a primal moment in humankind's early development when the brothers in the "primal horde" murder the father in order to gain freedom and women. A totem system emerges, one that reduplicates the crime but also puts in place prohibitions against the crime itself as well as the possession of women that made it necessary. From the primal horde emerged the "fraternal clan," and from this clan there ultimately emerged complex PATRIARCHAL social structures, religion, and morality. In *Civilization and Its Discontents*, one of his late works on the origins of civilization, Freud admits that "[w]e cannot get away from the assumption that man's sense of guilt springs from the Oedipus complex and was acquired at the killing of the father by the brothers banded together" (*SE* 21: 131).

It is only through psychoanalytic therapy that problems arising from sexual development, especially the Oedipus complex, can be brought to light. There can be complications, of course, including the analysand's resistance to the uncovering of repressed material and the process of *transference*, in which the patient rearticulates the structure of neurotic symptoms in terms of the analytical situation itself. In transference, libidinal investments in a repressed object (which is known at first only in terms of its displacement onto dream images or symptoms) are transferred to the analyst himself, who is then in a position to draw out, through association, the latent wish or desire that is at the root of the original neurosis. As Freud put it in the famous case history of Dora, transferences are "new editions or facsimiles of the impulses and phantasies which are aroused and made conscious during the progress of the analysis; but they have this peculiarity, which is characteristic for their species, that they replace some earlier person by the person of the physician" (SE 7: 116). This potentially problematic interaction between analyst and analysand is, in a sense, the goal of the analytical process itself, the point at which the analysand can be led to recognize his own repressed desires and confront them at the level of consciousness. Once confronted, these desires are no longer repressed and can no longer interfere with mental or bodily health by manifesting themselves as injurious symptoms.

As he developed the theory of the ego, especially in such controversial later works as *Beyond the Pleasure Principle* and *The Ego and the Id*, Freud formulated a "structural" theory of the mind, one in which the ego, the super-ego, and the id signified certain kinds of relationships between conscious and unconscious elements of the ego. According to this structural model, significant portions of the ego are unknown; in a sense, then, the subject is internally split and displaced. Fundamentally linked to the structural theory of the ego is the theory of instincts or drives. In the earlier topographical model, there were two primary instincts: *sexual*, linked to fantasy, wish fulfillment, and the pleasure principle; and *ego*, linked to consciousness and the reality principle. The revised theory of instincts offered in *Beyond the Pleasure Principle* subsumes the ego and sexual instincts into a single sexual instinct towards self-preservation (*Eros*) and offers a new category, the death instinct (*Thanatos*), which is dedicated to the paradoxical quest of short-circuiting the sexual instinct and ending life. "[A]n instinct is an urge inherent in organic life to restore an earlier state of things which the living entity has been obliged to abandon under the pressure of external disturbing forces; that is, it is a kind of organic elasticity, or, to put it another way, the expression of the inertia inherent in organic life." The death instinct seeks to return to an original *inorganic* state: "the aim of all life is death" (SE 18: 36, 38). The pleasure principle, because it seeks the repetition of desires and wishes that could bring harm to the individual, appears to be in the service of the death instinct. Because instincts constitute the limit of what can be studied scientifically, the aim of Psychoanalysis is restricted to "demonstrating the connection along the path of instinctual activity between a person's external experiences and his reactions" (*SE* 11: 136).

Though his later work, especially *Civilization and Its Discontents* and *Moses and Monotheism*, was highly speculative and dealt with the origins of civilization and religion rather than individual psychology, Freud believed that Psychoanalysis was a science. But not everyone agreed on the importance of key concepts (especially the Oedipus and castration complexes). Almost as soon as it became a legitimate field of study within the medical establishment (that is, around the time of the First World War), Psychoanalysis experienced schisms and factional movements that reduced Freud's centralizing authority and made Psychoanalysis more varied, more popular, and more accessible. Carl Jung's break with Freud in 1913 was due mainly to their divergent views on sexuality and the unconscious; because it occurred early in the development of Psychoanalysis, Jung's own subsequent work in "analytical psychology" is not usually regarded as revisionist Freudianism. The more serious threat to Freud's theoretical hegemony came from ego psychologists, like his daughter Anna, and object relations theorists like D. W. Winnicott, Otto Rank, and Melanie Klein. Ego psychologists tend to focus on the dynamic qualities of the ego, rather than on the id and the unconscious, while object relations theorists reject the priority of the Oedipus complex and emphasize instead the mother–child relationship. Object relations theory has been particularly influential. Other theorists attempted to regain the whole ego through a purging of the divided self, especially in the "self psychology" of R. D. Laing and Heinz Kohut. **Jacques Lacan** was critical of some of these developments, especially ego psychology, which for him had become distracted by the "sociological poem of the 'autonomous ego'" (*Écrit* 162). For this and other reasons, he encouraged a "return to Freud," specifically to fundamental concepts like the Oedipus complex and the unconscious.

Lacan's revolutionary rethinking of the SUBJECT and the construction of SUBJECTIVITY began with his theory of the "mirror stage" of childhood development. He argued that children at a certain age think they see themselves as an entire being, fully present before themselves (as in a mirror), disconnected from the oceanic unity of the maternal body. However, the image children see is not a true image, it obscures the figure of the mother-as-prop (or prosthesis), so that the image becomes a fantasy of the self. The mirror stage is a *mise-en-scène* of misrecognition (*méconnaissance*) that inaugurates the IMAGINARY order, a narcissistic realm of fantasy and imagination. Ultimately, the child will ascend to the SYMBOLIC order where he opens himself to language and the discourse of the OTHER and is allowed to hear from the Other what he recognizes as his desire. This ascension entails a transition from *demand*, associated with the Imaginary, to *desire*, where "lack" supersedes the dissatisfaction following upon unmet demands. For Lacan, lack, and the economies and structures of desire that attempt to fulfill it, defines human subjectivity. He also posits an order of the REAL, a domain of primal needs and the unattainable materiality of experience (as opposed to Symbolic or Imaginary representations of it). The Real designates all that falls outside the precincts of the Symbolic and the Imaginary. It is not a "thing-in-itself" in the Kantian sense, but a domain of experience; its inaccessibility has nothing to do with its ideal nature but rather with the opposite: it is the realm of the *un*ideal, the raw materiality of things before they have gotten a name or a purpose. Lacan, in the seminar on Freudian technique, describes the Real as that which "resists symbolization absolutely. In the end, doesn't the feeling of the real reach its high point in the pressing manifestation of an unreal, hallucinatory reality?" (*Seminar* 66). Even Lacan's attempts at defining the Real slip into the Symbolic register. "Drawing a clear line between the real and the symbolic," writes **Slavoj Žižek**, "is a symbolic operation *par excellen ce*. . . . [W]hat Lacan calls 'the real' is nothing beyond the symbolic, it's merely *the inherent inconsistency of the symbolic order itself*" ("Postscript" 41).

Lacan's poststructuralist revision of Freud, influenced by Saussurean linguistics and Lévi-Strauss's structuralist anthropology, revealed that the unconscious functioned like a language. For Lacan, the "letter" of the unconscious, like Edgar Allan Poe's "purloined letter," is manifest rather than latent, always in plain sight. The constitution of the subject in language takes place along a path of signification: "only signifier-to-signifier correlations provide the standard for any and every search for signification" (*Écrits* 145). Because only the signifier, the letter, is available to us, the signified effectively disappears *beneath* the signifier (hence Lacan's algorithm, S/s, in which the signified rests beneath the Signifier). "The notion of an incessant sliding of the signified under the signifier thus comes to the fore" (*Écrits* 145). This "signifying structure," which Lacan also finds in the symptom, signals "the omnipresence for human beings of the symbolic function stamped on the flesh" (*Écrits* 119). The symbolic function is itself symbolized by the PHALLUS. For Freud, the phallus was significant primarily for the role it played in the Oedipus and castration complexes. Lacan recognizes this important role, so much so that he equates the concept of the phallus with the concept of the TRANSCENDENTAL SIGNIFIER of authority, rationality (*logos*), and power. The phallus is not a fantasy, nor an object, nor an organ: For it is the signifier that is destined to designate meaning effects as a whole, insofar as the signifier conditions them by its presences as signifier" (*Écrits* 275). JOUISSANCE offers the only possible escape from the symbolic function. According to Madan Sarup, *jouissance* creates a space in which "the human subject is confronted by the unconscious which is striving to express what is really forbidden to the speaking subject – *jouissance* and death" (99). *Jouissance* takes the subject outside of subjectivity and language, that is, outside the Symbolic order of the phallus. Or, perhaps more accurately, *jouissance* enables the illusion of this stepping outside of language, for as some theorists have argued, *jouissance* is merely an instance of the Imaginary misrecognizing the Symbolic for the Real.

The role of woman (or, as Lacan puts it in *Feminine Sexuality*, ~~Woman~~) is to constitute and verify men, to serve as the other (*petit a*; lower case o) through which man constitutes himself *in* the Other (the unconscious). Lacan argues that the "I" (*je*; I) speaks only in order to secure an answer that validates, in the Symbolic order, what the self (*moi*; me) imagines itself as being; it seeks to elicit messages from the Other (through, for example, woman-as-other [*petit a*]) that the "paranoid" *moi* (the Imaginary conception of the self) needs to hear in order to believe in his existence. "The Other is, therefore, the locus in which is constituted the I who speaks along with he who hears, what is said by the one being already the reply, the other deciding, in hearing [*entendre*] it, whether the one has spoken or not" (*Écrits* 133). ~~Woman~~ is a symptom, a screen for the projection of lack, but also a space of desire fulfilled, the space of the Other/other in which man finds his identity and being. "What constitutes the symptom – that something which dallies with the unconscious – is that one believes in it. . . . [I]n the life of a man, a woman is something he believes in. He believes there is one, or at times two or three, but the interesting thing is that, unable to believe only in one, he believes in a species, rather like sylphs or water-sprites" (*Feminine* 168).

Many Feminists, including Juliet Mitchell, **Julia Kristeva, Luce Iriga-ray**, and Jane Gallop, were strongly influenced by Lacan's writings on female sexuality. Of crucial importance for Lacanian or post-Lacanian feminists was a reconsideration of the Oedipus complex and the role of the mother in pre-genital phases of development and object relations. The general tendency away from the Oedipus complex, especially in Kristeva, signals a repudiation of patriarchy and PHALLOGOCENTRIC thought and a privileging of the maternal body. In "Stabat Mater," Kristeva asks "[i]f it is not possible to say of a *woman* what she *is* (without running the risk of abolishing her difference), would it perhaps be different concerning the *mother*, since that is the only function of the 'other sex' to which we can definitely attribute existence?" (*Tales* 234). The problem with this argument is that it confuses the distinction between real experience and fantasy formations based on it; even for feminists this confusion leads to the rejection of motherhood as a model for feminine identity. Irigaray points to one reason why women and women's bodies are "excluded by the nature of things," as Lacan claimed. If they are associated with the material ground of existence, the non-essential ESSENCE that grounds male subjectivity, they cannot reflect (for) themselves. This would make woman a mere "speculum" or mirror for the production of male subjectivity. Irigaray asks, "Is [woman] the indispensable condition whereby the living entity retains and maintains and perfects himself in his self-likeness?" (*Speculum* 165).

Gilles Deleuze and **Félix Guattari** have mounted a similar attack against the centrality of the Oedipus complex. In *Anti-Oedipus* Deleuze and Guattari argue that the "oedipalized subject" is an imperialized subject, the perfect victim of capitalist and fascist states. "The Oedipal triangle ["mommy, daddy and me"] is the personal and private territoriality that corresponds to all of capitalism's efforts at social RETERRITORIALIZATION. Oedipus was always the displaced limit for every social formation, since it is the displaced represented of desire" (*Anti-Oedipus* 266). In other words, the mechanisms of repression and conscience that are unleashed by the Oedipus complex are perfectly suited to those of capitalism: both destroy traditional structures and both create new pathways and economies of desire. The emphasis on desire as the expression of lack found in both Freud and Lacan distracts us from the true nature of desire, which is not to be located in the feelings or experiences of the "oedipalized subject" but rather in a circulating flow of "intensities."

Human desire is only one kind of "desiring machine" that springs up spontaneously and without centralization, all over the social body. "If desire produces, its product is real. If desire is productive, it can be productive only in the real world and can produce only reality. . . . Desire and its object are one and the same thing: the machine, as a machine of a machine. Desire is a machine, and the object of desire is another machine connected to it" (26). The schizophrenic is especially sensitive to this conception of desire, and for this reason Deleuze and Guattari use the "schizo" rather than the neurotic as the basis for their critique of Psychoanalysis and its complicity with capitalism.

More recent critical interventions are no less idiosyncratic than *Anti-Oedipus* and also no less influential. Of particular interest is the adaptation of Lacanian ideas in critical and social theory. A good example is the Lacanian concept *point de capiton*, which refers to the points or nodes that connect the subject to a signifying economy. In **Judith Butler's** formulation, it refers to the situation in which "an arbitrary sign not only appears essential to what it signifies, but actively organizes the thing under the sign itself" (Butler et al. 26). Ernesto Laclau elaborates on the concept in terms of "the contingent imposition of limits or partial fixations" (Butler et al. 66) and the usefulness of such limits in a critique of hegemonic formations, while **Žižek** notes that the shark in *Jaws* serves just such a function in organizing free-floating fear and anxiety. Žižek has famously applied Lacanian theory to everything from Kant to Hitchcock and has developed a unique perspective on European nationalism indebted to Lacan's theory of lack and the relation of lack to the Symbolic order. His study of Lacan and Hollywood, *Enjoy Your Symptom!* (1992), has had an invigorating effect on how film is interpreted, especially with reference to the Lacanian concepts of the "gaze," repetition, and the Other.

Note. For more on Lacan, see Poststructuralism; on Irigaray, see Feminism; on Deleuze and Guattari, see Postmodernism; on Butler, Žižek, and Laclau, see Postmodernism and Critical Theory.

WORKS CITED

Judith Butler, Ernesto Laclau, and Slavoj Žižek. *Contingency, Hegemony, Universality: Contemporary Dialogues on the Left*. London and New York: Verso, 2000.

Deleuze, Gilles and Félix Guattari, *Anti-Oedipus: Capitalism and Schizophrenia.* 1977. Trans. Robert Hurley, Mark Seem, and Helen R. Lane. Minneapolis: University of Minnesota Press, 1983.

Freud, Sigmund. *Standard Edition of the Complete Psychological Works of Sigmund Freud.* Ed. James Strachey. 24 vols. London: Hogarth, 1953–74.

Kristeva, Julia. *Tales of Love.* Trans. Leon S. Roudiez. New York: Columbia University Press, 1987.

Irigaray, Luce. *Speculum of the Other Woman.* Trans. Gilliam C. Gill. Ithaca: Cornell University Press, 1985.

Lacan, Jacques. *Écrits: A Selection.* Trans. Bruce Fink. New York: Norton, 2002.

——. *Feminine Sexuality,* by Jacques Lacan and the *École Freudienne.* Eds. Juliet Mitchell and Jacqueline Rose. New York: Norton, 1982.

——. *The Seminar of Jacques Lacan.* Ed. Jacques-Alain Miller. Vol. 1. Trans. John Forrester. Cambridge: Cambridge University Press, 1988.

Sarup, Madan. *Jacques Lacan.* New York and London: Harvester Wheatsheaf, 1992.

Žižek, Slavoj. "Postscript." Interview. In *A Critical Sense: Interviews with Intellectuals.* Ed. Peter Osborne. London: Routledge, 1996. 36–44.

Reader-Response Theory

Reader-Response theory encompasses an array of approaches to literary and cultural texts that focus on the role of the reader in the creation of meaning. The importance of the reader in literary theory has long been acknowledged, but the reader's role has typically been subordinated to the qualities of TEXTUALITY. In formalist theories, including the New Criticism, the reader's experience is guided by formal cues inherent in the text; it is essentially a passive mode of reading that involves the discovery of the text's internal dynamics and structural unities. However, there were some figures in that movement who did significant work with reader response. For example, I. A. Richard's experiments in reading in his *Practical Criticism* (1929) took an "affective" approach that measured emotional responses and attitudes. As Stanley Fish has pointed out in *Is There a Text in This Class?* (1980), this method tends to separate referential or scientific language from "poetic" language, analysis from emotion. We might also regard William Empson's work on ambiguity in poetry as implicitly a theory of reading, though attention to formal structures leaves him little room to explore the reader's role in interpreting ambiguity, other than his own role as a kind of "master reader." Reader-Response theory, by contrast, is interested in the formal aspects of literary texts only insofar as they illustrate the way readers frame interpretations. Indeed, the ambit of Reader-Response theory is anti-formalist and process oriented.

Contemporary Reader-Response theory developed out of the philosophical hermeneutics and phenomenology of the 1950s. Then, the key question was establishing the "horizon" of the reader's consciousness in relation to a text perceived as a type of consciousness. Georges Poulet argued that the act of reading is a process of opening oneself up to an "alien" consciousness. In the act of reading, "I am aware of a rational being, of a consciousness; the consciousness of another, no different from the one I automatically assume in every human being I encounter, except in this case the consciousness is open to me, welcomes me, lets me look deep inside itself" ("Phenomenology" 54). Reading breaks down the barrier between subject and object in part by transforming the text-as-object into another subject, one that occupies the reader's consciousness, existing simultaneously within it. "You are inside [the text]; it is inside you; there is no longer either outside or inside" (54). In Poulet's phenomenology of reading, it is not the author's consciousness that occupies the reader's mind as subject, though such things as biographical and bibliographical information are certainly important to the reader. What penetrates the reader's mind and exists within it as an "alien subject," what effectively "loans" the reader's SUBJECTIVITY to the text is the consciousness of the text itself: "the subject which presides over the work can exist only in the work" (58). The "I" spoken in the reader's mind is the "I" of the work. There is a peculiar substantial existence accorded to the work in this process, for the text, in the act of reading, becomes a quite literal subject which takes on, as the reader does, its own objects. (On phenomenology, see p. 79.)

Poulet's phenomenological approach was influential among critics in the 1960s and '70s who were combating the Formalism of the New Criticism, though, as **Wolfgang Iser** has noted, Poulet's "substantialist conception of the consciousness that constitutes itself in the literary work" (293) was ultimately rejected in favor of more pragmatic conceptions of the relationship between reader and work. Despite this rejection, however, new developments in Reader-Response theory posited a similar breakdown in the subject–object relationship that characterized traditional rhetorical and formalist theories of the reading experience. Indeed, these theories rarely spoke of a reading experience as such but rather of certain protocols, of predictable reactions on the part of readers when presented with specific kinds of rhetorical or formal structures. Vladimir Propp's theory of the folktale is exemplary in this regard, for it argues that the folktale is structured in such a way as to inspire certain reactions in the reader according to the disposition of the formal elements of the tale. In structural SEMIOTICS, this relationship is theorized in terms of the reader's or addressee's function with respect to specific codes. Reading is not arbitrary or subjective; meaning is not a function of the individual reader's emotional or intellectual disposition but rather of her competence with respect to the codes employed in a given text or discourse. More precisely, meaning is a function of the disposition of the codes themselves, of the relation and interrelation of formal elements within a text; the reader's role is to capture this meaning by mastering the codes. Obviously, the reader is important in formalist and semiotic theories, for without the reader meaning would remain latent (and partial) in the text. But the tendency in such theories to constitute the reader as the "addressee" signals a desire to define an "implied" reader who is a function of the text, a formal necessity quite separate from the equally necessary existence of "real" readers. Gerald Prince, in discussing the role of the "narratee" in Narrative Theory, makes this point explicitly: "The reader of fiction, be it in prose or in verse, should not be mistaken for the narratee. The one is real, the other fictive. If it should occur that the reader bears an astonishing resemblance to the narratee, this is an exception and not the rule" ("Narratee" 9).

Umberto Eco's semiotic theory of reading similarly conscripts a "fictional" reader as part of the text's structure; however, because it is influenced by poststructuralist theories of language and textuality, his theory overcomes to some degree the limits of formalist models of the reading process. Eco remains committed to a semiotic structure of sender and addressee but defines them in terms of their "actantial roles" in the sentence, "not as *sujet de l'énonciation*, but as *sujet de l'énoncé*" (10). His theory of the *open text* makes room for a more productive relation for the reader. According to Eco, the open text makes available possibilities within "a given *field of relations*." The result of such openness is not chaos but an "organizing rule which governs these relations." The reader's freedom inheres in the task of completing the text: "[T]he author offers the interpreter, the performer, the addressee a work *to be completed*." And while the author cannot know how the work will be completed, it "will still be his own. It will not be a different work" (62). The open text is a "semantico-pragmatic process" in which the Model Reader makes decisions that are in fact a "component of [the text's] structural strategy" (9). Unlike a *closed text*, which may invite a variety of "aberrant" readings but only insofar as they are read independently of each other, the open text exhibits a plurality of possible interpretations and intertextual relations that coexist within the same act of reading. This plurality is governed only by rules of enunciation that originate in the confluence of codes and languages within socio-historical contexts. **Roland Barthes'** provocative and influential essay, "The Death of the Author," draws the inevitable conclusion from such textualist theories of reading: "[T]he reader is the space on which all the quotations that make up a writing are inscribed without any of them being lost; a text's unity lies not in its origin but in its destination. . . . [T]he birth of the reader must be at the cost of the death of the Author" (148).

The most significant and influential advances in Reader-Response theory came in the work of Iser and **Stanley Fish**. For these theorists, reading is fundamentally a process in which the reader activates or completes a text. Iser's phenomenological study of the novel builds on the work of Roman Ingarden, especially his theory of "concretization" or "realization," the dynamic process by which the reader participates in the creation of a text's potential meanings: "The convergence of the text and the reader brings the literary work into existence" (275). Iser postulates the existence of *expectations* (what the phenomenologist Edmund Husserl called *pre-intentions*) whose unfulfillment constitutes the structure of the literary text. Unlike a didactic text (for example, a cookbook or a chemistry textbook), the literary text is filled with gaps and blockages, "unexpected twists and turns, and frustration of expectations" (279). For this reason, it is constitutively indeterminate and inexhaustible. This explains why the same text can accommodate a variety of different interpretations. The literary text is far more than what is written in it; and this "far more" comes into existence precisely as part of a creative process whereby the reader's own faculties are brought into being. The reader's desire for consistency comes up against the text's own recalcitrance, its tendency to allow "alien associations" to interrupt the smooth, consistent flow of reading. However, while the illusion of consistency is continually being shattered, the need for it persists, in large measure, Iser argues, because it is tied up with our desire to interpret the world: "The need to decipher gives us the chance to formulate our own deciphering capacity – i.e., we bring to the fore an element of our being of which we are not directly conscious" (294). In this way, the "'reality' of the reading experience illuminates basic patterns of real experience"; it confers upon the text what Iser calls a "dynamic lifelikeness" that "enables us to absorb an unfamiliar experience into our personal world" (281, 288).

For Iser, the reader is a concrete historical subject who discovers as much about herself as about the text she reads. Hans Robert Jauss's work on reception theory focuses on this aspect of the reading process. For Jauss and other thinkers associated with the University of Constance, reception is a complex interaction of reading protocols and a sociohistorical "horizon of expectations" that together determine the "gestalt" that Iser identifies as the dynamic TOTALITY of the literary text. Even more than Iser, Jauss emphasizes the resistances that readers present to the literary text, resistances that are in part the function of historical context and contestation.

Like Iser, Stanley Fish believed that the reader is instrumental in the construction of meaningful texts. The only way to maneuver within a "scene of reading" riddled by contradictions, ellipses, gaps, and other inconsistencies was to learn the interpretive protocols of a given community of readers. Fish's first major book, *Surprised by Sin* (1967), argued that John Milton, in *Paradise Lost*, creates a form of empathy between the reader and Satan that leads the reader to experience the fall of Adam and Eve. The reader is thus in a position to grasp the powerful moral and religious lessons that their "fortunate fall" has to offer. In later essays, collected in *Is There a Text in This Class?*, Fish explores the dangers of succumbing to the "affective fallacy" and constituting meaning solely on the basis of subjective response. For Fish, "a stylistic fact is a fact of response" (65). Moreover, there can be no point in separating poetic from non-poetic styles. In his theory of "affective stylistics," he underscores the anti-formalist orientation of Reader-Response theory and argues, against critics like I. A. Richards and Michael Riffaterre, that the distinction between poetic and non-poetic language, and the consequent privileging of the former, limits the interpretive potential of language and texts. (On Richards, see pp. 123–4.) Fish offers a powerful hedge against subjectivism with his argument that the "informed" reader's response is not arbitrary or random, that there are " 'regularizing' constraints on response." These constraints are produced by "the system of rules all speakers share" and by various forms of linguistic and semantic competence honed within "interpretative communities" (44–45).

Like Iser, Fish argues that the meaning derived from literary texts is the product of a "joint responsibility." Meaning is thus "redefined as an event rather than an entity": "[T]he reader's response is not *to* the meaning; it *is* the meaning" (3). The "informed reader" learns the appropriate reading responses by being a member of an interpretive community "made up of those who share interpretive strategies" that "exist prior to the act of reading and therefore determine the shape of what is read rather than, as is usually assumed, the other way around" (171). Disagreements hinge not on a UNIVERSAL notion of the truth about texts or their meanings but rather on the conditioned and relative truth of each community. Thus, there can be both agreement among readers of the same community and principled disagreement between communities. Literary texts are always interpreted within the context of protocols and norms. There can be no such thing as a subjective reading (in the radical sense of a reading that emerges from a single person's own experience), nor can there be a reading that is based solely on the "given" structures of language or text. The meanings generated by these communities "are *both* subjective and objective: they are subjective because they inhere in a particular point of view and are therefore not universal; and they are objective because the point of view that delivers them is public and conventional rather than individual and unique" (335–36).

One of the most controversial developments within Reader-Response theory is the emergence of an "ethics of reading." This trend suggests that reading emerges out of communities and, at the same time, forms the ethical principles of those communities. But it also suggests that reading is an ethical encounter with the other embodied in the text, an idea that emerges in large part in response to Emmanuel Lévinas's work on ethics. **J. Hillis Miller's** understanding of the ethics of reading, however, moves in a quite different direction. For him, ethics is not a question of action in the social or political spheres but rather a question of the fundamental nature of language. Ethics in his view *is prior to* action precisely because it is embedded in language. And because reading is made possible by language and because human beings are confronted constantly with the task of reading, it follows that our ethical sense is a function of language and reading. "[E]ach reading is, strictly speaking, ethical, in the sense that it *has* to take place, by an implacable necessity, as the response to a categorical demand, and in the sense that the reader *must* take responsibility for it and for its consequences in the personal, social, and political worlds" (59). The problem with this approach, as Vincent Leitch has observed, is that it ignores precisely the social, political, and cultural contexts that structure our ways of reading. Leitch points out that, for Miller, reading makes social acts possible, that "social and political moments" are "all secondary, belated, SUPPLEMENTARY: first there is language and its law; then there is misreading and its ethical consequences. Evidently, after these come social, psychological, and political matters. Surely, Miller does not believe all this" (50). Well, assuming that he does, it should come as no surprise, especially in view of Fish's theory of interpretive communities. Miller belongs to a specific reading community for which the ethics of reading takes on a certain dimension, while Leitch belongs to another, quite different community.

That they can have a principled disagreement over the way reading and ethics intersect is the desirable outcome of a pluralistic intellectual universe in which different points of view coexist in peaceful disagreement.

WORKS CITED

Barthes, Roland. "The Death of the Author." In *Image-Music-Text*. Trans. Stephen Heath. 1977. New York: Hill and Wang, 1977. 142–48.

Eco, Umberto. *The Role of the Reader: Explorations in the Semiotics of Texts.* Bloomington: Indiana University Press, 1984.

Fish, Stanley. *Is There a Text in This Class?: The Authority of Interpretive Communities.* Cambridge, MA: Harvard University Press, 1980.

Iser, Wolfgang. *The Implied Reader: Patterns of Communication in Prose Fiction from Bunyan to Beckett.* Baltimore: Johns Hopkins University Press, 1974.

Leitch, Vincent B. "Taboo and Critique: Literary Criticism and Ethics." *ADE Bulletin* 90 (Fall 1988): 46–52.

Miller, J. Hillis. *The Ethics of Reading: Kant, de Man, Eliot, Trollope, James and Benjamin.* New York: Columbia University Press, 1987.

Poulet, Georges. "Phenomenology of Reading." *New Literary History* 1.1 (1969): 53–68.

Prince, Gerald. "Introduction to the Study of the Narratee." In *Reader-Response Criticism: From Formalism to Post-Structuralism.* Ed. Jane Tompkins. Baltimore: The Johns Hopkins University Press, 1980. 7–25.

Structuralism and Formalism

Though Structuralism and Formalism are highly differentiated theoretical fields, they share a dedication to the structural linguistics of Ferdinand de Saussure, whose *Course in General Linguistics* (1916) outlined a theory of the sign that transformed not only linguistics, but nearly every branch of the humanities and the social sciences. To some degree the relation between Formalism and Structuralism is historical, for it is possible to discern a progression from formalist studies of language to structuralist studies of society and culture. Though structuralist and formalist thought has been criticized for its inflexibility, especially by those who take the Saussurean paradigm in a rigid and doctrinaire fashion, the notions of *form* and *structure* are actually quite elastic and capable of myriad formulations, including social and historical ones.

Eighteenth- and nineteenth-century linguistics had concentrated on the study of grammar and philology, which emphasized logic and historical development, while comparative linguistics focused on analogy and homology. Saussure believed that language was more complex. For him, "[l]anguage has an individual aspect and a social aspect. One is not conceivable without the other." Also, language "involves an established system and an evolution. At any given time it is an institution in the present and a product of the past" (9). Saussure differentiated language as such (*langage*), the human ability to communicate with signs, from language as a system (*langue*) and both of these from individual instances of speech (*parole*). His work is mainly concerned with the difference between *langue* and *parole*, a difference, he argues, that enables us to distinguish "what is social from what is individual and . . . what is essential from what is ancillary and more or less accidental." *Langue* constitutes a system separate from the individual, "the product passively registered" without "premeditation" and without any reflection (except, of course, that of the linguist) (13–14). Most important of all, *langue* is "a series of phonetic differences matched with a series of conceptual differences." The "function of language as an institution is precisely to maintain these series of differences in parallel" (118–19). By contrast, *parole* "is an individual act of the will and the intelligence" (14). It is also "the sum total of what people say," comprising "individual combinations of words" and "acts of phonation": it is merely "an aggregate of particular cases" (19).

For Saussure, the social element of language, indeed of all sign-making practices, constitutes the field of *semiology*, which he defined as "a science which studies the role of signs as part of social life" (15). Though the terms SEMIOLOGY and SEMIOTICS are often used interchangeably, there are some significant differences. *Semiotics* refers to the general science of signs pioneered in the 1880s by Charles Sanders Peirce; in Peircean semiotics the focus is on the sign as a mark of reference to or representation of an object. *Semiology* is the theory of linguistic sign systems that Saussure investigates and is less interested in reference than in DIFFERENCE. In Saussurean semiology, the SIGN does not designate a link between a word and an object. Rather, it is a complex unity of a *concept* in the mind and a *sound pattern* that corresponds with it. The latter is not simply the vocalization of the concept. "A sound pattern is the hearer's psychological impression of a sound, as given to him by the evidence of his senses" (66). Saussure calls the sound pattern a *signal* (or SIGNIFIER) and the concept a *signification* (or SIGNIFIED), reserving the term *sign* for the combination of the two. Saussure has famously noted that the linguistic sign is arbitrary "in relation to its signification, with which it has no natural connexion in reality" (69). This is not to say that it is unfixed or free-floating or that the link between signal and signification is the "free choice" of the individual speaker, for "the individual has no power to alter a sign in any respect once it has become established in a linguistic community" (68). What can be said of the individual can also be said of the community, for the "complex mechanism" of a language prevents the community from changing it. By the same token, the fact that language is "something in which everyone participates all the time" means that "it is open to the influence of all." It is finally the community's "natural inertia" that guarantees a conservative influence and makes it impossible for a "linguistic revolution" to take place (73–4). From this conservative principle of language a second principle follows, that the signifier itself has a temporal aspect and produces a diachronic signifying chain. DIACHRONY refers to the linear and sequential relation of words in an utterance, while SYNCHRONY refers to a systematic whole existing at a given time. The combinations derived from relations of sequential interdependence Saussure called SYNTAGMATIC ("[a]lmost all linguistic units depend either on what precedes or follows in the spoken sequence"

[126]), while the relations within the system as a whole he called PARA-
DIGMATIC (i.e., "flexional paradigms" [133], the system of inflections,
declensions, synonyms, and so on that are both inferred and displaced
by words in syntagmatic combinations). This picture of language as at
once systematic and individual – existing as a whole entity of relations
but also as linear and sequential differences – revolutionized linguistics
and became the basis for structuralist theories of semiotics, anthropology, psychoanalysis, narrative, and a host of other fields.

The first to apply Saussure's ideas about language were the Russian
Formalists, especially Roman Jakobson, Boris Eichenbaum, Viktor
Shklovsky, and others associated with the Moscow Linguistic Circle.
Jakobson outlined the stages of formalist research: "(1) analysis of the
sound aspects of a literary work; (2) problems of meaning within the
framework of poetics; (3) integration of sound and meaning into an
inseparable whole" ("Dominant" 82). The formalist study of poetics
exists within the more general study of language, which Jakobson characterized in terms of its functions. The chief elements of this functional
system are the *addresser* (*emotive* function) and *addressee* (*conative* function); falling in between are a complex set of determinants that include
context (*referential* function), *message, contact* (*phatic* function: "a physical
channel and psychological connection between the addresser and
addressee"), and a *code* (*metalingual* function) known to both addresser
and addressee ("Closing Statement" 353–57). Jakobson emphasized the
poetic function of language, the "focus on the message for its own sake."
However, it is an oversimplification to reduce poetry to a poetic function.
"Poetic function is not the sole function of verbal art but only its dominant, determining function, whereas in all other verbal activities it acts
as a subsidiary, accessory constituent" ("Closing Statement" 356). Jakobson defines the *dominant* as the "focusing component of a work of art,"
which can include such things as rhyme, syllabic scheme, or metrical
structure; it "guarantees the integrity of the structure" ("Dominant" 82).
His distinction between *metaphoric* and *metonymic* poles of language
evolved out of Saussure's theory of synchronic (or paradigmatic) and diachronic (or syntagmatic) aspects of language systems and his own work
with aphasia. In the latter, he discovered two axes or levels of meaning
upon which poetry draws: the metaphoric and selective (or substitutive),
which operates synchronically, and the metonymic and combinative,
which operates diachronically. "The poetic function projects the

principle of equivalence from the axis of selection into the axis of combination" ("Closing Statement" 358). By this Jakobson means that in poetry, selections made on the level of metaphor are "superinduced" onto the level of metonymy where they are combined with other words to create poetic effects. Thus, if I write "my daughter blossoms," I am substituting "blossom" for a similar concept (grows, develops) and then combining it with "daughter" to suggest a flower-like opening up of young beauty. This form of projection "imparts to poetry its thoroughgoing symbolic, multiplex, polysemantic essence" ("Closing Statement" 370). Though the poetic function tends to draw out the latent metonymic quality of metaphor (and vice versa), the metaphoric pole tends to characterize poetry of a certain kind (e.g., Romantic and symbolist trends), while metonymy tends to characterize realistic forms (*Fundamentals* 90ff).

Viktor Shklovsky's work on prose as a formal device mirrors some of the innovations offered by Jakobson, his friend and colleague. His *Theory of Prose* (1925), which offered a systematic account of the way prose functioned, was to have a profound effect not only on Formalism but on the theory of the novel. Shklovsky held that the artistic work of art is autonomous, free from contingent social forces, and that prose is essentially *form* driven by artistic "devices." Though he believed in the AUTONOMY of art, he thought that the art work exhibited something of the struggle against social "automatization," which breeds alienation and fear. One way of combating alienation is "defamiliarization" (*ostranenie*, or estrangement), an artistic "device" that calls into question the alienating effect of things most familiar to us and indeed raises the question whether reality is not itself purely an effect. Another device that defamiliarizes the objects of representation is the "laying bare" of the author's techniques. Shklovsky's famous example is Laurence Sterne's *Tristram Shandy*, a novel that self-consciously addresses the reader and exposes the devices by which the author creates his effects.

Though not often regarded today as a formalist, **M. M. Bakhtin** was an influential figure in the Russian formalist movement. His *Problems of Dostoevsky's Poetics* (1929), and the materialist Formalism that it showcases, was well regarded and his own Circle flourished in Belarus and Leningrad throughout the 1920s. His essays of the 1930s and '40s, published in 1981 under the title *Dialogic Imagination*, went well beyond the limits of Formalism and postulated a new vocabulary for novelistic narrative. The convergence in his work of structural linguistics, poetics, and ideology critique challenged formalist assumptions about the autonomy of the work of the art. His interest in language was attuned to the subtle shifts and differences between dialects, jargons, and so-called standard speech as they were used in narrative representations of daily life. He was particularly interested in the *polyphony* that he discerned in novelists like Dickens and Dostoevsky: "A plurality of independent and unmerged voices and consciousnesses" (*Problems* 6). For Bakhtin, the object of formalist analysis is to identify the plurality of "authoritative ideological positions" (*Problems* 18) represented in the novel through narration (especially *skaz* or the oral idiom of the narrator), dialogue, parody, and other strategies. Bakhtin is not interested in language in the abstract, formal sense studied by linguists but rather in DISCOURSE, language understood "in its concrete living totality" (*Problems* 181). Like others in the Bakhtin Circle in the 1920s, Bakhtin was interested in the political ramifications of language and discourse; if he can properly be called a formalist, he is a *materialist* formalist, interested in the way material conditions, typically mediated by language, affect the perception and representation of forms. V. N. Voloshinov, for example, insisted that "[e]very sign is subject to the criteria of ideological evaluation (i.e., whether it is true, false, correct, fair, good, etc.). The domain of ideology coincides with the domain of signs. . . . *Everything ideological possesses semiotic value*" (*Marxism* 10). This perspective on the function of the sign accords with Bakhtinian DIALOGISM, the dynamic totality of linguistic possibilities that conditions individual utterances. For Bakhtin, discourse has a dialogic and "double-voiced" character, which lies outside the scope of conventional Marxist and formalist analysis. Double-voiced discourse is orientated in two different directions: to the "referential object of speech" and to *"another's discourse,* toward *someone else's speech"* (*Problems* 185). Bakhtin described two predominant forms of double-voiced discourse: *stylization,* in which another's discourse is appropriated to serve new ends, and *parody,* in which a similar appropriation takes place: "but, in contrast to stylization parody introduces into that discourse a semantic intention that is directly opposed to the original one" (*Problems* 193). The study of language must be conducted within its dialogic context "where discourse lives an authentic life" (*Problems* 202). Baktin's term for this context is DIALOGIZED HETEROGLOSSIA, "[t]he authentic environment of an utterance, the environment in which it lives and takes shape" (*Dialogic* 272). This environment is characterized by multiple and overlapping historical, cultural, and geographical "ideolects" that stratify and HYBRIDIZE linguistic expression.

Bakhtin's theories of language and discourse introduced an element of socio-historical embeddedness and pluralism that was missing from Formalism. Similar qualities can be found in the *functional structuralism* of the Prague Linguistic Circle, which was influenced by Jakobson, one of the founding members and vice-chairman. Functional structuralism, unlike Formalism, is primarily concerned with language as it is manifested in social contexts. It moves beyond the positivist orientation of Formalism, with its reliance on linguistic concepts and methodologies, and emphasizes instead a semiotics of social codes. "The semiotic concept of the literary work," writes Peter Steiner, "rendered it a social fact (i.e., a sign understood by the members of a given collectivity) and enabled the structuralists to relate the developmental changes in literary history to all other aspects of human culture." Steiner also points to the movement in Prague structuralism from poetics to aesthetics, a shift "from a concern with verbal art alone to a concern with all the arts and with extra-artistic esthetics as well" (177). This shift underscored the difference between the two movements with regard to the norms and values attached to language. For the formalist, all that matters are the facts of language, while for the structuralist "function (as crucial a concept as that of the sign) was inseparable from norms and values" (204).

The shift in emphasis among many European intellectuals from Formalism to Structuralism paved the way for structuralist approaches across the human and social sciences. Claude Lévi-Strauss, in his groundbreaking *Structural Anthropology* (1958), sums up the principles of structural linguistics: "First structural linguistics shifts from the study of *conscious* linguistic phenomena to study of their *unconscious* infrastructure; second, it does not treat *terms* as independent entities, taking instead as its basis of analysis the *relations* between terms; third, it introduces the concept of *system* . . . ; finally, structural linguistics aims at discovering *general laws*, either by induction 'or . . . by logical deduction, which would give them an absolute character'" (33; Lévi-Strauss quotes Nikolai Trubetzkoi). More than any other theorist, Lévi-Strauss demonstrated how structural linguistics could play a "renovating role" in the humanities and social sciences by providing a principled scientific method of analyzing literary and cultural texts. For, Lévi-Strauss, structure is "a model meeting with several requirements": first, it exhibits the characteristics of a system" in which no single element "can undergo a change without effecting changes in all the other elements." Second, "for any given model there should be a possibility of ordering a series of transformations resulting in a group of models of the same type." Third, "the above properties make it possible to predict how the model will react if one or more of its elements are submitted to certain modifications." Fourth, "the model should be constituted so as to make immediately intelligible all the observed facts" (279). Lévi-Strauss's study of kinship systems and mythology illuminates the specific ways that Structuralism can be applied to symbolic social systems. Using Structuralism in this way underscores one of Saussure's primary precepts, that context and precedence determine powerfully the place of the linguistic sign within a system. "The arbitrary character of the linguistic sign is thus only provisional," writes Lévi-Strauss. "Once a SIGN has been created its function becomes explicit, as related, on the one hand, to the biological structure of the brain and, on the other, to the aggregate of other signs – that is, to the linguistic universe, which always tends to be systematic" (94). Structuralism is especially useful in studying mythology, where meaning inheres not in isolated elements but in the way they are combined. The structure of myth is the organization of *mythemes*, the "gross constituent units" that make up the whole myth and that correspond to the phonemes, morphemes, and sememes found in linguistics. Unlike these linguistic units, however, which operate on the level of the word or the sound, mythemes operate on the level of the sentence. To understand the structure of a myth, the critic must "break[] down its story into the shortest possible sentences" (211) and then determine the function of each sentence and its relation to other sentences. Though myths function like languages, the language of myth "exhibits specific properties" and belongs to a "higher and more complex order" (210–11).

Lévi-Strauss's work had a profound effect on intellectual trends in the 1960s, especially in France. It stands behind such diverse developments as **Louis Althusser's** structuralist Marxism, **Jacque Lacan's** structuralist psychoanalysis, and Northrop Frye's rhetorical Formalism. One of the most prominent structuralists, certainly the most influential for literary theory, was **Roland Barthes**. Barthes' first major work, *Mythologies* (1957), approached cultural myths from a semiological perspective in which myth is regarded as a form of semiology, that "postulates a relation between two terms, a signifier and a signified" (*Mythologies* 111–12).

The message of myth lies in the significance of formal signifying relations. Barthes confesses to being impatient "at the sight of the 'naturalness' with which newspapers, art and common sense constantly dress up a reality which, even though it is the one we live in, is undoubtedly determined by history" (*Mythologies* 11). His provocative analyses of magazine covers, Latin grammar, detergent, toys, ornamental cookery, Gretta Garbo, plastic, and a variety of other "everyday" objects and themes reveal both the historical determinants of myths and the historical meanings generated by them. Both determination and meaning are made possible by the way the signifier functions in linguistic and mythic systems. A mythic signifier is formed by appropriating the linguistic SIGN (the unit composed of the SIGNIFIER and SIGNIFIED) and using it as a signifier for an entirely new signified. The original meaning of the linguistic sign, a meaning derived from historical embeddedness as well as from linguistic structure, undergoes a dialectical process of *deformation* when it is appropriated for mythic signification. The meaning of the linguistic sign is emptied of its history in order to provide a shallow, easily-filled form (a Latin sentence, a "Negro" soldier saluting on the cover of *Paris-Match*). This new form will in its turn be given new content, in the form of concepts that carry within them the kind of social and historical charge that had been leached out of the original sign: "this history which drains out of the form will be wholly absorbed by the concept. . . . Unlike the form, the concept is in no way abstract: it is filled with a situation. Through the concept, it is a whole new history which is implanted in the myth" (*Mythologies* 119). And while the creation of the mythic concept entails distortion of the original linguistic function, "this distortion is not an obliteration": "The concept, literally, deforms, but does not abolish the meaning; a word can perfectly render this contradiction: it alienates it" (*Mythologies* 122–23).

Though structural linguistics played a leading role in the development of semiology and semiotics, the latter are concerned with more than just language, as we have seen in Barthes' *Mythologies*. Indeed, semiotics in the 1960s and '70s was undergoing a transformation in the work of Umberto Eco, **Julia Kristeva**, and A. J. Greimas who redefined the object of semiotic analysis and, in the process, developed new semiotic systems. These developments pushed the field closer to structural linguistics and structuralist narratology. For example, Greimas developed a theory of *structural semantics* that emphasized the role of narrative in analysis. Every text contains a discursive level of *enunciation* (or *énon-ciation*) and a narrative level of *utterance* (or *énoncé*). (On these terms, see pp. 158–9, 176.) These correspond to the Saussurean terms *langue* and *parole*. Greimas and Joseph Courtés posit a deep level of narrative func-tioning which they call "narrativity": "the very organizing principle of all discourse, whether narrative (identified, in the first instance, as figu-rative discourse) or non-narrative" (209). Structuralist narratologists like Gerard Genette and, later, Gerald Prince, made similar claims about language and "narrativity." In his "Introduction to the Structural Analy-sis of Narrative" (1966), which was influential in the development of narratology, Barthes investigates the "functional syntax" of narrative structures, using a James Bond film to illustrate his points. Echoing Lévi-Strauss's theory of myths, he argues that narrative is structured like a sentence and that the relations between the various parts of a narrative have a syntactical form and value. "Structurally, narrative shares the characteristics of the sentence without ever being reducible to the simple sum of its sentences: a narrative is a long sentence, just as every consta-tive sentence is in a way the rough outline of a short narrative" (*Image* 84). Narrative discourse functions on three levels: on one level, narrative units are organized and distributed; on another, character functions as an index within a sequence; on still another, narration and reading take place. "These three levels are bound together according to a mode of progressive integration" (*Image* 88).

Though Barthes' structuralist theories are highly complex and employ a technical vocabulary, he does not commit the formalist mistake of ignoring context. Indeed, the structuralist emphasis on systems is, inevi-tably, an emphasis on systems *in the world*. Lévi-Strauss's structuralist anthropology is grounded on this fact, and Barthes' Structuralism is always aware of its historical moment: "Structuralism does not with-draw history from the world" (*Critical Essays* 219). The fact that narrative does not function MIMETICALLY – nothing takes place "from the referen-tial (reality) point of view" (*Image* 124) – does not mean that it does not acknowledge and make use of reality. When Barthes claims that "[i]t may be that men ceaselessly re-inject into narrative what they have known, what they have experienced" (*Image* 124), he reaffirms one of Saussure's principal points about language: that it is historically embedded. "Language," Saussure reminds us, "has an individual aspect and a social aspect. One is not conceivable without the other" (9).

Contrary to popular misconceptions, structuralism does not believe in an otherworldly realm of pure structure, but rather in the tendency of systems (natural and social) to exhibit structural relations. Structuralism is the study of these relations and the knowledge that they afford of the system itself. It is always the study of human being(s) in the world.

Note. For more on Propp, Barthes, and structuralist narratology, see Narrative Theory; on Kristeva, Eco, and semiotics, see Poststructuralism; on Althusser, see Marxist Theory; on Lacan, see Psychoanalysis and Poststructuralism.

WORKS CITED

Bakhtin, M. M. *Problems of Dostoevsky's Poetics.* Ed. and trans. Caryl Emerson. Minneapolis: University of Minnesota Press, 1984.

Barthes, Roland. *Critical Essays.* Trans. Richard Howard. Evanston: Northwestern University Press, 1972.

——. *Image-Music-Text.* Trans. Stephen Heath. New York: Hill and Wang, 1977.

——. *Mythologies.* 1957. Selected and Trans. Annette Lavers. New York: Hill and Wang, 1972.

Greimas, A. J. and J. Courtés. *Semiotics and Language: An Analytical Dictionary.* Bloomington: Indiana University, 1982.

Jakobson, Roman. "Dominant." In *Readings in Russian Poetics.* Eds. Ladislav Matejka, and Krystyna Pomorska. Ann Arbor: Michigan Slavic Publications, 1978. 82–7.

——. "Closing Statement: Linguistics and Poetics." In *Style in Language.* Ed. Thomas A. Sebeok. Cambridge, MA: MIT Press, 1960. 350–77.

—— and Morris Halle. *Fundamentals of Language.* 1956. 4th ed. The Hague: Mouton, 1980.

Lévi-Strauss, Claude. *Structural Anthropology.* Trans. Claire Jacobson and Brooke Grundfest Schoepf. New York: Basic Books, 1963.

Saussure, Ferdinand de. *Course in General Linguistics.* Ed. Charles Bally and Albert Sechehaye. Trans. Wade Baskin. New York: McGraw-Hill, 1966.

Steiner, Peter, ed. *The Prague School: Selected Writings, 1929–1946.* Trans. John Burbank, Olga Hasty, Manfred Jacobson, Bruce Kochis, and Wendy Steiner. Austin: University of Texas Press, 1982.

Voloshinov, V. N. *Marxism and the Philosophy of Language.* Trans. Ladislav Matejka and I. R. Titunik. New York: Seminar Press, 1973.

KEY FIGURES IN LITERARY THEORY

A shudder in the loins engenders there
The broken wall, the burning roof and tower
And Agamemnon dead.
W. B. Yeats, "Leda and the Swan"

Theodor Adorno (1903–69)

Theodor Adorno was born Theodor Ludwig Wiesengrund in Frankfurt, Germany, later taking on his mother's maiden name. His father was a Jewish convert to Protestantism and his mother a Catholic, though it would be his Jewish background that would prove influential in later life. He was a highly gifted student, studying Kant and Husserl at an early age. He attended the University of Frankfurt, where he received the doctorate in philosophy in 1924. He was also a musician and composer. In the mid-1920s, he traveled to Vienna, where he studied with the composer Alban Berg and became a devotee of Arnold Schoenberg, the great Modernist composer whose work had influenced Berg and, according to some critics, inspired some of the innovations in Adorno's philosophy.

Adorno began his academic career with a dissertation on the Danish philosopher Søren Kierkegaard, published in 1933. At this time, he was attached to the Institute for Social Research, which had been established ten years earlier. However, the Institute's work was disrupted by the rise to power of Hitler's National Socialist movement. Like so many other Jewish intellectuals at this time, Adorno went into exile, first at Oxford, later in the US. He was affiliated with Princeton University in the period 1938–41, then followed the Institute to Geneva and New York and finally to Los Angeles, where he became co-director with Max Horkheimer.

His first major publication, with Horkheimer, was *Dialectic of Enlightenment* (1944), a penetrating critique of the Enlightenment tradition of philosophy and literature and its consequences for contemporary culture, including the rise of the "culture industry," totalitarianism, and the commodification of art and AESTHETICS under capitalism. In 1958, he became the director of the Institute, and the ten years that followed, until his death in 1969, were the most productive of his career. In this period, he wrote his most important philosophical works, including *Negative Dialectics* (1966), *Minima Moralia* (1966), and *Aesthetic Theory* (1970). In these works, Adorno critiqued the German idealist tradition from Kant to Heidegger and offered a powerful new alternative to it, one that resisted ideological pressures and confronted the practical consequences that follow, or ought to follow, from the study of philosophy and critical theory. This confluence of theory and practice was made evident in 1969, when students influenced by him became involved in violent protest on the Frankfurt University campus against government emergency laws. During this tumultuous time, while vacationing in Switzerland, Adorno died of a heart attack after mountain climbing.

SELECTED BIBLIOGRAPHY

Adorno, Theodor. *The Adorno Reader*. Ed. Brian O'Connor. Oxford and Malden MA: Blackwell Publishers, 2000.

——. *Aesthetic Theory*. Ed. Gretel Adorno and Rolf Tiedemann and trans. Robert Hullot-Kentor. Minneapolis: University of Minnesota Press, 1997.

——. (with Max Horkheimer). *The Dialectic of Enlightenment*. Trans. John Cumming. New York: Herder and Herder, 1972.

——. *Minima Moralia: Reflections from Damaged Life*. Trans. E.F.N. Jephcott. London: Verso, 1974.

——. *Negative Dialectics*. Trans. E.B. Ashton. New York: Seabury Press, 1973.

——. *Prisms*. Trans. Samuel and Shierry Weber. Cambridge, MA: MIT Press, 1981.

Louis Althusser (1918–90)

Louis Althusser was born in Algeria and studied at the École Normale Supérieure in Paris. During the Second World War, he was involved in Catholic youth groups and became radicalized during the Nazi occupation of France. After a short time spent in a German concentration camp for his activities on behalf of the French Communist Party, he took his degree in 1948 and began teaching at the École, where he remained until 1980. One of his students in the early years of his tenure at the École was Michel Foucault, who was inspired by (if not converted to) Marxism under Althusser's tutelage. Althusser's form of "structuralist Marxism" was very much a product of the intellectual environment of France in the 1950s and early '60s. Rejecting the humanism of so much Marxist theory, but not its empiricism, Althusser insisted on the importance of IDEOLOGY and ideology critique. In *For Marx* (1965), he revised the idea of dialectical contradiction, stressing the condition of OVERDETERMINA-TION, an intensification of class contradictions at moments of social and economic crisis that leads to either "historical inhibition" or "revolutionary rupture." With Etienne Balibar, Althusser wrote *Reading "Capital"* (1968), a critique of classical economics and a close analysis of Marx's political economy. In this work, Althusser and Balibar reject the theory that Marxism is a species of historicism and put forward a scientific theory of Marx's thought.

The attempt to transform Marxism into a more rigorous science dedicated to the structuralist analysis of ideology is continued in Althusser's most famous and most influential work, the collection of essays, *Lenin and Philosophy* (1971). In "Ideology and Ideological State Apparatuses," Althusser argues that ideology "interpellates" or conscripts SUBJECTS into ideological discourses. Subjects are subjects precisely because of this interpellation. Also in *Lenin and Philosophy*, Althusser reflects on the importance of Freudian and Lacanian Psychoanalysis for a Marxist analysis of capitalism. Althusser continued to publish essays throughout the 1970s, but met with an infamous end to his career in 1980. In that year, Althusser murdered his wife and, after confessing to the crime, was committed to a psychiatric hospital where he spent the last ten years of his life. He told the story of the murder in his memoirs, *The Future Lasts a Long Time*.

SELECTED BIBLIOGRAPHY

Althusser, Louis. *Althusser: A Critical Reader*. Ed. Gregory Elliott. Oxford and Cambridge, MA: Blackwell Publishers, 1994.

——. *For Marx*. Trans. Ben Brewster. New York: Pantheon, 1969.

——. *Lenin and Philosophy, and Other Essays*. Trans. Ben Brewster. London: New Left Books, 1971.

—— and Etienne Balibar. *Reading "Capital."* Trans. Ben Brewster. 1968. London, NLB, 1970.

Mikhail Mikhailovich Bakhtin (1895–1975)

Mikhail Mikhailovich Bakhtin was born in Orel, Russia, and was educated at the University of St. Petersburg. In 1918, he left St. Petersburg, at the height of the Revolution, and settled in Vitebsk, where he worked as a school teacher. He also became the leading figure in the Bakhtin Circle, whose members combined formalist methods with ideological critique in the study of language, discourse, aesthetics, and literature. The writings of key members of this group, including P. N. Medvedev and V. N. Voloshinov, were once considered by scholars to have been written by Bakhtin, but the consensus now is that Medvedev and Voloshinov were responsible for the texts that bear their names. In 1924, Bakhtin moved to Leningrad, where he had difficulties finding employment due to his lack of enthusiasm for Marxism. By 1929, he had the misfortune of drawing the attention of Stalin's regime which, in those early years, conducted regular purges of intellectuals. He was accused of associating with the underground Orthodox Church, a charge that has never been substantiated or dismissed, and sentenced to internal exile, first in Kazakhstan (1930–36), where he worked on a collective farm, later in Mordovia (1937–69), where he taught at the Mordov Pedagogical Institute in Saransk. Throughout these years, Bakhtin suffered from poor health and in 1938 had to have one of his legs amputated.

In Leningrad, in the years before his exile, Bakhtin produced his first important work, *The Problems of Dostoevsky's Poetics* (1929), which explored the structures of novelistic prose and introduced the concept of DIALOGISM. In the 1930s and '40s, Bakhtin introduced two seminal concepts: HETEROGLOSSIA, a discourse "environment" characterized by polyphony, by multiple languages, dialects, jargons, and other discursive forms; and the CARNIVALESQUE, a mode of subversive representation based on the inversion of hierarchies. Also during this time, he began studying the *Bildungsroman*, but most of this work was destroyed when his publisher's premises was bombed by the Germans. Due to a shortage of cigarette paper, Bakhtin was forced to use the pages of the prospectus to roll cigarettes. Fragments of the work were published in *Speech Acts and Other Late Essays* (1979).

After Stalin's death in 1953, Bakhtin's work attracted more notice by scholars and by the late 1950s he was a well-known and respected figure among the Soviet intellectual elite as well as among European circles familiar with Russian Formalism. Though grounded in formalist thought, Bakhtin was primarily interested in the material implications of language and literature on social discourses. His was a *materialist* Formalism. In 1973, the essays on the novel written in the 1930s were published, and they solidified his reputation in the Soviet Union. Lionized and widely influential, Bakhtin died in 1975. These essays, translated into English as *The Dialogic Imagination* (1981), are Bakhtin's most important contribution to Poststructuralism and the theory of the novel.

SELECTED BIBLIOGRAPHY

Bakhtin, M. M. *The Dialogic Imagination.* Ed. Michael Holquist; Trans. Caryl Emerson and Michael Holquist. Austin: University of Austin Press, 1981.

——. *Problems of Dostoevsky's Poetics.* Trans. Caryl Emerson. Minneapolis: University of Minnesota Press, 1984.

——. *Rabelais and His World.* Trans. Hélène Iswolsky. Cambridge: The M.I.T. Press, 1968.

Roland Barthes (1915–80)

Roland Barthes was born in Cherbourg, northern France, but after his father's death in the First World War, his mother relocated to Bayonne. In 1924, the family moved to Paris, where Barthes studied classics, grammar, and philology at the Sorbonne University in Paris, receiving degrees in 1939 and 1943. In the mid-1930s and again in the 1940s, he spent time in sanatoriums suffering from tuberculosis. He taught at a number of lycées in Biarritz, Bayonne, and Paris, and, in the late 1940s, at the French Institute in Bucharest and the University of Alexandria in

Egypt. In the 1950s, he worked for the Direction Générale des Affaires Culturelles and held a research post with the Centre National de la Recherche Scientifique. His most important academic appointment was the director of studies at École Practique des Hautes Études (1960–76). He was a visiting professor at Johns Hopkins University (1967–68) and in the last four years of his life he chaired the department of literary semiology at the Collège de France.

Barthes' career traversed one of the most important literary epochs of the twentieth century. His work of his early period emphasized SEMIOLOGY and structural linguistics. *Writing Degree Zero* (1953) introduced the concepts of *écriture*, the "written" quality of language, while *Elements of Semiology* (1964) and *S/Z* (1970) focused on the structuralist analysis of literary texts. Barthes' unique mode of structuralist analysis was applied to a host of texts, including works by the Marquis de Sade and St. Ignatius of Loyola. In *Mythologies* (1958), he applied structuralist and semiological methods to a wide array of non-literary cultural texts, from wrestling and food to fashion and striptease. In 1966, he published the groundbreaking essay, "Introduction to the Structural Analysis of Narrative." In this essay, he used a sophisticated structuralist methodology to analyze the way narrative texts (literary and cinematic) function. Though grounded in structuralism and semiology, Barthes' work frequently challenged the limits of these fields. His most celebrated essay, "The Death of the Author" (1968), announced that the reader, the "modern scriptor," had overturned the traditional authority of author. In works like *The Pleasure of the Text* (1973), he transcended the limitations of structuralism and became a pioneer of Poststructuralism. Contrasting texts of *pleasure* (which conform to readers' expectations) with texts of *bliss* (which challenge or overturn these expectations), Barthes formulated a theory of textual eroticism, an attempt to explain how desire operates within language and dictates the way texts are written and read. His later essays continued this new trend in poststructuralist analysis. His last work, *Camera Lucinda* (1980), explored the communicative potential of photography, bringing to bear on that medium his unique brand of poststructuralist semiology. In that same year, Barthes was killed in a street accident in Paris. In a posthumously published memoir, *Incidents* (1983), Barthes told the story of a life filled with intellectual and sexual passions.

SELECTED BIBLIOGRAPHY

Barthes, Roland. *A Barthes Reader.* Ed. Susan Sontag. New York: Hill and Wang, 1982.

——. *Image-Music-Text.* Trans. Stephen Heath. New York: Hill and Wang, 1977.

——. *Mythologies.* Selected and trans. Annette Lavers. New York: Hill and Wang, 1972.

——. *The Pleasure of the Text.* Trans. Richard Miller. New York: Hill and Wang, 1975.

——. *Writing Degree Zero* and *Elements of Semiology.* Trans. Annette Lavers and Colin Smith. New York: Hill and Wang, 1968.

Jean Baudrillard (1929–)

Jean Baudrillard was born in Reims, France, and studied German at the Sorbonne University in Paris. He went on to teach German at the lycée level (1958–66) and later worked as a translator and critic while writing his doctoral dissertation, "The System of Objects," which he published in 1968. Until 1987, he taught at the University of Paris X (Nanterre) at various levels. He then served as scientific director at the Institut de Recherche et d'Information Socio-Économique at the University of Paris IX (Dauphine). Since 2001, he has been associated with the European Graduate School in Saas-Fee, Switzerland.

Baudrillard's work emerges at the intersection of SEMIOLOGY and the post-Marxism of the French avant-garde. His first major work, *The System of Objects*, with its emphasis on collecting, advertising, and consumption, argues that objects structure social life by signifying status and position within a general system of objectified relations. Important works of this period include *For a Critique of the Political Economy of the Sign* (1972) and *The Mirror of Production* (1973). The former develops a system of semiology that corresponds to categories of value: use value, exchange value, symbolic value, and sign value. The latter critiques the

Marxist conception of production and argues that radical politics must move beyond the conception of the worker as a "production machine"; it acknowledges the advent of a social system driven not by political economy but by signifying economies. In later works like *Simulations* (1981), which gained him academic acclaim and a certain degree of celebrity, Baudrillard defined Postmodern signifying economies in terms of "hyperreality" in which SIMULATIONS of the real displace reality. His most famous example is Disneyland, which exists in order to disguise the fact that it is itself the "real" America. His work in the 1990s continued this examination of Postmodern culture, especially in America. Perhaps his most controversial book is *The Gulf War Did Not Take Place* (1991), which argues that both sides of the conflict generated computer simulations that became the basis for "actual" events. Though much criticized for his "fatal" criticism, which some critics see as thinly disguised nostalgia for referentiality, Baudrillard's work has contributed to our understanding of the way signs and simulations function in media-saturated societies.

SELECTED BIBLIOGRAPHY

Baudrillard, Jean. *Baudrillard: A Critical Reader*. Ed. Douglas Kellner. Oxford and Cambridge MA: Blackwell Publishers, 1994.

———. *For a Critique of the Political Economy of the Sign*. 1972. Trans. Charles Levin. St. Louis: Telos Press, 1981.

———. *The Gulf War Did Not Take Place*. 1991. Trans. Paul Patton. Bloomington and Indianapolis: Indiana University Press; Sydney: Power Publications, 1994.

———. *Simulations*. Trans. Paul Foss, Paul Patton, and Philip Beitchman. New York: Semiotext(e), 1983.

Walter Benjamin (1892–1940)

Walter Benjamin was born in Berlin to a prosperous family and studied philosophy, receiving his doctorate in Bern, Switzerland, in 1919, though his *Habilitationsschrift* (thesis written as part of the qualification process, or *Habilitation*, to teach in a university), *The Origin of German Tragic Drama*, was rejected by the University of Frankfurt because of its unconventional use of quotation as a compositional method. It was published in 1928 and was the only book-length study he published in his lifetime. Because of his failure to earn his *Habilitation*, Benjamin was unable to find academic employment and so became a freelance critic and translator. Despite his rejection from the University of Frankfurt, he became associated with the theorists of the Frankfurt Institute for Social Research. He was especially close to **Theodor Adorno**, who disagreed with some of his ideas but formed a lasting intellectual bond with him. He was also close to the playwright Bertolt Brecht, who shared his skepticism about orthodox Marxism. He practiced forms of cultural and historical materialism, strongly influenced by his "messianic" vision of history as simultaneously materialist *and* transcendent of the present moment, the *now* which is the point of an infinite extension in time. The mystical elements of Benjamin's thought went against the grain of the CULTURAL MATERIALISM of most Frankfurt school theorists.

After Hitler and the National Socialists took power in 1933, Benjamin fled to Paris, where he found a congenial environment for his idiosyncratic method of cultural analysis. His reflections on the Parisian "arcades," indoor markets that extended for blocks and that contained a multitude of separate businesses, were meant to constitute his *magnum opus*, but were not published in his lifetime. Adorno, who corresponded with Benjamin from 1928 until his death, was fascinated with this project, but he was also frustrated with his friend's optimism, his recourse to mysticism, and his tendency toward a naïve form of positivism. In another of his posthumously published works, *Charles Baudelaire: Lyric Poet of High Capitalism* (1969), Benjamin elaborated on the important concept of the *flâneur*, that Modernist figure *par excellence*, at home in the city, moving among an endless array of spectacles and commodities. The *flâneur* gives form and substance to his own experience despite the crowd that flows continuously around him.

Events ultimately caught up with Benjamin. As the Nazis closed in on Paris in 1939, he fled to the Spanish frontier, hoping to make it to the US. Weakened because of heart trouble and in despair that he could not obtain a visa to enter Spain, Benjamin committed suicide. With the devoted attention of Adorno, Hannah Arendt, and others, Benjamin's arcades project and his numerous essays were finally published.

SELECTED BIBLIOGRAPHY

Benjamin, Walter. *The Arcades Project*. Trans. Howard Eiland and Kevin McLaughlin. Cambridge, MA and London: Belknap Press, 1999.

——. *Illuminations*. Ed. Hannah Arendt. Trans. Harry Zohn. New York: Harcourt, Brace & World, 1968.

——. *Reflections: Essays, Aphorisms and Autobiographical Writing*. Ed. Peter Demetz. Trans. Edmund Jephcott. New York: Schocken Books, 1986.

Homi Bhabha (1949–)

Homi Bhabha was born in Bombay, India, a member of the ancient Parsi community there. He studied at the University of Bombay, where he received his BA, and at Oxford University, where he completed his doctorate. He has held teaching positions at several English universities and at Princeton University, the University of Pennsylvania, and the University of Chicago. He is now Anne F. Rothenberg Professor of English and American Literature and Language at Harvard University and director of the Harvard Humanities Center.

Bhabha's analysis of colonial relations owed much to the work of **Frantz Fanon**, especially his theories of racial difference and mimicry, **Jacque Derrida**, **Michel Foucault**, and **Jacques Lacan**. His first major work, an edited volume of essays, *Nation and Narration*, brought together a wide variety of theorists who challenged the Enlightenment conception of nationalism and nationality and questioned the possibility of an ESSENTIALIST or UNIVERSALIST idea of the nation. Bhabha's contribution to the debate, "DissemiNation: Time, Narrative, and the Margins of the Modern Nation," used the tools of Poststructuralism, specifically Foucault's theories of power and discourse, to critique the Enlightenment tradition of historicism and to develop a theory of *emergence* to account for the wide variety of nations and nationalist movements. *The Location of Culture*, a collection of Bhabha's essays from the 1980s and early '90s, was an immense success and has remained influential in Postcolonial Studies. Bhabha advanced the concepts of HYBRIDITY and MIMICRY, which refer to the conditions of AMBIVALENCE that characterize colonial relations and colonial discourse. In the act of mimicry, the colonial subject inhabits and revises the "colonialist script," using it to express anti-colonial sentiments, even to serve as the rallying cry of insurrection. In the decade since the publication of *The Location of Culture*, Bhabha has continued to publish controversial works, but his reputation, powerful and wide-ranging, rests on a single collection of often brilliant essays.

SELECTED BIBLIOGRAPHY

Bhabha, Homi K. *The Location of Culture*. London and New York: Routledge, 1994.
——, ed. *Nation and Narration*. London: Routledge, 1990.
——. "Postcolonial Criticism." *Redrawing the Boundaries: The Transformation of English and American Studies*. Ed. Stephen Greenblatt and Giles Gunn. New York: MLA, 1992. 437–65.

Pierre Bourdieu (1930–2002)

Pierre Bourdieu was born in Denguin, a village in the Pyrenées in southern France, and attended school at the École Normale Supérieure in Paris, excelling at rugby and philosophy. Like **Jacques Derrida**, a fellow student at the École, Bourdieu studied the phenomenology of Merleau-Ponty, Heidegger, and Husserl. His thesis was a translation of and commentary on Leibniz's *Animadversiones* (1953). After a short stint in Algeria, serving in the French Army, he lectured at the University of Algiers (1959–60). He began his anthropological study of Berber culture at this time. The 1960s found him teaching at the University of Paris and the University of Lille and, from 1968, directing the Centre de Sociologie Européene. At the Centre, Bourdieu and his colleagues conducted research on the mechanisms of social power and its maintenance.

Bourdieu's early work in sociology focused on education and social environment. He developed the concept of HABITUS, or "socialized subjectivity," to describe the personal adaptations and motivations, attitudes, and modes of perception that arise as a result of individuals interacting in complex modern societies. His first major work, *Distinction* (1979), argues that social life is marked by the levels of distinction that attach to the individual by virtue of his or her manipulation of *habitus* within the broader social field. Like **Michel Foucault**'s theory of DISCURSIVE FORMATIONS, Bourdieu's theory of SOCIAL FIELD is an attempt to account for the complex interrelations and interconnections that constitute systems of social power. It posits a division in economic and cultural spheres, not unlike the Marxian base–superstructure model. Power and domination in the cultural sphere have their source in "cultural capital," which is itself the product of the individual's ability to manipulate *habitus* in order to achieve social distinction. Later works, like *The Field of Cultural Production*, explore the sociology of aesthetics, a form of reflexive analysis that regards the work of art as embedded within social fields and the systems dependent upon them. Bourdieu's work has influenced a broad array of disciplines, including anthropology, sociology, discourse theory, philosophy, and aesthetics. His work was driven by the same desire for social justice that motivated his commitment to local politics.

SELECTED BIBLIOGRAPHY

Bourdieu, Pierre. *Bourdieu: A Critical Reader.* Ed. Richard Shusterman. Oxford and Malden, MA: Blackwell Publishers, 1999.

——. *Distinction: A Social Critique of the Judgment of Taste.* Trans. Richard Nice. London: Routledge & Kegan Paul, 1984.

——. *The Field of Cultural Production: Essays on Art and Literature.* Ed. Randal Johnson. New York Columbia University Press, 1993.

——. *The Logic of Practice.* Trans. Richard Nice. Stanford: Stanford University Press, 1990.

Judith Butler (1956–)

Judith Butler was born in Cleveland, Ohio, and studied at Bennington College and Yale University, where she completed her doctorate in philosophy in 1984. She published her dissertation as *Subjects of Desire:*

Hegelian Reflections in Twentieth-Century France in 1987. She has held teaching positions at Wesleyan University and Johns Hopkins University, and is currently Chancellor Professor of Rhetoric and Comparative Literature at the University of California at Berkeley. Butler made her reputation in the 1990s with two important works on gender and sexuality. *Gender Trouble* (1990) critiqued the norm of compulsory heterosexuality and argued that IDENTITY was a function not of ESSENTIALIST gender roles or characteristics but rather of PERFORMATIVITY. Unlike performance, which is connected to traditional gender identity and presupposes a stable, essential SUBJECT, performativity challenges the very notion of such a subject. It also challenges the category of "sex." Butler argues that what we think of as biological sex is itself a function of gender. This argument was pursued further in *Bodies that Matter* (1993), a text that analyzes the status of sex as a regulatory social norm, with particular emphasis on how this norm is inscribed on the body, how it in fact animates and "materializes" the body.

With *Excitable Speech* (1997), Butler began to pursue questions of ethics, focusing on the ways that public speech can both cause social injury and mobilize individuals to take political action. At the turn of the twenty-first century, Butler collaborated with Ernest Laclau and **Slavoj Žižek** to produce a collection of essays on problems in Critical Theory, *Contingency, Hegemony, Universality* (2000). Butler's contributions address, among other things, the possibilities of "contingent universals" that could avoid the absolutism of Enlightenment traditions of critical thinking but that could also galvanize and consolidate movements for social change. *Precarious Life* (2004) examines the ethics of mourning in the wake of the attacks on the World Trade Center and the Pentagon in 2001. Butler's innovative critique of gender and ethics has made her something of a celebrity, despite the oft-cited difficulty of her work.

SELECTED BIBLIOGRAPHY

Butler, Judith. *Bodies that Matter: On the Discursive Limits of "Sex."* New York: Routledge, 1993

——. *Excitable Speech: A Politics of the Performative.* New York: Routledge, 1997.

——. *Gender Trouble: Feminism and the Subversion of Identity.* New York: Routledge, 1990.

——. *The Judith Butler Reader*. Ed. Sara Salih. Oxford and Malden, MA: Blackwell Publishers, 2004.

——. *Precarious Life: The Powers of Mourning and Violence*. London and New York: Verso, 2004.

Hazel Carby (1948–)

Hazel Carby was born in Britain of Jamaican and Welsh descent. She received her doctorate from the University of Birmingham in 1984. In the years before she entered graduate school, Carby taught high school English in East London. During this time, she also worked with local anti-racist groups. Her first faculty position was at Wesleyan University, which she held until 1989. In that year, she moved to Yale University, where she is currently Charles C. and Dorathea S. Dilley Professor and chair of the Department of African American studies. Her first major publication, *Reconstructing Womanhood*, was a revisionist reexamination of the tradition of African American writing by women. Like **bell hooks** and other feminist theorists of race, Carby insists on the social and historical determinations of racism and racial identity. In *Race Men*, she begins with a critique of W. E. B. Du Bois' *The Souls of Black Folk* and its representation of masculinity and then proceeds to analyze the repressed contradictions concealed by black male bodies as they are represented in literature and other media. Across the spectrum of representations of black masculinity Carby finds a rejection of the influence of black women and gay men.

Carby's work, like that of other theorists in Postcolonial Studies, focuses on racism as a colonial problem. Though she understands the determinations of local politics and social environments, she is also sensitive to how racism and racial identity are determined in global contexts. In *Cultures in Babylon*, she brings together her many essays on women and migration, black Feminism, and multiculturalism in "black Britain" and "African America." Carby's provocative critique of culture does not exclude the institutional contexts in which African American and black British literature is taught and canonized. Her work on the sexual politics in the UK and the science fiction writer Octavia Butler continues to test the boundaries of African American studies and to advocate a more open and inclusive study of contemporary Western cultures.

SELECTED BIBLIOGRAPHY

Carby, Hazel. *Cultures in Babylon: Black Britain and African America*. London: Verso, 1999.

———. *Race Men*. Cambridge, MA: Harvard University Press, 1998.

———. *Reconstructing Womanhood: The Emergence of the Afro-American Woman Novelist*. New York: Oxford University Press, 1987.

Hélène Cixous (1937–)

Hélène Cixous was born in Oran, Algeria. She studied in France and completed her doctorate in 1968. In the next year she published her dissertation, *The Exile of James Joyce*. She began teaching at the Université de Bordeaux and held positions at the Sorbonne and the University of Paris X (Nanterre). A year after the student uprisings in May 1968, Cixous was put in charge of developing curriculum for the new experimental University of Paris VIII (Vincennes). Along with Tzvetan Todorov and Gérard Genette, Cixous started *Poétique*, a journal for new criticism and theory.

Cixous was part of a generation of theorists on the rise during the turbulent 1960s. Her peers and colleagues at this time were **Michel Foucault, Jacques Derrida, Roland Barthes, Julia Kristeva**, and a host of others teaching in universities across France. She was especially close to Derrida, also born in Algeria of Jewish background. Cixous's literary theory was boldly innovative, as were her fiction and drama. In all of her writings, she resists the patriarchal power behind Western philosophical and theoretical traditions. "The Laugh of the Medusa" (1975) and *Three Steps on the Ladder of Writing* (1990) articulate her critique of these traditions and advocate an alternative discourse form, ÉCRITURE FEMININE (feminine writing, writing the body). *The Newly Born Woman* (1975), written with Catherine Clément, reconsiders the Freudian scenario in which the little girl seduces her father and suggests that it needs to be rewritten in terms of women seeking new representational forms based on their own "libidinal economies." Her later theoretical work focuses on aesthetics, epistemology, and ethics.

Throughout the 1970s and '80s, Cixous created innovative fictions like *The Book of Promethea* (1983), which shows the influence in her writing of Ukraine-born Brazilian novelist Clarise Lispector. Cixous' dramatic work also underwent a shift at this time after meeting Ariane Mnouchkine, experimental director at the Théâtre du Soleil to which she contributed several plays, including *The Terrible but Unfinished Story of Norodom Sihanouk, King of Cambodia* (produced in 1985), that explored the nature of power, responsibility, and memory. Cixous continues to write fiction and theory. In 2000, she published a collection of memoirs, *Daydreams of the Wild Woman*.

SELECTED BIBLIOGRAPHY

Cixous, Hélène. *"Coming to Writing" and Other Essays*. Ed. Deborah Jenson, Trans. Sarah Cornell, Deborah Jenson, Ann Liddle, Susan Sellers. Cambridge, MA: Harvard University Press, 1992.

——. *The Hélène Cixous Reader*. Ed. Susan Sellers. New York Routledge, 1994.

——. "The Laugh of the Medusa." *Signs* 1.4 (Summer 1976): 875–93.

——. *Three Steps on the Ladder of Writing*. Trans. Susan Sellers. New York: Columbia University Press, 1993.

—— and Catherine Clément. *The Newly Born Woman*. Trans. Betsy Wing. Minneapolis: University of Minnesota Press, 1986.

Teresa de Lauretis (1939–)

Teresa de Lauretis was born and educated in Italy, receiving her doctorate from Bocconi University, Milan. She taught widely in the United States and Europe before settling at the University of California, Santa Cruz, where she is a professor of the History of Consciousness. She wrote books in Italian on the novelist Italo Svevo and the semiotician and novelist Umberto Eco. Her first theoretical work in English, *Alice Doesn't: Feminism, Semiotics, Cinema* (1984), established her as a major figure in both Feminism and film studies. In this volume, she critiques the male gaze, using Lacanian psychoanalysis to formulate a conception of feminist gazing that "looks back" at the male subject, whose voyeuristic perspective characterizes Western art and culture. *Technologies of Gender* (1987), her most influential work, counters **Michel Foucault**'s tendency to distinguish bodies and pleasure from the "discourse of sexuality" with a theory of the body that situates it and its desire wholly in socio-historical contexts. In 1994, de Lauretis published an important work in queer theory, *The Practice of Love*, which draws on Psychoanalysis to explore the range of theories and practices associated with "lesbian sexuality and perverse desire." Since the late 1980s, de Lauretis has published essays and chapters on a wide variety of subjects, including Psychoanalysis, film, and the status of Feminism in Italy.

SELECTED BIBLIOGRAPHY

De Lauretis, Teresa. *Alice Doesn't: Feminism, Semiotics, Cinema.* Bloomington: Indiana University Press, 1984.
——. *The Practice of Love: Lesbian Sexuality and Perverse Desire.* Bloomington: Indiana University Press, 1994.
——. *Technologies of Gender: Essays on Theory, Film, and Fiction.* Bloomington: Indiana University Press, 1987.

Gilles Deleuze (1925–95)

and

Félix Guattari (1930–92)

It is rare in literary theory to come across a team of theorists whose work extends over a long period of time and focuses on a variety of complex problems in literature, psychoanalysis, Marxism, and philosophy. Gilles Deleuze and Félix Guattari are that rarity, and it is impossible to separate them when discussing their theoretical ideas.

Gilles Deleuze was born and educated in Paris. He studied philosophy at the Sorbonne and taught in Parisian lycées until 1957. At this time, he started teaching the history of philosophy at the Sorbonne and then worked as a researcher for the Centre National Recherche Scientifique (1960–64). He also taught at the University of Lyons, and then finally at the experimental University of Paris VIII (Vincennes), at the behest of **Michel Foucault**. He remained there until he retired in 1987. His earliest works were philosophical critiques of Nietzsche, Spinoza, Bergson, Kant, and others. In 1968, he published *Difference and Repetition*, which constituted the larger part of his dissertation. He also wrote on literary figures like Kafka and Proust.

Félix Guattari was born in Velleneuve-les-Sablons, France, and gravitated to the study of psychiatry as a young man of twenty. He practiced a form of psychiatry influenced by philosophy, linguistics, literature, and Lacanian psychoanalysis. Along with his collaborator, Jean Oury, he performed research and trained students in a private clinic, La Bord at Court-Cheverny. In the mid-1960s, he was active in the Association of Institutional Psychotherapy and along with others founded the Federation of Groups for Institutional Study and Research.

In May 1968, in the midst of student protests and rioting, the two men met at Vincennes. In the next few years they developed the material that became *Anti-Oedipus* (1977) and *Thousand Plateaus* (1983), which together constitute one of the most controversial and complex critiques of capitalist culture and its links to Psychoanalysis. Crucial to their understanding of the social body and social spaces are innovative concepts like TERRITORIALIZATION, which refers to the ways bodies and spaces are inscribed or demarcated by social, political, and cultural networks of power. Such networks are structured either hierarchically or "rhizomatically," with the latter's centerless, crabgrass-like extensions and complexities offering more freedom of expression and resistance. DETERRITORIALIZATION and RETERRITORIALIZATION are processes which erase or reconstruct, respectively, the limits and boundaries of the social space. Another important concept is the "body without organs," which Deleuze and Guattari argue is free of the repressive mechanisms of desire articulated in Psychoanalysis. In place of the psychoanalytic model of SUBJECTIVITY, signified by the Freudian theory of Oedipus, is the "anti-oedipal" condition of schizophrenia, a condition in which desire is the free and fluid expression of desiring machines along the surface of the body without organs. Deleuze and Guattari also worked together on other projects, notably *Kafka: Toward a Minor Literature* (1988), which explores the use of a dominant language (German) by the Jewish Czechoslovakian novelist, Franz Kafka. *Anti-Oedipus* remains their enduring contribution to literary and cultural theory.

SELECTED BIBLIOGRAPHY

Deleuze, Gilles. *The Deleuze Reader*. Ed. Constantin V. Boundas. New York: Columbia University Press, 1993.

Deleuze, Gilles and Felix Guattari, *Anti-Oedipus: Capitalism and Schizophrenia*. Trans. Robert Hurley, Mark Seem, and Helen R. Lane. Minneapolis: University of Minnesota Press, 1983.

———. *A Thousand Plateaus: Capitalism and Schizophrenia*. Trans. Brian Massumi. London: Athlone, 1988.

———. *Kafka: Toward a Minor Literature*. Trans. Dana Polan. Minneapolis: University of Minnesota Press, 1986.

Paul de Man (1919–83)

Paul de Man was born in Antwerp, Belgium, and came of age during a time of invasion and occupation by Nazi forces. During the war and for a time afterwards, he worked in journalism and publishing. He found his way to the US just after the war and received his doctorate from Harvard in the late 1950s. He taught at Cornell University and Johns Hopkins University before taking a position at Yale University in 1970, where he held the position of Sterling Professor of the Humanities at the time of his death.

Like many European theorists of his generation, de Man was steeped in the phenomenological tradition of philosophy and literary criticism. He met **Jacques Derrida** at a symposium on structuralism at the Johns Hopkins University Humanities Center in 1966. De Man came be known as one of the founders of Yale school Deconstruction. Although de Man's style was quite different from Derrida's, the two shared similar methods and objects of study. His preferred subjects were aesthetics, rhetoric, Romantic literature, especially the work of Jean-Jacques Rousseau, and Nietzsche's philosophy. In his first major work, *Blindness and Insight* (1971), he argues that criticism, due to a gap between its theoretical assumptions and its practice, is blind to its own insights. Blindness of the sort that de Man investigates often develops when rhetorical statements are mistaken for literal ones, and vice versa. In *Allegories of Reading* (1979), he uses this deconstructionist mode of analysis to explore the works of Rousseau, Nietzsche, Rilke, and Proust. In this volume, de Man emphasizes the vertiginous possibilities offered to the critic when confronted with a text that will not let the reader clearly decide between literal and figural (or rhetorical) readings. These two volumes of essays established de Man as a formidable and influential critic, despite his tendency to write essays rather than monographs. In his posthumously published *Aesthetic Ideology* (1992), he furthers his critique against universalist and idealist conceptions of aesthetics by applying his deconstructionist method of rhetorical analysis to the works of Kant, Hegel, and Schiller.

In 1987, four years after de Man's death, a Belgian researcher uncovered important information about de Man's war-time journalism career in Belgium. During the period 1940–42, de Man had published nearly 200 book reviews and short articles on literature and culture for *Le Soir* and *Het Vlaamsche Land*. These periodicals had come under the control of Nazi occupying forces and were therefore collaborationist and anti-Semitic in orientation. It was damaging enough simply to have written for such periodicals, but in at least one article, "Les Juifs dans la littéra-ture actuelle," de Man takes an anti-Semitic position when he argues that European literature will survive negative Jewish influence. The reaction among critics and scholars was complex and ambivalent, in part because it was difficult to reconcile de Man's tainted past with his brilliant academic career. Many readers, in and out of the academy, saw this episode as evidence of the nihilism and amorality of Deconstruction. Others, especially some of de Man's colleagues at Yale, sadly pointed out the irony of the situation, noting that his mode of Deconstruction, especially his critique of aesthetic ideology, was designed precisely to uncover the dangers of language when it is used to champion UNIVERSALIST ideals and social and cultural TOTALITY. De Man's life, tempered after death by the irony of his own past, exemplifies the very problematic nature of language and experience that his work strove to understand.

SELECTED BIBLIOGRAPHY

De Man, Paul. *Aesthetic Ideology*. Ed. Andrzej Warminski. Minneapolis: University of Minnesota Press, 1996.

——. *Allegories of Reading: Figural Language in Rousseau, Nietzsche, Rilke, and Proust*. New Haven: Yale University Press, 1979.

——. *Blindness and Insight: Essays in the Rhetoric of Contemporary Criticism*. New York: Oxford University Press, 1971.

——. *The Resistance to Theory*. Minneapolis: University of Minnesota Press, 1986.

Jacques Derrida (1930–2004)

Jacques Derrida was born in El Biar, Algeria, where his early education was interrupted when Algerian officials, acting on orders of the collaborationist Vichy government, expelled him from his lycée because he was Jewish. In 1949, he moved to France and by 1952 was enrolled in the École Normale Supérieure in Paris. While working toward his doctorate, he studied with **Michel Foucault** and **Louis Althusser**. He wrote a dissertation on the work of the phenomenologist Edmund Husserl, published in 2003. For two years in the late 1950s, he taught the children of soldiers in lieu of military service in Algeria, where the French Army was fighting against native Algerian forces. In 1960, he began teaching at the Sorbonne and in 1964 moved to the École Normale Supérieure, where he remained until 1984. After 1966, the year he presented, "Structure, Sign and Play in the Discourse of the Humanities" at Johns Hopkins University, Derrida was a regular speaker in forums worldwide and a visiting professor at many US universities. By the end of the 1960s, he had published several major works in French, including *Writing and Difference* and *Of Grammatology* (both 1967). In the 1970s, his reputation grew rapidly and widely throughout the US academy as his books were translated into English. This early work is concerned primarily with problems in philosophy and linguistics, but Derrida's deconstructionist critique of the problems of origin, ESSENCE, and PRESENCE caught the attention of critics and scholars who had become frustrated with limitations of New Criticism and Structuralism.

Margins of Philosophy (1972), a collection of essays, and *Disseminations* (1972), a meditation on Plato and Stéphan Mallarmé, solidified Derrida's reputation. In the mid-1970s, Derrida found himself in a public debate with analytical philosophy, a debate that produced *Limited Inc* (1977). In the 1980s, he wrote several major works, including *The Post Card* (1980), numerous essays on James Joyce and Heidegger, and a memoir for his friend, **Paul de Man**. In the 1990s, he published *Specters of Marx* (1993) and explored problems in Psychoanalysis and ethics. Of particular interest at this time was a series of books on the economies of the "gift" and the ethics of giving: *Given Time* (1992), *On the Name* (1995), and *The Gift of Death* (1995). In the last decade of his life, Derrida remained focused on ethics and memory, writing his *Adieu to Emmanuel Levinas* in 1997 and *The Work of Mourning* in 2001.

SELECTED BIBLIOGRAPHY

Derrida, Jacques. *A Derrida Reader: Between the Blinds*. Ed. Peggy Kamuf. New York: Columbia University Press, 1991.

——. *Dissemination*. Trans. Barbara Johnson. Chicago: University of Chicago Press, 1981.

——. *Margins of Philosophy*. Trans. Alan Bass. Chicago: University of Chicago Press, 1982.

——. *Of Grammatology*. Trans. Gayatri Chakravorty Spivak. Baltimore: Johns Hopkins University Press, 1976.

——. *Specters of Marx: The State of the Debt, the Work of Mourning and the New International*. Trans. Peggy Kamuf. New York: Routledge, 1994.

——. *Writing and Difference*. Trans. Alan Bass. Chicago: University of Chicago Press, 1978.

Terry Eagleton (1943–)

Terry Eagleton was born in Salford, England, and educated at Cambridge University. While at Cambridge, he was a student of **Raymond**

Williams, the most important Marxist critic of the era (1960s) and one of the founders of British Cultural Studies. Eagleton earned his doctoral degree at twenty-one and became a tutor of English at Wadham College, Oxford University. He has proven to be Williams's successor not only in Marxist literary theory but also, especially since the 1990s, in Cultural Studies.

Eagleton's early works were devoted to literature and society, with a focus on Shakespeare and the Brontës. His *Myths of Power* (1975) was a tour de force Marxist reading of the Brontë's works that made his reputation as a theorist. At this time, he also published important works on Marxist theory, including *Criticism and Ideology* (1976). In the 1980s, he produced monographs on a number of literary and theoretical figures, notably **Walter Benjamin** and Samuel Richardson. He also published his most widely-read book, *Literary Theory: An Introduction* (1983). No simple primer, *Literary Theory* begins by examining critically the concept of literature and the institutional setting in which it is taught. It then offers historically grounded surveys of the major theoretical fields, concluding with an appeal for "political criticism." The 1990s found Eagleton exploring aesthetics, nationalism, ideology, and Postmodernism. He contributed two volumes of essays on Irish literature and culture, *Heathcliff and the Great Hunger* (1995) and *Crazy John and the Bishop* (1998), both of which bear the distinct hallmarks of Williams and the English Marxist tradition. In the first few years of the twenty-first century, Eagleton wrote books on tragedy, literary theory, and the "idea of culture." In *After Theory* (2003), he announced the death of theory, though he continues to teach it at the University of Manchester.

SELECTED BIBLIOGRAPHY

Eagleton, Terry. *Criticism and Ideology: A Study in Marxist Literary Theory.* London: NLB; Atlantic Highlands: Humanities Press, 1976.

——. *The Eagleton Reader.* Ed. Stephen Regan. Oxford and Malden, MA: Blackwell Publishers, 1998.

——. *Heathcliff and the Great Hunger: Studies in Irish Culture.* London and New York: Verso, 1995.

——. *The Idea of Culture.* Oxford, UK and Malden, MA: Blackwell, 2000.

——. *Literary Theory: An Introduction.* 2nd ed. Minneapolis: University of Minnesota Press, 1983, 1996.

Frantz Fanon (1925–61)

Frantz Fanon was born in Martinique, in the French Caribbean, and studied at a lycée in Fort-de-France, where one of his teachers was Amié Césaire. During the Second World War, he served with the French Army in North Africa. He was wounded in 1944 and received the Croix de Guerre. After the war, he returned briefly to Martinique, where he worked on the parliamentary campaign of his former teacher, Césaire. They remained close friends. Fanon left for France, where he studied psychiatry in Paris and Lyons. At this time, he composed his first book, *Black Skin, White Masks* (1952), an investigation of colonialism from the perspective of race consciousness and race relations. In 1952, Fanon began practicing psychiatry in Algeria, at Blida-Joinville hospital, where he was director of the psychiatric ward. The war between French colonial forces and the National Liberation Front (NLF) began in 1954. By 1956, Fanon had resigned and begun his work with the liberation movement. He traveled all over North and Saharan African, visiting guerilla camps and training medical personnel. He also hid insurgents in his home. In the last few years of his life, in addition to writing several books, he worked as an ambassador of the provisional Algerian government to Ghana, edited a journal in Tunisia, and set up the first African psychiatric clinic. He died of leukemia in Washington, DC, but was buried in Algeria.

Fanon's work is largely concerned with African colonialism and the Algerian independence movement. *Toward an African Revolution*, published posthumously, brought together his shorter works published in NLF newspapers. Other essays on Algeria and the Algerian "national psyche" were compiled in *A Dying Colonialism* (1959). His most important work, *The Wretched of the Earth* (1961), was also his last. Unlike the essay collections, this volume presented a neo-Hegelian critique of colonialism, an integrated study of spontaneity and colonial violence, national consciousness, nationalist parties and leaders, the native intellectual, and the psychological trauma exacted by colonial wars. He was as critical of the nationalist bourgeoisie that inherited the privileges of the European colonizers as he was of the colonizers themselves. He understood that anti-colonial resistance could only succeed if the people were given the tools to "re-create" themselves as human beings. If necessary, they must do this through violence. The recognition and theorization of this hard necessity earned Fanon some criticism, but by and large his work and life have proven a positive inspiration for liberation groups worldwide and a valuable theoretical resource for Postcolonial Studies.

SELECTED BIBLIOGRAPHY

Fanon, Frantz. *Black Skin, White Masks*. Trans. Charles Lam Markmann. London: Pluto, 1986.
——. *Toward the African Revolution: Political Essays*. Trans. Haakon Chevalier. Harmondsworth: Penguin, 1970.
——. *The Wretched of the Earth*. Trans. Constance Farrington. New York: Grove Weidenfeld, 1963.
Gordon, Lewis R., T. Denean Sharpley-Whiting, and Renée T. White, eds. *Fanon: A Critical Reader*. Oxford and Cambridge, MA: Blackwell Publishers, 1996.

Stanley Fish (1938–)

Stanley Fish was born in Providence, Rhode Island, and educated at the University of Pennsylvania and Yale University. He received his doctorate in 1962 and soon began teaching at the University of California at Berkeley. He went on to teach at Johns Hopkins University and Duke University, where he was Arts and Sciences Professor of English and professor of law (1968–98).

Fish's early professional life was spent teaching medieval and seventeenth-century literature. His first major work, *Surprised by Sin* (1967), advanced a then-unique argument about the reader of *Paradise Lost*, who is seduced by Milton's language into experiencing Satan's temptation of Adam and Eve. Fish's "affective stylistics," which stresses the reader's response to a literary text, departed from the formalism of the New Critics. His next book, *Self-consuming Artifact* (1972), overcame some of the limitations of affective stylistics and offered a new theory of interpretive communities, cohorts of readers who agree, in principle, on a specific set of conventions and strategies. *Is There a Text in this Class?* brings together essays from the 1970s along with new material that contrasts his early conceptions of affective stylistics with his later formulations of reader response and interpretive communities. These later texts show the influence of **Wolfgang Iser** and Roman Ingarden who were developing similar projects in Europe at this time.

During the 1980s and '90s, Fish turned his attention to matters of law and legal theory, rhetoric, ethics, and the professionalization of literary studies. His interest in pragmatism and logic made him a formidable and often amusing interlocutor. Fish's attacks on Postmodernism were eloquent reminders that principles and standards are inevitable in human society and that the important issue is not protesting their existence but in constructing smart and tolerable ones. In 1989, Fish published *Doing What Comes Naturally*, a seminal work in the Critical Legal Studies movement. This was followed by his controversial volume on the first amendment, *There's No Such Thing as Free Speech: and It's a Good Thing, Too* (1994). From the mid-1990s, Fish's career settled into legal studies and administration. He served as Dean of Arts and Sciences at the University of Illinois, Chicago (1999–2004). In 2005, he joined the faculty of Florida International University College of Law, where he is Davidson-Kahn Distinguished University Professor of Humanities and Law.

SELECTED BIBLIOGRAPHY

Fish, Stanley. *Doing What Comes Naturally: Change, Rhetoric, and the Practice of Theory in Literary and Legal Studies*. Durham: Duke University Press, 1989.

——. *Is There a Text in This Class?: The Authority of Interpretive Communities*. Cambridge, MA: Harvard University Press, 1980.

——. *Professional Correctness: Literary Studies and Political Change*. New York: Clarendon Press, 1995.

——. *The Stanley Fish Reader*. Ed. H. Aram Veeser. Malden MA: Blackwell Publishers, 1999.

——. *Surprised by Sin: The Reader in* Paradise Lost. 2nd ed. Cambridge, MA: Harvard University Press, 1967, 1998.

Michel Foucault (1926–84)

Michel Foucault was born and educated in Poitiers, France, then sent to the prestigious Lycée Henry IV in Paris. He entered the École Normale Supérieure in 1946 and earned his "agrégation de philosophie" in 1951. At the École and at the Sorbonne, Foucault came into contact with leading intellectuals of the day, including Jean Hippolyte and **Louis Althusser**, and became a communist (though he left the Party in 1953). In 1952, he received his diploma in psychopathology from the University of Paris. After teaching briefly at the École and the University of Lille, Foucault spent three years at the University of Uppsala (1955–58), then one year directing the French Institute in Hamburg. His doctoral dissertation was published as *Madness and Civilization* in 1961. In the next five years, he published *The Birth of the Clinic* (1963) and *The Order of Things* (1966). These early texts exemplify the ARCHAEOLOGICAL method of history and sociology presented systematically in *Archaeology of Knowledge* (1969). Foucault was not interested in traditional historiographic methods that relied on cause and effect and chronological temporality. Drawing on the "anti-historicism" of Nietzschean GENEALOGY, he developed a way of talking about history that avoided the causal implications of the "event" and emphasized instead the fundamental role of interpretation in the emergence of law and morality. These "emergences" are not events in the conventional sense, and representing them requires new techniques of selection and explication, new conceptions of language, text, discourse, and archive.

Whether he studied clinics, insane asylums, economics, grammar, biology, or education, Foucault was interested in analyzing the discursive pathways by which POWER circulates within formations and traditions. His conception of power is an elaboration of the Nietzschean "will to power" and refers first and foremost to the representation of social AGENCY. Power is always a matter of using language, information, and images. Power is knowledge, and nowhere is this more clearly the case than in DISCURSIVE FORMATIONS that constitute "discipline." Foucault famously analyzed the nature of disciplinary power in *Discipline and Punish* (1975), his account of the development of imprisonment and punishment as expressions of social power. In 1976, the first volume of the

History of Sexuality appeared and introduced a new focus on sexuality and power, specifically the way that the nineteenth-century "discourse on sex" regulated and defused sexual activity. In addition to his involvement with liberation groups in Iran and Poland, Foucault spent the late 1970s and early '80s finishing two additional volumes of the *History of Sexuality* and writing essays on the relationship between power and the subject of knowledge. He gradually came to reject his own early position that the subject was in thrall to social discourses and began to theorize new forms of positive social agency. This work was cut short by Foucault's death in 1984, of an AIDS-related neurological disorder.

SELECTED BIBLIOGRAPHY

Foucault, Michel. *The Archaeology of Knowledge and the Discourse on Language.* Trans. A. M. Sheridan Smith. New York: Pantheon, 1972.

——. *Discipline and Punish: The Birth of the Prison.* Trans. Alan Sheridan. New York: Vintage Books, 1979, 1977.

——. *The Foucault Reader.* Ed. Paul Rabinow. New York: Pantheon Books, 1984.

——. *The History of Sexuality.* 3 vols. Trans. Robert Hurley. New York: Pantheon Books, 1978–88.

——. *The Order of Things: An Archaeology of the Human Sciences.* New York: Vintage Books, 1994.

Henry Louis Gates (1950–)

Henry Louis Gates was born in Keyser, West Virginia, and attended Yale University and Cambridge University. He completed his doctoral degree in 1979, the first black person ever to receive one from Cambridge. While at Cambridge, Gates became friends with the Nigerian playwright Wole Soyinka, who tutored him in the cultural traditions and language of the Yoruba tribe. After teaching at Cornell University and Yale, he joined the faculty at Harvard University, where he currently serves as the W. E. B. Du Bois Professor of the Humanities.

Gates studied widely in African American, African and Caribbean cultures and literatures. He made his reputation with the republication of Harriet E. Wilson's *Our Nig*, the first novel published in the US by an African American. His reputation was confirmed with the publication of two studies in black literary theory: *Figures in Black* (1987), a reconsideration of the nativist strand of influence in African American literature, and *The Signifying Monkey* (1988), an in-depth study of a native black rhetorical tradition of "Signifyin(g)" rooted in the mythologies and story-telling practices of West Africa. These works established Gates as a major figure in African American studies. His other major work at this time, an edited volume of essays, *"Race," Writing, and Difference* (1986), brought together a number of established theorists, including **Jacques Derrida**, **Homi Bhabha**, and **Gayatri Chakravorty Spivak**. Many of the essays explored the intersection of Poststructuralism and historicist theories of race and racial difference.

In the 1990s, Gates edited an important anthology of black feminist writings and wrote or edited many volumes on African American autobiography, Langston Hughes, Richard Wright, and Zora Neale Hurston. He was co-editor, with Nellie Y. McKay, of the *Norton Anthology of African American Literature* (1997). An important work in this period was *Thirteen Ways of Looking at a Black Man*, a series of interviews with prominent black men who reflect on their experiences with race and racism. In 1999, Gates and Kwame Anthony Appiah published, in conjunction with Microsoft, *Encarta Africana 2000*, an electronic resource on all things African. Also at this time, Gates wrote *Wonders of the African World* (1999), the companion to a BBC/PBS series. Gates continues to make significant contributions to African American studies.

SELECTED BIBLIOGRAPHY

Gates, Henry Louis. *Figures in Black: Words, Signs and the "Racial" Self.* New York: Oxford University Press, 1987.

——. *The Signifying Monkey: A Theory of Afro-American Literary Criticism.* New York: Oxford University Press, 1988.

——. *Thirteen Ways of Looking at a Black Man.* New York: Random House, 1997.

——, ed. *"Race," Writing, and Difference*. Chicago: University of Chicago Press, 1986.

—— and Kwame Anthony Appiah, eds. *Microsoft Encarta Africana 2000*. Electronic Resource. Redmond, WA: Microsoft, 1999.

Sandra Gilbert (1936–)

and

Susan Gubar (1944–)

The collaboration of Sandra Gilbert and Susan Gubar constitutes one of the foundation stones for feminist literary theory in the US. Sandra Gilbert was born in New York City and was educated at Cornell and New York University. She received her doctorate from Columbia University in 1968. After teaching at a number of schools, she took a position in 1975 at the University of California at Davis. After four years in the mid-1980s teaching at Princeton University, Gilbert returned to Davis where she continues to teach.

Susan Gubar was born in Brooklyn, New York, and was educated at the City University of New York and the University of Michigan. She received her doctorate from the University of Iowa in 1972. Within a year, Gubar joined the faculty of Indiana University. She is presently Distinguished Professor of English and Women's Studies at Indiana.

The two women met at Indiana University, where they designed a course on the feminist literary tradition and began a collaboration that would yield, in 1979, *The Madwoman in the Attic*. This was a groundbreaking work in literary criticism, but also a compelling revision of literary history. Gilbert and Gubar argued that women's writing in the nineteenth century constituted a feminist tradition of resistance to

PATRIARCHAL culture. This argument is extended in their three-volume study of twentieth-century women writers, *No Man's Land* (1988–94). In these volumes, they argue that Modernist and Postmodernist literature are comprehensible historically only if Feminism and writing by women are considered seriously as influences in literary traditions and CANONS. Through the 1980s and '90s, they edited many volumes together, including the *Norton Anthology of Literature by Women* (1985) and *The Female Imagination and the Modernist Aesthetic* (1986). They have also written a satire on the profession of teaching and canon formation, *Masterpiece Theatre: An Academic Melodrama* (1995).

Each of these women has been productive on their own as well. Gubar has published works in Cultural Studies, including *Racechanges* (1997), an analysis of "cross-racial masquerade." She has also published a volume on contemporary poetry, *Poetry After Auschwitz* (2003). Gilbert has written a study on the American poet H.D. and a memoir recounting her husband's death from cancer. She also published numerous books of poetry, including *Ghost Volcano* (1995), *Belongings* (2005), and *Kissing the Bread: New & Selected Poems, 1969–1999*.

SELECTED BIBLIOGRAPHY

Gilbert, Sandra and Susan Gubar. *The Madwoman in the Attic: The Woman Writer and the Nineteenth-Century Literary Imagination.* 2nd ed. New Haven and London: Yale University Press, 1979, 2000.

——. *No Man's Land: The Place of the Woman Writer in the Twentieth Century.* 3 vols. New Haven: Yale University Press, 1988–94.

——, eds. *The Female Imagination and the Modernist Aesthetic.* New York: Gordon and Breach Science Publishers, 1986.

Stephen Greenblatt (1943–)

Stephen Greenblatt was born in Cambridge, Massachusetts. He studied at Yale University and Cambridge University, receiving his doctorate from Yale in 1969. He began teaching at the University of California at

Berkeley that year and remained there until 1997, when he moved to Harvard University. In 2000, he became Cogan University Professor of the Humanities.

In his early years at Berkeley, Greenblatt was influenced by **Raymond Williams** and attended seminars given by **Michel Foucault**. The very different approaches to literary history and social theory represented by these theorists combined in Greenblatt's work to produce a nuanced style of close reading sensitive to the impact made on texts by social and historical forces. His third book, *Renaissance Self-Fashioning* (1980), drew on Foucault's ARCHAEOLOGICAL method of historical writing to describe the various ways that social power determines the subject and the representation of SUBJECTIVITY. It was widely read and regarded as a leading example of the New Historicism then emerging out of Renaissance studies. The New Historicist method was popularized in the pages of *Representations*, a journal co-founded by Greenblatt.

Greenblatt refined his new approach to mapping social power and its literary effects in *Shakespearean Negotiations* (1988). In addition to his editorial responsibilities with *Representations*, Greenblatt edited numerous volumes of essays. He also continued to produce scholarly studies of early modern literatures. Together with Catherine Gallagher, Greenblatt revisited the theoretical problems of New Historicism in *Practicing New Historicism* (2000). This text both situates New Historicism in the academic and social contexts of the late 1970s and '80s and offers virtuoso readings by acknowledged masters in the field. In 2004, Greenblatt made the headlines again with a new biography of Shakespeare, *Will in the World*, which was shortlisted for the National Book Award.

SELECTED BIBLIOGRAPHY

Gallagher, Catherine and Stephen Greenblatt. *Practicing New Historicism.* Chicago: University of Chicago Press, 2000.

Greenblatt, Stephen. *Greenblatt Reader.* Eds. Michael Payne and Stephen Greenblatt. Oxford: Blackwell Publishers, 2005.

——. *Learning to Curse: Essays in Early Modern Culture.* New York: Routledge, 1990.

——. *Renaissance Self-Fashioning: From More to Shakespeare.* Chicago: University of Chicago Press, 1980.

Stuart Hall (1932–)

Stuart Hall was born in Kingston, Jamaica, and moved to England in 1951. He was a Rhodes Scholar at Oxford University, where he received the MA degree. During the 1950s and early '60s, Hall was active in socialist movements and, together with Charles Taylor, Gabriel Pearson, and others, started a journal of art and criticism, *Universities and New Left Review*, which later became the *New Left Review*. After the publication of his first book, *The Popular Arts* (1965), Hall was invited to join the Centre for Contemporary Cultural Studies at the University of Birmingham in 1964. By 1968, he had taken over as director. During these years, British Cultural Studies was concerned primarily with sociological investigations of British society and the critique of IDEOLOGY. Hall's own work included a study of the SEMIOTICS of television in 1973 and a work done in collaboration with other members of the Centre, *Policing the Crisis*. This volume draws from Antonio Gramsci's interpretation of Marxism to argue that the racist representation of violent street crime by the British press in the 1970s masked economic and social crises.

By the time Hall moved to the Open University in 1979, where he was a professor of sociology until he retired, Cultural Studies was beginning to be recognized as a major theoretical field. In 1980, Hall published an important essay, "Cultural Studies: Two Paradigms," that sketched the history and theoretical influences on British Cultural Studies and suggested that there were two models from which to choose: culturalist and structuralist. Throughout the 1980s, Hall edited a number of volumes on Cultural Studies, sociology, the modern state, modernity, and Marxism. He also published *The Hard Road to Renewal*, a study of Margaret Thatcher's years as Prime Minister and the effects of those years on the British left. Hall's range of interests extended beyond the national context as well; his work on DIASPORIC IDENTITIES and immigration, for example, has contributed much to our understanding of the global ramifications of the modern multicultural state. Many of these issues are addressed in a collection of essays by and about Hall, *Critical Dialogues in Cultural Studies* (1996). Hall continues to be widely read and influential, as evidenced by the essay collection dedicated to him, *Without Guarantees: In Honour of Stuart Hall* (2000).

SELECTED BIBLIOGRAPHY

Hall, Stuart. *Critical Dialogues in Cultural Studies.* Ed. David Morely and Kuan-Hsing Chen. London and New York: Routledge, 1996.

——. "Cultural Studies: Two Paradigms." *Media, Culture and Society* 2 (1980): 57–72.

——. *The Hard Road to Renewal: Thatcherism and the Crisis of the Left.* London and New York: Verso, 1988.

—— et al., *Policing the Crisis: Mugging, the State and Law and Order.* New York: Holmes & Meier, 1978.

Donna Haraway (1944–)

Donna Haraway was born in Denver, Colorado, and studied zoology and philosophy at Colorado College. After a brief period as a Fulbright scholar studying evolutionary theory in Paris, she studied biology at Yale University, where she received her doctorate in 1972. After teaching at the University of Hawaii and Johns Hopkins University, Haraway joined the faculty of the History of Consciousness at the University of California, Santa Cruz, in 1980.

Haraway's interdisciplinary studies of technology and gender have had a powerful impact on Cultural Studies, Postmodernism, and Feminism. Her first book, *Crystals, Fabrics and Fields* (1976), based on her dissertation, concerned the way metaphors are used to describe organic development in biology. In her second book, *Primate Visions*, she began to explore the representation of gender and race in modern science. Haraway's Cultural Studies approach to science and its representations challenges our presuppositions about science, gender, nature, and humanity. Like **Michel Foucault** and other poststructuralists, Haraway is interested in the Nietzschean project of "overcoming" the Enlightenment and all of its intellectual categories. She is especially concerned with deconstructing ESSENTIALIST and UNIVERSALIST claims that human beings and nature are ontological and epistemological givens, prior to all construction or representation. "A Manifesto for Cyborgs" (1985) and *Simians, Cyborgs, and Women* (1991) counter these claims with a vision of the *cyborg*, a new model for describing the relationship in postmodernity between human beings and science. Haraway argues that this vision is especially valuable for socialism and radical Feminism, for the cyborg model is a powerful reminder that the SUBJECT and SUBJECTIVITY are hybrid creations – part nature, part machine – and subject to *re*-creation for revolutionary purposes.

Modest_Witness@Second_Millenium (1997) continues Haraway's exploration of Postmodern science. In this volume, she examines how genetic research creates the body as a kind of "hypertext" that requires a new form of "technoscience" to map and understand. Haraway's theories have proven immensely popular, as her speaking schedule and the websites devoted to her work amply demonstrate.

SELECTED BIBLIOGRAPHY

Haraway, Donna. *The Haraway Reader*. New York and London: Routledge, 2004.
——. *Modest_Witness@Second_Millenium.FemaleMan_Meets_OncoMouse: Feminism and Technoscience*. With paintings by Lynn M. Randolph. New York: Routledge, 1997.
——. *Simians, Cyborgs, and Women: The Reinvention of Nature*. New York: Routledge, 1991.

bell hooks (1952–)

bell hooks (née Gloria Watkins) was born in Hopkinsville, Kentucky, and was educated at Stanford University and the University of Wisconsin. She received her doctorate from the University of California, Santa Cruz, in 1983. After teaching at Yale University and Oberlin College, hooks began teaching at the City College of New York, where she is now a Distinguished Professor of English.

In her first book, *Ain't I a Woman* (1981), hooks argues that sexism and racism have the same cause – white PATRIARCHY – against which feminists and anti-racist groups need to forge a shared position. The point is carried further in her most influential book, *Feminist Theory: From Margin* to *Center* (1984). In this text, hooks systematically critiques mainstream European and US Feminism for neglecting the issue of racism and for refusing to see sexism as its corollary. She urges feminists to take up these issues if they hope to make substantial social changes. Throughout the 1980s and '90s, hooks published many volumes on issues concerning race, gender, representation, and art. In *Talking Back* (1989) and *Black Look* (1992), hooks emphasizes education as both an institutional impediment and a possible site of resistance to institutional power. She explores the margins of gender and sexual IDENTITY in *Outlaw Culture* (1994) and examines the interplay of sex and class in film in *Reel to Real* (1996). For hooks, the nature and direction of theory should tend towards a "passionate politics," a point she argues in *Feminism is for Everybody* (2000). In the late 1990s, hooks wrote two memoirs and in 2000 issued a second edition of her groundbreaking *Feminist Theory*. She continues to write on a variety of topics including self-esteem and education among African Americans (*Rock My Soul* and *Teaching Community*, both in 2003) and black masculinity (*We Real Cool*, in 2004). hooks has also forayed into the field of feminist popular psychology with well-regarded books on love and relationships, including *All About Love* (2000).

SELECTED BIBLIOGRAPHY

hooks, bell. *Black Looks: Race and Representation*. Boston: South End Press, 1992.

——. *Feminist Theory: From Margin to Center*. Cambridge, MA: South End Press, 1984, 2002.

——. *Outlaw Culture: Resisting Representations*. New York: Routledge, 1994.

——. *Talking Back: Thinking Feminism, Thinking Black*. Boston: South End Press, 1989.

Linda Hutcheon (1947–)

Linda Hutcheon was born in Toronto, Canada, and educated at Cornell University and the University of Toronto, where she received a doctorate in comparative literature in 1975. After teaching for twelve years at McMaster University in Hamilton, Ontario, she took a position in comparative literature at the University of Toronto. Her work in theory, beginning with *Narcissistic Narrative* (1980), established her as a significant voice in Postmodernism. In *A Theory of Parody* (1985), she argued that intertextuality was a form of METADISCURSIVE critique. Hutcheon made her reputation as a theorist on the basis of *A Poetics of Postmodernism* (1988), which argues for a Postmodern aesthetics based on intertextuality and a critical historicism. A follow-up to that book, *The Politics of Postmodernism* (1989), furthers the argument of *Poetics* in part by a deeper concern for the ideological and political ramifications of Postmodern theoretical positions, especially with respect to history and representation in the arts. Also at this time, Hutcheon contributed to the debate over the relevance of Postmodernism for Postcolonial Studies. Her essay, "'Circling the Downspout of Empire'" (1989), is a lucid argument for the progressive potential of Postmodernist strategies.

In the 1990s, Hutcheon pursued further her interest in a politicized rhetorical theory and published *Irony's Edge: The Theory and Politics of Irony* in 1994. With her husband, Michael Hutcheon, she wrote *Opera: Desire, Disease and Death* (1996), a study of the operatic representations of "classic" illnesses (tuberculosis and syphilis), epidemics, tobacco use, and AIDS (the "gay plague"). In a "crypto-ethnic confession" of 1998, widely available on the internet, Hutcheon reclaimed her Italian heritage (she was born Bortolotti) from the Anglo name she had taken from her husband. It is an illuminating meditation on ethnicity and the social forces and traditions that mask it. Conscious of her own performance of ethnicity, she is sensitive to the performances of others. She has written extensively on Canadian literature and the complexities of multiculturalism in Toronto and other cities. In 2005, she received the Killam Prize (2005), Canada's most prestigious award for outstanding career achievements in the humanities.

SELECTED BIBLIOGRAPHY

Hutcheon, Linda. *Irony's Edge: The Theory and Politics of Irony*. London and New York: Routledge, 1994.

———. *Narcissistic Narrative: The Metafictional Paradox.* Waterloo, Ont.: Wilfred Laurier University Press, 1980.

———. *A Poetics of Postmodernism: History, Theory, Fiction.* New York: Routledge, 1988.

———. *The Politics of Postmodernism.* 2nd ed. London: Routledge, 1989, 2002.

Luce Irigaray (1930–)

Luce Irigaray was born in Belgium and was educated at the University of Louvain, where she received an MA degree. After a short stint teaching high school in Brussels, she attended the University of Paris and received a second MA in psychology (1961), followed by a Diploma in psychotherapy (1962) and a doctorate in linguistics (1968). For two years, Irigaray worked for the Nationale de la Recherche Scientifique in Belgium, and in 1964 she began working for the Centre National de la Recherche Scientifique in Paris, where she is currently Director of Research. Throughout the 1960s, she trained as a psychoanalyst and was a member of **Jacques Lacan's** École Freudienne de Paris. In the late 1960s, she began teaching at the University of Paris VIII (Vincennes). Upon publication of her dissertation (for a second doctorate), *Speculum of the Other Woman* (1974), Irigaray was dismissed from her position at the University of Paris (and Lacan's École Freudienne de Paris), largely due to Lacan's disapproval of her work.

In *Speculum*, Irigaray argues that Western philosophy and Psychoanalysis regard women as mere reflecting surfaces on which masculine IDENTITY constitutes itself in a DIALECTICAL relation of dominance. In *This Sex Which Is Not One* (1977), she experimented with an innovative mode of ÉCRITURE FEMININE (feminine writing, writing the body). These works were committed to deconstructing the PHALLOGOCENTRIC traditions of Psychoanalysis, philosophy, and literature. Defying rhetorical, syntactical, and thematic conventions, Irigaray's theoretical writings offer a penetrating critique of those conventions as well as alternatives to them. In her subsequent works, Irigaray pursued questions of DIFFERENCE and alterity, especially as it concerned gender and sexual identity.

In the 1990s, she worked with the Commission for Equal Opportunities for the region of Emilia-Romagna in Italy, producing a report on the status of rights for women, *Democracy begins Between the Two* (1994). She also wrote many books exploring the ethical implications of gender difference, including *Je, Tu, Nous* (1990), a collection of essays on civil rights and biological difference, and *An Ethics of Sexual Difference* (1993), a study of the ethical tradition in philosophy and an elaboration of her own ethical vision. She also produced new works on philosophy, psychoanalytic method, and language, as well as a series of works on the role of the elements in the sensual life of philosophers, including *Marine Lover of Friedrich Nietzsche* (1991). In 2002, drawing on Eastern philosophy and yoga, she revisited the questions of gender and sexual difference that had first secured her reputation as a feminist philosopher.

SELECTED BIBLIOGRAPHY

Irigaray, Luce. *An Ethics of Sexual Difference*. Trans. Carolyn Burke and Gillian C. Gill. Ithaca: Cornell Univ. Press, 1993.

——. *The Irigaray Reader*. Ed. Margaret Whitford. Oxford and Cambridge, MA: Basil Blackwell, 1991.

——. *Je, Tu, Nous: Toward a Culture of Difference*. Trans. Alison Martin. New York: Routledge, 1993.

——. *This Sex Which Is Not One*. Trans. Catherine Porter. Ithaca: Cornell Univ. Press, 1985.

——. *Speculum of the Other Woman*. Trans. Gilliam C. Gill. Ithaca: Cornell University Press, 1985.

Wolfgang Iser (1926–)

Wolfgang Iser was born in Marienberg, Germany, and educated at the University of Heidelberg, where he received his doctorate. In the 1960s, he was involved in founding the experimental University of Konstanz. Ultimately, Konstanz would become closely associated with the

Reader-Response theory of Iser and the reception theory of Hans Robert Jauss. In addition to teaching at Konstanz, Iser has held a long-standing appointment at the University California, Irvine. His academic career began in earnest with the publication of *The Implied Reader* (1972), a work of literary criticism, and *The Act of Reading* (1976), a meditation on the theoretical principles of what came to be known as Reader-Response theory. Iser's work explores the problems faced by readers when confronted with literary texts. Following in the footsteps of Roman Ingarden, whose phenomenology of reading was well known by the Konstanz theorists, Iser argued that the literary work was the result of the reader's engagement with the text. The very process of taming the semantic and SEMIOTIC possibilities of the text awakens in the reader a profound understanding of what it means to confront an alien consciousness.

Throughout the late 1970s and '80s, Iser wrote on Walter Pater's aesthetics, Shakespeare, and Laurence Stern. At this time, he was also studying certain theoretical and critical implications of Reader-Response theory, specifically the process of self-discovery that it entails. In *Prospecting* (1989) and *The Fictive and the Imaginary* (1993), he developed a conception of "literary anthropology," a mode of fieldwork in which readers use the literary work as a basis for "staging" their own responses to being human. Reading helps to define social life; even more, it helps to define what it is to be human. Literature's role in this process is unique; no other linguistic artifact is capable of seducing the reader into an essentially anthropological experience. Iser's work continues to deepen our understanding of the social and historical implications of reading and of being in the world.

SELECTED BIBLIOGRAPHY

Iser, Wolfgang. *The Act of Reading: A Theory of Aesthetic Response.* Baltimore: The Johns Hopkins University Press, 1978.
———. *The Fictive and the Imaginary: Charting Literary Anthropology.* Baltimore and London: Johns Hopkins University Press, 1993.
———. *The Implied Reader: Patterns of Communication in Prose Fiction from Bunyan to Beckett.* Baltimore: Johns Hopkins University Press, 1974.
———. *Prospecting: From Reader Response to Literary Anthropology.* Baltimore: Johns Hopkins University Press, 1989.
———. *The Range of Interpretation.* New York: Columbia University Press, 2000.

Fredric Jameson (1934–)

Fredric Jameson was born in Cleveland, Ohio, and educated at Haverford College and Yale University. He received his doctorate in 1959 from Yale and began teaching at Harvard University. In 1967 he moved to the University of California, San Diego, where he taught French and comparative literature. In 1976 he returned to Yale as a professor of French, and remained until 1983. In that year, he moved to the University of California, Santa Cruz, where he taught in the History of Consciousness program. In 1986, he was named William A. Lane, Jr. Professor of Comparative Literature and director of the Graduate Program in Literature and Theory at Duke University.

His first book, *Sartre: The Origins of a Style*, focused on the politics and ethics of existential philosophy and their relation to the problem of style. His next two works, *Marxism and Form* (1971) and *The Prison House of Language* (1972), are steeped in Marxism and the Russian formalist tradition. His first major work, *The Political Unconscious* (1981), is a Marxist analysis of the early Modernist novel, stressing the ways in which ideological MASTER NARRATIVES operate at an unconscious level in the text. Following **Louis Althusser's** theories of IDEOLOGY and structural causality, Jameson regards the novel as the purveyor of ideological codes that can only be grasped by the critic capable of reading the text's "political unconscious."

Jameson's renown as a theorist came from his application of "post-Marxist" methodology to Postmodern cultural texts. In 1984, he published his landmark essay, "Postmodernism, or, The Cultural Logic of Late Capitalism," in the *New Left Review*. In this essay, he inaugurated a materialist critique of the Postmodern in literature, architecture, and the arts. The collection of essays by the same name, published in 1991, established Jameson as a leading theorist of Postmodernism. Much of his work in the 1990s was dedicated to the critique of Postmodernism and its relation to modernity and to a new analysis of MODERNISM, especially its relation to imperialism. Of special note is the collection of essays on the Postmodern, *The Cultural Turn* (1998) and a study of modernity and literary Modernism, *A Singular Modernity* (2002). Jameson continues to explore the implications of Postmodernism and to champion Marxism as a still-relevant approach to the study of society and culture.

SELECTED BIBLIOGRAPHY

Jameson, Fredric. *The Ideologies of Theory: Essays 1971–1986.* 2 vols. Minneapolis: University of Minnesota Press, 1988.

——. *The Jameson Reader.* Ed. Michael Hardt and Kathi Weeks. Oxford and Malden, MA: Blackwell Publishers, 2000.

——. *The Political Unconscious: Narrative as a Socially Symbolic Act.* Ithaca: Cornell University Press, 1981.

——. *Postmodernism, or, The Cultural Logic of Late Capitalism.* Durham: Duke University Press, 1991.

——. *A Singular Modernity: Essay on the Ontology of the Present.* London: Verso, 2002.

Julia Kristeva (1941–)

Julia Kristeva was born in Sliven, Bulgaria, and studied at the University of Sofia before moving to Paris in 1966. She studied linguistics and semiotics at the University of Paris VII (Denis Diderot) and the École des Hautes Études en Sciences Sociales, from which she received a doctorate in linguistics in 1973. In 1974, she became a "permanent" visiting professor in the department of French at Columbia University (a position she also enjoyed, after 1992, at the University of Toronto) and began her long career at University of Paris VII. In 1992, she became director of École Doctorale at Paris VII and is currently professor of literature and linguistics. In addition to her academic appointments, Kristeva has, since 1979, maintained a career in Psychoanalysis.

Kristeva's innovative combination of SEMIOTICS, literary theory, and psychoanalysis – "semanalysis" as she puts it – exemplifies the interdisciplinary nature of Poststructuralism. Her early linguistics and semiotics research found an audience among readers of the journal *Tel Quel*, whose editorial board she joined in 1969. In these years, she collaborated with **Roland Barthes** and Philippe Sollers (whom she eventually married). In 1974, she published her doctoral dissertation as *Revolution in Poetic Lan-*

guage, a study of semiotic poetics and nineteenth-century experimental poetry. Her most important early work involved an investigation of the semiotic *chora*, a pre-Oedipal space characterized by the dissolution of boundaries and signifying systems and a resistance to patriarchal discourse and authority. The *chora* privileges the maternal body and is the foundation for a feminist ethics. Kristeva's work in the 1970s concerned problems in linguistics and semiotics, though *About Chinese Women* (1977) looks ahead to her later works in feminist psychoanalysis. In the same year, *Polylogue* (1977), a collection of her early essays on semiotics and the novel appeared and, with some modifications, was translated as *Desire in Language* (1980). This text, especially its emphasis on Bakhtinian DIALOGISM, INTERTEXTUALITY, parody, and the maternal body, made her a major figure in Poststructuralist and Feminist Theory. In *Powers of Horror* (1980), she introduced the concept of "abjection," a condition resulting from the need, in patriarchal societies, to regard the maternal body as a threat to the development of normative SUBJECTIVITY.

Throughout the 1980s and '90s, Kristeva wrote on psychoanalysis, social alienation, nationalism, Proust, and a host of other topics. She also wrote fiction, with her *roman à clef, The Samurai*, attracting critical attention. Though she was influenced to some degree by **Jacques Lacan's** seminars of the 1970s, her own approach as an analyst was defined by a feminist resistance to some of his key formulations. Important psychoanalytic works include *Tales of Love* (1983) and *Black Sun* (1987), a study of depression and melancholy. In *New Maladies of the Soul* (1995), she brought together her essays from the previous two decades. This collection includes "Women's Time" (1977), one of her most important and influential feminist works. In 1998, Kristeva collaborated with Catherine Clément on *The Feminine and the Sacred* and, since 2000, she has written on Melanie Klein, Hannah Arendt, and Colette.

SELECTED BIBLIOGRAPHY

Kristeva, Julia. *The Kristeva Reader.* Ed. Toril Moi. New York: Columbia University Press, 1986.

——. *Powers of Horror: An Essay on Abjection.* Trans. Leon S. Roudiez. New York: Columbia University Press, 1982.

——. *Revolution in Poetic Language.* Trans. Margaret Waller. New York: Columbia University Press, 1984.

——. *Tales of Love*. Trans. Leon S. Roudiez. New York: Columbia University Press, 1987.

——. *New Maladies of the Soul*. Trans. Ross Guberman. New York: Columbia University Press, 1995.

Jacques Lacan (1901–81)

Jacques Lacan was born in Paris and educated in Jesuit schools before beginning his studies in medicine and psychiatry at the Faculté de Médecine de Paris. He started his clinical training in 1927, working on "automatism" and personality disorders. He received his doctorate in 1932 with a thesis on paranoid psychoses and the possibilities of combining psychiatry with Psychoanalysis. Two years later, he joined the Psychoanalytic Society of Paris and began undergoing psychoanalysis. During the Second World War, he protested the brutality of the Nazi occupiers of France by ceasing all professional work. In the decades following the war, he developed an interest in Structuralism and linguistics, arguing that these sciences shed light on the workings of the unconscious. His unorthodox theories of clinical practice led to his break from the International Psycho-Analytical Association (IPA) in 1953. In the same year, at a congress in Rome, Lacan read his most important early essay, "Function and Field of Speech in Psychoanalysis," which argues that the creation of the subject is fundamentally and unavoidably a process of immersion in linguistic structures. It followed that the unconscious must also operate according to this order.

For the next ten years or so, Lacan devoted his time to a project now referred to as the "return to Freud." As he readily admits, his discovery of the importance of structure and language in the unconscious was actually a working out of discoveries Freud himself had made without the benefit of the Saussurean linguistics that were necessary to understand them. The essays of this period, collected in *Écrits* (1966), form the basis of his early reputation, though his seminars, beginning in 1954, produced much of his work on Freudian theory. In *Écrits*, Lacan postulates a structural theory of language that permeates the ego's relations with the world, that indeed constructs the ego as a SUBJECTIVITY *in the* world. Lacan articulates this formation as a process in which the SUBJECT becomes constituted by her ascension to the SYMBOLIC order of language, law, and representation. In the Symbolic, desire displaces demand and institutes "lack" as the foundation of subjectivity. He also posited an IMAGINARY order, characterized by narcissistic desire and fantasy, and an order of the REAL where basic needs require and receive fulfillment. The Real is wholly external to the Symbolic and Imaginary orders, the unrepresentable ground of human experience.

In the early 1970s, Lacan and members of the *École freudienne de Paris*, which Lacan had formed in 1964, published *Feminine Sexuality* (1973). Since the early 1980s, translations of Lacan's seminars on psychoanalytic theory have steadily appeared, many of which were not published in any form in his lifetime. If the essays in *Écrits* established Lacan as the preeminent psychoanalytic theorist of the poststructuralist era, the seminars and later work confirmed the originality and critical power of his "return to Freud."

SELECTED BIBLIOGRAPHY

Lacan, Jacques. *Écrits: A Selection.* Trans. Alan Sheridan. New York: Norton, 1977.

——. *Feminine Sexuality: Jacques Lacan and the École Freudienne.* Ed. Juliet Mitchell and Jacqueline Rose. Trans. Jacqueline Rose. New York and London: Norton; New York: Pantheon Books, 1985.

——. *The Four Fundamental Concepts of Psycho-Analysis.* Ed. Jacques-Alain Miller. Trans. Alan Sheridan. New York: Norton, 1978.

——. "Desire and the Interpretation of Desire in Hamlet." Yale French Studies 55/56 (1980): 11–52.

——. *The Seminar of Jacques Lacan.* Ed. Jacques-Alain Miller. Trans. John Forrester. 2 vols. Cambridge: Cambridge University Press, 1988.

Jean-François Lyotard (1924–98)

Jean-François Lyotard was born in Vincennes, France, and studied philosophy and literature at Sorbonne University, where he met **Gilles**

Deleuze. In the last year of the war, Lyotard served as a first-aid volunteer in occupied Paris. After passing his *agrégation* in philosophy in 1950, he began teaching in a lycée in French-occupied Algeria. He became radicalized in the mid-1950s and joined the socialist collective *Socialisme et Barbarie*. By the early 1960s, he was lecturing at the Sorbonne, attending **Jacqaes Lacan**'s seminars and, later in the decade, teaching at the University of Paris X (Nanterre) and serving as director of research at the Centre National de la Recherche Scientifique. In 1971, Lyotard received his doctorate and began teaching at the University of Paris VII (Vincennes), where he remained until his retirement in 1987. Throughout the late 1980s and '90s, he lectured and taught all over the world and served as regular visiting professor at the University of California, Irvine.

After publishing a major work on phenomenology in 1954, Lyotard devoted much of his time to political journalism and Marxist essays on philosophical topics, publishing many of them in *Socialism et Barbarie*. In 1971 he published his doctoral thesis as *Discourse, figure*. This text is a response to Lacan's seminars and to Structuralism in general. Throughout the 1970s Lyotard continued to explore psychoanalytic questions, often alongside Marxist themes, as in *Dérive à partir de Marx et Freud* (1973). His most important work of this period was *Libidinal Economy* (1974), an innovative critique of philosophy and Marxism from the perspective of Freud's theory of desire. Lyotard's reputation as a Postmodernist was secured with *The Postmodern Condition* (1979), a study of Western knowledge and its transmission that focused on new forms of information analysis, especially game theory and pragmatics. His famous formulation of the Postmodern as that which, in the modern, resists representation has been widely adapted by theorists of postmodernity. Throughout the 1980s, he turned his attention to aesthetics, specifically the concept of the sublime, and to philosophical ethics. His work on the latter produced *Le Différend* (1983), which argues that social and cultural discourses often perpetuate a situation of incommensurability in which it is impossible to guarantee agreement in matters of justice, aesthetics, and moral philosophy. The *différend* marks this impossibility by naming the irreducible DIFFERENCE that defines it. Lyotard's theory of the Postmodern was developed throughout the 1980s and early '90s, issuing in two important essay collections, *The Postmodern Explained to Children* (1986) and *Toward the Postmodern* (1993). The last decade of his life saw a renewed interest in Kant's aesthetics and the publication, in 1994, of

Lessons on the Analytic of the Sublime. In this text, as in so many of his works at this time, Lyotard reminds us of postmodernity's lingering indebtedness to Enlightenment philosophy.

SELECTED BIBLIOGRAPHY

Lyotard, Jean-François. *The Differend: Phrases in Dispute.* Trans. Georges Van Den Abbeele. Minneapolis: University of Minnesota Press, 1988.

——. *Libidinal Economy.* Trans. Iain Hamilton Grant. Bloomington and Indianapolis: Indiana University Press, 1993.

——. *The Lyotard Reader.* Ed. Andrew Benjamin. Oxford and Cambridge, MA: Blackwell, 1989.

——. *The Postmodern Condition: A Report on Knowledge.* Trans. Geoff Bennington and Brian Massumi. Minneapolis: University of Minnesota Press, 1984.

——. *Toward the Postmodern.* Ed. Robert Harvey and Mark S. Roberts. Atlantic Highlands, NJ: Humanities Press, 1993.

J. Hillis Miller (1928–)

J. Hillis Miller was born in Newport News, Virginia, and studied at Oberlin College and Harvard University, where he received his doctorate in 1952. He taught for nearly twenty years at Johns Hopkins University (1953–72), then taught at Yale University (1972–86), where he held the Frederick W. Hilles Chair in English and Comparative Literature. In 1986, he left Yale for the University of California, Irvine, where he is currently UCI Distinguished Professor.

Miller's early work, especially *Charles Dickens: The World of His Novels* (1958), grew out of his interest in the Geneva school of phenomenological criticism, especially the ideas of Georges Poulet. Over the next ten years, Miller studied the nineteenth-century literary tradition, producing *The Disappearance of God* (1963) and *Poets of Reality* (1965), texts which examine the way God's absence and the "here and now" serve to ground literary vision. Through the late 1960s and '70s, he continued to write about the literary tradition, but also turned his attention to the problems that had arisen in the wake of Deconstruction and other poststructuralist theories. In "Ariadne's Thread" (1976), he argued that narratives do not proceed along straight lines but are rather structured like labyrinths. In "The Critic as Host" (1977), he defended Deconstruction against the charge of parasitism, and in the process deconstructed the binomial relationship of host–parasite. He followed up these extremely influential essays with *Fiction and Repetition* (1982), an important study of the novel that drew on Nietzschean and Deleuzean theories of DIFFERENCE and repetition to describe the two modes of repetition (unifying and differential) that construct novelistic narrative. In the 1980s, Miller began to explore a linguistically-based "ethics of reading," arguing that our compulsion to read enabled the development of an ethical sensibility. In 1990, Miller consolidated his position on the ethics of reading with three collections of essays, *Tropes, Parables, Performatives, Versions of Pygmalion*, and *Victorian Subjects*. These texts, with their emphasis on literature as a performative act involving the reader as collaborator, confirmed his reputation as a major innovator in deconstructionist and reader-response theories. In 1992, he published *Ariadne's Thread*, which explored further his earlier ideas about labyrinthine narratives in conjunction with his new performative theory of ethical reading. His work of the late 1990s tended toward studies of literature drawing on narrative theory and speech act theory. More than any other poststructuralist critic, Miller has taught us the myriad possibilities of an ethics of reading grounded in the openness of the text.

SELECTED BIBLIOGRAPHY

Miller, J. Hillis. *Ariadne's Thread: Story Lines*. New Haven: Yale University Press, 1992.

——. *The Ethics of Reading: Kant, de Man, Eliot, Trollope, James and Benjamin*. New York: Columbia University Press, 1987.

——. *Fiction and Repetition*. Cambridge: Harvard University Press, 1982.

——. *The J. Hillis Miller Reader*. Ed. Julian Wolfreys. Stanford: Stanford University Press, 2005.

——. *Tropes, Parables, Performatives: Essays on Twentieth-century Literature*. New York: Harvester Wheatsheaf, 1990.

Edward Said (1935–2003)

Edward Said was born in Jerusalem, British Occupied Palestine, and moved with his family to Cairo after the 1947 partition by Israel. He was educated in Cairo and the US, studying piano briefly at the Julliard School of Music. He received his BA degree from Princeton University (1957) and his doctorate from Harvard University (1964) and began his career at Columbia University, where he was teaching at the time of his death. He has held visiting professorships at a number of institutions, including Yale University and Stanford University. His dissertation was published in 1966 under the title *Joseph Conrad and the Fiction of Autobiography*. In the next year, after the outbreak of the Arab–Israel war in 1967, Said turned to a more politically charged critique. This trend in his thinking is notable in *Beginnings* (1975), a study of the novel influenced by Foucauldian theories of discourse analysis. His seminal study, *Orientalism* (1979), was his first major work to respond to the troubles in the Middle East. In this volume, he analyzes a vast structure of knowledge and power dedicated to representing and controlling the Orient. His critique of the binomial logic of "us and them" that subtends ORIENTALIST discourse was a foundational work for the emergent field of Postcolonial Studies and a powerful influence on **Homi Bhabha** and **Gayatri Chakravorty Spivak**.

In the 1980s, Said turned increasingly to the study of Palestine, challenging Western media stereotypes of the Middle East in *Covering Islam* (1981) and *After the Last Sky* (1986). He also elaborated on his theory of "secular criticism" in *The World, the Text and the Critic* (1983), a text that explored the cultural and political stakes of criticism and included the much-discussed essay, "Traveling Theory," a reflection on the globalization of theoretical discourse. Said wrote on a wide variety of topics through the 1980s and '90s, with many of his essays, including those on Jane Austen's representation of colonial economies, appearing in an important collection, *Culture and Imperialism* (1993). He continued to write about his involvement with the Palestinian Liberation Organization, with which he was affiliated throughout his career. He was also interested in the role of the intellectual and wrote many essays on the particular problems of intellectuals in colonial and postcolonial societies. In 1999, he published a memoir, *Out of Place*, that poignantly recounts the privileged yet traumatic upbringing he experienced in Palestine and Cairo, his involvement with Palestinian causes, and his long academic career in the US. In the last years of his life, he published collections of his essays and interviews on the Middle East peace process and other issues in contemporary politics. One of Said's last works, published the year after his death, *Humanism and Democratic Criticism* (2004), sums up his humanistic vision and reiterates the need for public intellectuals. Few literary theorists have been as passionately and consistently dedicated to the values of secularism and the free exchange of ideas.

SELECTED BIBLIOGRAPHY

Said, Edward W. *Beginnings: Intentions and Method.* New York: Columbia University Press, 1985.

——. *Culture and Imperialism.* New York: Knopf, 1993.

——. *The Edward Said Reader.* Ed. Moustafa Bayoumi and Andrew Rubin. New York: Vintage Books, 2000.

——. *Orientalism.* London: Penguin, 1985.

——. *The World, the Text and the Critic.* Cambridge, MA: Harvard University Press, 1983.

Eve Kosofsky Sedgwick (1950–)

Eve Kosofsky Sedgwick was born in Dayton, Ohio, and was educated at Cornell University and Yale University, where she received her doctorate in 1975. She has taught at a number of institutions, including Boston University, Dartmouth College, and Duke University, where she was the Newman Ivey White Professor of English. She now teaches in the Graduate Center of the City University of New York.

Sedgwick's early work was instrumental in establishing a theoretical vocabulary for queer theory. Of crucial importance was the concept of HOMOSOCIAL DESIRE which she introduced in her first book *Between Men* (1985). Drawing on the work of Gayle Rubin and René Girard, Sedgwick constructed a theory of "triangular desire," a relationship in which a woman serves as the conduit for a homosocial bond between men, a privileged access to social power that requires women and simultaneously excludes them. *Epistemology of the Closet* (1990) is a pioneering study of homosexuality in literature, focusing on Melville, Wilde, James, and Proust. Especially influential was Sedgwick's theory of "homosexual panic," a violent reaction against any manifestation of homoeroticism or "genitalized" homosexual behavior that might threaten homosocial bonds. In the early 1990s, she continued to pursue questions of queer identity in literature, causing something of a scandal with her controversial essay "Jane Austen and the Masturbating Girl" (1991). She also co-edited important essay collections, including *Performativity and Performance* (1995) and *Shame and Its Sister: A Silvan Tomkins Reader* (1995). The latter marks Sedgwick's interest in the work of Tomkins and his theories of innate primal affects, which she used to refine her own conception of "queer PERFORMATIVITY" in *Touching Feeling: Affect, Pedagogy, Performativity* (2003).

In addition to her groundbreaking theoretical work, Sedgwick has published a book of poems, *Fat Art, Thin Art* (1994), and an account of her experience with depression while recovering from breast cancer, *A Dialogue on Love* (1999). An experimental mélange of generic elements, her memoir seeks to understand the significance of therapy and the power of self-exploration.

SELECTED BIBLIOGRAPHY

Sedgwick, Eve Kosofsky. *Between Men: English Literature and Male Homosocial Desire.* New York: Columbia University Press, 1985.

——. *Epistemology of the Closet.* Berkeley: University of California Press, 1990.

——. *Tendencies.* Durham: Duke University Press, 1993.

——. *Touching Feeling: Affect, Pedagogy, Performativity.* Durham and London: Duke University Press, 2003.

Elaine Showalter (1941–)

Elaine Showalter was born in Cambridge, Massachusetts, and educated at Bryn Mawr College, Brandeis University, and the University of California at Davis in 1970. After teaching at a variety of institutions, including high school and adult education, she landed at Princeton University, where she is Avalon Foundation Professor Emerita. She has chaired the department of English at Princeton and served as president of the Modern Language Association (1997). She has been actively involved in writing for the popular press, with articles in *People*, *Vogue*, *The New Statesman*, the *London Review of Books*, and other periodicals, and appearing as a regular guest on television talk shows.

Showalter was one of the leading figures in US Feminism in the 1970s. She coined the term "gynocriticism," which refers to the study of the unique literary traditions of women writers. Her second and most influential work, *A Literature of Their Own* (1976), rewrote the literary history of the novel and developed a compelling alternative to the PATRIARCHAL tradition in fiction. Her theory of "the female aesthetic," influenced by French Feminism, especially the work of **Hélène Cixous**, argues for a vision of literary art in which language and narrative resist the constraints of patriarchal traditions. Showalter turned to cultural history in *The Female Malady* (1985), in which she critiqued the medical establishment, particularly psychiatry, and its attempt to define and control women by "medicalizing" personality traits and behaviors that violate heterosexual masculinist norms. Her next two books were elaborations on this critique. *Sexual Anarchy* (1990) continued her interest in the cultural history of women's experience, focusing on the psychology of gender in the 1890s. In *Hystories* (1997), Showalter continued the argument advanced in *Sexual Anarchy*, but went beyond the limits of her critique of gender to focus on chronic fatigue syndrome, Gulf War syndrome, recovered memory, satanic ritual abuse, and alien abduction. Her work in the twenty-first century has so far focused on pedagogy, feminist history, and the academic novel.

SELECTED BIBLIOGRAPHY

Showalter, Elaine. *The Female Malady: Women, Madness and English Culture, 1830–1980.* New York: Pantheon Books, 1985.

——. *Hystories: Hysterical Epidemics and Modern Culture.* New York: Columbia University Press, 1997.

——. *A Literature of Their Own: British Women Novelists from Brontë to Lessing.* 2nd Expanded Ed. Princeton: Princeton University Press, 1999.

——. *Sexual Anarchy: Gender and Culture at the Fin de Siècle.* New York: Viking, 1990.

——. *Teaching Literature.* Malden, MA: Blackwell Publishers, 2003.

Gayatri Chakravorty Spivak (1942–)

Gayatri Chakravorty Spivak was born in Calcutta, West Bengal, and educated at the University of Calcutta. She then moved to the US, where she studied comparative literature with **Paul de Man** at Cornell University. She began teaching at the University of Iowa in 1965, receiving her doctorate two years later. In her long and prestigious career, she has taught at a variety of institutions, including Brown University, the University of Texas, Austin, the University of Pittsburgh, and Emory University. She is currently Avalon Foundation Professor in the Humanities and the Director of the Center for Comparative Literature and Society at Columbia University.

Spivak published her dissertation on Yeats, *Myself Must I Remake: The Life and Poetry of W. B. Yeats,* in 1974, but her first major work was a translation of **Jacques Derrida's** *Of Grammatology* (1976). Her introduction to this volume acquired a notoriety of its own for its deft handling of Derrida's ideas and her complex and lively style. Throughout the late 1970s and '80s, Spivak published *In Other Worlds* (1987) and a number of important essays, including "Three Women's Texts and a Critique of Imperialism" (1985) and "Can the Subaltern Speak?" (1988). These essays combined an interest in Deconstruction and Marxism with a defiant resistance to PATRIARCHAL structures of knowledge and power. Of special importance was her attention to the problems of gender and SUBALTERN IDENTITY and her development of a feminist perspective sensitive to the political and cultural conditions of colonial and postcolonial societies. She also contributed a critical edge to the revisionist historiography coming out of the Subaltern Studies Group at this time. These early works established her as something of a celebrity, much sought after by interviewers. She was a willing, articulate, and quite charming subject, and a collection of her interviews, *The Post-Colonial Critic*, appeared in 1990.

Throughout the 1990s, Spivak pursued diverse interests within Postcolonial theory. Of special note is her work on pedagogy in *Outside In the Teaching Machine* (1993) and other texts, in which she reflects on the responsibilities of educators in multicultural societies, both western and postcolonial. Some of her work in this period was taken up and reframed in *A Critique of Postcolonial Reason* (1999). In 2000, she delivered the Wellek Library Lectures, published as *Death of a Discipline* (2003), in which she argues for a new conception of comparative literature, a "transnational cultural studies" that transcends traditional notions of nation and national boundary. In such provocative works, Spivak reminds us that the postcolonial world is *our* world.

SELECTED BIBLIOGRAPHY

Spivak, Gayatri Chakravorty. "Can the Subaltern Speak?" *Marxism and the Interpretation of Culture*. Ed. Cary Nelson and Lawrence Grossberg. Urbana: University of Illinois Press, 1988. 271–313.

——. *A Critique of Postcolonial Reason: Toward a History of the Vanishing Moment*. Cambridge, MA and London: Harvard University Press, 1999.

——. *In Other Worlds: Essays in Cultural Politics*. New York: Methuen, 1987.

——. *The Post-Colonial Critic: Interviews, Strategies, Dialogues*. Ed. Sarah Harasym. New York: Routledge, 1990.

——. *The Spivak Reader: Selected Works of Gayatri Chakravorty Spivak*. Ed. Donna Landry and Gerald MacLean. New York: Routledge, 1996.

Raymond Williams (1921–88)

Raymond Williams was born in Llanfihangel Crocorney, a small village in Wales. He began as a scholarship student at Trinity College, Cambridge University, in 1939. War service intervened on his education when, in 1941, he became a tank commander. He returned to Cambridge and received his MA in 1946. He began teaching at Oxford University as an extra-mural tutor in literature, mostly in adult education. In 1961, he became a Fellow at Jesus College, Oxford, only to return to Cambridge as a Reader in 1967. By 1974 he was Professor of Drama, a position he held until 1983.

Williams's earliest works were on modern drama, but his reputation began with two volumes of literary and cultural history, *Culture and Society: 1780–1950* (1958) and *The Long Revolution* (1961). These volumes are revisionist cultural histories in the New Left tradition of British CULTURAL MATERIALISM. *Culture and Society* reconsidered canonical literary and cultural works in terms of their role in the development of "culture," which he understood in Gramscian terms as a complex web of IDEOLOGICAL commitments and "structures of feeling." In *The Long Revolution*, Williams critiqued the concept of organicism that had shaped the conservative tradition of social theory that began with Edmund Burke. Of special importance was his analysis of English educational institutions and the role they play in the creation and preservation of culture.

These works form the basis of Williams's contribution to British Cultural Studies and cultural materialism. His work in the 1970s, beginning with *The English Novel from Dickens to Lawrence* (1970), continued the emphasis on cultural and literary history. This study was one of the first to submit the English novel tradition to a sustained materialist analysis. *The Country and the City* (1973), a penetrating analysis of the English pastoral tradition, highlights the political realities of both the country and the city. Other major works include *Keywords* (1985), an in-depth glossary of terms in cultural analysis, and *Marxism and Literature* (1977), one of the first general studies of Marxism and its uses for literary criticism.

Williams was also instrumental in developing programs in communications. His *Communications* (1967) became a textbook for new academic programs throughout the UK and the US. His later work focused on the popular media and the problems in cultural materialism. His last book, *The Politics of Modernism*, published the year after his death, explored the problematic relationship between radical politics and Modernism. Evidence of his continuing relevance for literary and cultural theory is the new revised edition of *Keywords* (2005).

SELECTED BIBLIOGRAPHY

Williams, Raymond. *Culture and Society: 1780–1950.* Rpt. New York: Columbia University Press, 1983.
——. *The Long Revolution.* New York: Columbia University Press; London: Chatto & Windus, 1961.
——. *Marxism and Literature.* Oxford: Oxford University Press, 1977.
——. *The Politics of Modernism: Against the New Conformists.* Ed. Tony Pinkney. London and New York: Verso, 1989.
——. *The Raymond Williams Reader.* Ed. John Higgins. Oxford and Malden, MA: Blackwell Publishers, 2001.

Slavoj Žižek (1949–)

Slavoj Žižek was born in Ljubljana, Slovenia, and studied philosophy at the University of Llubljana, where he received his doctorate. He also studied Psychoanalysis at the University of Paris and underwent analysis by Jacques Alain Miller, **Jacque Lacan's** son-in-law. In 1979, he became a researcher at the Institute for Sociology and Philosophy, at the University of Llubljana. He has lectured widely and served as a visiting professor in many US and European universities. In the 1980s, he was active in Slovenian politics, running for the presidency of the Republic of Slovenia in 1990. In addition to his duties at the Institute of Sociology, Žižek teaches at the European Graduate School in Saas-Fee, Switzerland.

Žižek is one of the most provocative and original thinkers to emerge in the 1990s and has written on a wide array of topics. From the beginning of his career, he has worked within two very different theoretical traditions: Critical Theory and poststructuralist Psychoanalysis. Following the lead of early theorists like Herbert Marcuse, he applied psychoanalytic theory to social and cultural phenomena. In the space of two years, he published *The Sublime Object of Ideology* (1989), a study of Marx and Hegel from a Lacanian perspective, and *Looking Awry* (1991), a Lacanian reading of popular culture, including the films of Alfred Hitchcock. These texts established Žižek as one of the most influential Lacanian theorists. *Tarrying with the Negative* (1993) uses Lacanian theories to understand the power and variety of contemporary ideologies. His study of the Lacanian "Thing" – the unknowable REAL object that serves as the magnetic center for unconscious thoughts – within a context of Eastern European nationalism was a signally important application of Psychoanalysis to social phenomena. In the 1990s, he wrote and edited numerous volumes on Psychoanalysis, and several works on the German Romantic critic F. W. J. von Schelling. In *Plague of Fantasies* (1997), he explored the breakdown of the centered psychological SUBJECT in the COMMODIFIED space of fantasy.

In the late 1990s and the first few years of the new millennium Žižek published books on political SUBJECTIVITY, David Lynch's *Lost Highway*, Christian belief, and totalitarianism. In *Contingency, Hegemony, Universality* (2000), he joined **Judith Butler** and Ernesto Laclau in an exploration of the uses of Kantian and Hegelian theories for leftist political theory. The essays in this volume critiqued the classical theories of universality and suggested that contingent forms of it might prove useful for political action. A similar argument is mounted in *The Fragile Absolute, Or, Why is the Christian Legacy Worth Fighting For?* (2000). In the wake of the attacks on the World Trade Center, Žižek has written on the occupation of Iraq, notably in *Welcome to the Desert of the Real!* (2002). His work demonstrates eloquently that theory has a vital role to play in contemporary politics.

SELECTED BIBLIOGRAPHY

Žižek, Slavoj. *Enjoy Your Symptom!: Jacques Lacan in Hollywood and Out.* New York: Routledge, 1992.

——. *Looking Awry: An Introduction to Jacques Lacan through Popular Culture.* Cambridge, MA: MIT Press, 1991.

——. *Tarrying with the Negative: Kant, Hegel, and the Critique of Ideology.* Durham: Duke University Press, 1993.

——. *Welcome to the Desert of the Real!: Five Essays on September 11 and Related Dates.* London and New York: Verso, 2002.

——. *The Žižek Reader.* Eds. Elizabeth Wright and Edmond Leo Wright. Oxford and Malden, MA: Blackwell Publishers, 1999.

READING WITH
LITERARY THEORY

Nor dare she trust a larger lay,
But rather loosens from the lip
Short swallow-flights of song, that dip
Their wings in tears, and skim away.
Tennyson, *In Memoriam*

In this section, I have chosen a dozen texts to illustrate the way literary theories work. These analyses are intended to exemplify the kinds of questions that a particular theory might ask of a particular text. To each text I apply three of the theories discussed in "The Scope of Literary Theory" (though in two cases, the sections on Conrad's *Heart of Darkness* and Brontë's *Jane Eyre*, I have used four). My choice of texts is based on a combination of factors, including availability, the likelihood that a given text will be regularly taught, and my own teaching and writing experience. Were there world enough and time, I would have included readings of film, advertising, romance and detective novels – the whole "readable" landscape of modern culture. As it is, the task is already daunting, even when confronted with that most traditional of artistic productions, the literary text.

My readings in this section, though crafted in their present short form for pedagogical purposes, give a fair sense of the variety of approaches to a single text. I have tried whenever possible to give an indication of how theories are combined in critical practice. The reader is invited to argue different points and to arrive at different conclusions.

I have included all the major literary genres and have tried to pick theories that seemed to me to have an affinity for a particular text

(Rushdie's *Midnight's Children* and Postcolonial Studies, for example, or Woolf's *To the Lighthouse* and Feminism). It may seem whimsical to speak of "affinities" in this context, but it is very often just that sense of intuitive connection that makes a given theoretical approach seem like the best one available. The reader should bear in mind that it is quite common for critical writers to draw on more than one theory. It is equally common for critics to disagree on the value of a particular theory or on how that theory ought to be applied. Critical debate has served a salutary role in the history of theory, not least because it advances the general principle that theory is a valuable tool in the analysis of literary and cultural texts.

Students who are beginning to use theory in their analysis of literary and cultural texts are not usually expected to do the kind of archival research demanded by New Historicism or to have the background in philosophy that distinguishes so many theorists of Deconstruction and Poststructuralism. Nor are students expected to have mastered technical knowledge of Psychoanalysis or Structuralism. Rather they are expected to keep an open mind and to experiment with the tools that they have at their disposal. They can also be expected to use their own resources, garnered from work in the classroom and the library, to build on the research that theorists have done. What the student brings to her own analyses of literary texts is a degree of curiosity about how theory might open up avenues of interpretation and a willingness to acquire a modest background in the theory in question. The *Blackwell Guide to Literary Theory* provides a starting point for this kind of work.

William Shakespeare, *The Tempest*

*Reader Response * New Historicism * Postcolonial Studies*

The Tempest was Shakespeare's last romance, written in 1611, and in it he meditates on the problems of power and "right rule." Readers (or spectators) of the play will regard the treatment of these issues in different ways, depending on the circumstances and conditions of their own experience. Reader-Response theory attempts to understand just these differences. Seventeenth-century readers would have understood the political point of *The Tempest* according to the "horizon" of their own experience and the specific nature of their "interpretive communities." They might see Prospero as a symbol of social harmony, civil justice, and dynastic succession. However, for modern readers schooled in the history of COLONIALISM and imperial expansion, Prospero is an oppressive colonist, using magic to mask social and political power. Similarly, while Shakespeare's own contemporaries might have regarded Caliban as an inhuman barbarian (or, at best, an early form of the Romantic "noble savage"), a modern reader is more likely to regard him sympathetically as the subject of colonial oppression and dispossession, of the inequality and discrimination at the heart of European power.

Reader-Response theory requires the reader of a literary text to make decisions about the significance of character, action, theme, and symbol. It assumes that the reader completes the text at hand, not by discovering "hidden" meanings but by interpreting gaps, contradictions, and ambiguities. Consider the following lines spoken by Caliban to Stephano, one of the men planning a revolt against Prospero:

> Why, as I told thee, 'tis a custom with him
> I' th' afternoon to sleep. There thou mayst brain him,
> Having first seized his books; or with a log
> Batter his skull, or paunch him with a stake,
> Or cut his weasand with thy knife. Remember
> First to possess his books, for without them
> He's but a sot, as I am, nor hath not
> One spirit to command. They all do hate him
> As rootedly as I. Burn but his books. (3.2.82–90)

It is difficult for a modern reader not to discern a certain resourceful-
ness behind Caliban's barbarism, evidence of the extent to which he has
learned the language of his oppressor. "You taught me language," he
tells Prospero, "and my profit on 182–83't/Is I know how to curse"
(I.2.364–65). But he knows more than how to curse. In the above-quoted
passage, the savage beast becomes the strategist, aware of Prospero's
weaknesses (his afternoon nap) but also aware that his books of magic
are the signs of his social authority. Readers are led to regard Caliban
not as a dangerous threat to social order but rather as a victim of that
order. But they are also led to regard Prospero, without his books, as
no better than Caliban: "without them/He's but a sot, as I am." The
reader of *The Tempest* must fill in gaps that have been created not only
by language (what exactly do "books" signify?) but by the "aesthetic
distance" between the play's historical context and the modern
reader.

The problem for the New Historicist critic is to determine the "historicity" of the text, the precise relation between the elements of the play
and the historical context in which it is embedded. Of particular importance for *The Tempest* is the New World, where early settlers were engaged
in Indian wars, and Ireland, which had experienced a major crisis in 1607
when the indigenous aristocracy fled to the Continent (the "flight of the
earls"), displaced by a huge influx of English "planters" into Ulster, Ireland's northern province. In addition to the colonial subtext is another,
which would have been more readily grasped by Shakespeare's contemporaries: the problem of proper governance and the right of succession,
especially with respect to the new Stuart regime. The play is framed by
comic scenes of monarchical infighting between the mutinous nobility
(Sebastian and Antonio) and the enlightened guardians of civil harmony
(Prospero and Gonzalo). This drama of internecine struggle is mirrored
by the farcical plot among Stephan, Trinculo, and Caliban to kill Prospero and take over the island (see 2.1.1–53). The comical struggles that
surround Prospero reflect dissatisfaction with the absolutism of James
the First, who ascended the throne in 1603 and whose relations with
Parliament were contentious. The masque in act four, which celebrates
Ferdinand and Miranda's engagement, solidifies power within a recognizable European tradition, but leaves open the question of whether this
power, entailing as it does the oppression of native peoples, constitutes
a "right to rule."

The important question is whether Shakespeare is defending the new king, and thus the Stuart line of succession, or if he is questioning not only his right to rule but also his policies of conquest. The inverse problem is also important: to what extent does Shakespeare's play exemplify the TEXTUALITY of history? For the New Historicist critic, interpreting *The Tempest* as a commentary on colonial expansion and monarchial absolutism amounts to opening up of history itself to interpretation. Indeed, it calls into question the possibility of a singular, irrefutable historical account.

For Postcolonial Studies, the issue is not proper governance or the right to rule within a context of orderly succession. The issue is rather one of colonial dispossession and the SOCIAL CONSTRUCTION of Caliban, represented as an abject, animal-like slave, as racially OTHER with respect to Europeans. Caliban thus becomes a screen on which the conquering Europeans project their own desire. "When thou didst not, savage,/ Know thine own meaning, but wouldst gabble like/A thing most brutish, I endowed thy purposes/With words that made them known" (1.2.358–61). Miranda speaks here, but she speaks for Prospero and for the West when she tells Caliban that his own "gabble" has been made "known" because she has taught him language. It is typical for the European colonizer to hear only silence from native peoples and to take them seriously only when they have accepted the language and culture of the colonizer. Miranda sums up this new political dispensation (which is really a "righting" of the old one, like the wrecked ship miraculously righted at the end) by seeing it as if it were new: "O brave new world/That has such people in 't!" (182–83). However, the civil unity that Miranda misreads has been achieved not only at her expense (she has been successfully married off), but mostly at Caliban's. In a final gesture, Ariel and Caliban are freed, but only Caliban is "claimed" by his master – "This thing of darkness I/Acknowledge mine" (5.1.275–76) – but in such a way as to suggest that Caliban's existence as an Other is essential to Prospero's identity as colonial ruler. For the modern reader, Shakespeare's play thus appears to critique the European colonial order at the very point in history when it was first gaining legitimacy by constructing an Other that requires conquest and conversion.

John Keats, "Ode on a Grecian Urn"

*Structuralism and Formalism * New Criticism * Poststructuralism*

John Keats's "Ode on a Grecian Urn" is one of the most famous and most puzzling Romantic poems. It is an example of a form known as *ekphrasis*, the representation in a literary work of an artistic work in another medium. A reading of the poem following Roman Jakobson's formalist theory would note how ekphrasis determines the formal structure of *addresser* and *addressee* and how the interaction of *context* and *code* determine meaning. The opening line – "Thou still unravish'd bride of quietness" – clearly indicates an addressee, presumably the urn, and an addresser, the "I" implied by the use of "thou." The scene of ekphrastic meditation splits this formal mode of address, directing a part of its *message* to the urn and another part to the reader. The poem is further complicated by an ekphrastic structure that doubles its referential ground: on one level, the poem represents an urn, but on another level, the urn serves as a reference point for another representation (i.e., what is inscribed upon it). The speaker's question about a ground for these representations – "What leaf-fring'd legend haunts about thy shape/Of deities or mortals, or of both"? – leads not to any definitive answer but to a litany of more questions. And it is unclear whether these questions are addressed to the reader or to the urn itself. The speaker's address to the urn in the second stanza is a rhetorical set-piece, a vividly painted scene of potential vibrancy awakened in the poet's imagination by the urn's silent history:

> Heard melodies are sweet, but those unheard
>   Are sweeter; therefore, ye soft pipes, play on;
> Not to the sensual ear, but, more endear'd,
>   Pipe to the spirit ditties of no tone:
> Fair youth, beneath the trees, thou canst not leave
>   Thy song, nor ever can those trees be bare;
>   Bold Lover, never, never canst thou kiss,
> Though winning near the goal – yet, do not grieve;
>   She cannot fade, though thou has not thy bliss,
>   For ever wilt thou love, and she be fair!

Keats's stanza form in this ode is a ten-line structure, the first four lines rhyming *abab*, the second six alternating in one form or another, as here *cdeced* – very much like a Petrarchan sonnet. The poet calls upon the formal limitations of this sonnet-like stanza to perform the same function as the urn itself: to capture a moment of longing and desire. The stanza is shot through with negatives – "unheard," "not," "no tone," "canst not," "nor ever," "never, never canst thou," "do not," "cannot," "not thy bliss." The cumulative effect of these negations is to cancel out the picture otherwise painted of fair youths and fair girls "winning near the goal." NEGATION structures a verbal form of painting: it simulates the stasis of action in representation. The poet's selection of metaphors (i.e., substitutions for ideas) – melodies, soft pipes, ditties – are "projected," as Jacobson would say, onto the level of metonymy (i.e., the world of extension, time, contiguity), which is also the level of cancellations and prohibitions. The poetic function, then, is precisely this invocation of metaphors that must be cancelled, in order to reproduce the effect of a "painted scene." This function is, indeed, the poem's message: immortality lies in the representation of immortality.

A New Critical reading of Keats's poem might focus on rhetorical figures, especially irony, PARADOX, and ambivalence, which give the poem its powerful but tentative formal unities. It opens on a significant AMBIVALENCE: the urn is referred to as a "bride of quietness," the "foster-child of silence" but also as a "Sylvan historian." Moreover, what the historian of silence tells us is ambivalently associated with "deities or mortals, or . . . both." The poem hangs on this ambivalence, because it creates the rhetorical grounds for the questions that conclude the first stanza. The poem's formal structure concentrates and intensifies verbal, prosodic, and rhetorical symmetries; this is especially the case in the second and third stanzas, where negations and ecstatic repetitions symbolize the contrapuntal energies unleashed in the process of artistic creation. The tension of opposites is resolved or reconciled in the unity of an aesthetic object (an urn, a poem). The persistently unanswered questions in the fourth stanza – "Who are these coming for the sacrifice?" – remind the reader of the fundamental strangeness of this artifact: it sends a message, but the original context (and addresser) is missing. Keats's poem transforms this puzzling message into a new context, harmonizing an authentic but lost meaning with a new meaning derived by the modern poet meditating on eternity and concluding, with Blake, that "eternity is in love with the productions of time." "Beauty is truth, truth beauty" the urn offers as its final, nearly neoclassical lesson; it is all we need to know.

The harmony of this lesson is undermined somewhat by an image of the "Cold Pastoral," another ekphrastic doubling that splits the pastoral into a scene on the urn and the speaker's (and reader's) more distanced "cooler" perspective meditating upon it. This short phrase reflects an aspect of the poem's ambivalence that in Poststructuralism is called "undecidability." The speaker (or reader) cannot decide with authority how to interpret the phrase. The most powerful example of this undecidability occurs in the last lines – " 'Beauty is truth, truth beauty' – that is all/Ye know on earth, and all ye need to know." This appears to be a message of startling simplicity and power, though it is a matter of fierce critical debate just what exactly the urn says (in part because in some editions the internal quotation marks enclose the last two lines, rather than the opening phrase of the penultimate one). This raises an important question: who or what speaks the quoted words about beauty and truth? This question signals an APORIA, a point at which contradiction expresses itself as an unsolvable puzzle, an incomprehensible script, an allegorical or coded message. The speaker reminds us that the urn's story is a fiction, a series of images, "with brede/Of marble men and maidens overwrought." Keats's ekphrastic meditation on a "painted scene" is thus a representation of a representation. On this view, a Poststructuralist reading of "Ode on a Grecian Urn" is redundant, since the poem is already deconstructing itself, drawing the reader's attention to its formal contradictions, its mirroring, and its ekphrastic doubling.

Charlotte Brontë, *Jane Eyre*

Feminist Theory * *New Historicism* * *Postcolonial Studies* *
Ethnic Studies

Charlotte Brontë's *Jane Eyre* offers the reader numerous avenues for interpretation. Most prominent since its publication in 1847 have been interpretations that focus on the representation of women. Feminist theory, particularly that form of it that emphasizes issues of social and sexual equality, has found a rich resource, even a kind of foundational text, in *Jane Eyre*. As a *Bildungsroman, Jane Eyre* records a young woman's self-formation, her struggle to harmonize her own desire with the demands placed on her by society. This struggle takes many different forms: reason *v.* passion, self *v.* society, self-fulfillment *v.* social duty, passive obedience *v.* active rebellion, self-mastery *v.* slavery, wife *v.* concubine. The polarized nature of these conflicts is symptomatic of the image we have of Jane and that she has of herself: a *divided self*, a SUBJECT torn between responsibilities to herself and to society. This self-division is reflected in her chosen occupation of governess, one of the few positions open to single women of modest means; but this role is ambiguous (she is both part of the household and an employee in it) and therefore stands for the uncertain and confusing status of women in Victorian society.

In the end, however, it is not clear if Jane ever effectively transcends or repairs her divided selfhood. Her desire for liberty – "I desired liberty; for liberty I gasped; for liberty I uttered a prayer" – is dampened and finally set aside in an unrelenting DIALECTIC of diminished choices. "I abandoned it and framed a humbler supplication; for change, stimulus: that petition, too, seemed swept off into vague space: 'Then,' I cried, half desperate, 'grant me at least a new servitude!'" (72). Jane's desire for a "new servitude" is to some degree a capitulation to the very PATRIARCHAL social order that restricts her life options to begin with. But it is also a sign of Jane's AGENCY, of her willful acceptance of social responsibility. Jane's powerful feelings for Rochester – "He stood between me and every thought of religion, as an eclipse intervenes between man and the broad sun" (234) – signal her enslavement to patriarchal authority. Indeed, Jane frequently uses the language of slavery to describe her relationship with Rochester. His Gothic intensity and energy "were more than beautiful to me" she notes: "they were full of an interest, an influence that quite mastered me" (149). However, it is possible to argue that Jane appropriates the language of slavery to assert her own authority and AUTONOMY. When Rochester makes an implicit comparison between her and "'the grand Turk's whole seraglio; gazelle-eyes, houri forms and all!,'" Jane responds in mutinous terms: "'I'll be preparing myself to go out as a missionary to preach liberty to them that are enslaved – your harem inmates amongst the rest.'" She adds that Rochester will find himself "fettered amongst our hands" and forced to "sign[] a charter, the most liberal that despot ever yet conferred'" (229–30). *Jane Eyre* is an AMBIVALENT text, unable decisively to assert Jane's dependence or independence.

As I have suggested above, Jane's ambivalence is partly a function of her position in Rochester's household. A New Historicist approach might focus on the socio-historical grounds for this ambivalence. In *Jane Eyre*, Brontë famously indicts institutions like Lowood School, dedicated to producing "proper" young ladies the best of whom, like Jane, go on to become governesses for the upper classes, teaching their students the same skills they themselves have learned. Jane attends a school populated by orphans and unwanted children and is fortunate enough to succeed and go on to teach herself. In the opening decades of the nineteenth century, the time-frame of *Jane Eyre*, there was no formal system of education available for women. After the formation of the national school system in the 1830s, there were some improvements. By the mid-1840s, when Brontë was writing, primary and some secondary education were fairly widely available. By setting her novel in the recent past, Brontë was able dramatically to point up the paucity of educational and occupational opportunities for women. Jane's relationship with her long-lost cousin, St. John Rivers, underscores another historical context in the novel. Rivers is a minister, and his Calvinism underscores both the social importance of religion, especially its missionary programs, and the severity of his religious authority. "'I am not a pagan,'" he tells Jane, "'but a Christian philosopher – a follower of the sect of Jesus. As His disciple I adopt His pure, His merciful, His benignant doctrines. I advocate them: I am sworn to spread them'" (320). His advocacy is very much a part of the patriarchal social order that limits Jane to subservient roles. Moreover, Rivers' insistence that she learn Hindustani in preparation to join him on a mission to India situates her within a specific historical context: the consolidation of British colonial power in India. That Jane resists the passive historical role foisted upon her is testimony not only to her strength of character, to her unwillingness to be conscripted into a colonialist enterprise, but also to Brontë's dissatisfaction with Protestant missionary activities. By depicting Jane's challenge to the limited agency offered to her by male authority figures (Rochester and Rivers), Brontë undermines the historical authority of the Church and the aristocracy. Though Jane's job as a schoolmistress, which she enters into while staying with her cousin, and her subsequent marriage to Rochester limit the efficacy of her challenge, her negotiation of these positions, together with her critique of patriarchy, calls into question the univocal authority of a historical narrative that subordinates women to male power.

Edward Said has argued that novels like Jane Austen's *Mansfield Park*, when subjected to critical examination, reveal the colonialist substructure of early nineteenth-century British society. A similar critical exposé is possible with *Jane Eyre*, for Rochester's fortune is derived from plantations he controls as a result of his marriage to Bertha Mason, a West Indian CREOLE (i.e., a European born in the Caribbean). On this view, Brontë's novel indirectly depicts the social impact of COLONIALISM on the English upper classes, specifically the way that colonial fortunes enabled those classes to maintain their social and cultural privileges. In *Jane Eyre*, Bertha is the "mad woman in the attic," a literal prisoner but also a powerful symbol for the colonial OTHERNESS that Rochester attempts to repress by locking her up. It is clear from Rochester's account of his marriage that he has been tricked into marrying a woman of mixed race. To Jane he speaks of "'vile discoveries'" and the "'treachery of concealment'"; her nature is "'wholly alien to mine,'" he confesses, "'her tastes obnoxious to me; her cast of mind common, low, narrow, and singularly incapable of being led to anything higher, expanded to anything larger. . . . What a pigmy intellect she had – and what giant propensities!'" (261). Rochester's language identifies Bertha as *racially* Other; her "alien" nature and "pigmy" intellect, her sexual openness and fondness for alcohol, were at that time qualities typically associated with SUBALTERN peoples. Moreover, the contrast with Jane identifies Jane herself as a version of the emblematic "English lady," the symbol of English values, of what colonialism and Christian missionary work are meant to instill in the barbaric peoples of Africa, India, and the Caribbean. The rebellion that Jane threatens to instigate should Rochester try to entrap her in a harem-like subservience testifies to her unwillingness to be identified as a colonized Other. But her subsequent marriage to him undermines her rebellious intentions by suggesting that, in the end, Jane is complicit in a colonial social order. Once again, Jane's (and Brontë's) ambivalence challenges the master narrative of historical destiny according to which Europe takes upon itself the authority to rule the subaltern races of the world.

The postcolonial critique of *Jane Eyre* is deepened and extended when read alongside Jean Rhys's *Wide Sargasso Sea*, a novel that tells the repressed story of the colonized OTHER, Bertha Mason (whose real name, we discover, is Antoinette). Set mostly in the Caribbean, Rhys's novel attempts not only to give substance to Bertha's character but also to reveal the precise nature of Rochester's involvement in the plantation system in the West Indies. Rhys's postcolonial critique of *Jane Eyre* dovetails with an Ethnic Studies approach that emphasizes problems of race and miscegenation. *Wide Sargasso Sea* avoids the kind of character assassination we see in *Jane Eyre* and tackles the problem of Antoinette's racial heritage through a more or less straightforward exposition of her background. In a powerful scene, Rochester confronts Daniel Cosway, the man he believes to be Antoinette's brother, and becomes increasingly hysterical in his dealings with his wife. He is drawn to Antoinette's sensuality, but at the same time repelled by the Otherness that she represents. She is soon associated in his mind with an unfriendly native environment. Just before Antoinette tells her mother's story, Rochester thinks, "the feeling of something unknown and hostile was very strong." Then he tells her, "'I feel very much a stranger here . . . I feel that this place is my enemy and on your side'" (78). He tries to efface this Otherness (he renames her "Bertha"), but Antoinette is surrounded by women who remind him of it. Amelia, a young servant, represents an object of forbidden desire – the purely racial Other – on whom Rochester is able to displace his desire for the equally forbidden Antoinette. Christophine is a more troubling figure, for she is a self-reliant, independent native woman, a practitioner of *obeah*, an Afro-Caribbean form of shamanism that is used as a weapon of resistance to the colonial authority that Rochester represents. When Antoinette asks Christophine to use *obeah* to make Rochester love her, she is attempting to use native resources to overcome her husband's European prejudices. Christophine warns her against this strategy. " 'So you believe in that tim-tim story about obeah, you hear when you so high? All that foolishness and folly. Too besides, that is not for *béké* [white person]. Bad, bad trouble come when *béké* meddle with that' " (67–68). As a Creole, however, Antoinette is neither Afro-Caribbean nor *béké*, so it is unclear how she ought to understand Christophine's words. Her fall into madness is a psychic response, a turning inward and away from a social world in which she is neither native nor European, but rather a "white nigger" caught in the middle of a colonial DIALECTIC. Her mother was "driven" mad in a very similar way. But this madness is not a sign of "a pigmy intellect" or of "giant propensities," as Brontë has Rochester claim in *Jane Eyre*. It is rather a response to a profound sense of alienation and displacement. By the time Antoinette arrives in England, she succumbs to what Brontë herself called "moral madness" but she more closely resembles the Afro-Caribbean *zombi*, "a dead person who seems to be alive or a living person who is dead" (64). In the final scene, Antoinette (as Bertha) awakens after dreaming of Tia, the girl who had taunted her at the novel's beginning for being a "white nigger." She takes up her candle and with resolve sets out to set fire to Thornfield. As we know from a few short sentences in *Jane Eyre*, Bertha dies in the fire. Rhys rewrites this conclusion, suggesting identity or union with the native Other in a purgative fire that transforms painful ambivalence into a joyful unity of difference.

WORKS CITED

Brontë, Charlotte. *Jane Eyre*. Ed. Richard J. Dunn. 3rd ed. New York: Norton, 2001.

Rhys, Jean. *Wide Sargasso Sea*. New York: Norton, 1999.

Herman Melville, *Bartleby the Scrivener: A Story of Wall Street*

Critical Theory * Marxist Theory * Psychoanalytic Theory

Herman Melville's *Bartleby, the Scrivener*, published in 1853, is a story that captures what Critical Theory might call the ALIENATION of modernity. Sequestered in a suite of offices, where scriveners do nothing but copy and proofread legal documents, the narrator, "an eminently *safe*" lawyer, reflects on the "cool tranquility of [his] snug retreat" (20). Unlike Bartleby, whose alienation is expressed in terms of a near-autistic withdrawal from the world, the lawyer constructs a fantasy realm of "snugness" to protect him from the very social forces that guarantee his financial success. He is a prototype of what Herbert Marcuse calls the "one-dimensional man," whose function is to safeguard the interests of the ruling classes. The narrator's fondness for John Jacob Astor, one of the great early American capitalists, is based not on any sense of the man's character but rather on his name, which he loves to repeat, "for it hath a rounded and orbicular sound to it, and rings like unto bullion" (20). The rationalization typical of one-dimensional thought, which negates transcendental possibilities and restricts human activity to the sphere of material existence, here reduces Astor to the sound of money. In a quite similar fashion, the narrator portrays himself as equally empty of character, a nameless factotum – successful, highly regarded (or so he claims), articulate – but without emotional investments in the people around him. That is, until Bartleby comes to work for him. When confronted with his new employee's recalcitrance, his "preference" not to work, the narrator reflects on the human condition: "The bond of a common humanity now drew me irresistibly to gloom. A fraternal melancholy! For both I and Bartleby were sons of Adam" (45). The phrases simply do not ring true, especially when one remembers that just pages earlier the lawyer had contemplated the return on his investment in Bartleby: a "cheaply purchase[d] . . . delicious self-approval," a "morsel for my conscience" (38). Bartleby is "useful," not so much as a scrivener but as a reminder that the lawyer is in fact a human being. The pathos of the story depends in part on the gap between the lawyer's IDEOLOGICAL function in a modern capitalist society and the humanity of which Bartleby reminds him. The irony, of course, lies in the fact that Bartleby himself is even more profoundly alienated, a condition symbolized by his position "close up to a small side-window," with a view of a wall, surrounded by a "high green folding screen, which might entirely isolate Bartleby from [the lawyer's] sight." Though the narrator muses that in this manner "privacy and society were conjoined" (31), the main thrust of the story is to dramatize how forcefully he has replicated the rationalized, one-dimensional world for which he, as a member of the legal profession, is partly responsible.

From a Marxist point of view, the alienation represented in *Bartleby* is of a slightly different character. Melville presents the reader with a meditation on a crucial period for capitalist development, a period during which industrial capabilities were consolidated in monopolies and trusts, which required the services of law firms to guarantee their smooth operation and protect the private property derived from them, the "rich men's bonds and mortgages and title-deeds" (20) that are the lawyer's stock in trade. However, Melville's depiction of the law office, though rendered in comic terms, illustrates the ALIENATING effects of labor. The other scriveners – Nippers, Turkey, and Ginger Nut – are entirely cut off from the natural world in which they might create useful things and are also cut off from the legal materials that they are instrumental in constructing. Nippers and Turkey are half-men, each suffering from "eccentricities" that make them useless for half the day, victims of the mind-numbing work involved in copying documents. They are representatives of a class of literate clerical workers required by the industrial phase of capitalism. Their alienation is no different from the unskilled laborer, except insofar as it manifests itself in idiosyncratic behavior that is tolerated because they could, at least half the time, accomplish "a great deal of work in a style not easy to be matched" (23). Nippers and Turkey comically depict the dehumanization and alienation created by industrial capitalism and sustained by a legal IDE-OLOGY that protects and nurtures private property. Bartleby's dehumanization – his imprisonment in a "dead-wall reverie" (52) – results ultimately in a form of rebellion, a refusal to work. One of the strengths of Melville's story from a Marxist perspective is that it captures the complexities of class struggle, and it does so not by IDEALIZING the workers but by showing in realistic terms the effects of their exploitation. It also provides a glimpse into the lawyer's mind, exposing his high-handed justifications ("Bartleby was billeted upon me for some mysterious purpose of an all-wise Providence" [61]) as illusions designed to mystify the real nature of class struggle.

This alienation and dehumanization can also be explained in Psychoanalytic terms. On this view, the lawyer's alienation from his employees is a function of his narcissism. His high-handedness, his sense that Bartleby is "useful" to him, indicates a pathological inability to empathize, to create a libidinal bond beyond his own ego. The belief that he is providing sanctuary for Bartleby, so that he will not fall into the hands of "some less indulgent employer" (38), masks his own narcissistic gratifications according to which Bartleby's alienation provides a "morsel" for his conscience. Bartleby not only stands for the guilt engendered in modern civilized societies by the forces of repression but also for the super-ego that administers that guilt. He is a persistent reminder of the need for repression and the need to abide by social conventions. He is at once "perverse," "peculiar," and "unaccountable," like the repressed unconscious wishes and desires that populate dreams, and a "valuable acquisition," a model of acquiescence to the reality principle. However, Bartleby's curious refusal to work (indeed, to live) is a final relinquishment of reality. His own narcissistic tendencies lead not to a strict adherence to the reality principle, which we find in the lawyer's case, but rather to an unfettered acceptance of the pleasure principle. Through the compulsive repetition of his mantra – "I prefer not" – Bartleby relives in order to manage some unrecovered trauma, symbolized perhaps by his prior employment at the Dead Letter Office. It is no wonder that he succumbs to the pleasure principle and a radical flight from pain and tension that fuels what Freud calls the "death drive." For unlike the lawyer, whose adherence to the reality principle has resulted in the repression of desires that might threaten his livelihood, Bartleby opens himself up to the primal pleasure of death, to a return to the stasis and peace of an original inorganic state, a process hauntingly symbolized by his wasting away in the Tombs.

WORK CITED

Melville, Herman. *Bartleby the Scrivener: A Story of Wall Street.* New York: Simon and Schuster, 1997.

Joseph Conrad, *Heart of Darkness*

*Narrative Theory * Psychoanalysis * New Historicism **
Postcolonial Studies

Joseph Conrad's *Heart of Darkness* (1899) was written at a time when the late Victorian imperial romance was at the height of its popularity. Unlike other such tales of the era, like Ryder Haggard's *She* (1887), Conrad's novella is less interested in imperial adventures than in the study of IMPERIALISM as it is manifested in character. From the point of view of Narrative Theory, specifically the theory of the novel, Conrad's choice constitutes a hybrid form in which the emergent "psychological novel," pioneered by Henry James, combines with the more conventional romance narrative. His story concerns Charlie Marlow, an Englishman employed by a company with a concession to hunt ivory in the Congo, a possession of King Leopold of Belgium. His job is to retrieve Kurtz, a renegade trader. Conrad complicates the propulsive, paratactic movement of the romance narrative by heightening certain elements of the narration itself, especially Marlow's meditations on barbarism, civilization, human nature, and the importance of self-knowledge.

The story opens with an unnamed narrator who describes a group of unidentified people on the deck of "the *Nellie*, a cruising yawl," listening to a story told by Marlow. The unnamed narrator has command of our attention for about eight paragraphs and in this short space establishes that Marlow's stories are not typical: "to him the meaning of an episode was not inside like a kernel but outside, enveloping the tale which brought it out only as a glow brings out a haze, in the likeness of one of these misty halos that sometimes are made visible by the spectral illumination of moonshine" (9). Having served the purpose of establishing Marlow as an unreliable narrator, the unnamed narrator all but disappears, save for a brief resurgence a page or so later to supply one more telling detail about the storyteller: "he had the pose of a Buddha preaching in European clothes and without a lotus-flower" (10). The kind of expectations set up by the romance narrative are gratified by this reference to Marlow's "Eastern" character, but his story seems to bog down in lengthy descriptions of COLONIAL administrators and his own commentary on the difference between Europeans and Africans. Several times he meditates on the nature of storytelling and insists that no one can communicate the "truth" about lived experience. In one of the rare moments when Marlow directly addresses his listeners on the *Nellie*, he tries to communicate to them (and, indirectly, to the reader) this very impossibility. " 'Do you see anything? It seems to me I am trying to tell you a dream. . . . No, it is impossible; it is impossible to convey the life-sensation of any given epoch of one's existence – that which makes its truth, its meaning – its subtle and penetrating essence' " (30). With this statement, the reader is warned not to expect the kind of revelations typically found in romance narratives. The only message conveyed by Marlow's narration is an impression of his experience, not *the truth* of it, much less the truth of anything beyond it. In this way, Marlow's story – non-linear, digressive, overtly figural – achieves a kind of *expressive form*, shaping itself to the storyteller's "hazy" sense of the truth of his own experience.

Narrative Theory alerts us to other possible motifs, including journeying, questing, and wandering – all of which can add nuances to a reading focused on Marlow's impressionistic storytelling. More than one reader has been struck by the quest motif and the irony of substituting Kurtz, the renegade from reason and civilization, for the more exalted object of such narratives. The quest motif can also be regarded from the point of view of Psychoanalysis. Thus Marlow embarks on a metaphorical journey into the unconscious, both his own and his culture's. According to Freud, the unconscious contains traces of ancient prehistoric human experience, precisely the quality that most persistently attracts Marlow's notice about the Congo: " 'Going up river was like traveling back to the earliest beginnings of the world, when vegetation rioted on the earth and the big trees were kings' " (35). Passages like this invite us to see this journey as an exploration of the unconscious. Marlow's language – lushly modified with vaguely sinister adjectives and adverbs repeated in an incantatory style – gives us a sense of a strange, unearthly landscape: it is inscrutable, abominable, impalpable, ominous, timeless. Moreover, as Marlow himself suggests, his experience is like a dream, " 'that commingling of absurdity, surprise, and bewilderment in a tremor of struggling revolt, that notion of being captured by the incredible which is of the very essence of dreams' " (30). He regards his own memories of the past " 'in the shape of an unrestful and noisy dream' " (36). If the Congo symbolizes the unconscious, the elements that make up the landscape – the river, the jungle, the native inhabitants – symbolize repressed material ("latent content") that is transformed through "dream-work" into the "manifest content." Certainly there is a sense that the jungle withholds something from Marlow, something he suspects he may have repressed: "'I saw a face amongst the leaves on the level with my own, looking at me very fierce and steady . . . I made out, deep in the tangled gloom, naked breasts, arms, legs, glaring eyes'" (46). What is it that Marlow (that humanity) represses? His own OTHERNESS, perhaps, which is projected onto the African natives as *their* birthright but also as part of non-human nature. Marlow thinks he understands his glimpse into the unconscious; he sees that what he (and humanity) represses is his own "'remote kinship'" with "'this wild and passionate uproar'" (38). His championing of Kurtz, who in this reading might stand in for the id, the force of unconscious instinct, can be read as an act of displacement or disavowal, an attempt to acknowledge indirectly a part of his personality that he cannot confront openly. In ways like this, through various symbolic substitutions and exclusions, Marlow's experience attains the quality of a dream whose truth is impossible to share without distortion and misinterpretation.

Modern editions of *Heart of Darkness* often provide just the sort of context that makes New Historicist readings possible. Conrad had himself made a journey up the Congo working as a merchant marine, and there were a number of people who had an interest in exposing King Leopold's practice of awarding concessions to adventurers. Roger Casement, an Irishman serving as British consul in Africa, investigated conditions in the Congo in the 1890s and delivered a highly critical report to the British Parliament in 1903. Conrad's novel is not simply further evidence of what Casement discovered; it is a fictional version of the same anti-colonialist discourse. Casement criticized colonialist efforts to compel natives to harvest india rubber and regarded the atrocities in the region as a direct result of these efforts. This compulsion is nowhere more graphically expressed than in Marlow's impressions of the same colonial context: "'Six black men advanced in a file, toiling up the path. . . . Black rags were wound round their loins. . . . I could see every rib, the joints of their limbs were like knots in a rope; each had an iron collar on his neck. . . . They passed me within six inches, without a glance, with that complete, deathlike indifference of unhappy savages'" (19). Marlow's account of atrocities in the Congo joins Casement's as part of a larger discourse on African colonialism. Certainly the story's impressionistic manner and dream-like logic lend themselves to interpretations that extend beyond the Congo. For example, the Boer War (1899–1902) was being conducted during the same period Conrad was revising his serialized version of *Heart of Darkness*. This was not a popular war, especially among Liberal politicians and the intelligentsia, so it is conceivable that Conrad's critique of European imperialism is meant to indict British interests elsewhere in Africa. There is something almost allegorical (and thus transportable) about Conrad's historical vision, a feature that is brilliantly confirmed in Francis Ford Coppola's appropriation of the narrative structure of *Heart of Darkness* for his haunting portrayal of the Vietnam War in *Apocalypse Now*.

For a Postcolonial critic like Chinua Achebe, Conrad's novel is not a critique of colonialism but a symptom of it. Achebe's famous critical response to *Heart of Darkness*, "An Image of Africa" (1971), accuses Conrad of racism and of effectively silencing the African natives in his representation of the Congo. To be sure, Conrad's representations of Africans are problematic; by and large, they are rendered as SUBALTERN SUBJECTS, threatened by colonial violence and enslavement. There are very few instances in which an African speaks; one famously says, "'Mistah Kutz – he dead,'" "'in a tone of scathing contempt'" (68–69). There are no occasions on which Africans are presented as members of peaceful, organized, communicative societies. Too often, they are associated with "'a complaining clamor, modulated in savage discord'" or a "'tumult of angry and warlike yells'" (41, 47). To the Europeans in *Heart of Darkness*, the sound of drums is part of this general incomprehensible clamor produced by an insidious natural environment. Over against this silence, this wordless clamor, we have Marlow's obsession with Kurtz, his presence and authority guaranteed by the gift of his voice: "'He was very little more than a voice. And I heard – him – it – this – voice – other voices – all of them were so little more than voices'" (48). Achebe takes issue with this repression of the African voice in his essay as well as in his most famous novel, *Things Fall Apart* (1959). Though Achebe's novel is written in a recognizably realist style, it is an "appropriated" style, borrowed and modified for the purposes of COLONIAL MIMICRY. It is shot through with Ibo phrases, names, and proverbs that block any easy facility with realist conventions and at the same time communicates to the Western reader something of the materiality of Ibo culture. Narrative style is simple and direct, in contrast to the complex frame-narration of

Heart of Darkness, and the skeptical impressionism that suffuses Conrad's story is utterly missing from Achebe's. *Things Fall Apart* is told from the perspective of a self-assured, traditional culture whose proverbs "are the palmoil with which words are eaten" (7). In contrast to the angry discord Marlow hears, Achebe's characters hear familiar and comforting sounds: the air is "message-laden" with the sound of drums, a part of "the living village": "It was like the pulsation of its heart. It throbbed in the air, in the sunshine, and even in the trees, and filled the village with excitement" (120, 44).

The traditional world articulated by these meaningful drums begins to deteriorate with the encroachment of Christian missionaries on tribal lands. Okonkwo, the protagonist, values the traditions of his own culture, but he is also a victim of one of its most serious taboos. He kills a neighbor's son accidentally and receives the ultimate punishment. "It was a crime against the earth goddess to kill a clansman, and a man who committed it must flee from the land" (124). From his position in exile with his mother's kinsmen, Okonkwo grows increasingly disturbed about the influence of the Christian missionaries and ultimately becomes involved in a violent and impetuous act of anti-colonial resistance. Upon hearing of Okonkwo's suicide, the white District Commissioner "changed instantaneously" from the "resolute administrator . . . to the student of primitive customs" (207). The novel ends with the Commissioner meditating on the "reasonable paragraph" that Okonkwo's story will fill in his book, *"The Pacification of the Primitive Tribes of the Lower Niger."* These words, the echo of a white man's colonial desire, conclude Achebe's novel and reinforce what the reader already knows: the people of Umuofia will never be the same again. Achebe's message is one that Frantz Fanon had himself conveyed just a few years earlier: only when the West recognizes the humanity of primitive "savages" can it begin to undo the dehumanizing legacy of colonialism.

WORKS CITED

Conrad, Joseph. *Heart of Darkness*. Ed. Robert Kimbrough. 3rd ed. New York: Norton, 1988.

Achebe, Chinua. *Things Fall Apart*. New York: Anchor 1994.

James Joyce, *Ulysses*

*Reader Response * Cultural Studies * Poststructuralism*

Each of the eighteen chapters of James Joyce's *Ulysses* (1922) is written in a different style and each invites different kinds of critical and theoretical attention. For a Reader-Response critic, the sheer diversity of styles, together with the often extreme experimentation that characterizes many of them, poses a major obstacle to even the most "informed" literary reader. The careful reader is caught off guard in the opening pages of the first episode, "Telemachus," in which Stephen Dedalus and his friend, Buck Mulligan, eat breakfast and go for a swim. At one point, Mulligan is berating Stephen for not asking their English friend for "a guinea" in exchange for a witticism he had made about Irish art. In between two blocks of Mulligan's reported dialogue we find the phrase, "Cranly's arm. His arm" (6). What is the reader to make of this enigmatic phrase interrupting an otherwise realistic passage of dialogue? Reader-Response theory calls for an active intervention at this point; the reader must become a participant in the process of making meaning. Specifically, the reader must decode this fragment that appears to come from nowhere. It is not part of a third-person narrator's exposition of the scene. As *Ulysses* throws up more of these fragments, the reader soon realizes that they are bits (or streams) of conscious thought, the unmediated report of Stephen's own thinking process. The "ideal reader" implied by the styles of *Ulysses* would know that this phrase refers to Joyce's *A Portrait of the Artist as a Young Man* (1916), at the conclusion of which Stephen's friend Cranly tries to convince him not to leave the Church to pursue his artistic vision. Stephen regards this moment, like the moment in "Telemachus," as an instance of betrayal. In both cases, betrayal comes in the form of glib attempts at intimacy. By solving the puzzles presented by textual gaps and complex knots of allusion, the reader grasps the narrative situation: Stephen has returned home from abroad to find his family fragmented and his place in society usurped by his friends.

A Cultural Studies approach to *Ulysses* is confronted with an embarrassment of riches. The novel depicts the actions of a single day, but the events of that day are drawn so vividly that the reader is tempted to believe Joyce's boast that Dublin could be rebuilt out of the pages of his book. It is not that Joyce describes Dublin scenes or landscapes particularly well – he does very little describing, actually – it is a question rather of reproducing cultural DISCOURSES within the texture of his narrative. A good deal of the stylistic innovation across the episodes has to do with this appropriation and parody of cultural codes. For example, in the first part of the "Nausicaa" episode, Gerty MacDowell is lounging on the strand and her experience is represented entirely in the language of fashion magazines, local folklore, and popular romance. She is a "sterling good daughter," "a ministering angel too with a little heart worth its weight in gold" (291); she is "Greekly perfect" with hands of "finely veined alabaster." But she also worries about "those discharges she used to get and that tired feeling" (286). Rather than present a character with the usual subjective "depth," Joyce parodies depth in the mimicry of cultural codes. Gerty is in fact an advertisement for the products she uses, the magazines she reads, and the shops she patronizes. But even more than this, she advertises an attitude and by so doing becomes a symbol of new possibilities for young women in the West at the turn of the twentieth century. She becomes an icon of the independent, risqué "seaside girl," made famous in product advertisements and music hall songs. One of these songs, "Seaside Girls" (1899) by Harry Norris, wends its way throughout the narrative of *Ulysses*: "*Those girls, those girls, those lovely seaside girls, / All dimples, smiles, and curls – your head it simply whirls!*" It is a leitmotif, a thematic thread, but it also indexes cultural trends. Gerty is emotionally invested in the cultural image of the seaside girl, as is Leopold Bloom, who observes Gerty as she lounges on the strand, masturbating and meditating on the erotic representation of women: "Do they snapshot those girls or is it all a fake? *Lingerie* does it. Felt for the curves inside her *deshabille*. Excites them also when they're. I'm all clean come and dirty me" (301–302). It should come as no surprise that cultural codes are gendered, that Bloom's commentary on and critique of Gerty's sexual roles is riddled with pornographic stereotypes and projections.

The appropriation of cultural codes in *Ulysses* is a specific effect of Joyce's more general critique of language, specifically as it is used in realistic fiction. On this view, the stylistic innovations of *Ulysses* deconstruct realism by exploiting the inherent playfulness of language. The Derridean conception of PLAY governs the text's stylistic DIFFÉRANCE. Freed from the burden of MIMESIS, of anchoring language to a referent outside the context of the narrative, Joyce's text is able to explore the possibilities of anchoring language in language itself. Another facet of Joyce's experimental style is INTERTEXTUALITY, a complex web of relations with other texts and traditions that is neither referential (or citational) nor influential. Joyce contrasts these different kinds of relation in a passage that relies on intertextual links to Shakespeare:

> Urbane, to comfort them, the quaker librarian purred:
> – And we have, have we not, those priceless pages of *Wilhelm Meister*. A great poet on a great brother poet. A hesitating soul taking arms against a sea of troubles, torn by conflicting doubts, as one sees in real life.
> He came a step a sinkapace forward on neatsleather creaking and a step backward a sinkapace on the solemn floor. (151)

This passage, at the beginning of the "Scylla and Charybdis" episode, introduces a reference to Goethe's novel, in which the influence of Shakespeare is a dominant theme, as well as a citation from *Hamlet* ("a sea of troubles"). The final sentence, with its evocative "sinkapace" and "neatsleather," registers through intertextual echo two other Shakespeare plays, *Twelfth Night* and *Julius Caesar*. There is no sense that the narrator who "speaks" such lines is referring to the external world. In keeping with the intertextual polyphony of the later episodes of *Ulysses*, Joyce here severs textuality from an existential ground. The final episode, "Penelope," Molly Bloom's monologue, returns us not to an original ground, Molly's consciousness, but rather to another scene of representation, where language and identity become one and the same.

WORK CITED

Joyce, James. *Ulysses*. New York: Random House, 1990.

Virginia Woolf, *To the Lighthouse*

*Feminist Theory * Psychoanalysis * Deconstruction*

Virginia Woolf's *To the Lighthouse* presents a challenge to Feminism. Mrs. Ramsey is in many ways typical of Woolf's protagonists: middle class, married and somewhat matronly, strong willed, imaginative but not quite artistic, socially confident but AMBIVALENT in deeply ingrained but deeply hidden ways about her own needs and desires. She is beautiful and possesses an almost childlike wonder about the people in her life. "Her simplicity fathomed what clever people falsified" (29), the narrator tells us, and it is this simplicity that makes it possible for her to get at "the still space that lies about the heart of things" (105). As her young house guest, Lily Briscoe, observes, she has the artist's power to transform the world through aesthetic vision. "In the midst of chaos there was shape; this eternal passing and flowing (she looked at the clouds going and the leaves shaking) was struck into stability. Life stand still here, Mrs. Ramsay said" (161). At the same time, Mrs. Ramsey is devoted to her philosopher husband and longs for her children to marry and lead exemplary conventional lives. Her attitude towards her husband's line of work – his students are always studying "the influence of something upon somebody" (12) – reveals a gulf between his rationalist sensibility and her own intuitiveness and maternal solicitude. One can read Mrs. Ramsey as a complacent middle-class woman who has sacrificed her own creative energies in order to support her husband's career. But it is also possible to regard her without recourse to stereotypes about housewives. Her desire to bring people together for a meal or a marriage signals not complicity with PATRIARCHAL authority but an assertion of an alternative to the ALIENATING effects of the rationality that characterizes that authority. "They all sat separate. And the whole of the effort of merging and flowing and creating rested on her. Again she felt, as a fact without hostility, the sterility of men" (83). Mrs. Ramsey's power, as the artist Lily knows best, lies in her ability to create – not simply the maternal power to reproduce, but the human power to create social bonds within a community.

Woolf's concern for personal relationships – a concern that characterized the Bloomsbury group of writers gathered around Woolf and her sister – invites psychoanalytic readings of a novel so obviously indebted to the Oedipus and castration complexes. The story opens with James, the Ramsey's youngest child, at his mother's feet, both of them posing for Lily. Meanwhile, Mr. Ramsey storms about the house and yard declaiming that there will be no trip to the lighthouse, a journey James very much wants to take. The weather will be fine, his mother murmurs, but his father contradicts her, "it won't be fine" (4). The bond with the mother is looked upon jealously by the powerful father who symbolically withholds the PHALLUS/lighthouse, the means by which James can win his mother's heart but also the sign of his ascension to the SYMBOLIC order. This threat of castration should initiate the normative process of development in which the male child learns to identify with the father and to transfer his desire to a more appropriate love object. Ten years later we discover the outcome of James's development. He is sixteen now, and his mother is dead. He has clearly not resolved the Oedipal conflicts that had surfaced so long before. "He had always kept this old symbol of taking a knife and striking his father to the heart" (184). The imagery is appropriate, especially when we recall that the narrator frequently refers to Mr. Ramsey's presence as an "arid scimitar," a reference to his ability to use reason, the sine qua non of the Symbolic order, to dismantle reality into its constituent parts. His son appropriates this same image in order to do away with what it represents: the relentless tearing apart of the world under the illusion of understanding its secrets. That James may be moving towards resolution is suggested by his dissociation of his father – "an old man, very sad, reading his book" – from the tyrannical authority that he once wielded: "that fierce sudden black-winged harpy, with its talons and its beak all cold and hard. . . . That he would kill, that he would strike to the heart" (184). It is odd that he would associate this authority with a "harpy," a legendary creature with the body of a vulture and the head and breasts of a woman. Perhaps for James male authority and power are a distortion of some primal femininity that he associates with his mother, a most unharpy-like woman. This aligns with a Lacanian reading of Woman as the screen on which men project their desires and from which they receive their sense of masculine identity. The arrival at the lighthouse suggests that the tyrant has been dispatched, the mother is no longer a screen or a threat or an object of desire, and the phallus can now be handed on to James without his father fearing for his own position. "There!" his sister, Cam thinks, as they land. "You've got it at last. For she knew that this was what James had been wanting. . . . His father had praised him" (206). The scene ends with Mr. Ramsey standing in the bow of the boat "as if he were saying, 'There is no God' " (207). For James, the father is no longer a god-like tyrant, and there appears to be no longer any obstacle to James identifying with him.

The reader may well wonder about Cam's own relation to her father, and to some degree we get a glimmer of it in the final paragraphs in which Lily Briscoe completes her abstract portrait of Mrs. Ramsey and James from ten years before. In a sense, Lily Deconstructs the novel's Oedipal dynamic, the severing and dis-articulating power of castrating reason in an artistic context that exploits a quite opposite power of knitting together, of rearticulating and unifying in an IMAGINARY register what is forestalled at the level of the Symbolic. In Mr. Ramsey's rationalist view, a line is a division and demarcation, knife-like and phallic, not at all like a dome or a triangle or a wedge (images associated with Mrs. Ramsey). It is also the "bar" that separates binomial opposites (man/ woman, adult/child, inside/outside, picture/frame, reality/image). The line is decisive, but it cuts two ways, for the same line that cleaves apart and separates can also cleave things to each other. The moment James lands at the lighthouse, Lily, echoing Cam, says, "It is finished." She has finally harmonized the "nervous lines" she had laid down earlier (158). Now a single line centers and balances her vision: "With a sudden intensity, as if she saw it clear for a second, she drew a line there, in the centre. It was done; it was finished. . . . I have had my vision" (209). Lily's creative inspiration puts "under erasure" the other sense of the line, cancels it but leaves it legible as a constituent element of her vision. The same line that draws distinctions (e.g., between genders), that places woman "below the bar" (in the manner of Jacque Lacan's algorithms in which the signified "slides under" the signifier), can also eliminate the bar by transforming it into a space for "merging and flowing and creating."

WORK CITED

Woolf, Virginia. *To the Lighthouse*. New York: HJB, 1989.

Zora Neale Hurston, *Their Eyes Were Watching God*

*Feminist Theory * Ethnic Studies * Narrative Theory*

For a Feminist critic, Zora Neale Hurston's *Their Eyes Were Watching God* (1937) represents a landmark achievement, for it offers the perspective of an independent-minded black woman, Janie Crawford, who tells the story of her life and loves. Though now regarded as one of the most acclaimed works of the Harlem Renaissance, it was neglected after its first publication, only to be rediscovered and promoted over forty years later by Alice Walker. One of the things that impressed Walker was Hurston's representation of Janie and the women in her life on their own terms and in their own language. Her uncompromising representation of a black woman's self-formation was a direct challenge both to the prejudices of white readers and the literary standards of black male writers. Just before her first marriage, Janie's grandmother, Nanny, tells the story of her escape from slavery and the violent circumstances of her granddaughter's birth: "'Dat school teacher had done hid her [Janie's mother] in de woods all night long, and he had done raped mah baby and run on off just before day'" (19). A legacy of slavery and sexual violence does not prevent Janie from exploring her own sexuality and eagerly awaiting the day when she might discover the joys of marriage. At first, she experiences a rush of delight at the thought: "She saw a dust-bearing bee sink into the sanctum of a bloom; the thousand sister-calyxes arch to meet the love embrace and the ecstatic shiver of the tree from root to tiniest branch creaming in every blossom and frothing with delight. So this was a marriage!" (11). However, after her first marriage to Logan Killicks, a local man with a bit of property, she has another revelation: "She knew now that marriage did not make love. Janie's first dream was dead, so she became a woman" (25). Her second husband, Joe Starks, is more ambitious and exciting, a vibrant force behind a new town founded by black people. But Janie soon discovers she is meant to be a silent and passive wife among men who do not understand the desires of women. To her husband and his friends she says, "'how surprised y'all is goin' tuh be if you ever find out you don't know half as much 'bout [womenfolks] as you think you do'" (75).

A feminist reading of *Their Eyes Were Watching God* inevitably dove-tails with an Ethnic Studies approach. Hurston addresses the issue of race as inextricably bound up with gender identity, and constructs the relationship between Janie and Tea Cake, her third husband, around the same PROBLEMATIC that we find in Nella Larson's *Passing*: the identity and self-formation of light-skinned black women. Janie's friend Mrs. Turner makes note of her "coffee-and-cream complexion and her luxurious hair" but cannot "forgive her for marrying a man as dark as Tea Cake" (140). Unlike Larson's protagonist, Janie embraces blackness, primarily in the form of the carefree, exciting, and unpredictable Tea Cake. With him she seeks to affirm a particular vision of being black, one that she formed in the wake of her disappointments with Logan and Joe. She did not want to be the kind of black woman who marries for social status. When she longs for love and desire to enter her relationship with Logan, her Nanny exclaims, " 'Lawd have mussy! Dat's de very prong all us black women gits hung on. Dis love! Dat's just whut's got us uh pullin' and uh haulin' and sweatin' and doin' from can't see in de mornin' till can't see at night' " (23). Janie defies her grandmother's wisdom and seeks to define love and marriage for herself. Though life with Tea Cake is rough, Janie feels a "self-crushing love" (128) for him in large measure because she can speak her mind with him. When things go badly for them it is not the result of an accident, nor a loss of love. A dog bite infects Tea Cake with rabies and during one of his "fits of gagging and choking" (177) Janie kills him in self-defense. She is acquitted of murder, though some people believe that her light-skinned appearance rather than Tea Cake's condition was the cause. " 'Well, you know whut dey say,' " she overhears one man say to another, " ' "uh white man and uh nigger woman is de freest thing on earth." Dey do as dey please' " (189). But what these men do not realize is how strongly Janie had identified, through her intense love, with a black man. "Of course he wasn't dead," she thinks to herself. "He could never be dead until she herself had finished feeling and thinking." Janie's appeal lies in her will to consolidate racial and gender DIFFERENCES: "She pulled in her horizon like a great fish-net. . . . So much of life in its meshes!" (193).

The final words of the novel just quoted are transmitted by the narrator, but they are spoken from Janie's point of view and are informed by her style and word choices. In Narrative Theory, this is known as a variation of third-person perspective (or "voice"), *free indirect discourse.*

The bulk of the novel is narrated this way, with point of view shifting from an omniscient voice to one that sounds a lot like Janie. Describing her in her Jacksonville boarding house, the narrator concludes, "But, don't care how firm your determination is, you can't keep turning round in one place like a horse grinding sugar cane. So Janie took to sitting over the room. . . ." (118). The third-person point of view is here permeated by Janie's sensibility, though there is no trace of the dialectal forms Hurston uses when she records speech. Free indirect discourse gives the reader access to a character's consciousness without surrendering a vantage point outside of it. Another important facet of Hurston's narrative style is the use of dialect. Hurston studied anthropology under Franz Boas and possessed a sensitive and intuitive ear for folklore, especially the performances of "mule-talkers" and "big picture talkers" who used "a side of the world for a canvas" (54). Lengthy portions of *Their Eyes Were Watching God* are given over to speakers whose words are rendered in dialectal form. A notable example is Nanny's story in chapter two. A Formalist approach to narrative might concentrate on *skaz*, a technique for rendering precisely the speech characteristics of an oral storyteller. In the examples quoted above, *skaz* calls our attention to the individualized teller, as opposed to the omniscient narrator. This narrative polyphony, which M. M. Bakhtin called HETEROGLOSSIA, undermines the dominance of an omniscient narrator and creates a dynamic, DIALOGIC space in which Janie's own voice can be discovered, heard, and appreciated.

WORK CITED

Hurston, Zora Neale. *Their Eyes Were Watching God*. New York: HarperPerennial, 1998.

William Butler Yeats, "Leda and the Swan"

Structuralism and Formalism * *New Criticism* *
Gender and Sexuality

William Butler Yeats's "Leda and the Swan" was originally published in response to a request for a political poem. Though the legend of Leda and Zeus overshadows any political point Yeats tried to make, the poem retains a powerfully mythologized vision of violent historical transformation. It derives its power largely by virtue of the Formal limits within which it articulates its meaning. As William Wordsworth famously noted, in a sonnet on the sonnet, "nuns fret not at their convent's narrow rooms;/and hermits are contented with their cells." The sonnet form affords unsuspected expansion of thought and feeling, and this is nowhere more evident than in Yeats's "Leda," which adheres strictly to the conventions of the form. Rhyme is regular, with only one falling rhyme (tower/power) and only the slightest vowel difference (up/drop). Other sound qualities link semantic and phonemic patterns, as in the second quatrain, where the hard consonants in ll. 5–6 contrast dramatically with the masses of open vowels: "How can those terrified vague fingers push/The feathered glory from her loosening thighs?" These lines evoke the struggle between god and mortal in terms that stress the combination of decisive violence and feathery vagueness. The poet uses stresses in a similar manner, clustering them to imitate action – "A sudden blow: the great wings beating still," "the strange heart beating" – using triple meters ("the staggering girl," "being so caught up") to suggest urgency and dizzying activity. He also uses the bipartite structure of the Petrarchan sonnet to create a sense of narrative propulsion: in the octet, the attack on Leda in the first quatrain is followed by questions in the second that qualify the attack and suggest that the "staggering girl" is less a victim of Zeus's desire than a half-willing conduit for his creative energy. The sestet records the consequences of this energy: from Zeus's rape of Leda emerged Western civilization, symbolized by her offspring: Helen, whose beauty launched a thousand ships, and Clytemnestra, who murdered Agamemnon and set in motion a series of tragic events. SYNCHRONIC-ALLY, the poem proceeds according to a series of metaphoric substitutions, Zeus and Leda in the sestet, "[t]he broken wall, the burning roof and tower" in the octet; at the level of the word and phoneme, however, the poem moves DIACHRONICALLY to suggest the historicity of this brutal moment in the air. The interchange between these two levels, the movement of metaphor onto the metonymic thrust of historical process, mimics the strange and violent transformation illustrated in the myth.

For the New Critic, the formal unity of the sonnet is of paramount importance, but this unity is only partially achieved through attention to structural aspects like rhyme, meter, stanza, and phonemic values. It is primarily achieved by balancing tensions created by irony, ambiguity, and AMBIVALENCE. The first quatrain generates an ambiguity that characterizes the entire poem:

> A sudden blow: the great wings beating still
> Above the staggering girl, her thighs caressed
> By the dark webs, her nape caught in his bill,
> He holds her helpless breast upon his breast.

Are the great wings "still" beating, after all this time? Or are they paradoxically both beating and remaining still? It could be that they beating in order to hold Zeus "still" "above the staggering girl"? The word "still" is poised on the turning point of an enjambment, which causes the slightest hesitation, the slightest doubt as to how this word functions. The uncertainty whether it is Leda who is "helpless" or only her breast (i.e., her heart) compounds the initial ambiguity and establishes a pattern of effects that draws the various syntactical and semantic elements of the poem into a web-like unity. The ambiguities pile up in the second quatrain, with "terrified vague fingers" and "loosening thighs": what exactly is Leda experiencing? Does she resist or capitulate or willingly comply? It is impossible to tell what the poet means when he asks how "body" can "[b]ut feel the strange heart beating where it lies." Whose body? Whose heart? The poem at this point appears to conflate the attacker and his victim in a "white rush" of sensual activity. The opening lines of the sestet introduce an irony, for Zeus's procreative act ("a shudder in the loins") has led only to destruction and death; but implicit in this ironic outcome is another, more surprising irony: out of the destruction of Troy and the death of Agamemnon sprang Homer and the culture of Western civilization. In two and a half lines, Yeats captures the "terrible beauty" of violent historical transformation. He returns to Leda, "mastered by the brute blood of the air," and poses his final question: "Did she put on his knowledge with his power/Before the indifferent beak could let her drop?" The verbal ambiguities throughout the poem here coalesce into a thematic ambivalence that gets to the heart of Yeats's historical vision: is Leda aware of her historical agency? In this coalescence, in which secondary ambiguities are resolved in the articulation of a primary ambivalence, we find the poem's unity, a gestalt of rhetorical effects reinforced by the sonnet's formal limits.

The conclusion of "Leda and the Swan" raises the question of the gendered subject: why did Yeats choose to represent his philosophy of history with an image of rape? Part of the answer lies in Yeats's belief that pivotal historical events (the fall of Troy, the birth of Christ) are moments of violent transformation. The sexual contact between a male god (standing in for the historical spirit) and a female mortal (standing in for all historical SUBJECTS) thus represents the violence of historical annunciation: a force, gendered male, subjects the individual, gendered female, to an overpowering submission. In this parable, the very nature of historical SUBJECTIVITY and AGENCY is gendered female, which is not surprising, given that Yeats was himself conditioned to use women to represent the Irish nation (e.g., Cathleen ní Houlihan). Leda is an icon of human agency; she is both passionate and pliable, essential to knowledge (she is its ESSENCE or ground) but debarred from that same knowledge because of her gender. The violent rape depicted in the poem is complicated by the ambiguities that force the reader to ask whether Leda has consented in some way to this attack, or whether she is ambivalent about her own desire and thus her own will to resist it. Like so many of Yeats's female protagonists, Leda is a powerful woman despite herself: her pliability and her passionate vagueness, which recall the feminine ideal of the Pre-Raphaelite movement, mask world-shattering power. The Olympian view the sonnet offers grows hazy in the concluding question, which betrays a hint of anxiety that Leda was never pliable or vague, that she had access herself to Zeus' terrible power. It is this kind of historical subjectivity that contemporary Feminists and theorists of Gender and Sexuality combat as a legacy of PATRIARCHAL violence.

Samuel Beckett, *Endgame*

*Critical Theory * Marxist Theory * Postmodernism*

Samuel Beckett's *Endgame* (1958) has been praised as an unflinching commentary on the human condition in the wake of the Second World War and the horrors of the Holocaust. From a perspective informed by Critical Theory, Beckett's play critiques the UNIVERSAL values of Enlightenment humanism, which are exposed as self-serving mystifications that rationalize and instrumentalize the practices of social life. **Theodor Adorno**, who found Beckett to be one of the few "authentic" artists in the modern era, famously noted that "[t]o write poetry after Auschwitz is barbaric." However, he also praised artists like Beckett, who were able to wring poetry out of the desolation, despair, and dehumanization resulting from the humanist project of Enlightenment. *Endgame* is a glimpse into a world where the dignity and majesty of humanity – its ideals, aspirations, philosophies and discoveries, its spirituality and high mindedness – are stripped away. Dreams of a benign humanism are mercilessly pilloried by Hamm: "Use your head, can't you, use your head, you're on earth, there's no cure for that!" (53). The reduction of human existence to a disease and human aspirations to a mundane concern for the epiphenomena of material social conditions is dramatized in spare stage settings and a small random collection of objects – ladder, alarm clock, toy dog, telescope – that serve primarily to underscore the utter lack of a meaningful human social context. This new condition is symbolized by the views afforded by two windows: a "zero" world in which the earth and the sea (the "without") lack light and living inhabitants. As Clov puts it, "the earth is extinguished though I never saw it lit" (81). Despite this dismal outlook, he and Hamm manage to remain together (for "the dialogue," Hamm claims), barely maintaining the belief that "we're getting on" (14), that "something is taking its course" (11), that they might someday "mean something" (32).

The impoverished human condition Beckett dramatizes invites a Marxist reading in which the relationship between Hamm and Clov allegorizes the class struggle between capitalists and the proletariat. Hamm's mistreatment of Clov in this reading would signify the capitalist's dehumanizing domination of his workers. Their complementary deformities – Clov cannot sit, Hamm cannot stand or see – comically renders the unceasing labor of the worker and the insulation from labor of the capitalist class. Hamm's insistence on being in the precise center of the room signifies both his tyrannical power and Clov's servile submission to that power. Both capitalist and worker are represented as estranged from the human values of work and reduced to mindless functionaries: "Every man his speciality" (10). This is certainly a plausible, if "vulgar," reading, which lacks the kind of nuance that would capture the ways in which Beckett's characters are entirely caught up in the dehumanized social world of which they appear to mourn the loss. We could instead read *Endgame* in terms of the "post-Marxist" critique of HEGEMONY, in which case the relationship between Hamm and Clov signifies not class struggle but rather the power of IDEOLOGY to achieve a non-coercive form of consensus. On this reading, Hamm's authority over Clov is ideological; it is not a function of brute force (his physical disabilities preclude it) but rather of a process whereby Hamm convinces Clov that his view of the world is the most reasonable, even natural one. As he looks out the window, Clov tells Hamm: "I warn you. I'm going to look at this filth since it's an order. But it's the last time" (78). Of course, it is not the last time, because he has already offered up his consent to a "one-dimensional world."

In some respects, a Marxist reading is foreclosed by the lack of any clear historical context. Beckett's play is precisely about this lack of context, this lack of any meaningful historical consciousness. Hamm and Clov thus allegorize the "Postmodern condition," which is characterized by immobility, passivity, incompleteness, lack of desire, and "affect": "Is it not time for my pain-killer?" Hamm asks (7). It is a *general* condition, as Hamm reminds Clov: "One day you'll be blind like me" (36). This thematic insistence on Postmodern meaninglessness is reflected in the play's deconstruction of dramaturgy. Dialogue is desultory, repetitive, fragmented, often monosyllabic. There is no "point," no rising action, no action at all, really, aside from Clov's attempt to kill a rat (which takes place off-stage). There are no complications, no crisis, no dénouement, no decisive conclusion, no patterns of significance. *Endgame* opens with a parody of Calvary: "Finished, it's finished, nearly finished, it must be nearly finished" (1). These lines both cite the Passion of Christ, a foundational MASTER NARRATIVE of Western culture, and announce its inadequacy as a meaningful narrative legitimation of contemporary society. They signal the impossibility of finishing or, worse, the probability that things are already finished. In any case, it is the outcome of what **Jean-François Lyotard** calls *delegitimation*, the process by which master narratives lose their power to legitimize social, political, and cultural discourses. All that is left are dreams – "What dreams! What forests!" (3) – and the ineffectual invocation of nature goddesses: "Flora! Pomona!" (39). The past is reduced to "yesterday" (15), "that bloody awful day, long ago, before this bloody awful day. I use the words you taught me" (43–44). Tradition is fragmented and misquoted, as with the echo of Shakespeare's *Richard III*: "My kingdom for a nightman" (23). The delegitimation of master narratives and other forms of cultural authority does not mean the end of stories, however, for it is precisely stories, paltry though they may be, that bind these characters together. Aimless, episodic anecdotes of a barely remembered life constitute a precarious bond, a social contract for a "post-human" era. "[W]e are obliged to each other," Hamm says at the conclusion of the play, caught up in an interminable endgame, whose outcome is implicit in its beginnings: "old endgame lost of old, play and lose and have done with losing" (82). In Beckett's Postmodern universe, the "old endgame" is reduced to a "little turn. . . . right round the world! . . . Hug the walls then back to the center again" (25). There are no grand strategies, no winning or losing, nothing really but "getting on."

WORK CITED

Beckett, Samuel. *Endgame* and *Act without Words*. New York: Grove Press, 1958.

Salman Rushdie, *Midnight's Children*

Postcolonial Studies * *Postmodernism* * *Ethnic Studies*

Salman Rushdie's *Midnight's Children* (1980), one of the most influential postcolonial novels, is a sprawling narrative told by Saleem Sinai. It begins with his grandfather in 1915, in the princely state of Kashmir, and proceeds through the major events of Indian history, beginning with the Amritsar massacre of 1919 then moving to Bombay and the creation of the Indian State (and the simultaneous partitioning of Pakistan), the Indo-Pakistan war, and the creation of Bangladesh out of East Pakistan. From a Postcolonial Studies point of view, Rushdie's treatment of these historical events constitutes a revisionist critique of COLONIALIST and nationalist visions of India. Rushdie embraces the idea that "there are as many versions of India as Indians" (323). One version is offered up by Dr. Narlikar, who invents a concrete tetrapod to be used in land reclamation. (Bombay was erected on land reclaimed from the sea.) These lingam-like structures prompt him to meditate on the "old dark priapic forces of ancient, procreative India" (209). Dr. Narlikar is able to sustain in his imagination, simultaneously, a pre-colonial conception of India and a vision of a project that will help usher India into modernity. Rushdie operates in a similar fashion, appropriating a wide range of native cultural discourses (including Vedic texts, Bollywood films, the *Arabian Nights*, pop songs and magic shows, advertisements for wise men like Lord Khusro Khusrovani, and on and on) in creating his postcolonial fable, which links his novel to the story cycle of Scheherazade. In other ways, Rushdie appropriates narrative forms from Western traditions, including the multi-generational saga form favored by novelists, including D. H. Lawrence and John Forsythe, and the *Bildungsroman*. In Rushdie's version, the narrative dynamics of the European *Bildungsroman* – a representation of the bourgeois SUBJECT's harmonious self-formation – undergo a convulsive reorganization. Rather than occupy its own AUTONOMOUS narrative space, Saleem's *Bildung* unfolds within a dense historical and familial context. He is "buffeted by too much history" (37). Saleem is born at midnight, August 15, 1947, the very moment of India's independence. His ability to connect telepathically, via his hypersensitive nose, with the hundreds of other children born at midnight, all of whom also possess magical gifts, links his development to that of the new Indian nation. The "children of midnight were also the children *of the time*," writes Saleem. "[F]athered, you understand, by history" (137). His narrative is a "long-winded autobiography" (548).

Rushdie's Postmodernist critique of history takes the form of anonymous letters fashioned from newspaper cut-outs, which Saleem uses to gratify his desire for love and vengeance: "Cutting up history to fit my nefarious purpose" (311). This instance of *citation* is joined by many others in which Saleem creates a network of INTERTEXTUAL references, or nodal points, which offer the reader alternative modes of constructing the narrative logic of the text. A good example is Aadam Aziz, Saleem's grandfather, who signals an intertextual relation with E. M. Forster's *Passage to India*. Forster's protagonist, Aziz, is not only a doctor but a Muslim, and shares many of Aadam's attitudes. For example, Aadam IDEALIZES the "Kashmiri girl" (33), echoing Forster's Aziz who waxes eloquent on the independence of Indian women. This and other intertextual connections to colonialist literature suggest to the reader a buried history of colonial and postcolonial India. Intertextuality also contributes to the METAFICTIONAL quality of Rushdie's text. Through ludic strategies of digression, repetition, summary, and prolepsis, the narrator draws the reader's attention to the artifice of narrative, "laying bare" the devices by which the text is created as a work of art. Saleem himself refers to his "miracle-laden omniscience" (177), a phrase that captures well the quality of Rushdie's *magic realism*. In this regard, *Midnight's Children* resembles Gabriel García Márquez's *One Hundred Years of Solitude*, another novel with a strong Postmodern orientation towards magical, anti-realistic representation. Some postcolonial critics condemn Rushdie's use of Postmodernist techniques of representation, claiming they are signs of a commitment to European intellectual values. Others would claim that these same techniques make possible a strategy of "writing for resistance" that we find in many postcolonial texts. Saleem himself provides a wonderful conceit, in the Snakes and Ladders game, for a narrative PERFORMANCE that negotiates between magic realism and historical mimesis. "[I]mplicit in the game is the unchanging twoness of things, the duality of up against down, good against evil; the solid rationality of ladders balances the occult sinuosities of the serpent" (167). Snakes and Ladders vividly models the HYBRID nature of postcolonial life and offers a profoundly *anti*-narrative model for representing human experience: the interminable up-and-down of a Manichaean dualism and the "sinuous" path of resistance to dualities of all kinds. In this case, Rushdie's postcolonial HISTORICISM – his "chutnification of history" – complements a Postmodern critique of history, for both are combating the influence of deterministic MASTER NARRATIVES.

Colonial and postcolonial SUBJECTS come of age in an environment in which identity is fractured along national, religious, and ethnic lines. Saleem is born on the hour of independence and lives to see his family claim Pakistan as its home. Can ethnic identities survive the breakdown of traditional geographical, linguistic, and cultural boundaries? Can they survive the militancy of "language marchers" who use language as a litmus test for national autonomy? There is also the question of Saleem's patrimony. A disgruntled family retainer had switched Amina Sinai's baby for another. Saleem, it turns out, is the son of a low-cast Hindu woman and an Englishman. Due to the "accidents" of history, Saleem embodies the multiplicity of India, with its "infinity of alternative realities" (389). Negotiating a plurality of identities, some illusory, complicates self-formation, but it also suggests new modes of collectivity. One of the consequences of his *Bildung*-plot, entangled as it is with the history of the nation, is that his own racial and ethnic identity is HYBRIDIZED. Saleem's hybrid condition is dramatized by his ability to be a "receptor" for all of midnight's children: "I decided to form . . . a gang which was spread over the length and breadth of the country, and whose headquarters were behind my eyebrows" (247). These children are the outcasts of history; they represent the historical realities of migrancy and DIASPORA, the geopolitical consequences of COLONIALISM and DECOLONIZATION. Saleem ultimately cracks under the burden of multiplicity: "fission of Saleem, I am the bomb of Bombay, watch me explode, bones splitting breaking beneath the awful pressure of the crowd" (552). Rushdie challenges his readers to figure out how to respond to this image of an annihilated SUBJECTIVITY.

WORK CITED

Rushdie, Salman. *Midnight's Children*. New York: Penguin, 1991.

Angela Carter, *Nights at the Circus*

*Gender and Sexuality * Postmodernism * Cultural Studies*

Angela Carter's *Nights at the Circus* (1984) frames questions of Gender and Sexuality in the context of the marginal world of circus performers in 1899. The protagonist, Sophia Fevvers, is an *aerialiste* whose talents are advertised by the slogan, "Is she fact or is she fiction?" This coy question refers to Fevvers' wings: are they real or not? Fevvers herself informs us in the first paragraph that she was "never docked via what you might call the *normal channels*, sir, oh, dear me, no; but, just like Helen of Troy, was *hatched*" (7). Carter's winged protagonist is an allegory of female AUTONOMY and self-reliance. For example, Ma Nelson, the Madame of a bordello where Fevvers spent her childhood, regards her young charge as a "pure child of the century that just now is waiting in the wings, the New Age in which no women will be bound down to the ground" (25). Fevvers blithely ignores socially-sanctioned gender roles and sexual IDENTITIES. Though she "served [her] apprenticeship in *being looked at* – at being the object of the eye of the beholder" (23), she was never quite the object upon which men thought they were fixing their gaze. They thought they were seeing a young girl disguised as the goddess "Winged Victory," when in fact she was the "real thing." "We were all suffragists in that house," Fevvers recalls, during an interview with a young newsman, Jack Walser (38). The point is reinforced by the ambience of her room, "a mistresspiece of exquisitely feminine squalor" (9). Fevvers moves from one "wholly female world" to another (38). Her longest sojourn is with Colonel Kearney's circus as it crosses Russia on the way to Japan. Though strongly dominated by male figures, the circus soon takes on a feminist identity: Mignon, a street waif, and the "Princess of Abyssinia" soothe tigers with song, thus appropriating a masculine Orphic tradition; Samson, the strong man, breaks down and decries his own masculinity. As for Walser, "'I'll *sit* on him, I'll hatch him out,'" Fevvers says, "'I'll make a new man of him. I'll make him into the New Man'" (281). As Simone de Beauvoir wrote, "one is not born, but becomes a woman." Carter's response is, yes, of course, and men must be *re*born in order to be become men.

Carter's Postmodernist fiction uses the fantastic to undermine conventions of perception and MIMETIC representation. Fevvers learns early on that reality is a fantasy, that what we typically regard as "real" is nothing more than a SIMULATION of the real. "'[O]h, indeed!'" she exclaims, speaking of the bordello, "'we knew we only sold the *simulacra*'" (39). Fevvers is herself caught up in the Postmodern condition of being unclearly distinguishable from a simulacrum of herself. Walser meditates on her "reality" while watching her perform, and notes that "in a secular age, an authentic miracle must purport to be a hoax, in order to gain credit in the world" (17). He reconsiders this paradox later and concludes that if she were a "prodigy" than she would no longer be a "wonder," an exceptional woman. Walser believes she should continue to be a "symbolic woman," rather than reveal her "real" self and be nothing but a "freak." "But what would she become, if she continued to be a woman?" (161). Walser himself, once he loses his memory, becomes bound up in the uncanny realm of simulation. He becomes a circus clown and experiences "the freedom that lies behind the mask, within dissimulation, the freedom to juggle with being, and, indeed, with the language which is vital to our being, that lies at the heart of burlesque" (103). Walser's distance from "reality" is dramatized when he is rescued in the Siberian wilderness, after the circus train is derailed, by a "forest dweller," a shaman, who finds Walser in a "permanent state of sanctified delirium" (254). The forest dwellers "shared a common dream, which was their world"; but this dream "did not, could not, take into account any other interpretation of the world, or dream, which was not their own one. Their dream was foolproof. An engine-turned fabrication. A closed system" (253). The same could be said for Ma Nelson's bordello or the circus. The Postmodern world is one of multiple and overlapping, in the end mutually exclusive, simulations of a reality that no one can know in an unmediated fashion.

From a Cultural Studies perspective, *Nights at the Circus* is a meditation on popular spectacles and the journalism that supports them. Walser is, in some ways, no different from Colonel Kearney. In Carter's view, newspapers and circuses appeal in the same way to the same audience. Walser, hoping to follow Fevvers to St. Petersburg, proposes to his editor that he join the circus incognito and write "a series of inside stories of the exotic, of the marvellous, of laughter and tears and thrills and all" (90). He knows just the sort of sentimental, gullible reader that would "thrill" to his account. Colonel Kearney, for his part, is a quintessential American huckster, whose pet pig once taught him a valuable lesson: "Never give a sucker an even break!" (175). His "Ludic Game" is a kind of adventurous, extravagant form of global capitalism, Barnum and Bailey style: "High-wire walkers, earth-shaking elephants – no end to the marvels the Colonel intended to transport about the globe, joined together in amity at the sight of the dollar bill" (99). Like Djuna Barnes in *Nightwood*, Carter situates her marginal figures in an exorbitant *demimonde*, where the barriers between man and woman, beast and human break down. Carter's depiction of the circus deconstructs our sense of culture by forcing us to rethink our idea of nature. Walser has a confrontation with one of "Lamarck's Educated Apes," an "inhabitant of the magic circle of difference, unreachable . . . but not unknowable." The chimp, "as if acknowledging their meeting across the gulf of strangeness, pressed his tough forefinger down on Walser's painted smile, bidding him be silent" (108). If Walser can reach across the species divide and connect with an ape, then perhaps he can become the New Man Fevver's desires. In Carter's phantasmagoria, the conventional distinctions between high and low cultural values are easily upended. In *Nights at the Circus*, popular culture is no longer marginal. Bordellos, circuses, penitentiaries, forest dwellers – all present their own simulations, their own dreams of the world, as if there were no "normative" standard. Or, more accurately, as if their simulations *were* the standard. As Fevvers says, in her send off, "'To think I really fooled you. . . . It just goes to show there's nothing like confidence'" (295).

WORK CITED

Carter, Angela. *Nights at the Circus*. New York: Penguin, 1985.

CONCLUSION: READING LITERARY THEORY

all words, there's nothing else,
you must go on, that's all I know
Beckett, *The Unnameable*

Readers confronted with literary theory often feel overwhelmed by technical language and a style of writing that can often be dense or opaque. As I have indicated throughout this *Guide*, many literary and cultural theories emerged out of philosophy and other technical fields. Difficulties in reading theory often result from a lack of knowledge of these fields. But they can also result from stylistic strategies that are calculated to keep readers from falling into the traps of conventional thinking. At its best, theory employs complex terminologies and writing styles in a principled attempt to explain ideas that cannot be explained in any other way. Many theorists invent new terms to accommodate new methods, techniques, and objects of study. Indeed, inventing or modifying terms may be the most important part of the work of contemporary theory, in large measure because they designate new or modified concepts and ideas.

In some cases, problems of comprehension are due to cultural and linguistic differences. Translation, of course, introduces special difficulties. What sounds familiar to French or German readers with even a slight knowledge of philosophical traditions may sound dauntingly unfamiliar to British or US readers relying on translations. Whenever possible, consult the translator's introduction or preface; these sections often contain explanations of important concepts and provide historical and cultural contexts. Writers like **Jacques Derrida** and **Theodor Adorno** are difficult for British and US readers in part because of the latter's unfamiliarity with French and German philosophical styles of writing. Aside from taking a detour into the works of Hegel and Heidegger, the reader could consult a resource (e.g., this *Guide* and, if necessary, an encyclopedia of philosophy, many of which are readily available on-line) that explains important terms and concepts. It is not necessary to be fluent in the philosophical traditions from which theorists draw their ideas; it is enough to be familiar with them in a general (but accurate) way. For example, the concept of DIALECTICS comes up time and again in literary and cultural theory, often as the object of critique. Though the word *dialectic* can be found in a dictionary, the definition given there will not be enough; the reader needs to find more focused and in-depth resources. A working understanding of Hegelian dialectics can be achieved by a targeted search in reliable resources, beginning with this *Guide*. A small amount of time spent consulting such resources would yield enough background knowledge to enable most readers to comprehend what Derrida and Adorno mean when they critique dialectical thinking.

Nearly every theory explored in this *Guide* owes an important debt to philosophy from which many of the terms used to talk about gender, sexuality, language, race, textuality, and a host of other themes and problems have been borrowed and adapted for new uses, sometimes *radically* new uses. Theoretical thought, in order to articulate generalizations and assumptions with any precision, must call into play such terms to achieve a particular force in analysis. Terms denote fundamental concepts within a theoretical discourse. Knowing them and their functions can allow the reader to deduce the nature of a given theory, its major concepts, key principles and assumptions, permissible strategies and techniques, and sometimes the kinds of relations that might obtain between one theory and another. The function of terminology is to *mediate* between the reader and the theoretical concepts employed by the author. Some terms are so general (e.g., SUBJECT, AGENCY, DISCOURSE) that there is no one theory that could be said to have given rise to them, while others (e.g., DIFFÉRANCE, ÉCRITURE FEMININE, HOMOSOCIAL DESIRE, and HYBRIDITY) have much more decisive points of emergence (e.g., Deconstruction, Feminism, theories of Gender and Sexuality, and Postcolonial Studies). The complexity and subtlety of theoretical terms are therefore *not* an effect of the terms themselves but of some aspect or operation of the theory in which they perform a specific function. Sometimes the confusion and irritation that readers experience when they encounter theory is due to vague, inconsistent, or ambiguous use of terms in the material they are assigned to read or come across in the course of research. *Jargon* is what occurs when otherwise useful terms have been uprooted from their contexts and become part of a pseudo-theoretical discourse in which they are used inconsistently and incoherently.

Another important aspect of theoretical discourse is style. Many theorists (e.g., **Jacques Lacan, Luce Irigaray, Gilles Deleuze** and **Félix Guattari**) write in an elliptical style; they are intentionally subverting the standards of academic prose, in large part because they are critiquing the criteria of logic, rationality, and sequential presentation of information that underwrite clear and accessible prose. So how does one follow this kind of theoretical discourse? The first step, which this *Guide* is designed to provide, is for the reader to become familiar with the broad contours of a particular theory. The second step is to develop a method of reading that is appropriate for the difficulties presented by that theory. When one reads a difficult text only once and stops frequently to puzzle over terminology or difficulties in phrasing, there will be inevitable problems following the thread of the argument. Therefore, it might be best to read theoretical texts twice. The first reading should be done without pausing (no matter how difficult it might seem), in order to get a feel for the rhythm and texture of the prose. Readers would be surprised, I think, at how much can be picked up in a first reading; very often a general sense of the argument can be gleaned, which can then be fleshed out in the second, more careful reading. In this second, more deliberative reading, the reader should highlight the author's thesis/ argument, which is often stated overtly, and try to identify key points that follow from it. Though many key points can be located at the beginning or end of subsections, it is nevertheless the case that they may not be as clearly marked as an initial statement of the argument. But despite the difficulties, trying to identify them engages the reader more closely with the details of the text.

Readers should be aware of key terms. Use a glossary like the one in this *Guide* to define specialized terms. Many of the important terms in a given theoretical argument will be repeated, so the reader should be watchful for repetitions and mark them. (Light pencil in library books, please!) Being aware of these repetitions will not only allow the reader to become familiar with them but will clarify the contexts in which they are used. The same idea applies to phrases (e.g., signifying practices, ideological hegemony): once the reader has defined the terms, the ways in which they are used in such phrases (and in larger contexts) can be more easily determined.

The extra time taken to read in this fashion will be worth it in the long run, because it mitigates frustration and leaves the reader feeling more engaged with theoretical ideas. By and large, literary and cultural theories are worth the candle. By following some of the practical tips I have provided here, and by being aware of the special status of theoretical terms, readers should feel less anxiety and gain greater clarity from the texts they read. The point is not to understand every single sentence encountered in theoretical texts but rather to comprehend the arguments within which each sentence can, given world enough and time, be rendered comprehensible. This *Guide* was designed to facilitate this process by providing a first step toward greater understanding of literary and cultural theory.

RECOMMENDATIONS FOR FURTHER STUDY

Note. See the Works Cited appended to the entries in the sections "The Scope of Literary Theory" and "Key Figures in Literary Theory" for additional titles.

Critical Theory

Arato, Andrew and Eike Gebhardt, eds. *The Essential Frankfurt School Reader.* 2nd ed. New York: Continuum, 1993.

Bernstein, Jay, ed. *The Frankfurt School: Critical Assessments.* 6 vols. London and New York: Routledge, 1994.

Habermas, Jürgen. *Legitimation Crisis.* Trans. Thomas McCarthy. Boston: Beacon, 1975.

——. *The Philosophical Discourse of Modernity: Twelve Lectures.* 1985. Trans. Frederick Lawrence. Cambridge, MA: MIT Press, 1987.

Kellner, Douglas. *Critical Theory, Marxism and Modernity.* Baltimore: Johns Hopkins University Press, 1989.

Laclau, Ernesto and Chantal Mouffe. *Hegemony and Socialist Strategy: Towards a Radical Democratic Politics.* 2nd ed. London and New York: Verso, 2001.

Tallack, Douglas, ed. *Critical Theory: A Reader.* New York: Harvester Wheatsheaf, 1995.

Cultural Studies

Bennett, Tony, Graham Martin, Colin Mercer, and Janet Woollacott, eds. *Culture, Ideology and Social Process: A Reader*. London: Batsford Academic and Educational, Ltd., 1981.

Brantlinger, Patrick. *Crusoe's Footprints: Cultural Studies in Britain and America*. New York: Routledge, 1990.

Grossberg, Lawrence, Cary Nelson, and Paula A. Treichler, eds. *Cultural Studies*. New York and London: Routledge, 1992.

Miller, Toby, ed. *A Companion to Cultural Studies*. Malden, MA: Blackwell, 2000.

Warren, Catherine A. and Mary Douglas, eds. *American Cultural Studies*. Urbana: University of Illinois Press, 2002.

Williams, Raymond. *New Keywords: A Revised Vocabulary of Culture and Society*. Ed. Tony Bennett, Lawrence Grossberg, and Meaghan Morris. Malden, MA: Blackwell, 2005.

Deconstruction

Cohen, Tom, ed. *Jacques Derrida and the Humanities: A Critical Reader*. Cambridge: Cambridge University Press, 2001.

Culler, Jonathan. *On Deconstruction: Theory and Criticism After Structuralism*. Ithaca: Cornell University Press, 1982.

Norris, Christopher. *Deconstruction: Theory and Practice*. 1982. 3rd ed. London and New York: Routledge, 2002.

Ryan, Michael. *Marxism and Deconstruction: A Critical Articulation*. Baltimore: Johns Hopkins University Press, 1982.

Wood, David, ed. *Derrida: A Critical Reader*. Oxford and Cambridge, MA: Blackwell, 1992.

Ethnic Studies

Appiah, Kwame Anthony and Henry Louis Gates, eds. *Africana: The Encyclopedia of the African and African American Experience*. 2nd ed. Oxford and New York: Oxford University Press, 2005.

Baker, Houston. *Afro-American Poetics: Revisions of Harlem and the Black Aesthetic*. Madison: University of Wisconsin, 1988.

Brown, Dee. *Bury My Heart at Wounded Knee: An Indian History of the American West.* New York: Holt, Rinehart & Winston, 1970.

Gates, Henry Louis, ed. *"Race," Writing, and Difference.* Chicago: University of Chicago Press, 1986.

Goldberg, David Theo and John Solomos, eds. *A Companion to Racial and Ethnic Studies.* Malden, MA: Blackwell, 2002.

Moraga, Cherríe and Gloria Anzaldúa, eds. *This Bridge Called My Back: Writings by Radical Women of Color.* 2nd ed. New York: Kitchen Table, Women of Color Press, 1983.

Spillers, Hortense J. *Black, White, and In Color: Essays on American Literature and Culture.* Chicago and London: University of Chicago Press, 2003.

Susser, Ida and Thomas C. Patterson, eds. *Cultural Diversity in the United States: A Critical Reader.* Malden, MA: Blackwell, 2001.

Feminism

Butler, Judith and Joan W. Scott, eds. *Feminists Theorize the Political.* New York: Routledge, 1992.

Collins, Patricia Hill. *Black Feminist Thought: Knowledge, Consciousness, and the Politics of Empowerment.* 2nd ed. New York and London: Routledge, 2000.

Cudd, Ann E. and Robin O. Andreasen, eds. *Feminist Theory: A Philosophical Anthology.* Malden, MA: Blackwell, 2005.

Ferguson, Margaret and Jennifer Wicke, eds. *Feminism and Postmodernism.* Durham: Duke University Press, 1994.

Hull, Gloria T., Patricia Bell Scott, and Barbara Smith. *All the Women are White, All the Blacks are Men, But Some of Us are Brave: Black Women's Studies.* Old Westbury, NY: Feminist Press, 1982.

Moi, Tori. *Sexual/Textual Politics: Feminist Literary Theory.* 2nd ed. London and New York: Routledge, 2002.

Rayna R. Reitor, ed. *Toward an Anthropology of Women.* New York: Monthly Review Press, 1975.

Gender and Sexuality

De Lauretis, Teresa. *The Practice of Love: Lesbian Sexuality and Perverse Desire.* Bloomington: Indiana University Press, 1994.

Dollimore, Jonathan. *Sexual Dissidence: Augustine to Wilde, Freud to Foucault.* Oxford: Clarendon Press; New York: Oxford University Press, 1991.

Edelman, Lee. *Homographies: Essays in Gay Literary and Cultural Theory.* New York: Routledge, 1994.

Essed, Philomena, David Theo Goldberg, and Audrey Kobayashi, eds. *A Companion to Gender Studies.* Malden, MA and Oxford: Blackwell, 2005.

Grosz, Elizabeth. *Space, Time, and Perversion: Essays on the Politics of Bodies.* New York: Routledge, 1995.

Hart, Lynda. *Fatal Women: Lesbian Sexuality and the Mark of Aggression.* Princeton: Princeton University Press, 1994.

Koestenbaum, Wayne. *Double Talk: The Erotics of Male Literary Collaboration.* New York: Routledge, 1989.

Marxist Theory

Eagleton, Terry and Drew Milne, eds. *Marxist Literary Theory: A Reader.* Oxford and Cambridge, MA: Blackwell, 1996.

Gramsci, Antonio. *A Gramsci Reader: Selected Writings, 1916–1935.* Ed. David Forgasc. London: Lawrence and Wishart. 1999.

Jameson, Fredric. *The Political Unconscious: Narrative as a Socially Symbolic Act.* Ithaca: Cornell University Press, 1981.

Mandel, Ernest. *Late Capitalism.* 1972. Trans. Joris De Bres. London: Verso, 1978.

Marx, Karl and Fredrick Engels. *The German Ideology.* Ed. C. J. Arthur. New York, International, 1972.

Nelson, Cary and Lawrence Grossberg, eds. *Marxism and the Interpretation of Culture.* Urbana: University of Illinois Press, 1988.

Williams, Raymond. *Marxism and Literature.* Oxford: Oxford University Press, 1977.

Narrative Theory

Booth, Wayne. *The Rhetoric of Fiction.* 1966. 2nd ed. Chicago: University of Chicago Press, 1983.

McKeon, Michael, ed. *Theory of the Novel: A Historical Approach.* Baltimore: Johns Hopkins University Press, 2000.

Mitchell. W. J. T., ed. *On Narrative*. Chicago: University of Chicago Press, 1981.

Phelan, James and Peter Rabinowitz, eds. *A Companion to Narrative Theory*. Malden, MA: Blackwell, 2005.

Prince, Gerald. *Narratology: The Form and Functioning of Narrative*. Berlin and New York: Mouton, 1982.

Todorov, Tzvetan. *The Poetics of Prose*. Trans. Richard Howard. Ithaca: Cornell University Press, 1977.

Watt, Ian. *The Rise of the Novel*. Berkeley: University of California Press, 1957.

New Criticism

Burke, Kenneth. *Counter-Statement*. 1931. 2nd ed. Los Altos, CA: Hermes Publications, 1953.

Jancovich, Mark. *The Cultural Politics of the New Criticism*. Cambridge: Cambridge University Press, 1993.

Leavis, F. R., ed. *A Selection from Scrutiny*. 2 vols. London and New York: Cambridge University Press, 1968.

Ransom, John Crow. *The New Criticism*. Norfolk, CT: New Directions, 1941.

Spurlin, William J. and Michael Fisher, eds. *The New Criticism and Contemporary Literary Theory: Connections and Continuities*. New York and London: Garland Publishing, 1995

Wellek, Rene and Austin Warren. *Theory of Literature*. London: Cape, 1949.

New Historicism

Dollimore, Jonathan. *Radical Tragedy: Religion, Ideology, and Power in the Drama of Shakespeare and his Contemporaries*. 3rd Edition. Durham, NC: Duke University Press, 2004.

Gallagher, Catherine and Stephen Greenblatt. *Practicing New Historicism*. Chicago: University of Chicago Press, 2000.

Goldberg, Jonathan. *James I and the Politics of Literature: Jonson, Shakespeare, Donne, and their Contemporaries*. Baltimore: Johns Hopkins University Press, 1983.

Montrose, Louis. *The Purpose of Playing: Shakespeare and the Cultural Politics of the Elizabethan Theatre*. Chicago: University of Chicago Press, 1996.

Ryan, Kiernan, ed. *New Historicism and Cultural Materialism: A Reader.* London and New York: Arnold, 1996.

Veeser, H. Aram, ed. *The New Historicism Reader.* New York: Routledge, 1994.

Postcolonial Studies

Ashcroft, W.D, Gareth Griffiths, and Helen Tiffin. *The Empire Writes Back: Theory and Practice in Post-colonial Literatures.* 1989. 2nd ed. London and New York: Routledge, 2002.

Castle, Gregory, ed. *Postcolonial Discourses: An Anthology.* Oxford: Blackwell, 2001.

Guha, Ranajit and Gayatri Spivak, eds. *Selected Subaltern Studies.* Delhi and New York: Oxford University Press, 1988.

Schwarz, Henry and Sangeeta Ray. *A Companion to Postcolonial Studies.* Malden, MA: Blackwell, 2000.

Spivak, Gayatri Chakravorty. *A Critique of Postcolonial Reason: Toward a History of the Vanishing Present.* Cambridge, MA and London: Harvard University Press, 1999.

Williams, Patrick and Laura Chrisman, eds. *Colonial Discourse and Post-Colonial Theory: A Reader.* New York: Columbia University Press, 1994.

Young, Robert J.C. *Postcolonialism: An Historical Introduction.* Oxford; Malden, MA: Blackwell, 2001.

Postmodernism

Connor, Steve. *Postmodernist Culture: An Introduction to Theories of the Contemporary.* 2nd ed. Oxford: Blackwell, 1997.

Docherty, Thomas, ed. *Postmodernism: A Reader.* New York. Harvester Wheatsheaf, 1993.

Ferguson, Margaret and Jennifer Wicke, eds. *Feminism and Postmodernism.* Durham: Duke University Press, 1994.

Hassan, Ihab. *The Dismemberment of Orpheus: Toward a Postmodern Literature.* 2nd ed. Madison: University of Wisconsin Press, 1982.

Kaplan, Ann, ed. *Postmodernism and Its Discontents: Theories, Practices.* London and New York: Verso, 1988.

Lucy, Niall. *Postmodern Literary Theory: An Introduction.* Oxford: Blackwell, 1997.

Natoli, Joseph and Linda Hutcheon, eds. *A Postmodern Reader*. Albany: State University of New York Press, 1993.
Seidman, Steven. *Contested Knowledge: Social Theory in the Postmodern Era*. Oxford and Cambridge, MA: Blackwell, 1994.

Poststructuralism

Bakhtin, M. M. *The Dialogic Imagination*. Ed. Michael Holquist; Trans. Caryl Emerson and Michael Holquist. Austin: University of Austin Press, 1981.
Barthes, Roland. *Critical Essays*. 1964. Trans. Richard Howard. Evanston: Northwestern University Press, 1972.
Derrida, Jacques. *Of Grammatology*. Trans. Gayatri Chakravorty Spivak. Baltimore: Johns Hopkins University Press, 1976.
Felperin, Howard. *Beyond Deconstruction: The Uses and Abuses of Literary Theory*. Oxford: Clarendon Press, 1985.
Foucault, Michel. *Language, Counter-Memory, Practice: Selected Essays and Interviews*. Ed. Donald F. Bouchard. Trans. Donald F. Bouchard and Sherry Simon. Ithaca: Cornell University Press, 1977.
Lotringer, Sylvère and Sande Cohen. *French Theory in America*. New York and London: Routledge, 2001.
Macksey, Richard and Eugenio Donato, eds. *The Structuralist Controversy: The Languages of Criticism and the Sciences of Man*. 1970. Baltimore: The Johns Hopkins University Press, 1972.
Sarup, Madan. *Poststructuralism and Postmodernism*. 2nd ed. Athens: University of Georgia Press, 1993.

Psychoanalysis

Felman, Shoshana. *Literature and Psychoanalysis: The Question of Reading: Otherwise*. Baltimore and London: The Johns Hopkins University Press, 1982.
Freud, Sigmund. *The Freud Reader*. Ed. Peter Gay. New York: W.W. Norton, 1995.
Laplanche, J. and J.-B. Pontalis. *The Language of Psycho-Analysis*. Trans. Donald Nicholson-Smith. New York: Norton, 1974.
Mitchell, Juliet. *Psychoanalysis and Feminism*. New York: Vintage Books, 1975.
Sarup, Madan. *Jacques Lacan*. New York and London: Harvester Wheatsheaf, 1992.

Vice, Sue, ed. *Psychoanalytic Criticism: A Reader*. Cambridge, England: Polity Press; Cambridge, MA: Blackwell, 1996.

Žižek, Slavoj. *Enjoy Your Symptom!: Jacques Lacan in Hollywood and Out*. Rev. ed. New York and London: Routledge, 2001.

Reader-Response Theory

Ingarden, Roman. *The Cognition of the Literary Work of Art*. Trans. Ruth Ann Crowley and Kenneth R. Olson. Evanston: Northwestern University Press, 1973.

Jauss, Hans Robert. *Toward An Aesthetic of Reception*. Trans. Timothy Bahti. Minneapolis: University of Minnesota Press, 1982.

Machor, James L. and Philip Goldstein, eds. *Reception Study: From Literary Theory to Cultural Studies*. New York: Routledge, 2001.

Phelan, James, ed. *Reading Narrative: Form, Ethics, Ideology*. Columbus: Ohio State University Press, 1989.

Tompkins, Jane, ed. *Reader-Response Criticism: From Formalism to Post-Structuralism*. Baltimore: The Johns Hopkins University Press, 1980.

Structuralism and Formalism

Culler, Jonathan. *Structuralist Poetics: Structuralism, Linguistics and the Study of Literature*. Ithaca: Cornell University Press, 1976.

Dosse, François. *History of Structuralism*. 2 vols. Trans. Deborah Glassman. Minneapolis: University of Minnesota Press, 1997.

Hawkes, Terence. *Structuralism and Semiotics*. Berkeley: University of California Press, 1977.

Jameson, Fredric. *The Prison-House of Language: A Critical Account of Structuralism and Russian Formalism*. Princeton, NJ: Princeton University Press, 1972.

Lane, Michael, ed. *Structuralism: A Reader*. London: Cape, 1970.

Matejka, Ladislav and Krystyna Pomorska, eds. *Readings in Russian Poetics: Formalist and Structuralist Views*. Ann Arbor: Michigan Slavic Publications, 1978.

Scholes, Robert. *Structuralism in Literature: An Introduction*. New Haven: Yale University Press, 1974.

Shklovsky, Viktor. *Theory of Prose*. 1925. Trans. Benjamin Sher. Elmwood Park, IL: Dalkey Archive Press, 1990.

GLOSSARY

Note. Terms that designate a movement or major trend covered in "The Scope of Literary Theory" (e.g., Poststructuralism, Deconstruction, Psychoanalysis, and so on) are not included in this glossary. Terms in small caps within the definitions below have their own entries. As elsewhere in this *Guide*, boldface indicates that additional discussions of the theorist in question can be found in "Key Figures in Literary Theory." The index will direct readers to further discussion of many of these terms as well as to those terms of a highly specialized nature (e.g., those found in psychoanalytic theory).

AESTHETIC THEORY, AESTHETICS.   Generally, these terms refer to theories of artistic value, production, and judgment. Theories of aesthetics began with Aristotle's *Poetics*, and most philosophers to follow him have written on the subject. The Enlightenment aesthetics of writers like Edmund Burke and Immanual Kant identify *beauty* and the *sublime* as the two chief aesthetic responses. A Kantian tradition in aesthetics predominated in the nineteenth and twentieth centuries. In recent years, Postmodernists like **Jean-François Lyotard** have championed an aesthetics that locates the sublime experience in "perpetual negation," the unrepresentable difference of language and pure *figurality*.

AESTHETICISM.   Typically used to designate a movement, associated with Charles Baudelaire, Theophile Gautier and Oscar Wilde, *aestheticism* celebrates "art for art's sake." It privileges beauty above all things and insists on the AUTONOMY of art. Within the *aesthete* movement there coexisted a trend towards *décadence*, which regards the perverse and the decayed, the malformed and merely natural, as themselves objects of beauty. Both *aestheticism* and *décadence* are retreats from realism and naturalism and from the sentimental moralizing attendant upon both. See AESTHETIC THEORY.

AGENCY.   The power of a human SUBJECT to exert his or her will in the social world. To have *agency* is to have social power; to lack it is to be ignored or subjugated by others who possess it. Typically, *agency* is associated with the subject of Western discourses and historical *agency* is perhaps the most important form. To acquire *agency* outside of or in conflict with these discourses is considered by many to be a political, even an insurrectionary act. See PERFORMANCE.

ALIENATION.   A multifaceted term, with wide currency in literary and cultural theory. The general concept stems from the Marxist notion that workers cannot enjoy the fruits of their labor and are thus alienated from the objective world they help to create. In many cases, this term is used with a psychological emphasis and denotes experiences of anomie, disconnection, and isolation.

AMBIVALENCE.   This term derives from Psychoanalysis and refers to the unstable nature of IDENTITY when the norms governing sexual choice do not function predictably. In general, it refers to the failure of language or DISCOURSE to settle on a single definitive meaning. Rhetorically, *ambivalence* resembles *irony*, which marks a gap between a thing said and a thing done or between intention and effect. Cf. TOTALITY and UNIVERSALISM.

APORIA.   From the Greek, *a-byssos*, without depth or bottom. Typically, this term refers to textual instances of doubt or uncertainty about meaning, an unsolvable puzzle, a gap or ellipsis. Many poststructuralists hold that language itself, by virtue of its quality of DIFFERENCE, is *aporetic*.

ARCHAEOLOGY.   Associated with **Michel Foucault**, *archaeology* refers to a SYNCHRONIC mode of DISCOURSE ANLAYSIS that eschews conventional historical methodologies and focuses on ruptures and discontinuities in order to come to an understanding of the emergence of statements and events within DISCURSIVE FORMATIONS. A crucial function of *archaeology* is the interrogation of documents and the status of the historical "event." Cf. the diachronic method of GENEALOGY.

AUTONOMY, AUTONOMOUS, AUTONOMIZATION.   These terms refer to the possibility of grounding subjectivity or aesthetic production beyond the influence of social, political, and cultural forces. The bourgeois SUBJECT is often described as *autonomous* in this sense. Some theorists speak of a process of *autonomization* by which the illusion of *autonomy* is maintained in both theory and practice.

BASE/SUPERSTRUCTURE.   In classical Marxism, *base* refers to the modes of production, while *superstructure* refers to the aggregate of social, cultural, political, and commercial institutions and practices that are supported by the base. The precise nature of the relationship varies from school to school within Marxism. A mechanistic relationship would yield a predictable superstructure, which is clearly not the case. Post-Marxist theories of *structural causality* are concerned with IDEO-LOGICAL determinations within the *superstructure* itself rather than with direct expressions of economic forces deriving from the *base*. See CULTURAL MATERIALISM and HISTORICAL DETERMINISM.

CANON.   A term used to designate an authoritative body of work in a given field. It emerged from religious studies where it refers to a law or system of laws as well as to the selection of texts that make up the Holy Scriptures (the "sacred canon"). In literary studies, the term *canon* is used to designate the most important texts in a particular literary tradition. In recent years, the very idea of a literary *canon* has been called into question, in part because it is thought to exclude women and ethnic minorities. The so-called "canon wars" of the 1980s and '90s were a sign of deep cultural division, especially in the US and Britain.

CARNIVALESQUE.   Associated with the work of **M. M. Bakhtin**, the *carnivalesque* designates a subversion of social norms in ritual spectacles, comic overturnings, and scatological representations. Linked to the early Christian notion of *carnival*, a time of feasting and merriment before the sacrifices of Lent.

COLONIAL DISCOURSE.   A discursive form of DOMINATION. *Colonial discourse* consists of all those texts, documents, art works, and other means of expression that relate directly and indirectly to colonial rule. *Colonial discourse* is the object of certain forms of discourse analysis, for example ORIENTALISM. See also MIMICRY.

COLONIALISM.   Colonialism is the process whereby imperial states acquire new territories and exploit them for land, raw materials, and human labor. *Administered colonies* like India were in large part driven by commerce in native produce, but they were also major centers of imperial power. The colonial bureaucracy was large and offered advancement to Europeans, but it also created the need for native civil servants. By contrast, *settler colonies* involve the extensive settlement of Europeans, either through the establishment of penal colonies, as in Australia, or the appropriation of arable land, as in Ireland, the Caribbean, and parts of Africa. DECOLONIZATION is a period of intense social contradiction and conflict that typically ends in an anti-colonial resistance and the creation of independent nations. NEOCOLONIALISM refers to the continuation of European exploitation of former colonies and implies, on the part of those colonies, either economic helplessness or collusion. Due to its geographical and cultural proximity to the center of empire, Ireland is sometimes called a *metrocolony*. See MET-ROPOLITAN CULTURE.

COLONIAL MIMICRY.   See MIMICRY.

COMMODITY, COMMODIFICATION.   Terms developed in Marxist theory that refer to the process by which the products of human labor are transformed into what Marx called the "mysterious" concept of the *commodity*. The *commodity* is an object produced from nature but one bearing the "stamp" of a social relation (i.e., relations of *use* and *exchange*) that severs the commodity once and for all from the body of the producer.

CONSTELLATION.   A mode of philosophical reflection in which the SUBJECT arranges the experiences of multiple perceptions (texts, ideas, phenomena) in such a way that draws out a general idea or truth. A *constellation* is subjective in the sense that it is not a function of the quality of the experiences, but of the critic's understanding of their true idea. It is also provisional: it *might* reveal an idea.

COUNTER-HEGEMONY.   See HEGEMONY.

CREOLE, CREOLIZATION.   See HYBRIDITY.

CULTURAL MATERIALISM.   A mode of analysis that focuses on how ideas, beliefs, and IDEOLOGIES are formed by material conditions, by constraints imposed by social, cultural, and political policies and forces. *Cultural materialism* holds that social and cultural artifacts are sites of ideological conflict; in such artifacts, the reader can discern the figural expression of social contradictions. It is grounded in the Marxist theory of materialism according to which the modes of production and material conditions are chiefly responsible for determining social, cultural, and political institutions and practices. See BASE/SUPER-STRUCTURE and DIALECTIC.

CULTURAL POETICS, POETICS OF CULTURE. Often used to describe the methodologies of cultural criticism in New Historicism and textualist anthropology. Sometimes referred to as *poetics of culture*, this perspective calls into question the objectivity or scientific status that anthropology and other disciplines claim for their representations. It argues that all representations of culture are determined by the same linguistic constraints and freedoms that govern aesthetic discourse.

DECOLONIZATION. See COLONIALISM.

DETERMINATION. See HISTORICAL DETERMINISM and NEGATION.

DETERRITORIALIZATION. See TERRITORIALIZATION.

DIACHRONY/SYNCHRONY. *Diachrony* is a temporal progression moving in sequence, typically chronologically, within a system. Cf. *synchrony*, a spatial dimension extending in all possible directions from any single point; it thus designates the totality of a system. The former tends to be associated with traditional history and the logic of causality, the latter with atemporal or spatial representations that do not heed causality, sequence, or priority.

DIALECTICS, DIALECTICAL MATERIALISM. These terms refer both to a kind of process and to a mode of analysis. The former goes back to Plato and the Socratic dialogues, in which logical propositions are formulated through the give-and-take of discussion. Hegel made famous the idea of an interplay between thesis and antithesis that yielded a new synthesis, while Marx put this idea into materialist terms when he theorized a dialectical struggle between classes that yielded a classless society. A *dialectical materialist* mode of analysis concentrates on the process of class struggle and its social, economic, and political effects. A dialectical logic underwrites most varieties of *cultural materialism*. See NEGATION.

DIALOGISM. The dynamic totality of linguistic possibilities that condition individual utterances within social or cultural discourses. Dialogized discourse is open to multiple historical and social contexts, a condition **M. M. Bakhtin** called HETEROGLOSSIA.

DIASPORA, DIASPORIC IDENTITIES. See HYBRIDITY.

DIFFERENCE, *DIFFÉRANCE*. A principle according to which language makes meaning by virtue of the *difference* between signs within a system rather than the similarity between a sign and its external referent. *Difference* in this sense evolved from **Jacques Derrida's** notion of *différance*, which combines the meanings "to defer" and "to differ." It has come to have a general application in the study of gender, sexuality, race, and other topics. See SIGN and PLAY.

DISCOURSE.   Refers primarily to SIGNIFYING SYSTEMS, typically linguistic, within the limits of a particular field of study or knowledge (e.g., medical discourse, literary discourse). For some formalist theorists, *discourse* signifies a linguistic system constituting a dynamic totality. **Michel Foucault** has proposed the idea of the DISCURSIVE FORMATION, a term which refers to the aggregate of statements made about a given idea (madness, sexuality, punishment). *Discourse analysis* is a mode of interpretation that stresses the textual and linguistic expression of social and cultural power within such formations. See COLONIAL DISCOURSE, MASTER NARRATIVE, ORIENTALISM, and SOCIAL FIELD.

DISCOURSE ANALYSIS.   See DISCOURSE.

DISCURSIVE FORMATION.   Associated with the work of **Michel Foucault**, this term refers to a field of statements and textual "events" that reflect relations of social and cultural power. Many such formations are structured hierarchically and reinforce established traditions and dominant IDEOLOGIES. They are characterized also by the creation of rules of exclusion and, to this extent, are self-regulating systems. The unity or coherence of *discursive formations* is dependent not on the unity or coherence of particular ideas but rather on their emergence and transformation within the formation. *Discursive practices* are those textual and linguistic enunciations that enforce these rules in specific, disciplined fashion. They can, however, be exploited for subversive purposes, as in COLONIAL MIMICRY and in Foucault's own analytical methods, ARCHAEOLOGY and GENEALOGY. See DISCOURSE and SOCIAL FIELD.

DOMINATION.   In Marxist theory, this term refers to a social condition in which power is exerted over others by material (i.e., military or police) force. Cf. HEGEMONY, which is a non-coercive form of social control.

ÉCRITURE FEMININE.   A form of strategic ESSENTIALISM, which revalues women's bodies and identities outside of hegemonic discursive practices. It is an acknowledgment of the body as the mystical or spiritual ground for a specifically female *essence*, and thus as the origin and legitimation of a new form of writing. Literally, "feminine writing," it is typically translated, "writing the body."

ESSENCE, ESSENTIAL, ESSENTIALISM. The essence of a thing is what is inherent, indivisible, immutable about it, what it must possess in order to be *a thing*. It is the chief assumption behind biologistic theories of race and gender and it drives certain theories of literature and culture that rest on moral and ethical premises. Such theories are often referred to as *essentialist*. Opposed concepts include SOCIAL CONSTRUCTIONISM and ÉCRITURE FEMININE.

FABULATION. See METAFICTION.

GENEALOGY. A mode of historical analysis devised by Friedrich Nietzsche and later used by **Michel Foucault** to chart the DIACHRONIC emergence of specific concepts and forms of knowledge (punishment, sexuality, mental health) through institutional practices. It is concerned not with natural or divine origins or with chronological, sequential, or causal development over time but rather with the specific points of emergence or transformation or interpretation of POWER. In Foucault's thought, *genealogy* represents a turn away from discourse towards power and the subject of power. It is to some degree a refinement of the SYNCHRONIC method known as ARCHAEOLOGY.

GLOBALIZATION. A term that encompasses a number of theories concerning the international extension of political, technological, and economic capital, in association with a form of cultural imperialism that seeks a UNIVERSALIZED consumer culture. A *globalized* economy or a global culture is one in which difference is minimized and standardization the norm.

HABITUS. Associated with **Pierre Bourdieu**, *habitus* refers to a social practice, the construction of a subjectivity within the rules and limits of a SOCIAL FIELD. These rules and limits are not arbitrary or externally applied but are rather the result of the aggregate of practices, habits, beliefs, and general knowledge that individuals acquire living in specific social environments. The ability successfully to manipulate *habitus* guarantees the individual social *distinction*.

HEGEMONY. The process by which the IDEOLOGY of dominant classes exerts control through social, political, and cultural institutions. *Ideological hegemony* is a form of non-coercive social control achieved through consensus rather than through direct and material coercion (e.g., military and police force). That this *hegemony* is achieved without force does not mean that it is thus benign. *Counter-hegemony* refers to attempts to critique or dismantle hegemonic power. See DOMINATION and IDEOLOGY.

HETEROGLOSSIA. A condition of language, determined by DIALOGISM, that is open to multiple historical and social determinations. Associated with **M. M. Bakhtin**, this term typically refers to the linguistic stratification of discourses characterized by the inclusion of diverse dialects, ideolects, jargons, and other speech forms.

HISTORICAL DETERMINISM. A theory of history that holds that all human events are affected in material ways by the economic sphere of society (i.e., the modes of production in classical Marxism). History is therefore the history of *determinations* made by productive forces. Of course, such determinations are complex, especially in advanced industrial societies. For "post-Marxists," the most important *determinations* occur at the superstructural level (i.e., media, social and cultural institutions, ideologies); for them, the relationship is not deterministic or mechanistic but HEGEMONIC. *Overdetermination* refers to an intensification of class contradictions which can lead (as Lenin said of Russia) to revolution. See BASE/SUPERSTRUCTURE and NEGATION.

HISTORICISM. A view of history and historiography according to which social, cultural, philosophical, and religious values have meaning only when grasped as part of the historical moment in which they arise. For some philosophers of history, it refers to the laws of development that characterize historical processes. In some cases, as in Marxist *historicism*, history is understood as functioning according to a theory of DIALECTICAL MATERIALISM.

HOMOSOCIAL DESIRE. This concept emerged out of the work of Gayle Rubin and **Eve Kosofsky Sedgwick**. It designates a social relationship in which a woman, real or figurative, serves as a conduit for the desire, social or sexual, of two men. To varying degrees, the desire of men for other men is thus sublimated and recast as the competition between men for a woman. Women thus become tokens in an exchange that really has nothing to do with them. At a certain extreme, *homosocial desire* can manifest itself as *homophobia*.

HYBRIDITY, HYBRIDIZATION. A term associated with Postcolonial Studies, where it is used to describe the multitude of subject positions and identities in colonial and, especially, postcolonial societies. **Homi**

Bhabha describes it as an "affect" of COLONIAL MIMICRY, in which the subject is doubled in a transgressive rewriting of colonial discourse. It can also result from immigration and migration, especially the form known as *diaspora*, in which large numbers of a people are dispersed across wide geographical areas. Examples include the Jewish diasporas throughout history, the African diaspora that began with the slave trade, and the Irish diaspora that followed the famine of the 1840s. *Diasporic identities* are those formed along multiple geographical locations, the result of slavery, exile, expulsion, or emigration. These identities may be formed and nourished in enclaves or they may develop along cosmopolitan, multi-racial, and multilingual lines. *Hybridity* thus refers to a pluralized identity, open to contingency and change, to linguistic, ethnic, and racial merger. *Creole* is often used to indicate a racially hybrid people (for example, the Cajuns of Louisiana), but this is a potentially misleading term in Postcolonial and Ethnic Studies. The word *creole* has a long and complex history. In the Caribbean colonies, it came to refer to any person, native, African, or European, who had been born (or "seasoned") in the region. In linguistics, it is used to describe a new indigenous language formed by mixing several other languages. *Creolization*, whether it refers to the process of acclimation to a foreign environment or to linguistic, ethnic and racial mixing, constitutes a common form of hybrid social and cultural development.

IDEALIZE, IDEALIZATION.   A practice in which something (an object, place, concept, or person) is represented in its most highly evolved and perfected (*ideal*) form. *Idealization* is a form of symbolic representation, whereby the *ideal* of a thing is substituted for the thing itself. *Idealizations* are often invested with a value that has little to do with the thing represented, as when an emergent nation symbolizes its sovereignty as a stylized and perfected woman. A related term comes from Psychoanalysis; the *ego-ideal* is what one thinks oneself to be: the *ideal* form of oneself. *Idealizations* generally are fantasy constructions, but they can have a profound impact on personal, social, and cultural life.

IDENTITY.   A term that traditionally has designated the distinct and stable "personality" or "character" of an individual, both as it is conceived by others in social environments and as it is conceived by the individual herself. *Identity* is often spoken of in terms of its SOCIAL CONSTRUCTION or its gender and sexual determinations. Important for many theorists is the relationship between *identity* and IDEOLOGY. *Self-identity* refers to the awareness of one's own identity as a stable and singular entity. In metaphysical philosophy, it refers to the possibility of a thing according perfectly with its idea, of the sublation of difference within absolute sameness. *Nonidentity* is a term from DIALECTICS that refers to the opposite pole of *identity*; in dialectical operations, nonidentity is subsumed into the construction of identity. See PRESENCE and NEGATION.

IDEOLOGICAL HEGEMONY. See HEGEMONY.

IDEOLOGY. In Marxist theory, a set of beliefs, laws, statutes, principles, practices, and traditions proclaimed by a dominant class in order to rule other classes. Some theorists believe that *ideology* is an "unscientific" point of view, a form of "false consciousness" because it obscures the reality of historical processes. But *ideology* can also refer to *any* set of beliefs, laws, statutes, and the like; thus, we can speak of "working-class ideology" or "socialist ideology." Some theorists hold that *ideology* is precisely the process of representing ideas and beliefs in SIGNIFYING SYSTEMS, of making meaning in a social context. **Louis Althusser's** influential conception emphasizes the idea of *ideological state apparatuses* (e.g., bureaucracies, schools, universities, the police and military) and the production of *ideology* as an all-encompassing social demand on individuals. See BASE/SUPERSTRUCTURE.

IMAGINARY, SYMBOLIC, REAL. Orders of reality proposed by **Jacques Lacan**. The *Symbolic* designates the realm of law, language, reason, metaphysics, the PHALLUS, and so on. The *Imaginary* is the order of fantasy, of pre-Oedipal merger (mother and child bond) and lack of differentiation, JOUISSANCE, DIFFÉRANCE. Some theorists argue that the Imaginary is, in fundamental ways, a misrecognition of the Symbolic. The *Real* designates what cannot be designated, what cannot be thought or known via the Symbolic or the Imaginary. But its persistence, as in the Freudian unconscious, can be felt as symptoms in the Symbolic and, more effectively, the Imaginary order.

IMPERIALISM. If COLONIALISM refers to the administration of foreign territories, *imperialism* refers to the social and political objectives of colonialism and the economic and political consequences of competition with other European states. It also specifies a phase of capitalist development in which markets and labor shift to peripheral territories. *Imperialism* also designates a complex matrix of cultural codes and practices grounded in the social, political, and economic realities of colonialism. *Neoimperialism* designates the continuation of these codes and practices after the imperial era, a situation which leaves the postcolony in a familiar state of dependency. Often used interchangeably with NEOCOLONIALISM.

INTERTEXTUALITY.   A theory of textual reference which holds that the relationship between texts within and between DISCURSIVE FORMATIONS is partly determined by citations and allusions. For **M. M. Bakhtin**, *intertextuality* is the inevitable result of DIALOGIZED HETEROGLOSSIA, of languages stratified and coded with a multitude of dialects, jargons, and other speech forms. Building on Bakhtin, other theorists have linked stratified and dialogized language to the desiring subject (the reader, the writer). Still others have regard *intertextuality* as a form of auto-critique, of discourse policing itself, of plagiarism, cannibalism, and other forms of consumption. This term should not be confused with *influence* or standard forms of scholarly reference, for they imply a level of intentionality not typically associated with *intertextuality*.

JOUISSANCE.   Often associated with sexual pleasure and death, *jouissance* (from the French *jouir*, to enjoy) refers to the unknown and inexpressible aspects of unconscious experience and desire. In **Jacques Lacan**'s terms, it is the IMAGINARY mis-recognition of the SYMBOLIC in which intense pleasures are decoupled from the "law of the signifier." *Jouissance* is therefore that which is *not* known, that which is beyond knowledge, beyond the SUBJECT of knowledge.

LOGOCENTRISM.   This term refers to the primacy, in Western cultures, of *logos* (literarily, "word"), specifically of discourses characterized by reason, logic, and rationality. Often modified as PHALLOGOCENTRISM to emphasize the underlying patriarchal and masculinist authority of such discourses.

MANICHEANISM.   In its ancient Persian religious context, *Manicheanism* refers to the division of the world into good and evil forces that battle for the possession of humanity. In literary and cultural theory, it designates a binary relation of power characterized by ESSENTIAL difference (e.g., primitive/civilized, male/female, nature/culture), polarization, and inequality. Abdul JanMohamed coined the term "Manichean allegory" to express the relations of power between colonizer and colonized.

MASTER NARRATIVE. Popularized by **Jean-François Lyotard**, this term refers to the authoritative or foundational narratives of Western societies, specifically the narratives of emancipation and knowledge. Such narratives serve to *legitimate* the power of dominant social classes; their failure results in a process Lyotard calls *delegimitation*. The term is commonly used to refer to any dominant discourse, but especially those that lend themselves to narrative treatment (e.g., Homeric return, Christian Providence, Hegelian world Spirit, Marxist class struggle). See DISCOURSE.

MATERIALISM. See CULTURAL MATERIALISM and DIALECTIC.

METADISCOURSE. Any discourse that comments upon or governs another discourse. For example, *meta-linguistics* would refer to a technical discourse that reflected upon the way linguistics is discussed and its findings presented. See METAFICTION.

METAFICTION. A quality of Postmodern fiction whereby narrative reflects upon its own status as fictional. It can take the form of structural self-reflection (**Linda Hutcheon's** "narcissistic narrative") or a "laying bare" of the devices by which novelists traditionally achieve their effects. A related term is Robert Schole's *fabulation*, which refers to the complex patterns and arrangements of language and image often found in Postmodern and contemporary fiction. See METADISCOURSE.

METROCOLONY. See METROPOLITAN CULTURE, COLONIALISM.

METROPOLITAN CULTURE. Typically used to refer to an imperial capital (e.g., New York, London, Paris, Amsterdam) and is used in contrast to a COLONY or periphery. A *metrocolony* is a large, and largely urban, colony in close proximity to the *metropolitan* center. Ireland is a classic example. See COLONIALISM.

MIMESIS. A theory of representation according to which an object is faithfully imitated or copied, with mirror-like accuracy. Literary *realism* in its conventional mode is often referred to as *mimetic* in that it creates the illusion in language of a faithful reflection of the world.

MIMICRY. A concept pioneered by **Frantz Fanon**, who argued that colonized people, forced to abandon traditional notions of selfhood and national identity, learn to *mimic* their colonial masters. **Homi Bhabha** modified the concept to emphasize its critical and productive potential. COLONIAL MIMICRY entails an act of subverting COLONIAL DISCOURSE by exploiting the AMBIVALENCE at its heart, its unstable, contradictory, nonidentical potentiality. It results in HYBRID IDENTITIES. The term *mimicry* now broadly refers to acts of appropriation that result in the SOCIAL CONSTRUCTION or PERFORMANCE of identity. The term is frequently used in a more general sense to designate any sort of critical parody.

MODERNISM, MODERNIZATION. See MODERNITY.

MODERNITY. Refers to a period after the decline of feudalism in which we see the rise of secular science, technology, and rational philosophy. It embraces the Renaissance, the Enlightenment, the nineteenth-century Age of Progress, and the triumphs of the early twentieth century. It is grounded in secularism, humanism, and an openness to innovation in all spheres. Key features of *modernity* include industrial capitalism, the nation-state, the development of governmental bureaucracies, the development and refinement of educational systems, and the emergence of the SUBJECT as sovereign and self-identical. *Modernization* refers to the material processes that ensure scientific and technological advancement. It refers also to a condition of rapid and pervasive social and cultural development. *Postmodernity*, in historical terms, begins with or shortly after the Second World War. It is at the same time a general critique of *modernity* and the articulation of radically new ways of seeing and knowing the world. Technology plays a decisive role in many theories of postmodernity. On *Modernism*, see "The Rise of Literary Theory," pp. 21–4; on *Postmodernism*, see "The Scope of Literary Theory," pp. 144–53.

NEGATION. In DIALECTICS, a process by which the negative term of a logical process is sublated in the other, positive term, thus creating a new term that will logically attract its own negation. In logic and philosophy, this is known as *negation of the negation*. The process of *negation* is a necessary and constitutive one for all syntheses; it does not designate the absence of elements. This form of *negation* should not be confused with "negative" in the mathematical sense of subtraction or in the moral/ethic sense of "not good." The term *determinate negation* refers to the process by which negation *determines* the outcome of the dialectical interplay. *Negative dialectics* seeks to subvert the classical *negation of the negation* by seeking its preservation as the *non-identical* outside the limits of dialectical sublation. See DIALECTICS, HISTORICAL DETERMINISM.

NEGATIVE.　See NEGATION.

NEGATIVE DIALECTICS.　See NEGATION.

NEOCOLONIALISM.　See COLONIALISM.

NONIDENTITY.　See IDENTITY.

ONTOLOGY.　The study of the nature of being, often associated with a belief in PRESENCE, in the absolute fullness of things, absolute SELF-IDENTITY.

ORIENTALISM.　Associated with the work of **Edward Said**, this term refers to the authoritative discourses on the East (or Orient) produced by the West (or Occident). These discourses include historical, linguistic, philological, and literary works and operate on latent and manifest levels. See DISCOURSE and COLONIAL DISCOURSE.

ORTHODOXY.　Rooted in the concept *doxa*, which means "opinion," *orthodoxy* has come to mean definitive or established truth, typically that of an institutional authority (e.g., the Roman Catholic Church). *Heterodoxy* indicates a deviance from "true opinion," while *paradox* refers to a situation in which contrary opinions appear to be true at the same time. In logic, a *paradox* is a contradictory statement. The New Criticism privileged *paradox* as one of the chief elements of poetry.

OTHER, OTHERNESS.　Term in widespread use that designate a variety of positions opposed to the *same* or the *self-same*. In Poststructuralism, the *other* refers to the negative pole of a dialectic, that which is sublated to fulfill the destiny of the positive term. It also refers to the difference in language or to the structure of a speech act or text in which there is a receiver of a statement. Ethical philosophy treats the *other* in a similar fashion, as the receiver of actions and attitudes. From Lacanian psychoanalysis, we get the sense of the *other* as the unconscious (Other) which speaks through instances of otherness generated by gender difference (other). For example, the "woman as other" refers to a situation in which a woman becomes a mere surface from which the male subject receives back his own vision of himself, which is generated from the unconscious (Other). Postcolonial theorists, influenced by Psychoanalysis, have developed theories of the *other* based on racial, ethnic, and cultural difference.

OVERDETERMINATION.   See HISTORICAL DETERMINISM.

PARADIGMATIC/SYNTAGMATIC.   *Paradigmatic* refers to the aggregate of relations among elements in a given SYNCHRONIC system. *Syntagmatic* refers to the combinations and relations of elements within DIACHRONIC sequences (e.g., sentences, narratives).

PARADOX.   See ORTHODOXY.

PATRIARCHY.   A social formation in which the father, or a father figure, is the supreme authority. More commonly, the term refers to complex societies in which social and cultural institutions are created and ruled by men, and in which women are accorded inferior or secondary status. *Patriarchal* societies are legitimated and sustained by political, psychological, and philosophical conceptions of the superiority of the PHALLUS and male subjectivity.

PERFORMANCE, PERFORMATIVITY.   These terms refer to a specific form of SOCIAL CONSTRUCTIONISM, the idea that IDENTITY is a function of the *performance* of gender and sexuality. **Judith Butler** usefully distinguishes between *performance* (the enactment of normative gender and sexual roles) and *performativity* (the subversion of these roles in a critical restaging of identity). See AGENCY.

PHALLUS, PHALLOGOCENTRISM.   *Phallus* refers to the abstract idea of male or PATRIARCHAL power. *Phallocentrism* refers to masculine and patriarchal foundations of western thought. A common variant, *phallogocentrism*, emphasizes that language and reason (*logos*) are implicated in a *phallic* economy of knowledge and power. See LOGOCENTRISM.

PLAY.   In Deconstruction, *play* refers to the relationships of DIFFERENCE that obtain within linguistic systems. Without a stable center in such systems, and without a predictable relationship between SIGNIFIER and SIGNIFIED, the signifying elements of the system (i.e., the signifiers) enter into *play*, free of any MIMETIC or referential connection to the external world. *Play* occurs by virtue of the arbitrary relationship between words and what they signify; we can never be sure, therefore, that our discourse refers to what we think it does. Opposed to the free *play* of the signifier, is the idea of pure PRESENCE.

POETICS OF CULTURE.   See CULTURAL POETICS.

POSTMODERNITY.   See MODERNITY.

POWER.   A term used by **Michel Foucault** and those influenced by him to refer to the expression of social and cultural forces (energy, libido) in the form of discourse and discursive formations. A notoriously ambiguous term, *power* (or "power/knowledge") can mean many things. It is analogous to IDEOLOGICAL HEGEMONY, but is generally depicted as indeterminate and diffuse, closer to Nietzsche's *will to power*, a non-hierarchical expression of "dynamic quanta." The roots and locations of *power* are amorphous, unpredictable, *rhizomatic* (like crabgrass). Some critics argue that Foucauldian and Nietzschean conceptions of *power* constitute new forms of metaphysical absolutism.

PRESENCE.   A philosophical concept that refers to Being as such, to the essence of a thing, to the present material reality of objects but also a transcendental reality (or Being), outside the realm of signifiers. These conceptions of *presence* provide the foundation for science, morality, aesthetics, religion, even language itself. **Jacques Derrida's** deconstructionist project was inaugurated with a critique of *presence* as a stable reference in linguistic and philosophical statements. Cf. PLAY.

PRIMITIVISM.   A form of COLONIAL DISCOURSE dependent upon a MANICHEAN distinction between civilization and savagery. It derives from scientific, historical, anthropological, philological, sociological, and imaginative texts whose common denominator is a vision of *primitive* peoples as childlike, feminine, irrational, superstitious, violent, garrulous, and genetically inferior. As part of the ideological structure of colonialism, *primitivism* played an important role in establishing the inhumanity of non-Western peoples, thus making it easier to subjugate, exploit, and exterminate them. Interest in *primitivism* was an important part of Modernist literature and art. See COLONIALISM and ORIENTALISM.

PROBLEMATIC.   Strictly speaking, this term refers to a delimited set of social or textual phenomena – contradictions or gaps in logic, sudden discontinuities or juxtapositions, inequalities or asymmetries – that, when taken together, suggest an opportunity for critical intervention. It is often used in less specialized ways as a synonym for the more prosaic "problem."

REAL. See IMAGINARY.

REIFICATION. In Marxist theory, *reification* refers to a process by which social practices are converted into abstractions and objectified, thus distorting the real nature of social conditions and forestalling the development of class consciousness. In this sense, see COMMODIFICATION. It is often regarded as a form of *depersonalization*. In logic, it is used to refer to a process by which abstractions are treated as if they were concrete material realities.

RETERRITORIALIZATION. See TERRITORIALIZATION.

SELF-IDENTITY. See IDENTITY.

SEMIOLOGY, SEMIOTICS. Both terms refer to the science of signs and signification. *Semiotics* is associated with the work of Charles Sanders Peirce and emphasizes reference and representation, while *semiology* is associated with the work of Ferdinand de Saussure and emphasizes difference. The terms are often used interchangeably, though the more common term in Continental European theory is *semiotics*. Some poststructuralist theorists (like **Julia Kristeva**) use it in tandem with other theoretical models to craft innovative, non-conventional strategies for analyzing signifying systems.

SETTLER COLONY. See COLONIALISM.

SIGN, SIGNIFIER, SIGNIFIED. In Saussurean linguistics, *signifier* refers to a word or sound-image within a linguistic system and *signified* refers to a concept that the signifier designates. Taken together, the two elements constitute a *sign*, which is itself arbitrary in its relation to external reality. A *signifying system* is one in which *signs*, linguistic or otherwise, constitute a single formation in which rules of enunciation and exclusion define the limits of the system. *Transcendental signifier* is the name given by some critics to a metaphysical *Sign* (e.g., God, Reason, the PHALLUS) that legitimates specific *signifying systems* (e.g., metaphysical philosophy, Psychoanalysis).

SIGNIFYING SYSTEM. See SIGN.

SIMULACRA, SIMULATION. Associated with the work of **Jean Baudrillard**, these terms refer to the idea that "signs of the real" substitute for reality. The "orders of simulation" extend from simple mimetic copies (i.e., exact representations of an external referent) to copies that have no referent at all, that create the illusion of reference and, thus, of reality.

SOCIAL CONSTRUCTIONISM. An epistemological theory according to which material forces emanating from social and cultural institutions *construct* individual IDENTITY and SUBJECTIVITY. It stands in opposition to ESSENTIALISM, which assumes that race, gender, and other features of identity are innate, non-contingent, beyond the influence of material social forces. To construct an identity, personal or national, is a matter of making choices from a wide array of models and combining choices in startling ways. This is most evident in the sphere of gender and sexual identity. See ÉCRITURE FEMININE.

SOCIAL FIELD. As used by **Pierre Bourdieu** this term refers to two forms of "social hierarchization": one that encompasses the modes of material and ideological domination while another encompasses cultural and symbolic production, which has its own forms of domination. Cf. DISCURSIVE FORMATION and HABITUS.

SOCIAL FORMATION. A *social formation* is the product of a specific mode of production (BASE) and the class relations that compose and sustain it. It is thus characterized by relations of ideological and material DOMINATION. See BASE/SUPERSTRUCTURE.

SUBALTERN, SUBALTERN SUBJECT. These terms refer to social groups – e.g., migrants, shantytown dwellers, displaced tribes, refugees, untouchable castes, the homeless – that either do not possess or are prevented from possessing class consciousness and who are in any case prevented from mobilizing as organized groups. In this limited sense, *subalternity* refers to many but not all strata of colonized peoples. Antonio Gramsci introduced the current critical meaning, but the term is grounded in the idea of *subject races*, a term put forward by Lord Cromer in 1907 to refer to non-European peoples. The colonialist frame of reference that envisioned subaltern races could do so only because it was supported by a MANICHEAN IDEOLOGY of racial DIFFERENCE. See SUBJECT.

SUBJECT, SUBJECTIVITY. These terms typically refer to Western traditions of citizenship, selfhood, and consciousness. The *subject* of modern Western societies is often referred to as the *subject of knowledge* (i.e., of a specific epistemological framework) or the *universal subject* and is regarded as autonomous, sovereign, and self-determining. Many theorists challenge these characteristics when they become normative, regulative, or repressive. For them, the *subject* is at the mercy of social forces that determine it, more or less completely. *Subjectivity* is the condition of being a *subject*, specifically the condition of self-identity (i.e., self-awareness), and the ability not only to recognize oneself as a *subject* (agent or citizen) but also to regulate one's actions accordingly. To be capable of conscious action and social and historical AGENCY, the *subject* must occupy a recognizable and legitimate *subject position* within a specific social context. See SUBALTERN.

SUBJECT POSITION.   See SUBJECT.

SUPERSTRUCTURE.   See BASE/SUPERSTRUCTURE.

SUPPLEMENT, SUPPLEMENTATION.   In the special sense given it by **Jacques Derrida**, this term refers to the ambivalence of language understood both as an addition to the full PRESENCE of the world of objects and as a substitute for that presence which is thus deferred indefinitely in the free PLAY of SIGNS as *supplements*.

SYMBOLIC.   See IMAGINARY.

SYNCHRONY.   See DIACHRONY.

SYNTAGMATIC.   See PARADIGMATIC.

TELOS, TELEOLOGY.   *Telos* means end or termination. *Teleology* is typically used with reference to a form of HISTORICAL DETERMINISM in which the end-point of history justifies and legitimizes in advance the means of attaining it.

TERRITORIALIZATION.   Associated with the work of **Gilles Deleuze** and **Félix Guattari**, *territorialization* refers to the demarcation of social and cultural spaces by principles of law and rationality (i.e., the SYMBOLIC). To *deterritorialize* is to remove these demarcations, while to *reterritorialize* is to inscribe new demarcations in place of the old. These processes are associated with the imposition of dominant ideologies, especially fascism and colonialism.

TEXTUALISM, TEXTUALITY.   In literary theory, a *text* is not simply a book. It is rather a complex, unstable, and unpredictable site, where a number of operations take place: the reader's engagement with the author's words, the PLAY of DIFFERENCES in the language apart from any authorial (or readerly) intent, the INTERTEXTUAL connections with other *texts*, the DETERMINATIONS of social and cultural institutions and traditions. *Textuality* refers to this multivalent aspect of *texts*, to this quality of playfulness and instability. *Textualism*, especially in fields like history and anthropology, refers to the process by which one's consciousness of the world is mediated by written texts.

TOTALITY, TOTALIZE. *Totality* refers to a structural concept of perfect unity, inclusion, or completeness. In philosophy, it refers to the fullness of a concept. To *totalize* is to represent a complex entity or unfinished process as if it were a complete and unified object. Because totalizing visions always come at the expense of other visions, to totalize is, paradoxically, to exclude. In classical Marxism, *totality* refers to the aggregate of social relations that constitute a SOCIAL FORMATION. For analytic purposes, a theory of *totality* is required to give social contradictions their true meaning. See UNIVERSALITY.

TRANSCENDENTAL SIGNIFIER. See SIGN.

UNIVERSAL SUBJECT. See SUBJECT.

UNIVERSALITY. A term that refers to the general or absolute existence of an idea (e.g., humanism, liberalism, democracy, white supremacy). *Universality* emerged in the early Enlightenment as way to describe mathematical, logical, and ethical absolutes. Especially important was the idea of *universal* values, which were in fact the values of a few elevated to general status. In this sense, *universalist* thinking is, paradoxically, provincial. Some theorists have developed *contingent universals* that serve to galvanize support for specific strategic ends. See SUBJECT and TOTALITY.

INDEX